LEONARD KRIEGER, who has taught at Yale
University and Columbia University, is
University Professor of History at the
University of Chicago. He has been a fellow at
the Center for Advanced Study in the
Behavioral Sciences in Palo Alto, and a
member of the Institute for Advanced Study
in Princeton. General editor of the Classic
European Historians series published by the
University of Chicago Press, he is the author of
*The Politics of Discretion, An Essay on the
Theory of Enlightened Despotism,* and *The
German Idea of Freedom,* all published by the
University of Chicago Press.

D1564869

Ranke The Meaning of History

THE UNIVERSITY OF CHICAGO PRESS • CHICAGO AND LONDON

Ranke
The Meaning
of History

Leonard Krieger

D
15
.R3
K74

The University of Chicago Press, Chicago 60637
The University of Chicago Press, Ltd., London

82 81 80 79 78 77   9 8 7 6 5 4 3 2 1

Library of Congress Cataloging in Publication Data

Krieger, Leonard.
  Ranke: the meaning of history.

  Bibliography: p.
  Includes index.
  1. Ranke, Leopold von, 1795–1886. 2. History
—Philosophy. 3. Historicism. 4. Historians—
Germany—Biography.
D15.R3K74   907'.2'024   76-25633
ISBN 0-226-45349-9

Parts of chapters 7 and 8 of the present work appeared in a slightly different version in *History and Theory*, Beiheft 14 (1975): 1–15. © 1975 by Wesleyan University.

Leonard Krieger is University Professor of History at the University of Chicago. He is author of several books, including *The German Idea of Freedom* (2d printing, 1973) and *An Essay on the Theory of Enlightened Despotism* (1975).

To the Memory of Hajo Holborn

Contents

Contents (Continued)

Preface

This book is the resultant of two related questions. First, how did Leopold Ranke, commonly acknowledged to be the father of modern scientific history, manage to combine the scientific dimension which has been the model for controlled research into the particular facts of history with the ideal dimension, indubitably established by recent commentators, which testifies to his lifelong devotion to universal values? Second, in view of the current crisis of historical study, highlighted especially by the growing conviction that history has no meaning for man's living and by the consequent decline of interest in the schools, can we learn anything about possible meanings of history from what it has meant to men in ages more congenial to it? Since the dualities in Ranke's approach to history reflected profound divisions in his attitude to life in general, and since he found the meaning of history to consist precisely in the capacity of history to reconcile what remained irreconcilable for him outside it, it is clear that the answer to the first question is also an answer to the second—that the way in which Ranke reconciled the dualities in his history also defined the meaning that history had for his life in general. And since the conditions of his life, however much they may have differed from our own in their religious, moral, and political content, share a crucial fragmentation with our age, inference may well be made from the meaning of history for him to the meaning of history for us.

The organization of the book follows from the substance of the Ranke problem, so conceived, and from the pattern of solution stipulated by Ranke himself. When Ranke's approach to history is analyzed from his own several theoretical statements about it, the conclusion must be the frustrating dualism which is so familiar in his legacy. The transcendence of the dualism and the ascertainment of his integrity ensue when application is made of his own practical recipe to himself and his career is treated historically, with his life and his historical work providing the explanatory circumstances of his various theoretical positions and softening their apparently frictional edges. Hence the first part of this study is addressed to Ranke's well-known theoretical pronunciamentos about history with a view to showing their discordant confrontation on this level. The second, and much lengthier, section is devoted to the history of Ranke and of his historical work with a view to showing the integrity of both the man and his production on this level and to reinterpreting the theory from this point of view. The repetition of doctrinal propositions is thus intentional, for the historical conditions of their second appearance is designed to revise the impression given by the analytical format of their first.

Given the problematic orientation, need it be added that this book is not the full-dress biography or the complete historiographical study of Ranke that has so often been called for? Until they appear, the reader who is interested in a straight biographical and historiographical sketch would be well advised to consult the extended introduction in Georg G. Iggers' and Konrad von Moltke's selected edition of Ranke as *The Theory and Practice of History* (Indianapolis, 1973); Theodore Von Laue's exemplary study of Ranke's early life and career, *Leopold Ranke: The Formative Years* (Princeton, 1950); and the myriad commentaries, specially on Ranke or on more general themes notably including Ranke, that are selectively listed in the bibliography.

My focus is rather on a distinctive level within Ranke, a level which lay between his theory and practice of history and which may perhaps be best characterized as his attitude toward history. This focus entails a definite way of looking at Ranke's thinking and his career, for it makes his perception of his environment much more relevant than this environment itself, and it assesses his historical writings rather for their intellectual meaning than for their historiographical validity. What should be looked for in the following pages, then, is subjectified—i.e., Rankeified—rather than objective contexts and a stress rather on the revealing than on the informing aspects of his histories.

From this point of view, for example, what matters about the provenance of Ranke's famous doctrine of ideas in history was not the real course that led from Plato to Kant, Humboldt, and Hegel (a provenance that has, incidentally, been often described) but Ranke's conscious absorption of it in the form he took from Luther and Fichte. Again, *we* can see that Ranke's emphasis on universal history was a commonplace of his day, for it was a staple genre of a German historiographical tradition that included the most prominent of eighteenth- and early nineteenth-century historians— Gatterer, Schlözer, Schlosser, Heeren, and Johannes von Müller— but for Ranke the tradition was irrelevant, for he considered his approach to universal history to be idiosyncratic.* He knew many of the names and works in the tradition, of course, and he even expressed admiration for Müller. But even in Müller's case Ranke seems to have been impressed more by the Swiss historian's personal spirit and colorful style than by his ideas about history, and he accorded even less recognition to the others.** "We in Germany possess no universal history of real historical merit," he wrote summarily just as he was beginning his own universal history, and he dismissed Friedrich Christoph Schlosser in this context as an historian who "has vast erudition; whose work should always be consulted but is incomplete."†

---

*For Ranke's unenthusiastic attitude toward the tradition of universal history, see his casual—and critical—discussion of its chief practitioners in a "digression" attached to the lecture notes of a course on ancient history in 1848. In Ranke, *Aus Werk und Nachlass*, ed. Walther Peter Fuchs and Theodor Schieder (4 vols., Munich, 1964-75), 4:209-10.

**"In the final analysis," he wrote about Johannes von Müller, "I believe that Müller has had more effect through his letters than through all his works." Ranke to Heinrich Ranke, Feb. 26, 1835 in Ranke, *Das Briefwerk,* ed. Walther Peter Fuchs (Hamburg, 1949), p. 267.

†Ranke to Cleuthere Thomas, Nov. 14, 1879, in Ranke, *Neue Briefe*, ed. Bernhard Hoeft and Hans Herzfeld (Hamburg, 1949), p. 682.

From our internal perspective, moreover, Ranke's own works merit attention of a different kind and in different proportions than their variable quality usually evokes. Thus those of his studies which are generally recognized as historical classics—such as the *History of the Popes,* the *German History in the Age of the Reformation,* the *French History,* and the *English History*—are viewed here not so much for the history that they tell as for the attitude toward history which they contain, and the same standard confers an unwonted prominence on those of his histories—such as the lectures *On the Epochs of Modern History* and that unfinished product of his old age, the *World History*—in which little historical value is acknowledged.

I dedicate this book to the late Hajo Holborn, my old mentor, who modernized and liberalized Ranke and who, more than any historian I have ever known or read, realized the Rankean ideal of applying the conscience of the historian to combine exact scholarship with the discovery of universal meaning in the human past. At the time of his death he was about to make his own assessment of Ranke, and the origins of this book—albeit not its interpretations—stem from my assumption of this commission. Hajo Holborn's would have been a much more magisterial performance, and we shall always be the poorer for having to do without it. But he always delighted in the independence of his students, and I like to think that however he might have judged the results, he would smilingly have approved my writing on his cherished Ranke in my way rather than his. Despite the considerable difference in our approaches to Ranke, the debt that I owe Hajo Holborn on this as on so many other scores is immeasurable, and I can myself not discern the point which separates what I have absorbed from what I have elaborated upon him.

About other obligations I can be more precise. To my wife I am especially beholden, not only for her usual perceptive contributions as discussant, editor, and communicator but for her unfailing attention, so singularly valuable, in a study like this, to keeping Ranke in due perspective as an intellectual figure and to remembering always the man behind the historian. Richard Barnes, Otto Pflanze, and Fritz Stern referred me to contemporary observations on Ranke in sources which I should not otherwise have consulted. Mrs. Adlyn Evans showed remarkable patience in producing a legible typescript from a difficult original.

Part One
The Theory

1
The Dubious Legacy

The historian is the ghostwriter of the past. He memorializes the deeds and thoughts of others, and he establishes, for the personages and the events he publicizes, a lasting identity in which his own is submerged. In part the historian's comparative anonymity is the inevitable result of the secondhand living which is his business, but in part too it is the intended effect of a conscious principle which proportions historical truth to the distance from the personality of its recorder. Histories, consequently, are read by men from many walks of life, but historians are usually of interest only to other historians—when they are of interest to anyone at all.

Of the few historians whose persons have attracted long-range fame (or notoriety), some—such as Augustine, Machiavelli, Hume, Marx, Croce—owe their longevity to other capacities without which the personal tribute of posterity would be unthinkable. Others—the likes of Voltaire, Schiller, Carlyle—have written history as a species of literature and are valued for their artistry. Limited indeed, both in numbers and in cultural range, is the residue of historians who have themselves been accorded the immortal rights of historical personages by the simple virtue of the history they have written, for better or for worse. But they do exist, and the interest in them has become paradoxically greater than the interest in the history for which they are remembered. This group includes Thucydides, Guicciardini, Gibbon, Herder—and Leopold von Ranke.

Ranke's then, is one of the great names in the history of history. His reputation stems not only from historians' explicit attribution to him of a decisive new direction within their discipline but from his representation of the discipline to the culture at large, plotting a new role for history in that culture. The outer marks of his accomplishments have become truisms in the profession and models of the profession for those outside it. He propounded a science of history, based upon the critical study of its sources and upon the organization of these sources into a hierarchy with its apex in the original document contemporary with the historicized event, as close as possible to the historical actor and as distant as possible from the historian. He developed a method for this critical study, using all possible knowledge of the source to discredit distortions of it and to isolate its true content. He directed this method to the materials of modern history (to history, that is, since the beginning of the sixteenth century), thereby detaching the method from its association with philology, law, and theology in ancient and medieval history, making its modern application a model for universal history, and thus turning it into an autonomous method coextensive with the liberated historical discipline as such. He exemplified his methodical scientific history in a stupendous series of historical works which traversed the histories of the chief European nations between the sixteenth and the eighteenth centuries, each in its own terms and from sources appropriate to it, leading up to the climactic and long anticipated attempt at a universal history—in all a massive performance occupying the bulk of the fifty-four volumes which comprise the incomplete edition of his collected works. Ranke devised, finally, the educational institution appropriate to the perpetuation of his new science—the historical seminar, or "exercises," as he revealingly called it, in which students practiced the new critical history under the supervision of the master.

No one can quarrel with the tributes which have been paid Ranke on the score of the sheer bulk and range of his historical writing, since his successive adoptions of the language, sources, and attitudes of nation after nation, state after state, add up to a virtuoso performance without precedent or sequel. But the rest of his accomplishment is not quite so obvious. What is not clear, in the first instance, is the character of the presumed innovation which has secured for him roughly the same place in historical knowledge as Copernicus has in astronomy and Kant in philosophy. The fact is that neither the critical attitude toward sources, nor the insistence upon original documents, nor even the application of the philological method to the writing and teaching of history was new with Ranke. The first dated back to Thucydides;[1] the second had been a mainstay of humanism since the fifteenth century and was made the focus of collection and scientific analysis by Jean Mabillon and the Maurists of the seventeenth; the third, shifting the basis of judging testimony about the past from probable reasons and common sense to the internal comprehension of meaning in the terms and conditions of the testimony itself, had been announced in principle by Hamann and Herder during the eighteenth century, developed in the philological seminars of the early nineteenth, and spectacularly applied to Roman history by Barthold Georg Niebuhr, whom Ranke explicitly acknowledged as mentor.[2]

It would seem, then, that Ranke's contributions, both to history as a discipline and to the historical dimension of our culture, lay not in any single breakthrough but rather in the unprecedented way he put familiar notions together and in the new contexts he found for them. Thus he applied to *modern* history the documentary and philological methods which had been specifically devised for penetration into remote ages. He thereby created an independent historical discipline which absorbed the otherness derived from the experience of ancient and medieval history and the continuity derived from the experience of contemporary history but which avoided the antiquarian specificity associated with the one and the pragmatic participation associated with the other. In its modern application under his guidance, the combination of original sources and critical approach served not only the familiar negative purpose of safeguarding the authenticity of reports but the novel, positive method of reconstructing the life of the mediate past. Ranke looked in documents not only for their veracity but for their vitality. He asserted frankly that, while he would not allow himself to be lied to, he looked above all in his criticism for "originality, characteristic attitude, fullness of life." Because he actually built his history on the reality which pulsed in the sources and utilized scientific techniques to proceed from the documents to that reality, he contributed a new substantive component to historical criticism. It has been well said of him that, starting from his very first book, what was exemplary in Ranke was his "combination of presentation and criticism," wherein the criticism, "rightly applied, enhances not only the authenticity but the lifelikeness of the presentation."[3]

Further, Ranke's incremental historical criticism converted principles which had been the tenets of individual historians into a paradigm which could be communicated to an entire profession as its distinctive collective identification. Science in its modern connotation is characterized precisely by the collective prosecution of a singular method, and it is in this sense that Ranke initiated the modern science of history. In Acton's well-known obituary judgment of 1886, Ranke's achievement lay less in "the display of extraordinary faculties" than in his having "written a larger number of mostly excellent books than any man that ever lived" and in his having "taken pains from the first to explain how the thing is done."[4]

An essential feature of the communicability which was so important to Ranke's role in the launching of history as an independent and specialized science was the set of categorical and quotable propositions in which he articulated the fundamental tenets of scientific history, for these propositions were detachable from any particular context in Ranke and came to serve other generations as general directions for the prosecution of any historical study. The four Rankean principles which have constituted the canon of scientific history are the objectivity of historical truth, the priority of facts over concepts, the equivalent uniqueness of all historical events, and the centrality of politics—and each of them Ranke immortalized in a memorable formulation.

The ideal of the historian's objectivity evoked from Ranke the most famous statement in all historiography: "History has had assigned to it the task of judging the past, of instructing the present for the benefit of ages to come. The present study does not assume such a high office; it wants to show only what actually happened" (*wie es eigentlich gewesen*).[5] In his published lectures and correspondence, moreover, he expanded on this sentiment to show that by it he meant not merely to defend the autonomy of history against its pragmatic subordination, as the context might imply, but to make "objectivity" the "task" and "aim" which "the historian . . . must set for himself all the more since personal limitation hinders him from attaining it. The ideal of historical education would consist in training the subject to make himself wholly into the organ of the object, that is, of science (*Wissenschaft*) itself, without being hindered from knowing and presenting the complete truth by the natural or fortuitous limits of human existence."[6] For Ranke neither language, nor art, nor politics—the main concerns of history—can be understood unless one "immerses oneself in the object . . . and grasps its inner necessity, for it carries its own law within itself."[7] He found an equally trenchant expression for his own application of the principle when he declared of his *English History* that in it he had tried "to extinguish my own self, as it were, to let the things speak and the mighty forces appear which have arisen in the course of the centuries."[8]

Ranke's testimonials to the primacy of facts—the second canon of his scientific history—were both autobiographical and principled. He characterized his own political activity after 1830 by his decision not to make theory "but to get to know and to present the facts (*Fakten*) as they are, just as in history. True doctrine lies in the knowledge of the facts. . . . An idea cannot be given in general; the thing (*die Sache*) itself must express it."[9] "From the particular," he opined philosophically, "you can perhaps ascend . . . to the general. But there is no way of leading from general theory to the perception of the particular."[10] And in history itself the rule is the same: "Strict presentation of the facts, conditional and unattractive though they may be, is unquestionably the supreme law, for historical research is oriented by its very nature to the particular."[11] Moreover, factuality and objectivity—his two leading principles of scientific history—went together. "God grant that I bring to light the facts, I hope, as they were, without any deception whether of my own or of others." "All my conclusions," he wrote in rejection both of abstraction and of subjectivity, "go *a posteriori*."[12]

A corollary of Ranke's factuality was the most effective prescription of his critical method: return to the sources. For him, all knowledge "is documentary," but it was especially "to get at the truth of the facts," "to establish the particular precisely," that he required the historian to depend primarily on original documents. He aligned himself, in a well-known statement, with the historians "who intend only to transmit what happened; they are aided by eye-witnesses delivering reports. The actors speak; documents, alleged and authentic, are present in masses." The critical method in this perspective consisted, moreover, not only in the approach to the historical fact itself through the primary documents it produced and the immediate reports from those who witnessed it, but also in the evaluation of more remote historical commentaries by the light of the facts in the documents. "Before one makes historical use of a work, one must sometime investigate the extent to which it can maintain itself vis-à-vis the truth of the documents."[13]

The third great dogma of the Rankean scientific doctrine—the unique and autonomous individuality of all historical forms—was also enshrined in a memorable formula: "Every epoch is directly under God, and its value depends not on what comes from it but in its existence itself, in its own self. Thereby the consideration of history, and indeed of the individual life in history, acquires a wholly distinctive stimulus, since each epoch must be seen as something valid for its own sake and as most worthy of consideration.... All generations of mankind are equally justified in the sight of God, and so must the historian view the thing."[14] This dogma of the uniqueness in the products of history was clearly associated in Ranke's mind with the aforementioned dogmas of objectivity and factuality, since the unique object can only be understood by the submission of the subject to it and by its immunity to classificatory concepts. "A work should never be viewed as a type [Gattung] into which we may intrude our own contribution," he wrote about the classics, significantly associating general concepts with subjectivity, "but rather as an individual [Individuum], with its own root, atmosphere, nature, and existence."[15] Nor did he hesitate to make the same point for the specific profession of history: one of the two essential qualifications of "the true historian" is "participation and joy in the particular, in and for itself ... without ulterior purpose, simply out of joy in the particular life—just as one enjoys flowers without thinking of which Linnaean class they belong to."[16] The other qualification stipulated by Ranke—the possession of an "eye for generality" in history—[17] would carry him beyond this ideal juncture of individuality and objectivity, but Ranke's telling formulations of this side of his ideal reflected his certainty about it: the historian's objective view of the unique individual in history—whether a person, an institution, or an era—would always be the firm basis of all the historian's operations.

The fourth and final tenet which Ranke enshrined in a haunting phrase directed the historian to focus on past politics. States, he wrote, are "ideas of God." By this he meant to indicate both that as "spiritual substances" states are themselves "individualities," each, like other historical agents, "a living thing, . . . an unique self," and that states are a special kind of individual through which the collective historical destinies of men can be followed, since each state in its own way manifests "the idea that inspires and dominates the whole" of human institutions, determines "the personalities of all citizens," and embodies the discoverable "laws of growth." "Behold them, these celestial bodies, in their cycles, their mutual gravitation, their systems!"[18]

But despite this apparent symmetry of Ranke's legacy to and his prescription for empirical scientific history, there is something wrong with the picture. For one thing, Ranke always insisted that history was an art as well as a science, and he even implied that it was rather as an art than as a science that history was most distinctive and autonomous.[19] Nor was this aesthetic emphasis a matter merely of general profession. He often confessed his ambition to compose works that were beautiful in form as well as sound of substance, and he aimed frankly at a broad and popular rather than a special and academic audience.[20] When we look to his works themselves, we find ample evidence of the success of his effort: what remains most vital about them is the perceptive and imaginative portraiture, especially of individuals but also of groups, for which they are still read.

The addition of an artistic to the scientific facet of his history is but an overt expression, in Ranke, of a temperament which belied the linear character to be expected in the leader of a scientific revolution in history. Ranke by fundamental disposition abhorred extremes and ever sought middle grounds which would account for as many positions as were possible within their mutually inclusive

limits. Thus he was addicted to the both-and rather than the
either-or: he tended to reject all doctrine and even, in principle, all
categorical concepts precisely because they were exclusive and
hence, by his definition, partisan extremes. He deplored the
historical novel and drama, depreciated academic monography,
and yet combined elements from both genres. In politics he
opposed and was opposed by both radical left and radical right,
and came to favor a constitutional monarchy somewhat to the right
of center making a national appeal somewhat to the left of center.
In religion he turned down every dogma, and yet accounted
himself a Lutheran with "some Catholic and perhaps even heath-
enish leaven" who found the Koran "enchanting and transport-
ing" and was "determined to admit the validity of every position."[21]

Such a disposition squared well with the impartiality of Ranke's
scientific history but hardly with the narrow doctrine of objective
and factual political history with which it has been associated in
the Rankean canon. And in truth this inherited canon does turn
out to be a selection from a much larger complex of Ranke's
principles—principles which transcend the range of the canonical
scientific quartet, attenuate the connections between its propositions, and seriously compromise scientific history as a coherent
doctrine. Each of its four principles, indeed, was paired in Ranke
with an opposite principle, not so happily formulated but equally
authentic, and whether this second set be viewed as the complement or the antinomy of the first, it modifies its meaning
essentially. When the whole corpus of Ranke's historical principles
is taken into account, he appears no longer as the father of the
definite scientific, scholarly, professionalized history about whom
schools of disciples and opponents have passionately fought
sectarian academic wars, but rather as an ambiguous Ranke who
emerges from the recent scholarship of reassessment reflecting the
ambivalences of his early nineteenth-century age, at once romantic
and science-minded, and bequeathing to posterity a more encum-
bered inheritance than the deceptively simple method he seemed
to settle upon it.

That the original Ranke was more complicated than the symbol
he became is clear enough; and so is the selective effect of his
successors' increasing scientism in making him a symbol and

simplifying his influence. What is not so clear, however, is the implicit coherence, the hidden unity, behind Ranke's combination of principles. For if they did not supply a rigorous scientific doctrine, neither were they merely a collection of ideas from which successors could pick and choose at will. They were subtly joined by Ranke's own continuing quest for coherence and unity in the historical principles whose mutual tension he himself acknowledged, as well as by his fundamental and indirectly articulated commitment to history as the key to the whole knowledge of man; and the reconstruction of this matrix is important not only for the understanding of the real Ranke but also for the revision of his legacy. Since Ranke's principles were rooted in a pervasive attitude from which they could not be simply detached and appropriated, the selective harvesting of them by posterity carried with it more of the Rankean substratum than appeared on the surface. Along with the legacy of scientific history, we have inherited, subliminally, something of the generic Rankean attitude to history, and it is to the reconstruction of this that we now turn.

First we shall characterize the alternate set of formal principles which accompanied his principles of scientific history in order to comprehend the full range of his theorizing about history. But Ranke's whole attitude toward history is not to be comprehended in such theoretical principles, however complete: the rhetoric of the striking phrase and the distortions of a categorical philosophy which produced the static antitheses in his general statements about history obscured the flexible connection between principles in his practice of history, and it is hardly surprising that his theory of history has been the open quarry from which historians of different vintages have taken what they wanted. The theoretical principles are indeed useful as definitions of the poles around which Ranke's historical attitude revolved, but once they have been identified we may then proceed to reconstitute the conditions and the experience which related the divergent poles of his thinking in the integral attitude to history which has been Ranke's actual contribution to our culture.

2
The Unscientific Counterpoint

Ranke announced four principles of philosophical or theological history
which may be placed in explicit counterpoint to his four principles
of scientific history.

First, with regard to the ideal of objective history Ranke
acknowledged the constructive role of the subject qua historian—
not merely in the sense of inevitable private limitations, but in
principle. To be sure, Ranke followed Niebuhr in his confidence
that through the philological version of the critical method not
only could the fidelity of the source be judged but the original
truth of the described event could be discovered. Hence Ranke's
preference for terms like "bring to light" and "unriddle" to
indicate that the object of his historical research was there to be
uncovered. But the object to be uncovered was not ready-made in
the past, lying there to be simply copied by the historian; the
historian's activity was necessary to its constitution as a historical
object. "Since everything comes from God," wrote the young
Ranke, "what matters is not the material of existence but the eye
for the material; when we remove the shells from things and turn
out what is essential in them, it happens that in our own selves
essence, spiritual life, soul, and the breath of God take wing, or at
least have existence."[1] The divine truth is not only objectified in

the historical process but subjectified in the historian. It is obscured by human frailties in the agents as in the observers of history, and if the historian must purge himself by immersion in the past, he must also unravel the essentially true historical object from the inessential appearances in which past men enveloped it. Ranke correspondingly characterized his own role, as historian of Prussia, in activistic terms as "raising myself above the gossip which surrounds the living and which easily fixes itself for posterity as accepted tradition, and finding the right track among the thousandfold expressions of the agent himself, which often seem to contradict one another."[2]

This qualification of historical objectivity has two radically opposed sets of implications, and the revealing thing is that Ranke drew them both, though in different contexts. Insofar as objective historical truth was originated by God and produced by men in the past, the task of the historian was "to attach himself to the object" by "grasping" (*fassen*) the outer forms in which events made their appearance and, through those forms, to secure the essence which was continuous with them.[3] In such contexts Ranke thought of himself as a simple discoverer of what existed but was unknown—as a "Columbus" or as "a kind of Cook for so many beautiful, unknown islands of world history."[4] But in other contexts objective historical truth was not so much in the deeds and ideas produced by past men as it was a different kind of existence, which only the activity of the historian could distill from them. On this level Ranke could express himself in terms of a categorical dualism, with its justification of subjective construction, which was so foreign to his comprehensive receptivity as a working historian. "Over against the world of truth there is a world of appearance which also goes to the roots and develops an ever more profound appearance until it ends in phantasy [*Wesenlosigkeit*]. . . . Talent is an intimation [*Ahnung*], an immediate empathy with essence. I scent the track of the spirit. . . . The spirit from which things come, and the knower, will be one. In this theory of knowledge the most subjective is at the same time the most general truth."[5] When he thought on this cosmic level, Ranke thought in terms of the creative function of the historian: "I should like to appropriate everything great and beautiful that the world, past and present, has brought forth, and to view the course of eternal destiny with an unerring eye, and in this spirit to produce, myself, noble and beautiful works."[6]

Behind the apparent ambiguity in Ranke's famed doctrine of historical objectivity lay a fact that is crucial to the understanding both of him and of his legacy: ideas that were antithetical for life in general became reconcilable and complementary for life in history. Thus appearances and essences which were fatally divorced in his philosophy yielded to the smooth sequence of critical research, intuition, and combination in his historical method. As a historian, consequently, Ranke had no trouble in drawing from his doctrine of objectivity a conclusion which may have been difficult to sustain in logic but which made sense to him as a historical practitioner: historical truth itself was objective but many-faceted, and he illuminated the side of it that was appropriate to his own nature. "I can claim no right other than to be what I am and to think as I think, and to combine both of these in words and in the perception of my material.... My happiness is to observe the world, past and present, from this point on which I stand, and to absorb it into myself, insofar as it is congruent [homogen] with me."[7]

The ambiguities in Ranke's approach to objectivity were connected with the limits which he placed upon his addiction to "facts" in history. Not only were historical facts for him instrumental to a kind of understanding that transcended factuality, but this larger meaning was what the historian had in common with the otherness of the historical fact and what thus made the knowledge of the fact possible at all. Ranke addressed himself to the historical "grasp of men's factual circumstances" (Zustände) because he felt that it offered the best path to the understanding of "our inborn way of looking at things" (Sinnesweise) and to "the knowledge of essential being."[8] It was, indeed, only a general spiritual object that could absorb the subject while yet preserving him and thus mediate between the historian-subject and the specific historical object. "Real joy is to forget oneself, to give oneself, to become more conscious of oneself in the larger whole."[9] Thus he insisted that "the particular can never appear in full clarity unless it is grasped in its general relations."[10]

For Ranke, then, what was beyond the fact was more valuable than the fact itself. When he showed the similarity of history and

natural science it was not their analogous procedures for ascertain-
ing facts that he emphasized but rather "the higher principle"
to which they were equally dedicated—"the search for causes"
and "beginnings," for "the deeper sources" of nature and
of life.[11] He lamented, early on, that "the revealing of certain
secrets, the illumination of a thing which is obscure, is the only
thing that I can hope for in this life," when his real desire was to
write a work which "contains the fullness of the spiritual life of
history."[12] This larger purpose of his history was of a different
order than the discrete reality of events. Rather was it in the nature
of "relation" or "connection." In his dramatic invocation of
history as the dwelling place and revelation of God he paid full
honor to "every act" and "every moment" as "His witness"; but
he distinguished from these acts and moments "the connectedness
[Zusammenhang] of history in the large," which, he wrote,
witnessed Him "most of all." It was this coherence of history,
"standing there like a holy hieroglyph," which we should "decipher" and "thus serve God."[13] These relations or connections
could be, to be sure, mere combinations, contexts, or abstracts of
events. But they also could be realities in their own right, higher
indeed than the empirical reality of discrete events. They were
"dominant ideas" (die leitenden Ideen) or "dominant tendencies," and from Ranke's conclusion that their "general movement
is the really vital force in history" one commentator has gone so far
as to claim that his contribution has been "not a new method of
using sources but the infusion of new spiritual principles into the
writing of history, principles . . . which forge its external sequences
of events into internal unities."[14]

Just as Ranke's renowned emphasis on factuality had its methodological corollary in his prescription of the historian's immersion
in documentary sources for the ascertainment of the "truth of the
facts," so did his countervailing transcendence of the facts have its
corresponding principle in historical empathy—a principle that
seemed at odds with the documentary discrimination of truth from
falsity but was equally indispensable for the critical method. Ranke
developed his approach to history out of the attitudes he absorbed
from classical philology—even late in life he would instruct
historians "to fulfill the requirements of criticism and scholarship
somewhat in the manner of a philological work"[15]—and his idea

of criticism always included the imputation of relative truth to all utterances, as was taught in the philology of his day. It was this principle indeed—that all historical statements are true in the ideas and feelings they express and in the circumstances that they reflect, over and above the truthfulness of the facts they purport to convey—that turned out to be a Rankean contribution to historical method even more distinctive than Ranke's rigorous dependence upon unpublished archival sources for the discovery of unknown or reliable fact. It was characteristic of Ranke, when he was exercising his method from this perspective, to discount "innumerable errors of detail" and to assert of a historian that "on the whole he is more one-sided than false"—that his "basic standpoint . . . has its truth." Perhaps the most extreme example of this employment was Ranke's defense of Saint-Simon's notoriously unreliable memoirs. Admitting that they could not be used "as a source of pure historical instruction," he yet asserted them to have "an authenticity," not only as a product of the court society that faithfully and immediately transmitted the "one-sided" and "slanderous" attitude of these "acting persons," but even more as the expression of a higher moral truth. Saint-Simon asserted a "pointed and strict morality in a decadent age"; he "spoke for the ennobling movements of the human soul."[16]

Ranke's commitment to both facts and ideas in this sense was but one version of his profound conjoint belief in both particularity and generality as ultimate forms of truth, in both individuality and universality as ultimate forms of reality, in both freedom and necessity as ultimate conditions of action, and in both national and world history as ultimate frames of disciplined knowledge. The crucial question for the understanding of Ranke is, of course, the question of how he conceived the poles in each of these sets to be related, and here both the evidence in Ranke and the verdicts about him vary widely. There are good grounds for saying, with some, that Ranke treated the opposite terms in each of these sets—especially particular and general truths—as complements, and there are equally good grounds for saying, with others, that there was a running tension in Ranke between them.[17]

On the complementary side there was his early conviction that "all is one, and one all"; that "the activity and effect of general life is always present in the smallest details and can be known in them"; that during historical research "often from a torn, lost word a whóle form rises in shining beauty, and every day there rises too just one idea, which refers to the authentic life of the world, to the inner life of nations, and therewith to God," and that "historical personality" belongs to those individuals who make "the personal self the epitome of the general interest"—that is, who identify themselves with the universal principles of their age.[18]

On the other side Ranke not only vacillated between the primacy of the particular and of the universal principle but even acknowledged—sometimes frankly and sometimes implicitly— their incompatibility. In his reconstituted journals, for example, he seems to have noted in quick succession, first that "the precise research of the particular is always more secure" (than our dedication solely to the general), and second that "the general tendency always prevails, for only in general combinations do we get to know the nature of things."[19] When musing on religion, he thus sometimes found personality—the human embodiment of particularity—to be problematical or contingent in the light of the universal. In this context, he doubted "whether the personal is more that the necessity of earthly existence."[20] He humbly admitted, moreover, that "one lives more in the whole than in the person. . . . Often one has almost lost the awareness of having a personality. One is no longer an ego. The eternal Father of all things, who gives life to all, draws us to Him without resistance."[21]

The answer to the puzzle is that for Ranke there was no answer on this conceptual level. The imprecision of his abstract categories and the uncongeniality of his thinking in this vein obscured the crucial distinction which he made concretely between the priority of particulars in the method of knowledge and the priority of universals in the substance of knowledge.[22] Since particularity was for him the special domain of history, and since he ultimately found it easier to go from the method to the substance of knowledge than in the converse direction, once more we find in the practice of history an operational solution for a problem which he left unresolved in its own theoretical terms.

The third of Ranke's celebrated doctrines—the historicist doctrine of the unique and independent value of every historical form—was similarly qualified by Ranke's passion for a total view of things. To be sure, he would always be disposed to "enjoy every individual life" and to "admit the validity of every position,"[23] but he always postulated too the idea of a developmental totality which was axiologically superior to his individuals and made some of them more valuable than others in the light of it. Ranke's commitment to universal history, literally fulfilled only toward the end of his long life, was paramount for him in principle from the very beginning of his career as an historian.[24] Not only was his correspondence filled with testimonials to "world history" as "certainly the finest and most noteworthy history that ever happened," but he lectured on it from the time of his appointment to the University of Berlin in 1824.[25] And from the beginning this commitment was intimately tied up with his striving for knowledge of human nature and of human development as a whole—a kind of knowledge which he himself recognized to be categorically different from the knowledge of particular history. As early as 1826, when he was but thirty-one years old, he was referring to his "old purpose of discovering the tale [*Mär*] of world history" and describing it as "that course of events and developments of our species which is to be seen as its real content, as its center and its essence." Soon afterward he was announcing that this old purpose—to grasp "the whole" (*das Ganze*) of "the course of human development"—had become his real goal as a historian.[26] He came more and more strongly to feel "what sublime stuff is universal history, from which I can only with violence tear myself away to some particular study," and ultimately he even acknowledged, beyond humanity, the historical relevance of "the eternal ideas which condition the spiritual life of mankind."[27]

Thus Ranke applied to history the antinomy characteristic of his romantic age: the idea of an individual reality which was at one and the same time unique in itself and, like other individuals, a manifestation of a universal principle. It is hardly surprising, then, to find Ranke having recourse to the time-tested argument from ignorance and admitting that, however "unknown to us" they might be, there were "laws, more mysterious and greater than one usually thinks," which "govern the appearance of the infinite variety of developments inherent in mankind" and which thus implicitly interrupt the immediacy and the autonomy of these variegated appearances.[28]

It can be argued—indeed, it usually has been argued—that Ranke's commitment to "eternal ideas," "moral laws," and "universal history" confirmed rather than abridged the sovereign particularity and individuality of historical events, since, for him, general ideas and laws were unknowable in themselves and were knowable only as functions of the particular data and individual agents in which they were exclusively manifested. From this point of view "the tale of universal history," to which he was metaphorically committed, faithfully reflected Ranke's notion of general truth as a multiform resultant of the kaleidoscopic movements and intersections of myriad individual actions. This point of view is supported, moreover, by Ranke's arguments against both kinds of the general truths which he explicitly identified as challenges to the unique individuality of historical events: against synchronic "dominant ideas" as "something conceptual" which reduces men to "mere shadows or schemata incorporating the concept"; and against the diachronic "concept of progress," which reduces the history of one generation to "a stage of the next."[29] Instead of dominant ideas, he endorsed descriptive "tendencies," which he could distill from events; and instead of progress, he proposed the amorphous "course and movement of the human race," as a general theme which would be consonant with the individuality of men's creative acts and with their "independence from what precedes and what follows."[30]

But this familiar nominalistic interpretation of Ranke is deceptive, for he also explicitly and emphatically asserted the historical validity both of dominant ideas and of progress over and above the validity of individual events. Despite his objections to the synchronic subsumption of particular facts under abstract ideas, not only did Ranke develop (consistently in his thinking if not in his terminology) a notion of individuality which was categorically distinguished from particularity precisely by its perspective upon "universality" (*das Allgemeine*) and by its generalizing hierarchy of individual persons, individual states, and individual epochs, but he also specified the historical relevance of eternal ideas independently of any embodiment in historical individuals. The distinctive tendency and ideal which the historian discovers in each age, he wrote, is "apart from certain unchanging, eternal dominant ideas [*Hauptideen*], such as moral ideas," and he applied the principle regularly in the moral judgments which he deemed

the historian qualified to pronounce upon the past on behalf of
the universal human reality transcending each of its individual
expressions. As he would dramatize the principle in his condemnation of the Saint Bartholomew Massacre, "Men may blind themselves for a time, but they cannot disturb the moral laws on which
their existence reposes; these rule with a necessity as inevitable as
that which regulates the course of the stars."[31]

Nor did Ranke leave the idea of progress an unqualified victim
of the uniqueness and equivalence of individuals in history. His
general argument against progress in history, and especially against
any progress in "the true morality and religion," was misleading,
for he himself appended to it a countervailing argument which set
up a general level of history where progress did apply against the
individual level where it did not. Thus, when he spelled out his
concession of "a progress in material things," it grew to mean "an
unconditional progress in the development and application of the
exact sciences and even in the diffusion of the idea of humanity
and of culture to the various nations and individuals," including,
specifically, "the expansion of moral and religious ideas." However selective and irregular the process, Ranke concluded that man
has acquired "in the course of the centuries a possession which
consists in material and social progress, but especially also in
religious development." In short, "the human spirit is caught up
in an infinite progress." The task of the universal historian is to
trace as a "vital totality" the "historical life which moves progressively from one nation to another" and to approach the individual
state itself as "a living being which by its nature incessantly grows
and irresistibly progresses . . . toward its ideas, toward greater
perfection." Progress may be irrelevant to the individual, but it
does pertain to "humanity."[32]

Now the connection between the Ranke who did not believe in
the historical validity of transcendent ideas and of progress and the
Ranke who did believe in it is hard to explain. What Ranke did not
believe in was the combination of transcendent ideas and progress;
what he did believe in was each separately. The confusion about
this solution in Ranke stems from his apparently separate discussions of "dominant ideas" and "progress," but the context of his
discussion makes it clear that when he rejected either, it was always
on the assumption of its conjunction with the other.[33] What he

objected to in this conjunction, which he saw in the form of Hegel's or Schelling's philosophy of history, was its construction of a distinct, logically sequential level of ideal history above and independent of the empirical level of particular historical facts and individual historical events. But he could approve transcendent ideas that were unchanging and therefore dependent upon individual actors for their historization, as he could, analogously, approve an empirical idea of progress bereft of the linear and determined qualities stemming from a logical association with a transcendent idea. His universal history could therefore evince, in Masur's trenchant phrase, "a teleology without a telos."[34] Ranke did then believe in eternal ideas and in historical progress which, however empirically rooted they must be for their relevance to history, respectively stood over against individual acts as the constant conditions of these evanescent acts and bestowed on some historical periods a greater value than on others. They were beliefs that created tension not between what was and what was not history but between the general and the individual principles within history itself, and only there was it resolved.

The fourth and, for our purpose, final item of the Rankean heritage has been the focus on the political dimension of history, and here too there is evidence in Ranke himself that points another way. To be sure, states were the primary units of his history; their movements and relations formed the core of knowable human activity in the past with which he was concerned. But in two important respects this concentration upon the state went beyond the emphasis upon governmental measures and policies—particularly in war and diplomacy—which it has often been taken to justify. First, Ranke's working notion of the state included much more than its government. Second, he included in his history activities that were outside the state. His idea of the state as the primary historical unit meant not that it was the only historical unit but that it was the universally relevant one and that the other dimensions of men's activity should be viewed in relation to their politics. On the first count—his large definition of states—the state is a "modification" of both the nation and humanity: it is man in his orientation toward "the common good." Nations, in this view, are the organizations of humanity through which its universal history as a whole must be studied; states are the national organizations (albeit the connection between states and nations is not a one-to-one correspondence) through which the history of nations—and thus of humanity—in modern times must be studied, since "the rejuvenation of the state by the national principle . . .—by the essential, actual nationality that is expressed in the state—"has determined recent history.[35] Nations and states, as articulations of humanity, are universal in their comprehension of all men, and, like humanity, they too are spiritual in essence. The relationship between politics and culture (that is, religion and the arts), which is external in the loosely coherent nation, becomes integrated within the nationally integrated modern state. National culture has become a generator of political vitality.

On the second count—the validation of men's social and cultural activities in history outside of but conjointly with their politics—we must note that Ranke's nations persisted as historical units in modern times, even if they had become secondary, for historical study, to the states from which he distinguished them. Consequently, he declared his interest in modern Italian art and literature as the means of getting at "the history of the inner existence of the nation," and he even wrote history in those fields.[36] But consistently enough it was in his approach to world history as a totality, in which he deemed nations and humanity to be the dialectical subjects, that he defined the historian's field in a way far transcending men's past politics. All the fields of history are "always conjoined and mutually conditioning," he wrote in his notes of the 1830s—the same decade in which he was developing his theory of the state as the idea of God.[37] The "specific principle" of the "common life" which is the substance of universal history is the history of "civilization," a category which includes the arts, sciences, religion, and the state. As "the free development of all these forces looking to the ideal," civilization is itself "the foremost acquisition and possession of humanity handed on and augmented from generation to generation" and is "inseparably bound together with politics and war and with all the events which constitute the facts of history.[38]

Ranke's unscientific counterpoint has been summed up in the problematic reinterpretation of his renowned scientific dictum that history aims at "what actually happened." It no longer means the objective reporting of past facts in the documents; it refers, rather, to the reconstruction of the past life behind the documents.

3
The Limits of Theory

Thus did Ranke summarize his position that the general, progressive, and cultural development of man was as essential to the study of history as the objective, critically ascertained unique facts of individual states and equivalent epochs with which it was somehow joined. It should be clear, from the foregoing, that both levels of history were of crucial importance to Ranke, and it should also be clear that along these theoretical lines he neither could nor would develop their relationship and therewith an integral idea of history. But although Ranke did not himself relate his two theoretical levels, and although the final answer to the question of his historical integrity is not to be found in them, we can adduce three rational explanations of their coexistence and an additional one of their mutual historical conditioning which constitute the beginnings of an answer. For these explanations show the function which such principles, through their very diversity, played in his idea of history.

I   First, the discrepancy between the two sets of Ranke's historical principles was connected with the nugatory role of theoretical principles as such for him. He did not believe that abstract concepts could touch truth, and he would hardly have been able to account for his own dicta about history in general. History

subsumed under concepts was for him the enslavement of history
by philosophy, and he announced plainly that the way to truth
through the relations of general propositions was not for him as a
historian.[1] His inconsistencies, therefore, stemmed from the contradictions within his theory itself, and these, in turn, stemmed
from his deliberate neglect of its internal relations; his theoretical
propositions were aligned not with one another but rather with the
specific facets of actual history that instigated them, and what were
differences in the degree of generality for actual history became
categorical differences of kind in the derivative theory. Ranke was,
in short, an ad hoc theorist and an integral practitioner of history;
the internal connection between the different levels of history he
worked with cannot be found in any logical coherence, which he
did not even attempt, but in a temporal coherence, which he could
not avoid.

Striking indeed is the contrast between the fragmentary, sporadic pattern of his theorizing and the continuity of his lifelong
commitment to the substance of both particular and universal
history. What passes for Ranke's philosophy of history—a label
which he characteristically rejected as an invention of philosophers
for their domination over history—is drawn from sources of three
kinds: from isolated comments scattered through his notebooks,
correspondence, and prefaces; from the manuscript lecture notes
for his general history courses, composed largely (albeit not
exclusively) in the decade of the 1830s; and from the articles of the
same short period, when he was completing his maturation as a
person and attaining the peak of his historical power and when he
apparently did turn his attention to the formulation of a coherent
theory of history for the general public.

The propositions from the first kind of source are occasional
statements of belief rather than reasoned arguments. In each
instance he tailored his remarks to the requirements of the
particular situation or to the individual character of his interlocu-
tor. Even the lengthier introductory remarks of 1854, in Ranke's
private lectures to Bavaria's King Maximilian II on general modern
history, were ex cathedra pronouncements by the renowned professor which he modified or complicated rather than developed
under the questioning of the king.[2]

The other kinds of source comprise informal and unpublished

essays, designed as sketches of introductory classroom lectures, on the nature of history and its place in the constellation of organized knowledge, and of published essays on the great powers (*Die grossen Mächte*, 1832), on the nature of the state via a dialogue on politics (*Politisches Gespräch*, 1836), and on his "reflections" (from the political journal, *Historisch-Politische Zeitschrift*, which Ranke edited from 1832 to 1836). From these sources comes much of the evidence for Ranke as the theorist of historical individuality and of the sanctity of political history, but upon closer inspection it is clear that these essays too—philosophical and political alike— were occasional pieces whose theoretical emphases were partial generalizations of Ranke's contemporary academic and practical concerns. They were triggered by the fact of interdisciplinary feud and the threat of revolutionary conflict, and their common denominator was the stress upon the actual and the individual in history for the purpose of rejecting the general and abstract theories which he found common to his opponents in politics, philosophy, and theology. Ranke combined two concerns in these essays: he meant to exclude political, philosophical, and theological doctrine from the interpretation of history, and he meant to make this autonomous history, with its conservative and empirical character, the core of new political, philosophical, and theological doctrine.

To accomplish these purposes Ranke could not deny theory— since he needed to counter theory with theory—but he depreciated it: he defined historical reality in terms of particular events and institutions, and he asserted his theory of historical individuality as a derivation from this actuality. Thus, when he indicated that historical knowledge should be independent of politics but should itself search out the hidden causes of events and so become the basis of politics, he was committing himself to a theory of history which exalted historically rooted facts over any theory to be drawn from history.[3] His declarations during this period all tended to validate general truths both in history and about history only as functions of the particular facts which for this purpose and at this time dominated his idea of history. Authentic theory, he affirmed, was a matter not of the application of general categories to discrete phenomena but of the "vital insight" (*lebendige Ansicht*) into the "inner essence of existence and its laws."[4] He made it quite clear, moreover, that history was the only medium in which individual things could maintain this priority over general ideas—in which the facts themselves determined the ideas. "There are just two ways to get to learn human things—knowledge of the particular and abstraction" he wrote at this time. "The latter is the way of philosophy, the former the way of history. There is no other way." And he now classified "philosophy of history" as philosophy, not history.[5]

Thus even in his theoretically most coherent phase Ranke's theory of history was dominated by his view of historical reality, and his view of historical reality was dominated by the sovereignty of particular facts over the kind of general truths which could serve as a basis for autonomous theory. "A history of the most important moments of recent times is being put together almost without my assistance," he remarked at the beginning of the 1830s,[6] and this feeling of being borne along by a current of historical facts carried over into his theory to make it a self-denying celebration of its own impotence. Since this theory was first conceived during the period in which the practical considerations it reflected were governed by the supreme standards of particularity and variety, and since it had no intellectual warrant of its own to transcend these standards, the bits of generality and synthesis which embodied Ranke's wistful search for an ideal history surfaced in the theory as distant objectives, separated by far from the main flow. What value the theory has is not any service it performed for Ranke's history but the light that its unbalanced duality between a predominant emphasis on individuality and a subordinate but persistent acknowledgment of universality throws on the assumptions of his historical practice. What integrity the theory has lies not in any analytical relationship of its dual factors but in Ranke's own history, for it was their joint conditioning by the situation of the 1830s that formed the substratal connection between both.[7]

II The second contributory answer to the question posed by the co-existence of Ranke's two layers of history is the necessity of an historiographical scaffolding. Ranke could not, in the early nineteenth century, demand the loving care for the brute historical fact that he required of himself, his students, and his readers, without bringing to bear a whole traditional framework of spiritual support to infuse it with a worthy meaning. Thus Ranke associated divine purpose with world history and used both to cradle "the core, nature, and life of the individual" (*Individuums*), which was the immediate object of his historical studies. At the very outset of his career he declared his mission to be the exposition of "men's divine nature" through the demonstration of "the esteem and the love which they bear for the individuality [*Eigentümlichkeit*] that God has given them," and he announced his intention of revealing this divine quality in human nature through its history, where "God lives and is to be known," where "every deed witnesses Him and every moment preaches His name." Nor did he ever drop this early motif. Whether by invocation of God or of humanity he would continue to subsume the particular results of his specialized research under a higher category that gave it meaning. Thus he would justify his research by referring to its view of "the immediate working, the visible action of God"; to its revelation of a "human history" that shows "the ideality of an original and forever God-related existence, ... seeking the ocean drop by drop, a harmony raised in a thousand dissonances"; to its "continuous pursuit of a greater universal purpose"; to its principle that "only from the depths of the most thorough research is it possible to investigate the secret traces of God in history"; and to its tenet that only from the history of the individual nations and their interaction "does the history of humanity appear."[8]

By this explanation, Ranke's generalizing and individualizing ideas of history could coexist because, however anomalous abstractly, operationally they acted on different planes—the one served the other. Universal principle neither qualified nor limited the principle of individuality but rather was a hermeneutic instrument for its interpretation in an age which could not yet accept particular things and individual persons as ends in themselves with meanings for themselves.

III The third of the analytical explanations that serve as partial answers to the question of the relations between principle and fact in Ranke's history has to do with his distinctive religiosity, which posited a God who not only functioned as a prop for history (a position not in itself very distinctive) but was dependent upon history to be known and worshiped (a position certainly distinctive). The character of Ranke's Christianity is perhaps the most frequently and thoroughly given of all the interpretations of his approach to history,[9] and the fitness of the religious interpretation is beyond dispute. Ranke was a Lutheran, but one for whom God's inscrutability was so cardinal a tenet that he rejected all doctrine, not only orthodox dogma but also his brother Heinrich's pietistic Biblicism, simply because they presumed a definite conceptual knowledge of God—because, as Ranke put it, in doctrine "the understanding makes itself at home under prepared ideas . . . and must reject any opposition."[10] "Religion rests primarily on the uninhibited truth of the inner sense," and for Ranke this sense dictated the absolute faith in "the certainty of His existence and His participation in life," a faith without which "I could not live."[11] This God expressed Himself in history and was accessible only through history. "I hope," Ranke wrote at an early, revealing moment, "ever to know God and the human race, and nations and history—yet no, to know not God but the rest through the sensing of Him" (*im Gefühl von ihm das übrige*).[12] For "the spirit cannot be touched with the hands or perceived with the eyes; it is known in its results and in its activity" (*Wirkung*).[13] To know history in the consciousness of the meaning bestowed upon human events by a God who expressed Himself only thus, and thereby to know all there is to know of God—this was Ranke's historical faith. This faith it was that led him to exult, as an ordained historian, to his clerical brother: "I am certain of the omnipresence of God and think that one can grasp Him definitely with one's hands. In my present mood I swear to myself a thousand times that I shall spend my life in the fear of God and in history."[14]

Clearly, Ranke's piety was of a kind that led him to seek God in history through what he variously called His "finger," His "destiny" (*Geschick*), His "traces," His "Providence." Clearly too, the element in Ranke's piety which led him from the old Lutheran belief in the unknowability of God's nature to the positive and exclusive faith in history as the way to knowledge of His works was his assumption that God was accessible to man only through His gift of life, of movement, of creativity. God consequently can be grasped, not directly through concepts in dogmas, but indirectly through the spontaneous individual acts and the mobile developments in history which are the appropriate human symbols of His essential vitality. Ranke's most revealing term for the divine presence in the world was God's "breath," and this "source of life active behind the appearance—understanding, love, soul"—was witnessed, for Ranke, by "the stream of human history, now rushing and wild, now peaceful and quiet." In Ranke's religiosity the particular events and the general developments of history met; both kinds of history bore witness to God and were parts of His "eternal revelation."[15] Ranke's religion confirmed rather than resolved the duality of his historical principles.

IV From whatever angle we have inspected Ranke's theoretical ideas *about* history—as rationalizations, as hermeneutics, and as exercises in piety—we have been referred to his operational views *of* history itself, to his views of what was in history and how the historian could know it. For Ranke committed himself immediately to the stuff and method of history: he found in the actual process of history a satisfaction of his political, religious, and philosophical needs which he could find neither in absolute principle nor even in any conception of the meaning of history, and above all he found in actual history a working interaction of the diverse principles which remained disengaged polarities outside of history. To understand a view of history which made the events of the past the pattern of human destiny and the historian's knowledge of those events the key to his own identity, we must turn away from Ranke's principles of history to the experience which directed him to it as his primary commitment. The elements that went into Ranke's commitment to history were supplied by the atmosphere in which he matured, but the exclusive commitment itself was distinctive and came out of his own experience.

According to his own retrospective testimony, he absorbed two kinds of contemporary historical attitudes into his own approach to history during the Restoration from 1815 to 1830, the period of European stabilization which coincided with his formative period. He was imbued with the appreciation of history diffused by the romantic school, particularly by the philosopher Fichte, who would be listed by Ranke along with Thucydides, Niebuhr, and

Luther as one of his main intellectual creditors for whatever impact he had "on the science of history"; and he claimed to be profoundly moved toward the study of "historical institutions" by the continuing threat posed to them by revolution.[16] Actually, the two reminiscences are of unequal value: Ranke's recollection of his sensitivity to the romantic mentality was entirely accurate; his recollection of his susceptibility to the counterrevolutionary politics of the Restoration was anachronistic, relocating a political concern which really seized him only subsequently.[17]

Ranke's early notes and correspondence confirm his testimony that he felt Fichte speaking to him directly as a scholar. His excerpts of the philosopher's obviously relevant essays, *The Way to the Blessed Life* and *On the Nature of the Scholar,* show his reception of their moral that the academic calling is sanctified by its task in this world, that the "divine idea" appears in the world as "divine life," that the law of divine life is "development," that "all philosophical knowledge is by its very nature not factual but genetic," that the mission of the scholar is to comprehend and to represent the divine idea by producing and constructing it from its vitalizing function in the world of appearances, and that therefore, in Ranke's recollection of the application of Fichte's moral to history, the "love of a past life—that is, of its idea, . . . leads to God."[18] Ranke also took from Fichte an even more distinctive piece of the romantic mentality: although the historian did not buy the whole of the philosopher's radical subjectivity, since he insisted, explicitly against Fichte, on the necessity of "the perception of another" to the ego's gaining consciousness of its own identity, yet he admitted, with Fichte, that the ego's identity itself "must precede every such perception . . . and makes it possible." Ranke's later profession of the submersion of the subject in the object should be understood against the background of his early Fichtean belief in the bond of the common Divine "spirit" which required the action of each upon the other while preserving the integrity of each in the other.[19]

Nor was Fichte the only conduit from romanticism. Ranke took extensive notes on language, art, and the philosophy of spirit from such luminaries of the movement as Hamann, Friedrich Heinrich Jacobi, Friedrich Schlegel, Jean Paul, Jacob Grimm, and Schelling.

With the philosophers—Jacobi, Schelling, Schlegel, and even
Fichte at times—he wrestled, as befitted his inherent distaste for
speculation and his suspicion of its results, but he never visited on
them the fundamental condemnations which he reserved, from
time to time and despite his general recognition of their achievements, for such stellar lights of the German classical school as Kant
("Godless and hopeless"), Hegel ("the new scholasticism," "the
sophistic philosophy effective only through the incantation of odd
formulas"), Schiller ("had no vocation as a writer of history"),
and even Goethe ("violates us in his application of natural laws to
spiritual love").[20] However sporadic these outbursts were and
however plausible the subliminal influence of their targets upon
him may have been, the kind of rational and aesthetic syntheses
which these classicists had sought or achieved kept Ranke an
outsider. Of romantics like Heine, Schelling, and Schleiermacher,
on the contrary, he wrote warmly, and with the latter two he was
tied in personal friendship.[21]

The bond with Friedrich Schleiermacher especially was revealing
of the intellectual sustenance which Ranke was drawing from his
environment. In the academic politics of the University of Berlin,
Ranke sided with Schleiermacher against Hegel, and this party
lineup was expressive of a deeper intellectual relationship. Schleiermacher, the renovator of Protestantism, articulated in his theology and philosophy the same doctrine that appeared in Ranke as a
summary assumption of his history. This doctrine, which may be
labeled dialectical dualism, set up the fundamental terms of
life—God and the world, religion and culture, the ideal and the
real, feeling and understanding, the general and the individual—
as polar opposites in continual and reciprocal interaction and
posited Christianity as the active, living spirit ("galvanic soul," in
Schleiermacher's words) which both preserved the separate identities of the two terms in each of these sets and sparked their
evanescent fusions, in an infinite rhythm of determinate and
mediated antitheses without a synthesis. Like Ranke's too, Schleiermacher's God was a conceptually unknowable deity, and the
theologian explicated the implication of such a God for history
when he declared that the conjunctions of the general ideal and
the individual reality through which He could be perceived were
essentially irrational and must be empirically intuited.

Although there is no conclusive evidence of a literal influence upon Ranke by Schleiermacher, the striking similarities of the terms and the tensions of their thinking point to a common root in the romantic propensity for spiritualizing natural existence, naturalizing the spiritual life, and yet maintaining the respective integrity of both the natural and the spiritual principles.[22] The experience of revolution and attempted reconstruction was built into this perspective upon the world, and it was thus, secondhand through his cultural atmosphere rather than first-hand through political experience, that the young Ranke absorbed the circumstantial influences of his environment and, consistent with their indirect path to him, applied them indirectly—not to his participation in the present but to his understanding of the past of his own age.

Ranke's single-minded application of the familiar romantic mentality to history affords a collateral confirmation of what we have seen demonstrated repeatedly in his own creed—that his distinctive quality lay not in his ideas about life and history but in his reference of all his ideas about life *to* history before he could give them substance, understand them, and organize them. Where others of his generation raised the status of history, as a concrete manifestation of spirit, to an honorable place among the many mansions of the spirit because it was found suitable to the new emphasis on the dynamism and mobility of the spirit, Ranke went beyond them to historicize all that we can know about spirit and thus to make history no longer *an* arena where integral principles were actualized but now *the* dimension where actual principles were integrated. In short, Ranke's environment predisposed him to value history as an equivalent mode of knowledge. But it was the mold of his own experience and his own thinking that would dispose him to value history as a superior mode of knowledge.

Thus there is a kind of symmetry between the substance of the Ranke problem and the method through which it can be fruitfully approached. The materials for the exhibition of the tension in him between particular and general truth may be most advantageously displayed in the analysis of his theoretical principles about history, but the materials for the resolution of the tension are most appropriately displayed through the actual history of Ranke and of his histories. Now the principles of Ranke's historical theory, telling as their formulations are, reveal more about the later generations that abstracted them than they do about their meaning for the Rankean generation that produced them. If we approach Ranke through the history that he wrote and the history that he lived rather than through the theoretical categories of both that he conceived, we should gain far better access not only to the concretions that held him together but even to the genesis of the very categories that rent him.

We shall meet many of these theoretical positions again in our journey along the path of Ranke's own historical development, but under conditions and in contexts that should make their frictions and imbalances both explicable and meaningful.

Part Two
The History

4
The Preconditions of History
(1795–1817)

We must ask first, then, how history grew, in Ranke's hands, from a distinct field of knowledge among others to a perspective upon all reality—the only perspective from which the opposing principles of life could be perceived in constructive interaction. The answer lies in his personal history and in his developing view of human nature. He could preach the saving medium of history in the realm of knowledge because it had in fact saved him and enabled him to live with the centrifugal tendencies in his own soul. And once professed, history could become the prism through which he would filter all his subsequent experience because history, and history alone, provided coherent access to the contradictory nature of man and thereby to the contradictory philosophical and religious principles which were the abstractions from it. Ranke's biography helps to explain his historiographical principles. His view of man helps to explain his interpretation of the historical process. The complete identification of Ranke the man with Ranke the historian helps to explain the congruence of his historiography and his history—helps to explain, that is, why his provocative combination of individuality and universality was a combination which he both required in the method of the historian and found in the actual pattern of the past.

Ranke lived an uneventful life in a most eventful age, originally by circumstance and subsequently by choice. However uninteresting biographically, the fact is crucial intellectually, for it was the chronic condition that fostered and conserved his disposition to history. At least since Rousseau and Kant, men had resorted to the requirements of human action for the necessary organization of ideas which were heterogeneous or contradictory in principle, and Ranke's own inaction led him all the more to depend upon the vicarious acts of man in history for the integration of his own divided self. For his was a riven spirit indeed. The same circumstances that suspended him from the activity of his early nineteenth-century world immersed him in its psychic duality, and even after he discovered a bridge in history and a haven in conservative politics, the tension between his principles persisted within these practical media.

These two dimensions of the mature Ranke—his penchant for life's manifold conflicts and his recurrent insistence upon their resolution in the stability of academic profession and political tradition—has each produced a version of his early years which serves as the backdrop to it. The generally accepted view of his youth, consistent with in own reminiscences of it, is geared to his persistent drive toward stability and tradition. The recent revision of this view furnishes biographical support for his equally persistent appreciation of human reality's disorderly manifold and its incessant movement.

The established biographical interpretation illuminates those aspects in Ranke's breeding that contributed a lasting cushion of protective safety to his temperament. Born on December 21, 1795, in the small rural Thuringian valley town of Wiehe, he was descended from a long line of Lutheran pastors which had made, in the person of Leopold's father, the not infrequent middle-class German transition to the profession of law and the civil service. To the security of the locally established paternal family was added the comfortable property from the maternal side, and in the rural section of electoral Saxony to which the town and family belonged, Leopold grew up amid an unshaken traditional social order and far removed from the convulsions of the period's revolutionary and international politics. Affection for his native neighborhood, loyalty to family, and visceral attachment to the

peace and security of traditional ways remained with him throughout his life and undoubtedly contributed to that veneration of old
established institutions which led him to seek out their historical
origins and development. "We [Rankes]," he would write to a
brother in later life, "are all by nature averse to destruction, and
desire to root tradition [*das Erhaltene*] in our knowledge of actual
existence and in our insight into its essence."[1]

But the social structure of Ranke's home town also possessed, in
addition to the stability of the hierarchical principle, features
which gave a distinctive turn to the historical conservatism it
otherwise bred. It was a local administrative rather than commer-
cial center, and it was dominated by an educated middle-class
elite—officials, pastors, and professional men—whose unquestioning support of the existing order was accompanied by a firm
commitment to intellectual vocations and to their value for the
society. Ranke associated his family and himself with this elite of
old families and literate vocations,[2] and the schools he attended,
populated in the main by its scions, intensified his experience of its
ethos. These Saxon schools admitted their students on nomination
of the authorities, segregated them from the outside world, and
taught them a traditional Lutheran humanism, of Melanchthonian
origins and spiked with a moderate dosage of pietism, which
consecrated learning in the practical form of preparing their young
men for the posts that required it.[3]

That these conditions of his nurture settled into the permanent
frame of Ranke's mentality is patent from the halcyonic tones of
the nostalgia which he cherished toward the settled order and the
intellectual dedication of his family and its social environs his long
life through. But there was another side of his early conditioning
which he elided in his reminiscences, and this harsher aspect of his
youth, so different from the testimony of his conscious recollection, exercised a contrapuntal unsettling pressure upon his formation.[4] The Ranke family appears to have been much less solidly
entrenched and more perilously unorthodox than either Ranke's
memory or the compatible biographic analyses took it to have
been. Not only did neither side of his family belong to the "old
families" of Wiehe—the settlement there of Ranke's paternal
ancestors went back only four generations and that of his maternal
forebears three, shallow roots by the customary standards of such a

static locale—but the family's place on the social ladder was far from assured. Both Ranke's father and his grandfather were half-orphaned and torn early from their parental homes by the premature deaths of their mothers, and both responded by exhibiting maverick tendencies that certainly cast doubt upon their respectability as this quality was measured by the hierarchical society of their day. The grandfather was almost committed to an artisan's trade and showed diversionary ambitions for a teaching and academic career when he did return to the pastoral calling of his forefathers. Ranke's father fomented a family crisis when he broke with family tradition and turned from the ministry for which he was destined to the practice of law, a shift which contributed to his insecure social position in the community.

The nonconformist facet of Ranke's family background is most revisionist in the family's religious heterodoxy, for the solid trans-mission of an evangelical Lutheran Christianity was supposed to be the continuous heritage which, again according to Ranke and the main line of his commentators, sustained him through his sundry spiritual crises until the apotheosis of his religious piety in the sanctuary of an inscrutable divine history. In fact, however, the parental home perpetuated only faint traces of orthodox Lutheran-ism, for religion as such did not permeate the atmosphere, and what there was of it was dominated by the ill-assorted but equally disreputable elements of utilitarian rational moralism from the father's partiality for Enlightenment theology and of the uncon-fined emotional transports from the ecstatic enthusiasm of the mother. For what they are worth, extant papers which the child Leopold Ranke wrote in elementary school reveal a practical, progressive, worldly point of view which points to influence by the simplistic paternal brand of Enlightenment.[5]

Now one need not accept the theses that have accompanied the revision—the thesis of the essential incompatibility between the versions of the secure and the insecure background and the thesis of Ranke's intentional distortion of his family background to obscure its originality and heighten his own individuality[6]—to find meaning in the facts to which the revision calls attention. Not only do these facts confirm the conversion of religious into academic callings which the traditional interpretation of Ranke's early background also highlights, but both sides of this background are required for an adequate genetic account of the two-sided mature Ranke. Like the grown man, the very young Ranke inhabited situations of insecurity and struggle in which he discerned the outlines of a blessed harmonious order. The connection between the orderliness of the adult and the orderliness in the youthful environs is overt, for it appears in the testimony of the adult Ranke himself. Any connection between the crisis-beset adult and the instability in the youthful environs, however, must be interpolated if it is to be made at all, since by its nature and by this quality of Ranke's early environment it could only have been made beneath the level of consciousness. He did betray the possibility of such a connection in his recollections, for there he acknowledged several of the single facts that together compose a social insecurity—the recency of his family's ascertainable genealogical record, the imminence of his grandfather's near descent into the artisanry, his father's susceptibility to the Enlightenment and withdrawal from the community into family life, the unsteadiness of his mother's religious faith—but he neither aligned them nor attributed any meaning to them.[7]

Yet one demonstrable connection with his later tensile mentality did come out of his early years. From a very young age he would turn his attention to politics primarily when crises broke in upon him, and in the first of these he revealed the original association of this concern for the explosive dimension of politics— a dimension which would remain the cynosure of his political interest all his life—with his insecurity about the constancy of the social hierarchy. The jejune essay "What Use Has the Learning of History for the Life of Man?" which he wrote as a twelve-year old schoolboy had little of his later approach to history, but it did articulate the visceral linkage between the dangers to the monarchical state and the social structure which was brought to the surface by his response to the French victory and the German crisis of 1806.[8] In this plastic period of his life, even before he had developed any but the most banal feelings about the pragmatic uses of the past, he was called by an external convulsion to make the first of what would be many connections between his fears for the fragility of his social order and his insight into the fundamental divisions of politics, and instinctively he turned to history for the confirmation of his equally strong conviction that social stability and political unity were ultimate and attainable realities. Already the two aspects of his being were so equally balanced that he could find the resolution of practical crises only in knowledge.

Ranke's experience at secondary school, too, was characterized by a feature which is evident enough in the contemporary evidence, which was dropped from the biographical reconstructions of the later Ranke, and which should be restored to provide genetic underpinning for an apparently spontaneous mature Rankean trait. Pforta, the secondary school he attended, has been well known, both from Ranke's recollections and biographers, for having plunged him into the ancient classics and for having stimulated his passion for the literary arts. But the notes and papers from the five years of his studying there also show an immersion in the literature of the modern German classical school—in Lessing, Schiller, Goethe, and above all in Herder—that was obscured by his later condemnation or neglect of these writers and his preference for the poets, critics, and philosophers of the rival romantic school.[9] His passion for Goethe and his reliance on Herder would outlast his school years, but ultimately their integration of history into larger schemes encompassing all nature, art, and thought would lead to their eclipse, during Ranke's own years of *Sturm und Drang*, in favor of the more open-ended and pluralistic tendency of the romantics. Yet, however transitional the young Ranke's addiction to the modern classical branch of the German aesthetic movement may have been, this recapitulation, in Ranke's ontogeny, of the nation's phylogenic cultural development from the dominance of Enlightenment through that of classicism to that of romanticism indicates a parallel absorption of what had superficially seemed to be superseded. For Ranke, as for his contemporary German culture as a whole, the classical bent toward the satisfying cloture of a total system that would accommodate the rich varieties of individual life was to persist within the romantic celebration of the natural and human manifold as the impulse toward the harmonious transcendence of its multifarious discords.

In 1814 Ranke left his native state of electoral Saxony to study at the university in royal Saxony, and he would never again return as permanent resident. During the next two decades, as student in Leipzig and teacher in Prussia, he would develop the substantive interests, ideas, and commitments that led him toward history and that determined the kind of historian he became. Just as the condition of his early years shaped his frame, the experiences of his subsequent youthful years gave him his direction. Of these experiences and his responses to them, three require particular attention, because they are so apt to be casually misunderstood and because they have a historiographical as much as a biographical resonance. Ranke's Prussianism, his religiosity, his joint passion for intangible unities and for concrete details: these would be constant themes in his life that came from the experience of his formative years, and it is worthwhile, for the illumination both of Ranke and of the human process generally, to see how events harden into attributes. These events fall into a chronological line extending from Ranke's departure from home for study at the University of Leipzig in 1814 to the convulsive—for him—revolution of 1830. The inquiry into the events and into the attributes they triggered is tantamount to an analytical biography of the youthful Ranke.

I   If the child's inbred tendency to accept the larger world around him and to look to the authorities for his blessings was confirmed in the small world of Ranke's rearing, so was his belief, as a member of the educated elite, in the special mission of the academically trained citizen and in the special sanctity of an aristocracy of merit. In Ranke's case this kind of nurture at home and at school inspired an aggressive drive which cut across his fealty to the political and social hierarchies and which helps to explain some of the surprising deficiencies in his allegiance. Ranke's political interest was rarely intense, chronically moderated as it was by his tendency to appreciate several sides of any issue, and it was usually secondary to his veneration of the academic calling in motivating his political and social commitments. Certainly Ranke was never wholeheartedly committed to the states he inhabited and served. This pattern was apparent from the beginning of his adult years, even when his primordial attachment to his homeland was freshest and while he was participating as an undergraduate in the energized atmosphere of Leipzig University from 1814 to 1818, during the tumultuous years of Napoleon's fall and Germany's reorganization. Ranke's attention was caught, to be sure, by the events—his immediate concern with politics would always be sporadic, rising in the crises of 1814–15, 1830–31, 1847–48, 1870–71, and ebbing in between—but his contemporary jottings indicate an engagement that was milder and more indecisive than his retrospective reminiscences claimed. Although he favored the German mobilization to defeat Napoleon, he was also appreciative of the Saxons' continued loyalty to their king, Napoleon's former ally; and although he did have something of the awareness, which he would later exaggerate, of German-European relations as a general problem, it was rather the local issue of the Thuringian subjection to Prussia that aroused his transitory youthful passion.[10] But despite the fulsome poem of filial devotion which he addressed to his Saxon Elector Frederick August in 1815, Ranke followed his father's advice and transferred his loyalty, without any apparent qualms, to Prussia when that state absorbed electoral Saxony by the terms of the Vienna settlement during the same year. What weighed more heavily than any naturalized local patriotism for him (as for his father) was the higher level of the Prussian civil service and in particular the greater opportunity offered by its teaching corps. He subsequently (in 1818) became a Prussian high school teacher, but when his professional interest seemed threatened, as it did by a Prussian decree of 1822 against teachers' tenure, Ranke did not hesitate to put out feelers for a post in Bavaria on grounds which exhibited the vocational cast of his public ethics. "It is intolerable to live in a state which pulls from under one's feet the moral foundation on which one rests," he declaimed loftily. "It [Prussia] is not really my fatherland: I have no obligation to it." And to his brother he went even further, warning in high dudgeon on the same occasion: "I only wish that you do not take the same path that makes us nothing but public slaves." What inspired this moral repulsion in Ranke was a simple professional issue—that by dint of the decree Prussia "has broken the contract which I concluded with it on the basis of an earlier law" and "denies me" the possibility of completing a serious work of scholarship.[11]

Even after his acceptance of an associate professorship at the University of Berlin in 1825, Ranke indicated his willingness to leave Prussia for Munich because "I hope to find in Munich more support for my work than here."[12] And later, when he was well settled in Berlin and was appointed official Prussian state historian in 1841, the same kind of consideration moderated his allegiance to his adopted country. He appreciated Prussia for its libraries and its authorities for their support of his teaching and research.[13] Characteristic of his pragmatic patriotism was his expression of the "profound feeling of scientific gratitude" which he felt toward Prussia because his scholarly work "would hardly have been possible for me under another government."[14] When in 1853 he declined the Munich professorship for which he had angled during the 1820s, before the Prussian ministry of education promoted and supported him to his satisfaction, he accompanied the pious invocation of his "primary duties . . . to the Prussian state" with a specific acknowledgment of the honor he rendered the Prussian king "who now shows me such good will, even grace."[15] And even after the Austro-Prussian War of 1866, on the occasion of congratulating King William I on his successful military career, Ranke could not refrain from invoking the Prussian promotion of scholarship as a function and a justification of the state's martial character: "Without the protection of Your Majesty and your blessed arms we scholars would not be able to write our books and no one would want to read them; in the public mind [*Publikum*] other attitudes would prevail."[16]

There is evidence, moreover, that this functional dimension of Ranke's commitment to established government went beyond the ingredients of his personal loyalty to Prussia in particular and was built into his notoriously exalted theory of the state in general as the sole union of power and spirit and as the historical focus of human culture. In October 1824, almost a decade prior to his formulation of this theory and almost simultaneously with his completion of the book—his first—on which his ambitions for promotion to a university post rested, the young teacher delivered an anniversary lecture to his high school in which he articulated what he would carry implicitly into his later general political attitude: that the state's promotion of scholarship was the heart of its responsibility to protect spirit and to advance culture. Confessing his own pleasant surprise that the state had actually transcended the expected practicality of its educational interest in inculcating good citizenship and in training qualified officials, Ranke aligned the state with scholarship (*Wissenschaft*) and the teaching corps, and he identified the "public" (in Ranke's usage reminiscent of Hegel's "civil society") with civic and vocational training and the student body. Once having asserted these factual connections, moreover, he then proceeded to define scholarship and the commitment of teachers to it in the expanded terms not simply of humane education and of knowledge for its own sake but of "inquiry into the ground of all things" and of "spirit, vital, active, by nature attuned to everything good" through which "we reproduce spiritually the phenomena of the world." It is the protection of knowledge in this large cultural sense—"original truth . . . transmitted by one generation to the next"—that is "the noble calling conferred by God on the state."[17] Ranke's subsequent exaltation of the state to the status of "an idea of God" may well have had something of the Lutheran religious sanctity and the Neoplatonic ontological profundity that has been attributed to it, but the characterization also carried its early connotation of an *academic* idea, merited by government's welcoming admission of committed teachers and scholars like Leopold Ranke on their own terms into the orbit of the state.

The professional dimension of Ranke's political fidelity, moreover, extended to his social tastes. When he was a young bachelor in Berlin after his move to the university there in 1825, he frequented the lively and not wholly respectable salons of the liberal Jewess Rahel Varnhagen von Ense and the eccentric romanticist Bettina von Arnim (see below, more in chapter 5) because their intellectual and literary preoccupations fed his plastic approach to the scholarly life in general and the historical discipline in particular at that time. And later, after he had cracked what was even then called "high society,"[18] he was notably cool in his attitude toward the tone-setting hereditary aristocracy as such. He was a member of the conservative group at the court of Frederick William IV, and was himself ennobled in 1865, but his middle-class and bureaucratic ethic of performance persisted, and it was with high officials that he preferably consorted.

Again, his attitude toward the other end of the social scale was similarly dominated, in the final analysis, by professional considerations. He held the prejudicial views of Jews usual among European conservatives in the nineteenth century, agreeing that "the stock exchange" was "peculiarly congenial to them," noting enviously the large role which the criterion of "intellectual training" gave them in the administration and the courts, and discriminating them disapprovingly because in those areas "they have applied the nature peculiar to them in a way deviating from the idea of the Christian nation." Yet his censure of their "presumptions" was mild, and he showed understanding for their past oppressions and for "the profound clannish loyalty [*Stammesgefühl*] in their religion." The mellowness of his judgment was connected, to be sure, with his acknowledgment of the Jews' full performance of their "civil duty" and with his historically reinforced inclination to empathize with all national groups, but above all he himself traced his restraint to his experience with his compliant Jewish students, whom "I declared to be historical Christians because they must have absorbed the ideas of the middle ages and modern times which rest on Christianity."[19]

II Although Ranke's nurture and the persistent weakness of an independent political drive in him help to explain his commitment to a teacher-scholar's career as a secular version of the Protestant clerical calling, serving God's social order and yet with an independent mission transcending it, these genetic and political conditions do not yet explain his specific commitment to history as the field of this secularized calling. What brought him closer to such a commitment was the religious conversion associated with his Leipzig experience, for not only was he brought thereby to consider for the first time the composition of a historical work, but the substantive religious motif which exalted all the histories he would ever write into so many clues to a hidden God had its start with this conversion. It has been held indeed—with enough evidence to make its acceptance tempting—that Ranke's characteristic approach to history was actually a direct product of his religious conversion and that in the form of his "historical theology" his religion is the key to the understanding of his history.[20]

If, then, we find reason to doubt the grounding of Ranke's historical conversion in his religious conversion, the point is not a merely pedantic revision of a biographical sequence but an essentially altered view of what lay behind Ranke's primary commitment to history as a field of knowledge and to the historical profession as the calling appropriate to it. The fact is that Ranke's religious development during the years spanning his evangelical awakening of 1816 did not itself lead him into history but rather posed the urgent challenge which his subsequent turn to history met. It may even be said that Ranke's explicit commitment to history waxed as his preoccupation with religion waned. Certainly he carried into his history the combination of universal meaning and individual sanctity with which his religion dignified every natural thing and human deed on this mortal coil, but once more his easy quotability can yield a deceptively one-sided interpretation. From his early familiar exultations that "this love of a past life ... leads to God," and that the history where "God lives and is to be known" is "a holy hieroglyph" which "we serve God" by "revealing," to the memorable dictum of his declining years that "historical science and writing is an office which can only be compared with that of the priest, worldly though its materials [*Gegenstände*] may be," Ranke provided obvious support for the primarily religious interpretation of his approach to history and for the corollary that his commitment to history was a direct product of his youthful religious experience.[21]

But this summary evidence obscures the ambiguities in his religious position, ambiguities stemming from the irresolute relations between such antipodal elements as individuality and totality, subjectivity and objectivity, essence and appearance, which he combined in his religion. Experiences and ideas quite independent of this religion had to intervene before he settled on the study of history as the only medium for harmonizing the opposite factors of his uneasy religious combination. Something extrareligious had to happen before the open question posed by the young Ranke immediately following the conversion of his Leipzig years—"Is religion something objective or subjective?"—could harden into the dogmatic association of the priestly office of the historian with his obligation "to keep in mind only the object itself and nothing more, in all impartiality."[22]

What follows, then, is the account of both the achievements and the limits of Ranke's youthful religious conversion in its meaning for history. It must be an accounting rather for the inflection of religion toward history than for the production by religion of history.

Ranke's religious conversion was a mild one, as such inner convulsions go. It moved within the limits of the Lutheran faith that he professed both before and after the event, and it had enough preconditions to which it seemed an appropriate response for the characterization of this religious development as a "conversion," with the term's connotation of an integral mutation, to apply only in a special way.[23] Overtly, it was a sudden breakthrough into an immediate sense and total absorption of Luther's original spirituality that had all of the dramatic testimony and the mysterious spontaneity usually associated with conversions. More subtly, but still perceptibly, it jelled what had been fragmented into a new awareness of coherence that meant the arrival at a new stage on life's way.

The most obvious of the preconditions behind Ranke's religious crisis was his dissatisfaction with the combination of rational theology and official dogma which had come to dominate the established Lutheran church in which he was raised and which he found replicated at the university in Leipzig. Susceptible as he was to the strain of pietistic romanticism he found in Herder, Friedrich Schlegel, and Fichte, the rationalism and the conformism of orthodox Protestantism were to him complementary qualities of a dessicated and superficial religion. The evangelical direction of his reaction against this marriage of Enlightenment and ecclesiastical tradition was common enough in the Europe of his day. When he looked back upon his early discontent from the security of his successful old age, it was the rationalism and not its association with orthodoxy that he recalled as the source of his unease—in his words, "moderate rationalism, . . . to me unsatisfying, shallow, insipid," as against his own belief in "the unconditionally binding Truth (*Gültige*) which announces itself and is known in the word of God," a belief which he admitted "came from I know not where."[24] But contemporaneously with the event itself, during the months in which he was struggling to articulate for himself the implications of the difference he felt between the Lutheranism he was so enthusiastically reconstructing and the Lutheranism he found so inadequate, he was also aware of the anti-institutional dimension which certainly added an important level of depth to the dissatisfaction of one as temperamentally irenic as Ranke ever was. Now he cast the difference in the form of a distinction between "religion" and "a religion"; "a man of religion we call whoever attests through the living deed to a belief in divinity which is nourished in his innermost being and to a belief in the union of the human and the divine in moral reason, without giving any consideration to the external cult of which he is a member; a religion, on the contrary, we call merely the particular variety of external cult of which someone is a member or can be made a member."[25]

What gave his response the extra intensity that it possessed was the input of other, nonreligious pressures that found venting in a religious form. According to the recollections of the old Ranke, indeed, his concern with Luther was triggered "primarily" by his interest in language and literature, with his "concern for theological questions" playing an auxiliary role. In this reminiscent version, Ranke's early preoccupation with theology at Leipzig was diverted by his immersion in classical literature and philology and especially by his great admiration for Goethe; he was led to Luther by a confluence of these two literary passions. Goethe "was really too modern for me. Already at that time I sought for an older linguistic form, lying more in the depths of the nation. I seized on Luther at first only to learn German from him and to make my own the foundation of the modern German [neudeutschen] written language." The medium of the young Ranke's concern with Luther was the biography of the reformer that he started to write, and his memory of the occasion for the decision to write one supported his argument for a joint linguistic and religious motivation behind it. For the occasion was "the appearance of weak popular accounts" of Luther in the anniversary year of 1817, at a time "when I was studying the authentic documents," and on such an occasion both the literary and the theological appetites of the budding scholar might well be whetted.[26]

Doubt has recently been cast on this testimony of the old Ranke because the contemporary notebooks of the young Ranke belie its chronology: they show a profound engagement with Luther from late 1816 which nullifies the presumed causal validity of later literary events, such as the publication of the Luther memorials.[27] But if the details were wrong, the general fact remains true: whatever the succession of emphases in Ranke's formal studies and whatever the succession of specific events at the various stages of his interest in Luther, not only do his notebooks show him to have been continuously, intensely, and personally preoccupied with both religious and literary issues before, during, and after his intra-Lutheran conversion, but throughout the same period he also applied himself to studies and translations of that "zealous and devout [*gottinnigen und gottgläubigen*] antiquity" in which religion and classical philology met. He worked, for example, at a literary analysis of the Pauline letters and at a translation and philological study of the Psalms as "noteworthy memorials of high antiquity" at the same time as he was steeping himself in Greek philology and literature—in mythology, Pindar, Hesiod, and, above all, Thucydides.[28] Whether the confluence of classical and Hebraic-Christian motifs in his conception of antiquity was the cause or the effect of the veneration he felt for its literary treasures, there was a pious tone in his approach to the great "ancients" and a religious kind of seeking in his relations with them. In a notebook entry close to the outpouring that marked his religious conversion, Ranke invoked the undifferentiated heroes of ancient culture in intimate terms and with a personal need very like the one that was guiding his quest for religious renovation:

And if you would all come to speak at once, you famous ancients, you poets and artists, you story-tellers and wise men; and all those of greatness that the modern world has produced would join the chorus; and if you wished to raise your voices and to say what was your innermost idea, and thought to express it in the mortal medium: would that not be a concert in the most beautiful harmony, one tone, one breath, One single word! But we hear you all as separate individuals, and when we listen to you, in the final analysis we do not understand what you want and what you say with all your speeches and doings. Oh! Come to me! Talk with me! I am willing and I am silent! I should very much like to join in the almighty chorus too: for otherwise I know not what I am good for here.[29]

Less explicit for the retrospective Ranke but more explicit in the contemporary Ranke was the philosophical factor that entered into his religious conversion. At this time it was primarily the philosophy of Neoplatonism to which the young Ranke proved susceptible, and while his acquaintanceship with it in its original ancient classical expressions connected the philosophical with his literary and philological interests, it was in the recent version that he learned from Johann Gottlieb Fichte that Neoplatonism became the mold of the religious ideas and formulations most directly relevant to his conversion. The Fichte that Ranke appropriated at this time was the edifying "second" Fichte of *The Way to the Blessed Life* (*Die Anweisung zum seligen Leben*) and above all of the published lectures *On the Nature of the Scholar, and his Appearances in the Realm of Freedom* (*Über das Wesen des Gelehrten, und seine Erscheinungen in dem Gebiete der Freiheit*), works in which the metaphysical philosopher of the transcendental ego turned his attention to the manifestations of this God in the finite world and to the problem, at once moral and epistemological, of how to find Him there. Fichte in these writings and Ranke in his copious excerpts from them were concerned in the abstract with the relations between God's inner absolute Being and His external, manifold existence, the only form in which human knowledge of His Being was possible; and more concretely with "the divine idea of the world" (*die göttliche Idee von der Welt*), that is, with the knowledge of God through the discernment of the Idea from its appearances in the temporal world, especially by the scholar, whose sacred function it is to penetrate through appearances with his science to the divine idea behind them—a function he can fulfill only by participating himself in the divine idea, by making "his own person simply the sensory appearance of this existence of the [eternal divine] idea."[30]

The Fichtean Neoplatonic approach to the problem of knowing God in the world entered into the way in which Ranke articulated his religious conversion, and it had several effects upon the form taken by that conversion, effects that would later enter into the influence of Ranke's religion upon his conception of history. First, it gave discursive content to the notion of a God whose nature was hidden from men and who was knowable by men only through the relations of seeming opposites—of outer appearances to their inner essences, of a manifold existence to its unitary principle, and of individual parts to their organic wholes. Second, the Neoplatonic tradition gave to Ranke not so much the concepts for such relations as the explicit symbols of the tree and the spring which furnished viable models of their working: the divine idea—at once essence, principle, and totality—manifested itself on earth as an invisible life force graspable only in the movement of its growth and its flow through the tangible opposites it vitalized.[31] Thus these symbols and the vitalism they signified appeared instead of conceptual exposition at fundamental points of Ranke's Luther fragment. The very entry in which Ranke confessed his penetration to the source of spirit—the conversion entry of December 20, 1816—conveyed Ranke's experience in a series of metaphors, starting from his favored spiritual "chorus" and proceeding to "the seed," "the One Sun," and finally to "the branch" (Ranke) who "clings to the trunk" (the harmony of the world's spirits) in order that he might grow like it.[32] In another entry, he expanded on the symbol in the course of explaining the meaning of Luther's message: "All life is in itself one [*einiges*], invisible: it is above all appearance, and indeed precisely as that which appears in all appearance. Look at the growing tree! It shoots up, pushes out branches, boughs, leaves.... What is it then that drives the trunk up and produces branches and fruit? It is the secret life of the seed, it is a formative, plastic element in it which emerges in the appearance; it is invisible and yet it is there, not the tree itself but in the tree.... And so it is with everything living: so it is with the life of the human spirit." And in a variation to the alternative symbol, another notebook item of the period again used a Neoplatonic figure to indicate his faith in the ineffable unity behind multiplicity, and to indicate too the dynamic process behind one of his most-quoted conclusions: "This infinite force which courses through everything outside and inside us, this spring [*Quelle*], of which we are also a part, which creates and maintains all things, indestructible in itself, self-sustaining, inexhaustible! What a lofty and splendid idea it gives of what we call God and of what we and things are. All is one and one is all."[33]

In addition to the anti-establishmentarian, classicist, and philosophical influences upon Ranke's religious conversion, a fourth contribution was made by the need of the academic vocation, to which the young Ranke was already attracted, for an ultimate justification in his eyes; and here again Fichte provided the connection between a fundamental concern and a new approach to religion. Ranke's excerpts from *On the Nature of the Scholar* were much more copious than from *The Way to the Blessed Life*, and, unlike the latter, they were entered before Ranke's decisive spiritual experience of December 20, 1816. In this work Fichte treated all stages and types of the academic life—and he spiritualized them all. He glorified "the mature scholar" (whom Ranke hoped to become) as well as "the apprentice scholar" (with whom Ranke obviously then identified himself); among the mature scholars he included both rulers (who direct "real life and activity" in accord with the divine idea) and "scholars in the authentic sense" (who demonstrate "that there is a divine idea accessible to man, who clarify and specify it, and who pass it on in this improved form to posterity"); among the authentic scholars, in turn, he included both teachers and writers: and Ranke, who was otherwise so selective in his excerpting, was careful to note the functions of them all. Certainly the notion of the special "holiness of science," in Fichte's sense of the scholar's particular calling to use his discipline for penetrating beyond the outer shell of appearances to the higher meaning that was certainly invested in them, was a belief that consolidated the connotations of intellectual vocation from Ranke's childhood and that he would instill in the historical profession.[34]

But a word of caution should be added on the limits of the Fichtean influence. For Ranke's explicit rejection of one aspect and his implicit omission of another were of more than mere philosophical import—they prevented him from accepting Fichte's closed system of perfectly matching ideal and phenomenal realms under God, and they located the imbalance which would make his religious conversion as transitory a stage of his intellectual career as it turned out to be. Ranke's explicit doubt was of Fichte's inadequate empiricism, which in Ranke's eyes led the philosopher to distort reality by pre-treating existence. "Why a model people (*Normalvolk*) even for a Fichtean purpose?" he asked, in the context of studying Luther's diffusion of the Reformation through his "real education" of a German nation actuated by "receptivity, and also the need."[35]

As for Ranke's implicit omission, it derives from the general proposition that what a man does not select is as revealing of him as what he does. Ranke did not choose to record Fichte's striking and categorical argument against the individuality of the divine idea, although it was ensconced in the middle of a section that he did record. The categorical language of Fichte's argument could hardly have escaped a reader as interested in the problem of individuality as Ranke was then as well as later: "The idea is not an individual [*individueller*] ornament, since that which is individual [*Individuum*] as such does not in general inhere in the idea, but rather the idea strives to spread out into the whole human race. . . . This is the constant character of the idea; and what is without this character is not the idea. Therefore where it acquires a life, it strives through its own inner life, and in no way through individual life, irresistibly for this general efficacy. . . . Entirely by itself, and without needing any intention of the person, it never stops working and developing."[36] Of this argument, Ranke recorded only that "the idea strives irresistibly for general efficacy," neglecting the anti-individual argument, which, as the emphases of his conversion will show, must have made little sense to him.[37] In these limits of the Fichtean influence upon Ranke—limits which indicate Ranke's early reach for empirical truths and individual realities—we get a clue to the unsettling features in his conversion.

Overlapping these concerns with official Protestantism, with the Christian classics, with Neoplatonism, and with the dignity of the academic calling, in the background of Ranke's religious conversion and more explanatory than any of them were the youthful confusion and irresolution of Ranke's psychic orientation. Even in his later years, when he had quite outlived the torment of his student days, he recalled that however enthusiastically he had participated in the discrete theological, literary, and philosophical studies of his university years, in the final analysis he had found them "incoherent," and they were "far from occupying me fully."[38] What the young Ranke needed was precisely the coherence in his view of life that his formal studies failed to provide; the reading and thinking with which he proceeded to occupy himself were designed to produce such coherence, and his religious conversion may well be seen as the experience of sudden insight when everything seems to fall into place. The notebooks which he kept at Leipzig served him both as a kind of personal diary of the mind and as an outlet for spontaneous writing projects, and they show an inner struggle for which his sudden insight into Luther provided a settlement and his abortive biography of Luther a resumption on another plane.

What he yearned for above all, like so many other young men growing into their maturity, was release from solitude, for with his personal isolation he associated uncertainty, ambiguity, and contradiction in all things. During his college years, indeed at the very time of his conversion, Ranke was lamenting the growth of the individuality that was cutting him off from the fraternal community in which he had grown up. "We were so close as children," he mourned. "But as we grew, a kind of iron bar developed around each of us . . . ; the barrier of individuality, the closed stage of life is at hand and does not let the I out to the Thou." [39] It was not only the "weakened intimacy" itself that he bewailed; in his aloneness truth itself became dubious and unstable. "Oh that a God would save us from dreaming, . . . and offer us truth. But what is truth? The eternal, self-existent solidity [*das Feste*]: how can I know it?" [40] But he did not entirely despair. He felt that the reestablishment of community was possible, and with community he associated the capacity to know the divine harmony. "Can it not become so again?" he asked rhetorically of his old fraternal communion. "Can the fire of ardent love not melt the bars of separation?" [41] He invoked the aid of his brother to fight "the sons of the abyss," and, as we have seen him do, he listened for the message from the harmonious chorus of the ages. [42] He listened too—and here he approached the locus of his answer—for the beatitude in sacred music, "when your spirit has exalted itself quietly on the wondrous harmony of the joyous creation, perceives everything and makes it its own. . . . I call him happy who can open himself to the wonder-world of music when he will, and on its wings travel to God." [43]

But, as with the chorus of the ancients, the harmony may not come through; and when it does not, the dread failure is accountable, for Ranke, not to any contingent or voluntaristic default, but to discords rooted deep in the nature of things. "A remarkable twofold or even threefold division reveals itself in me to me," he noted in a characteristic discussion of the various kinds of "philosophy"—popular, critical, and constructive—and he concluded, just as characteristically, that "our knowledge is nothing; we listen to rumor alone." [44] "We can no longer tolerate

the contradiction in our knowledge'' that stems from the ''great
gulf dividing the life of the spirit and the daily business of
existence.... It is absolutely clear that we desire to grasp [*fassen*]
the world in a single perception [*Anschauung*]. We must do this;
it is a compulsive need.''[45] Behind the intolerable separation
which Ranke sensed in the kinds of men's knowledge lay his
acknowledgment of a fundamental tension between the antipodal
principles, both of life and of knowledge, which for him was posed
but only imperfectly resolved in the Neoplatonic tradition. Thus
between the inner and the outer: ''What exists internally desires to
have an external life; it can have this only in its own way.... But
to construct the internal from the external is not given to [every-
one].''[46] Between the ego and the world: ''The highest, indeed
the only, possible object of philosophical knowledge is the ego,
since the possibility of all other knowledge is conditioned by prior
knowledge of the ego''; but on the other hand ''I understand the
possibility of how a man through a one-sided philosophical
striving can fall on the idea of deriving everything from his narrow
ego, but when one considers the matter it is not formally possible
to maintain this, since the consciousness of our own self necessarily
assumes the consciousness of someone outside us.''[47] Between
individuality and universality in religious faith: ''Now whether or
not faith is something purely objective in itself, still man must
have an objective proposition to which he can hold, ... and this
object is only himself,'' so that ''in this respect one could indeed
say that faith is a subjective vision''; but, on the other hand,
''when God reveals Himself to us in the Word, He will have been
able to announce Himself to us through the collective mentality—
not through the idea that stews in the heads of individuals but
through the idea that is a property of the people and that is
universal.''[48]

   Whatever the particular fields of these reluctant confrontations,
the reiterated pattern points to a more general mental disposition
that underlay them all. He saw antitheses everywhere because he
was oppressed simultaneously by two different and fundamental
kinds of ruptures which must be repaired: within the realm of
spirit, individual agency must somehow be reconciled with universal guidelines of knowledge and action; between the realms of
spirit and appearance, the individual agents of the spirit must

engage the phenomenal world to penetrate it with spirit but must yet avoid being crushed by this world once the contact was made. Given these two axes of the problem, small wonder that Ranke looked for a resolution on both of these planes, with the individual the common and central element in both. "Must we not be free and on our own innermost ground if we are to know God aright?" he asked in a hortatory recapitulation of his dilemma. The rites of the external church leave one "oppressed"; "the wondrous harmony of the joyous creation" which yields the knowledge of God may be beyond the capacity of the isolated individual. Therefore, concluded Ranke, in a parable of his conversion, "if you cannot have it [knowledge of God through the harmony of nature], then go into the church of your confession, sit alone somewhere and listen to its song; . . . the community of the pious will soon throw its shadow over you, so that you join in the public hymn" (*in den lauten Lobgesang*).[49]

This, then, was the desideratum and the schema of Ranke's conversion: transfiguration of universal spirit by the individual into a force capable of vitalizing the external world. He found this schema realized in Luther and thenceforward could believe in a possibility he could not believe in before. His first indication of a convulsive experience was his intimation of how profound and how intimate was the impact of his sudden access to a model resolver. "And then the branch grew up," wrote Ranke, using his favorite image at the start of the decisive passage in his entry of December 20, 1816, "so it has already selected a trunk to grow on. . . . Already the trunk has nodded to the branch and spoken many a soft word down to it. How much the branch would now like to speak back up in confidential dialogue. Quiet! Quiet! I shall yet betray my secret, oh the most secret secret, which only the seething drops of blood tell about in the heart and bear on further in quiet circulation."[50] And more directly to Luther: "Now then, you holy shade, do not be angry with me because I speak of you . . .; should I be quiet, I who have approached you so often in my solitude, I who have implored you and have not desisted until I thought to have found the secret meaning of your life?"[51]

This meaning, for Ranke, consisted in two unequal lessons. First, there was an achievement of Luther's on which Ranke did not dwell, since it involved the centrality of scripture, a commitment for which Ranke admired Luther but into which he could not himself, either then or later, enter unreservedly. Still, he did acknowledge that through this centrality Luther had accomplished an enviable feat: Luther showed how the individual could break through to absolute spirituality. "Oh lead me into the holy kingdom where the one eternal ground of things dwells and is complete," pled Ranke. "In that will I rest, in the timeless."[52] Luther led by choosing "the ideal life" over "the historical life" of time and circumstance, and by "pressing on only to faith, present, ever new, vital." This faith, moreover, restored "the secret free life of the spirit" and "recognized no limit" but yet had its "supreme principle" (*Grundsatz*) in the authority of scripture, which "resolved all conflict for him" and which "could become general."[53] Ranke tried to explain this synthesis of "innermost individuality" and universal principle in Luther as "the medium" (*das Element*) which, as against the supremacy of the Church, was at once truest to Luther's "internal act" and most communicable to his "century." But the young convert had to protest bravely: "if it could resolve every conflict for him, so it can for me; for both of us have a good will."[54] Despite Ranke's veneration of Luther's triumph in this respect for having "ordered the intellectual under the moral" and thereby satisfied Ranke's quest of "an *a priori* containing the common forms for spiritual, moral experience, . . . therewith proving the possibility of transcendental knowledge," scripture could not, in the event, do for Ranke what it had done for Luther.[55]

The real meaning of Ranke's conversion lay rather in a second aspect of his insight into Luther—in his flashing realization that the reformer's marvelous achievement of communicating his personal internal vision to all of Europe was the model synthesis of spirit and appearance—and it was this active aspect of Luther's spirituality that had such a shattering impact on the young Ranke. For even stronger than the youth's yearning to find security in the eternal was his striving to activate the eternal in this world. After declaring his intention "to live as a member of the moral and supersensory world order," he immediately expressed the fervent wish: "Oh that I could join action [*die That*] with this holy yearning."[56] And it was precisely this juncture that he celebrated in Luther. For Ranke's Luther, "every representation [*Darstellung*] must manifest the spiritual," and the "new point of view" that we gain over "all action" from Luther is precisely this unification of spirit and appearance in the world through human activity. "What speaks out of man, and what acts out of him? Have his words a meaning, his deeds a basis and a purpose? Whence meaning, basis, purpose? Everything from the secret life of the human spirit. Word is appearance, act appearance, they would be null if something did not appear in them. They are our branches, the secret inner life of the spirit shoots them out. Therefore, as one is, so does he speak and so does he act."[57]

How did Luther accomplish this stupendous feat? Ranke's answer to this question explains the individualistic overbalance of his early life and career, for his answer showed "the secret meaning" of Luther's life—the solution to the mystery of how "the vital word of his spirit could inspire the innermost spirit everywhere"—to consist in Luther's demonstration that the integrity of the human spirit, "which is identical to itself," was refracted on earth into the many spirits internal to individuals, and that this human identity could therefore be made manifest only in the direct communication between the most intimate and essential core of one individual and the most intimate and essential core of another. "Oh, what is it then that binds souls to this internality and this essentiality? It is the internality and the essentiality in ourselves. Thence stems whatever great has happened, and everything good."[58] This moral union of vital individuals must be distinguished in principle, consequently, from the intellectual "conviction of the world," and Luther's penetration of the world with his "glowing heart" in the former sense did not prevent him from fighting for "his own internally most private conviction" against the conviction of the world.[59] What maintained Luther against the papacy, according to Ranke, was "the force of his private, inner life." What Luther said and did came from "his innermost source," and if "from this one point a convulsion spread over all Europe," it was because "his words encountered kindred hearts . . . , since these words were based on the divine element in the nature of man—that is, on the revealed word of God." Only thus, by "striking root" in individual souls, did the message from Luther's own individual internality become externalized.[60]

But the opposition that Luther faced showed the limits of his achievement, and the limits of his achievement marked the limits of Ranke's conversion. For Ranke saw Luther's conflicts as products of fundamental relations in the structure of the human world, relations which placed deep-lying restrictions on the desirable merger of spirit and appearances. Ranke generalized the counter-forces to Luther's activity into two principles—one explicit, the other implicit—and both principles, like the indelible religious conversion itself—would ultimately bear on his approach to history. The first, explicit, principle which Ranke derived from the resistance to Luther's vital spirituality was the recalcitrance of outer appearance as an autonomous reality of this world. "Were the life of the spirit unrestricted, were it not inhibited by an opposing element," wrote Ranke in connection with papal opposition to Luther, "its infinite formative force would have originally raised everything to the Ideal; we would all already live in the perfect state; we would already have had the perfect science. But it is not so. To say it briefly, appearance has its own principle, precisely as appearance. Man forgets the life of the spirit, the circumstantial element takes him captive, he falls away from the godly and becomes a sinner."[61] And as Ranke delved into the Reformation he began to see that this principle applied not only to the papacy, which persisted in this kind of sin, but to the Protestants, who inexorably developed it in the form of dogma and political involvement, who whereby became a kind of mirror image of the Catholic party, and who, in the process, departed from Luther's original spirituality. As Ranke epitomized the process: "The external powers—existence—set themselves against Luther's doctrine. They could hinder nothing as long as the spirit flowed and was felt. But the spirit turned into stone, the doctrine into dogma: how could a stone flow?"[62] In the general ramifications of this alternation between the immanent spirituality and the autonomous materiality of earthly appearances —an alternation which we may call Ranke's law of the phenomenon —lay the seeds of the historian's later insistence on the dual requirements of historical method. The apparent paradox which characterized his combination of imaginative reconstruction and critical approach as the twin pillars of scientific history becomes explicable by the combined susceptibility and recalcitrance to spirit in all the deeds of this world.

Lying athwart this law of the phenomenon was a second,

implicit principle of limitation which Ranke glimpsed seriatim in Luther but which he could not yet admit as such. This was a limitation within Luther's spirit itself, deriving from a crippling opposition between the individual and the universal aspects of spirit. Ranke verged on the principle in other contexts, as in his characterization of the two Protestant parties in the Reformation as "one which had the individual [das Individuum] in mind, the other the whole [das Ganze]," and in his repeated admonitions that Charles V must be interpreted in terms of the inner conflict of his ideas rather than from "external grounds."[63] But on these occasions Ranke invariably confused the issue by aligning one side of the spiritual division with some honorable exterior motive of long-range circumstance, such as peace or national unity, and the other with the requirements of authentic religiosity. Only in the case of Luther did Ranke face, however fleetingly, the issue of a fundamental division within the purely spiritual realm. Scripture for Ranke, be it recalled, meant the mediation of God's word through "the common conviction" or "the general voice": in short, it represented the universal facet of spirit. Despite his admiration of Luther's appropriation of it to fulfill his own individuality, Ranke sensed that universal spirit in the form of scripture failed at precisely the point that marked the highest achievement of Luther's individual spirituality—it failed to penetrate and to vitalize the outer forms and appearance of this world. Ranke summarized the attainment of the one and the insufficiency of the other in staccato style: "Luther had repealed the authority of the church but he clung to scripture.... As soon as one depends only on scripture he is an exegete of scripture: otherwise it is the church. The church was canceled; the exegesis did not suffice; some ideas that were circulated from Wittenberg forcefully contradicted the existing form; the conflict was practically inevitable. The form was dissolved; only revelations were left."[64] Indeed, Ranke even perceived that for Luther there was an essential correlation between the internal integrity of his individual spirit and the recalcitrance of outer forms to universal spirit. Thus "the chasm within Luther" that was created by "the contrast between his morality and his intellectual training" was bridged only by the "infinite passion for truth" that was fired by the "conflict between his own conviction and the conviction of the world''; as a result, ''by fighting against the external world he came—led by the most profound idea—ever more into harmony with and clear consciousness of himself.''[65] The notion that universal spirit could vitalize human existence only through the activities of the individual and that the individual therefore would be pre-eminent in the earthly world of conflict would become a dominant assumption of Ranke's initial stage as a committed historian.

But this stage had not begun yet. Despite the illusion cast by Ranke's occasional reference to his abortive Luther biography as a ''history of Luther'' (*Luthers Geschichte*) and by the several notebook entries on the nature of history which he made simultaneously with the Luther project and sometimes in conjunction with it, neither the positive qualities nor the acknowledged limits of his religious conversion led Ranke directly to history.[66] Certainly he was aware of history as an area of knowledge, and he listed it along with nature and humanity as a field in which art could make concrete representations of spirit[67]—but history was not at this time a privileged area for him. History, like the other areas, was subordinate to religion in its spirituality, and insofar as it manifested the divine spirit it repeated rather than resolved the limitations of religion. This derivative character of Ranke's history at this time was evident on two levels—on the actual level of the Reformation history that he tried to write, and on the theoretical level of the propositions about history in general that he enunciated.

The notes that constitute Ranke's ''Luther-fragment''—his passionate but unfinished investigation of Luther's career—underline his vacillation between ''biography'' (*Lebensbeschreibung*) and ''history'' in his classification of it. For the notes were of two radically distinct kinds, only one of which dealt with the events of the Reformation and was recognizably historical. The other kind of note, whose tone gave evidence of Ranke's primary commitment, articulated his empathetic internal understanding of Luther. A mix of theology, philosophy, and poetry in its formulations, not only was this part of the Luther project itself unhistorical but the content of Ranke's notes attributed to Luther an ultimately and explicitly antihistorical stance that patently embodied something of Ranke's own. His tone was admiring when he recognized that for the sake of "present [*gegenwärtigen*] faith" Luther "did not concern himself with the historical [*das Historische*]," and in his comment on the opposition of Luther and the German humanist Eobanus Hess he permitted himself a pejorative generalization on the comparative value of history: "Where a histor[ical] science gains the upper hand, the absolutes like the arts must sink. . . . On the contrary, where philosophy and art gain the upper hand, all science must necessarily flourish."[68]

The other category of Ranke's Luther notes was in a drastically different mode of thought and language. They were long, detailed accounts of events and activities—capriciously interlarded with Ranke's own observations evidently produced by thought association—concerning the Imperial, Catholic, and Protestant parties who responded to Luther's message, but hardly mentioning Luther himself; they were identifiable pieces of what we would call a history of the German Reformation. But it was precisely this kind of historical material which Ranke could not yet manage—that is, which he could not yet turn into history. Almost half a century later he would remember that with this project "I had . . . undertaken too much—my equipment (*Mittel*) began to fail me," and this memory is confirmed both by the disjointedness of the several narrative pieces and by the evident desperation with which Ranke confronted the historical process of increasing fragmentation evident in his texts. It was, he confided in one of his final entries, "the state of war of all against all"—and in a precocious adumbration of the conservative patriot he would become he blamed the whole condition on France.[69]

In any case, this abortive historical project had little connection with the history he would later write. In substance, the radical disjunction between the ideal coherence he found in Luther and the consequently incoherent fragments he found to be the pattern of external events differed widely from the struggle to combine the two motifs which informed his characteristic histories. In form, his heavy reliance, in the youthful Luther project, upon authoritative chroniclers and commentators of the sixteenth century differed essentially from the critical approach to contemporary historians which led to his characteristic reliance upon primary sources. And in actuality it has become clear that Ranke did not use any of these notes for the history of the same subject—the Reformation in Germany—that he would write some twenty years afterward.[70]

Ranke was also doing some thinking about history in general at the time of his obsession with Luther; but it was a kind of thinking that showed the derivative status of history for him, since he saw it as the locus of the same kind of problems that beset him in other areas of knowledge—that is, in theology, philosophy, and art. If at times history did preoccupy him distinctively, indeed, it was because history was outstandingly worse than the other disciplines —because his generic problem of grasping spirit in the shell of appearance was peculiarly difficult of solution in an historical realm which was dominated by fissiparous appearances. Even in retrospect, despite his anachronistic reading back into this period an immersion in the Roman history of Niebuhr which actually came later, Ranke avowed that amid all his appreciation of his philological, philosophical, and theological studies at Leipzig, he "was rather alienated from history," repelled by the obscurity and aridity of the textbooks.[71] In the jottings about history which he made in conjunction or at least contemporaneously with his Luther project, Ranke applied to it his familiar problematical categories of ideals versus phenomena and totalities versus individuals; and in both cases he found history far overbalanced in the direction of particularity. "Since history is an empirical science," he opined generally, "it happens only too often that it is split into trivial details and is far from what has always been praised in it—the formation of men. Only he who marries that empirical trait to the idea can really bring in spirit."[72] Nor was this reproach merely a recall from a bad practice to a sound norm of history, for in an emotional invocation of Goethe—the subsumption of history under art was characteristic of Ranke at this stage—he bemoaned the same deficiency in his own questing approach to history: "Oh that the development of this life would become as clear to me as this life itself has been...; oh that the Ideal may truly raise itself on the firm basis of the historical; that from the given forms what is not given may spring."[73]

The failure of historical knowledge to grasp the spirit behind the facts had its parallel in Ranke's characteristic perception of the predominance of individuals over totalities in historical reality.

"The sense for the single is less inspired for the manifold," he lamented in a fragmentary Latin verse, and in other entries he prosaically rooted this epistemological imbalance in the very nature of the historical process. "What has been really great in the history of man," Ranke expounded, "has been created and maintained" both "through the gradual formative striving of the many and through one single energetic force"—that is, both through the "unity somehow constructed" out of the "heterogeneous activity of the many, arisen from multiple motives and directed to various purposes," and through "the individual, purified by destiny, inspired to the highest, and denying himself and everything earthly."[74] But although "the divine idea reveals itself in both cases," Ranke's further expatiation, in this entry and others, makes it clear that the respective ways in which the divine spirit acts in history make individuals much more susceptible to historical knowledge than are totalities.

It was in this context that he asserted "the explanation of the web of individual actions only from the attitudes of individuals, and from the education of each individual in the spirit of the age." Contending that "the psychological development of the characters of history" was "most necessary in great, active, agitated periods" like the Reformation, he prescribed "precise research on individuals" for such periods. He admitted at the same time that historians had a complementary function—the explanation of events by something transcending their explanation "by the attitudes of the individual agents" and referring to "that higher development of human life which extends over the whole age in which persons live, to the great events in which they participate, and to the overview of the general destiny of humanity"—but the terms in which he characterized the object of this alternate function betray why he neither elaborated upon it nor gave a prescription for it. "There must be something that is over the individual agents of history and rules them—destiny, Providence, God, as men call it."[75] Such hypothetical unities could hardly be the objects of research because, unlike individuals, they had no appropriate empirical form. The difference in epistemological status between collectivities and individuals, despite the equal investment of the divine idea in both, slipped out of the young Ranke in the gradations of his language descriptive of the revelations: whereas the divinity merely "announces itself in the many," it "stands incarnate and vital before us in the individual." [76]

Only in the context of art—in the perceptions of the poet rather than the historian—did he augur that the representational unity of the past might be found in the logic of development, that is, in "the appearance to the poet of what follows out of what precedes according to strict logical principles," and in "the bright common [gemeinschaftliches] light shed by what follows upon what has immediately preceded." [77] Like the ideal of universality, the reality of individuality, and the problematic knowledge of spirit through appearance, the idea of development in his student years had its locus in a realm that was larger and more essential than the historical world it subsumed. The categories which the young man then grasped would indeed become dominant categories in his approach to history after he became committed to it, but personal factors from the separate tracks of his religious, aesthetic, and philological concerns would have to enter his experience before he would concentrate on history as the realm in which these tensile categories could apply and be harmonized.

5
The Conditions of History
(1818–31)

To search for the roots of an intellectual or professional attitude in the personality of its holder is usually a risky procedure, as the safeguards currently under construction around psychohistory confirm, but in Ranke's case the procedure is both requisite and legitimate. It is requisite because the prevalent monistic interpretation of Ranke's general sense of scholarly mission and specific dedication to the truth of historical particularity in terms of his religious and romantic reverence for the divine-idea-in-the-world is itself certainly personal, albeit the adduced facets of personality are of the traditionally respectable kind for historians; any direct emendation of this interpretation, then, must be equally personal if not quite so respectable. The resort to the more elemental facets of personality is incontestably legitimate in Ranke's case, moreover, because the interpenetration of his professional and his private life, which is easily demonstrable from the perspective of the pervasion of his private existence by his professional, also validates the reciprocal relevance of the whole range of Ranke's personality to the vocational and historical commitments that he absorbed into it.

I   There was an erotic tone in Ranke's exultations about documents and archives that was an expression at least as much of relocated libido as of carnalized piety.[1] For there was in his psyche a kind of vacuum that exercised suction upon his commitment to history, making it an accessible object of his otherwise frustrated desires, as certainly as there was spiritual pressure upon this commitment which made it the incarnation of his faith. From this perspective, history was even more of a vicarious living for Ranke than was politics—not only because its greater comprehensiveness, malleability, and temporality made it a more appropriate receptacle for the variety of his personal interests, but also because in times of crisis politics would break in upon him, rupturing the vicarious barrier and requiring conversion into contemporary history to remove it to its normal alignment alongside remote history as Ranke's filtered experience of life's glorious manifold.

Everything that we know about the personal Ranke indicates that his sexual transference to the veiled facts of history belonged to a larger pattern of sublimation. Until he succeeded in completely identifying his private desires with his professional achievements, his reach ever exceeded his personal grasp, and this gap effected a continuous pull upon his historical commitment toward its personalization. The changing psychic relationship between his drive and his capacity at first paralleled and then interacted with the professional relationship between particular and universal history. In his early years, when the personal discrepancy was at its greatest, so was his professional emphasis upon differentiated, multifarious, particularized history. Then, as the process of sublimation gradually took hold, his personal integration and his reconciliation of particular and universal history proceeded apace in tandem.

But constant throughout the whole process, and helping to spark it, was the mode of behavior through which the fragile vessel of the outer Ranke handled the surplus freight of feeling and thinking which it had to bear: the mode of alternation which spaced out along a temporal axis the varieties of motifs unmanageable for him in the mode of the coherence and continuity required for action and discourse (for him a kind of action). "Ranke is a small, insignificant-looking man," his English translator wrote disappointedly after their first personal meeting. "His articulation is bad.... He is not so good as his books." Behind this judgment was the perception of two opposite traits, exhibited by Ranke successively. First he was "abashed"— "he thought that people were looking at him, and therefore he hardly spoke to me." Then he was conceited, "his manner not pleasant or gentlemanlike."[2] Nor were the observations isolated ones, for their general tenor was confirmed on other occasions by more interested parties. At the Varnhagen and Arnim salons, where he was once welcome, he ended by being alternately resented and derided. And however effective he may have been in the seminar rooms, he lacked the equipment for a successful lecturer—he spoke too fast, too inaudibly, too incomprehensibly. Ranke was, moreover, all too aware of his social incapacities, of the reactions they provoked, and even of their relations with his historical work. "I have remarked," he wrote to Varnhagen von Ense in response to a stylistic criticism of the recently published *Serbian Revolution*, "that whatever one's qualities, and annoying as they may be in private [*Haus und Stube*], they always come out in literary works, however one dissembles. . . . I imagine indeed that I have improved a bit. . . ; but still I feel . . . that I cannot claim to move easily and freely either for a whole evening long in a salon or at an elegant dinner party. How should this not show in what I write?"[3] As for the teaching function, which he acknowledged to be the mediation between science and society, he acknowledged that he was "not the man to assume the noble position of the true teacher," and it bothered him that his lectures were not well attended.[4]

For the young Ranke the limits of personality took the primary form of an uncertain identity, and his social as well as his historical activity was correspondingly directed at a fullness and variety of experience that reflected the diffraction of his own self. Whether as cause or as effect, his internal ambiguity went along with the combination of his extraordinary susceptibility to influence by his human environment and of his equally extraordinary dissatisfaction with this environment which drove him to move beyond it. During the period of Ranke's early growth into a historian and as a historian—a period roughly congruent with the age of Restoration in European culture—his personal susceptibility influenced the kind of professional activities he was undertaking at the time, and his personal dissatisfaction influenced the kind of professional activities he would develop subsequently.

II The pattern emerged with the very beginnings of his evolution into the historical calling, for his personality played an important role in both the religious orientation and the vocational interests that directed this evolution. Ranke's Lutheran religiosity, with its ultimate encouragement of historical study through its direction of attention to the internal side of human action as the spiritual manifestation of an inscrutable God, was closely connected with his intimate relationship with his younger brother, Friedrich Heinrich (called Heinrich) , and the form of Leopold's piety varies with the intimacy of the personal relationship. Heinrich had moved to the environs of Leipzig, to be close to Leopold during the latter's student years, and had shared with him the conversion experience during 1817. Leopold himself had been well aware of how essential this fraternal relationship was to his personal salvation. In an unpublished sonnet from his Leipzig years on the transparent theme of a knight's search for a beautiful island, the threatening spirits against which the knight ''longs for help'' are banished by ''the playing of a gay flute'' and by the conclusive hope that ''perhaps two brothers, bound eternally, will find the island.''⁵

But Heinrich's religious experience, it turned out, went far beyond Leopold's in its pietism, its orthodoxy, and its permanence; when he followed his older and more flexible brother to Frankfurt in 1818, it was as the sustaining influence in their common Christianity. The fraternal influence upon Leopold Ranke was confirmed by the uncharacteristically liberal political stance which he took for the first and only time in his life and which was a function not of any genuinely political interest but of the resentment of an older brother against the Prussian government for its oppressive treatment of a younger on account of the latter's German patriotic activities in support of the nationalistic organization of youth associated with the presumed subversive, Friedrich Ludwig ''Father'' Jahn.

Leopold's gradual turn to the vocation of historian between 1819 and 1822, when he began writing his first historical book, went *pari passu* with his outgrowing of literal Christianity and with his ever stronger belief in religion as ''the uninhibited truth of the inner sense'' that is knowable not from ''*a priori* ideas''—even in ''the Word''—but from ''God's presence in all things, . . .*a posteriori.''*[6] This attenuation—or more precisely this diffusion—of Leopold's piety, in turn, went *pari passu* with a definite estrangement from his intensely evangelical brother, and neither the diffusion nor the estrangement was entirely doctrinal. Both Leopold's restless, temperamental drive for ever more varied and concrete manifestations of spirit, and the final departure in January 1820 of brother Heinrich, with his constant pressuring influence, from Frankfurt, were involved in Leopold's change of convictions and sense of vocation, and both factors referred to an irreducible personal basis of the professional development.

The other facet of the young Ranke in Frankfurt, his career as a high school teacher between 1818 and 1825, entailed an analogously asymmetrical personal factor in his movement toward history as a discipline and historical scholarship as a career. Both in terms of his relations with his peers and in terms of his approach to his pedagogical vocation he manifested an unstable blend of susceptibility and dissatisfaction.

One side of Ranke's relationship to Frankfurt friends and school was open and positive. He usually perceived himself as an active participating member of a lively company formed by the young teachers of the gymnasium—those "most excellent friends," in his roseate remembrance of them.[7] His contributions to their conversations were on the subject of contemporary literature, the subject most congenial to him during this entire period and most closely related to the classical literature of the ancients, which was the main focus of his teaching. His sympathetic vibrations with the nationalistic agitation of his brother on the Father Jahn model, moreover, lent a liberal tone to his political attitude at this time, recessive as it was, and this too made for an affable community with his colleagues. Like them, he complained of repression by the German extreme right, whom he associated with "the Ultras in France," and he aligned himself with "the liberal-minded men" who must protest this reactionary "conspiracy."[8]

Ranke's growing commitment to history during his Frankfurt years was also conditioned by his accommodation to the congenial gymnasial environment. Until close to the very end of his stay in Frankfurt, history had a parallel hybrid function both for Ranke and for the local academic community, and certainly he was encouraged by the supportive atmosphere to center on history a kind of respectability by association—by association, that is, both with a reputable institution and with the venerable subjects of a classical education. For history was, to this community, but one interest among many, a branch of study taking the forms of classical, literary, and world history and in each of these forms retaining the indissoluble ties to classical antiquity, to ancient and modern languages and literatures, to patriotic civics and to Stoic ethics—in short, to the stock-in-trade of neohumanist pedagogy that had supplied principles and values to the study of history for some three centuries. But if the role of history in the philosophy of classical education thus persisted, the Frankfurt gymnasium also registered the new curricular dignity and autonomy which the culture of the early nineteenth century was bringing to historical study: its director, E. F. Poppo, projected its organization into a separate department, alongside the classical languages and mathematics. What made this delicate modulation, which entailed history's axiological dependence and organizational independence, especially relevant to Ranke were Poppo's explicit assignment of its application to his new teacher and the latter's actual appropriation of all the history courses given at the school.[9] Ranke's own approach to history during these years of his Frankfurt engagement (1818–24) fit neatly into the standards and requirements of his institution.

Like the school's scale of priorities, Ranke's primary commitments remained literary and classical, while the historical dimension of those commitments got an ever greater share of his professional attention. Out of school, his characteristic contributions to the social evenings of his Frankfurt sodality were discussions of contemporary literature.[10] In school, the range of his history courses may have extended impressively until they covered Greek, Roman, medieval European, German, and world history, but they always remained subordinate in his teaching load to his instruction of classical and German languages and literatures. The same blend of a growing historicity and a timeless literary humanism, moreover, informed his explicit discussions of history at this stage, and clearly the viability of the blend in its external institutional employment helped to make it intellectually plausible. In a public address on Greek, Roman, and German ideals of education which Ranke delivered at the annual convocation of the Frankfurt gymnasium on October 12, 1818, soon after his arrival, he faithfully conformed to Poppo's plans for him by recommending "the study of history"—in addition to religion, the arts and sciences, and physical education—as "something new that lies particularly close to my heart." The novelty was the recommendation of history as an autonomous discipline apparently equal in rank and subsequent only in emphasis—a kind of secundus inter pares—to the study of classical antiquity: " We Germans shape the ideal of education first through the study of the ancients, second through the study of history."[11] But once more it would be a mistake to be too literal about Ranke's early references to history. It is as misleading to read Ranke's later hypostatization of history back into the Frankfurt situation of 1818 as into his Leipzig situation of the year before: if the theosophical context of 1817 shows the limited function of the abortive Reformation history, the humanistic context of 1818 shows the principled subordination of presumptively autonomous general history. For the primary purpose of Ranke's address was to demonstrate that "essentially" ancient and modern ideals of education are the same—the formation of self-governing individuals who are wholeheartedly participant in their "fatherland" —and the study of history takes its character from the kind of service it renders to this constant humanistic ideal. Not only is the studied communion with the souls of classical antiquity, as distinguished from history, "first and foremost" in value as well as in emphasis for its capacity to make "creative spirit" an active reality in the present, but the function of history is tailored to the external service of freeing men from "alien impulse" by recognizing what has been authentic and what imitative in the life of the nation. Historical study, then, is a surrogate for the actual integrity of a national life that the ancients had and the modern Germans do not, and it has the limited purpose of separating out the congruent communal values from the inhibiting foreign excrescences for the humanist ethic. The study of history, moreover, is itself infiltrated by the suprahistorical principles of its external relations.

The motive for historical study is not, as it would be later for Ranke, understanding of the past in its own terms and for its own sake but, on the contrary, "the extirpation of the evil in the overpowering influence which the past exercises upon us." And the effect of historical study, similarly, is the demonstration not so much of what changes in time but of what underlies such changes and is constant through time—not so much of public events as of national character. "However much events and times change in the history of the German people, yet wherever the spirit actively produces it does so in a distinctive form, ever in the same way. The colors change, but it is the same light that is refracted in them."[12] The figure has shifted from the tree trunks and leaves of the previous year, and the transcendent spirit is now social rather than metaphysical; but the extrahistorical chrysalis of history clearly persisted into Ranke's Frankfurt years, nourished, like the increasing emphasis upon history with which it was educationally compatible, by the institutional matrix of the gymnasium.

There are clear signs that this humanistic osmosis from his daily environment persisted throughout the whole Frankfurt period of Ranke's historical incubation. Although the crystallization of his historical interests around the origins of the modern age undoubtedly reflected his growing sense of the intellectual distinctiveness characterizing his activity as a historian, he also paid increasing attention to the historical dimension of classical studies and frequently operated on a level which made history and the classics interactive and compatible. At the start of the (untitled) anniversary address which he gave at the Frankfurt gymnasium in 1821, he promised to treat his subject—the relationship of the school's function to "fundamental human action and nature"—"historically" (*geschichtweis*), but the address itself indicated that by "history" in this context Ranke meant story, or exemplary fable on the classical model, with only as much orthodox connotation as would lend his story versimilitude. The setting, indeed, was a or the (unspecified) past German "civil war," but the format was a dialogue in the ancient manner, the theme was the age-old quest for permanence and essence vis-à-vis the transitory and the apparent in nature, and the resolution was the familiar humanistic appeal to the immortal deed through which "the soul joins the fathers, the real men, the heroes," and through the striving for immortality and fame creates "the truth of the eternal present."[13] This was a peculiar approach to "history" for Ranke, to be sure, but it was conceivable because it was the pastness, or the historicity, óf the classics that guaranteed the eternity of the creative human values which were Ranke's primary concern. Small wonder that he taught the classics with the same focus on the sources and the same attention to contemporaneity that he would emphasize for modern history. "Among the preventatives against the misuse of the ancients, the one I hold to be the best is: so to read them as they might have read one another."[14] Small wonder, too, that as late as 1824, in the very letter which announced his commitment to the historical discipline and his intention to publish his first historical work, he would still accompany his announcement with a small caveat: "It is certain that I was born for studying and am good for nothing else in this world: but it is not so certain that I was born for the study of history."[15]

To stress the duality in Ranke's vocational loyalty during his Frankfurt period is not mere pedantry. His susceptibility to his ambivalent teaching conditions had the effect of impressing his developing historical sense with qualities absorbed from his concomitant classical and literary commitments—qualities which would characteristically inform the history he later wrote. First, it was in reference to the classics of antiquity that he first articulated the veneration for secular sources, understood in their own contemporary terms. From this classical literary background, indeed, came Ranke's effective limitation of historical sources to written documents and of historical truth to the contemporary meaning of the immediate written testimony. His later prescription of historiographical principle—"to stay with that which is verbally transmitted and which can be derived from the verbal transmission with rigorous certainty"[16]—revealed both the scientific advantage and the cultural limits of his early literary conditioning. But in any event the application of philological criteria to historical sources, which would constitute so prominent a part of Ranke's critical method, was mediated through the substance of classical literature.

Second, it was in reference to the ideal of the ancients, in its humanistic exegesis, that Ranke would retain the normative unity of human nature as the temporal expression of the *deus reconditus* in history. This faith in the transcendent moral integrity of humanity, however various and imperfect in its realizations, furnished a continuing support to the persistent themes of universality and coherence in Ranke's history. Third, it was as a complement to the explanatory power of the classical ethic and humanistic literature that Ranke first declared the essence of the historical to be something in events "which cannot be explained or derived but can only be known."[17] Ranke's characteristic stress on the autonomy of history thus had as its original context the inimitable immediacy of its distinctive reality and the countervailing recognition of other disciplines in charge of the more structured aspects of the human reality.

But there was a second, quite different side to Ranke's Frankfurt existence. As had been the case in his Leipzig religious conversion and would again be the case in his early Berlin years, some inner imbalance drove Ranke beyond his accommodation to the compatible Frankfurt situation and provided a personal stimulus to the gradual but insistent turn from classics to history as his primary profession. Perhaps it was the actuality of his social situation, as it looked to an outside observer, that broke through his usual determined cheerfulness about it. For Ernst Poppo, director of Ranke's gymnasium, testified that both in the school and in the town Ranke cut a relatively solitary figure.[18] The nostalgia which drew him repeatedly into the considerable trips, on horseback, from the Brandenburg city of Frankfurt on the Oder to the old homestead in Thuringian Wiehe may well have been a sign of unease, and certainly his feeler of April 1824 for a high school post in Bavaria indicated a particular discontent with his teaching situation in Frankfurt as much as a general dissatisfaction with Prussian repressive educational legislation. But neither factor would seem to have been the kind of fundamental goad to his specialization as an historian, the first because nostalgia for his native hearth would remain with him always and because in any case he was addicted to riding; the second because his later restlessness at Prussian Frankfurt was at least as much an effect as it was a cause of his commitment to historical scholarship, as shown by his expression of interest in the Munich library and his acceptance of an academic post at the University of Berlin, at the heart of the presumably detested Prussian state.[19] More fundamental, however, was the personal impact of the interaction between Ranke's religious development and his classical environment, for his susceptibility to both unstabilized each, with the effect of lead-

ing him every more definitely to historical scholarship as his
secure haven. "I hope ever for a life which would be childlike,
secure, active, and beyond all doubting," he confessed in 1820;[20]
but his piety, indissolubly linked for him with his brother
Heinrich, and his classical culture dissolubly linked with his
Frankfurt colleagues and vocation, canceled out each other's
security.

The breach in Leopold's relationship with Heinrich, openly
lamented by Leopold, he associated not only with the alternative
faith which led him to seek God rather in His multifarious
creation than in dogmatic formulations but also with a religious
"doubt" which grew precisely out of this search for God exclusively within the world. "What is this unbelieving, insane, vain
doubt in me? It rests wholly on worldliness and uprooted appearance."[21] But Heinrich, and the religiosity for which he stood, in
their turn alienated Leopold internally from the humanistic society
in which he moved and inserted a taint of suspicion between him
and his classical studies. Leopold warned time and again of the
perilous death of the soul to which the unaided study of the
ancient classics was subject.[22] He dreamed repeatedly of his absent
and diverging brother, always invoking his presence, and it was
hardly coincidental that the combination of fraternal distance and
the wish for its bridging should drive a wedge between Leopold
and his society, bringing forth in the context of the dreams and the
wishes Leopold's reiterated complaints of his utter solitude and
hopes for its supercession. "I can only assure you that I am very
lonely. My heart is so numb that it does not even complain much
about it. But there is a dialogue, coming from kindred hearts . . .
which lovingly guides contemplation ever higher until it finds
God and general truth. . . . This dialogue I miss."[23] His quest for
"God and general truth" poisoned his daily existence but was not
solid enough to replace it. "Our life is short and without particular
substance; my heart is hard and repels the world. . . . Otherwise
[aside from family concerns], my dear brother, I live not especially
ill, without happiness or misery, without love and friendship,
without failure, without success—like an Epicurean god who
hovers between worlds and like a stoic soul. The fog of enveloping,
habitual error still gives way but little. . . . If I only had your faith!
If I only were firm!"[24]

In this distraction of spirit, Leopold Ranke turned to historical study. He explicitly associated it with his need for communication and for certainty, finding in it a union of God and the world which he could find neither in religion nor in classical education. After admitting the cocoon of error in which he was enmeshed, he went on to write: "There must be people whose whole desire is to grasp a discipline [*Studium*], and I am one of them. My good fortune would be to complete something competent, and if that is denied me my good fortune would be to strive for something competent, and that I will not deny myself." In this context of a discipline Ranke lost his fear of uprooted and godless worldly appearances. "Is it [disciplined study] worldly, you ask? Is there really anything wholly worldly in the world, something really godless? Does not everything rest on the eternal Good, on the maternal soil and on Him who created it?"[25] "Every day I grow colder, although I have long been very cold already. . . . My love is fading away from the world," he wrote to his brother in January 1821, from the depths of his solitude and his "unworthiness." But even then, in the early stages of the research on his first history book, he balanced the confession with a hint at the scholarly resolution of his personal distraction. "My enthusiasm is directed exclusively toward the intellect (*auf die Einsicht*)."[26]

Two years later he was making the same connection, but more specifically and more unmistakably: "What shall I tell you of my life—of this infinitely distant goal and of the brief daily journeys toward it? And how I have only a single torment, which is I myself, and . . . a supreme pleasure, which are the small discoveries of human virtues, of human life, and of a human history which I make daily in the Berlin folios."[27] Less than a year after writing these words the transition was complete: he had made historical scholarship the center of his existence, no longer as a compensation for his problematic personal life but as the core around which he would organize it. The focus of his new single-mindedness not only made his teaching career at Frankfurt now intolerable but created a foundation from which he could dream once more of compatible community. He decided to publish what he had written at Frankfurt despite the admitted inadequacy of the research, precisely "because I can no longer leave these studies without committing suicide, and yet I cannot pursue them further without outside support''—requirements which, ''in the existing conditions of the academic world to which we must adapt ourselves,'' necessitated the wide reputation accruing to publication. A scholarly career, moreover, meant to him social as well as personal fulfillment. Since teaching influences students by the teacher as model and by the long-lived community of teacher and students, Ranke wrote, and since ''my model is almost useless and there is, in general, no community,'' he not only opined that his students would get more out of a good history book that he could write but also mused about the communication that could go into such a book. ''I would rather [than publish under Frankfurt conditions] have a few years of leisure and a room full of the books and documents which I need, and a friend—just one authentic human being—close by with whom I could refresh myself from time to time; then I imagine, I would make a tolerable book—no, not only that, but deliver a genuine report of true humanity, the true God, and of history as it actually happened (*wirklich geschehener Geschichte*).''[28] Thus the first formulation of Ranke's famous principle of scientific history had as its occasion his early awareness that only from the platform of a distinctive historical truth and an independent professional research into it could he manage the religious, social, and vocational doubts which were threatening to engulf him.

The specifically modern focus of his historical commitment, moreover, as well as the general fact of it is illuminated by its genesis in Ranke's Frankfurt locale. The illumination covers both the method and the substance of this focus. Methodologically, Ranke's interest in research had as its initial conditions the unusual library that had been bequeathed to his gymnasium by a grateful professor, the private reading he did in it, and the suspicions about the reliability of the sixteenth-century humanist historians Paolo Giovio and Francesco Guicciardini whom he found there—suspicions which led to the emphasis on primary sources and to the critical method for which he would soon become famous. Thus stimulated by the inconsistencies between the two Renaissance historians, his own first approach to history was a kind of literary criticism of classical emulators that was continuous with the philological analysis he practiced at Frankfurt.[29]

Substantively, it was the crossing of his humanistic and religious concerns at Frankfurt that led him to the origins of the modern era in the fifteenth and sixteenth centuries as the target of his first historical scholarship and to his lifelong definition of "modern history"—the era to which he primarily committed himself—in terms of what we call the early-modern centuries between the Renaissance and the French Revolution. "I should like," he wrote in an early formulation of this project for a general history of the fifteenth century," . . . to learn something of the subsequent growth of all the seeds sewn by antiquity," but he acknowledged that for such a history the classical approach to literature would not suffice. "I know from the Reformation" and "from the wholly different grounds on which the original revelation of the Gospel by God's grace to Luther and the subsequent success of its communication rest," he wrote in a meaningful allusion to the abortive religiohistorical project of his youthful piety, that "the formative striving and willing [behind the early-modern efflorescence of antiquity's dormant seeds] did not remain in the literary elite but in a certain form passed to the people. . . . Only dry wood takes the flame at once."[30] Thus humanistic studies, like his religious faith before it, proved inadequate to satisfy Ranke's passion for concreteness, his instinct for visual truths—it was not wholly fortuitous that he was always more sensitive to the sights of nature, the plastic arts, and written literature than to music and the spoken word. However "sweet" Ranke confessed it was "to revel in the treasures of the centuries, to see eye to eye with all the heroes and to relive their experiences," he added censoriously that it was also "diversionary" (*verführerisch*).[31] To know human reality the understanding of an original creative force did not suffice, whether that force was the divinely inspired utterance of a prophet knowable through religion or the morally inspired utterance of a seer knowable through the classics: what did suffice for the grasp of human reality was the variety of individual forms this force took in its dissemination to humanity at large, and this was knowable only through disciplined work in the historical documents produced by the authoritative institutions of mankind.

But however susceptible to the analogy of his prior fideism Ranke's humanistic interest may have been in its opening toward history, it differed from the model in one crucial respect: whereas he had not been able to make the transition from Luther's inspiration to Reformation history, he did in fact move successfully from his humanist point of departure to the finished works of history he published in 1824 while still in Frankfurt. Both substantively through the Italian focus of his history of the authoritative modern nations at the start of the modern period, and methodologically through his separately published critique of modern—and especially humanist—historical writers, Ranke took off into history from his classical and literary background.

The context of the early historical work helps to explain its character—the actual stress upon the vagarious succession of particular events and upon the internal criticism of individual writers—and it helps to explain therefore too Ranke's own reservations about the discrepancy betwen the specific truths he felt he had unearthed and the universal human truths at which he aimed. For his view of the ancient classics posited the approach to each work "as an individuality [*Individuum*] with its own roots, atmosphere, nature, and existence;"[32] his attitude toward religion embodied his sense of an unrealized totality in life. His view of the classics affected his actual approach to history; his attitude toward religion retained his awareness of an unfulfilled ideal. What drove Ranke to look for an escape from Frankfurt, indeed, was not only the ambitious quest for academic glory and not only the narrow range of the local library he had outstripped: it was, at least as much as either, his profound feeling that only a more immediate access to the sources of history would permit him to grasp the individuality of living beings in a form that allowed for the possibility of understanding their supervening harmony.

Hence Ranke greeted the project of a professorial appointment at the University of Berlin in 1825 with a euphoric announcement of his self-fulfillment that mixed the definite joys of particularistic scholarship and the indefinite opening toward the integral knowledge of humanity. The possibility of "doing research in the documents of modern history every day of my life [*Lebtag*]," he wrote, "is to me as if the gates to my authentic external life are finally opening, as if I might finally take wing," and he symptomatically associated this personal satisfaction with the historical benediction of Johannes von Müller, the Swiss historian whose combination of a vague belief in the ultimate meaningfulness of the divine plan for world history with a kaleidoscopic diffusiveness of historiographical practice could have been a model for the young Ranke. "Johann Müller says somewhere," the budding German historian recalled in the context of his own coming professorship, "that finally there must also be an archive of God's above in heaven," and as if to make explicit the covert sense of a transcendent unity stubbornly if unfruitfully present amid all the variety and vacillation of the famous Swiss historian, the young Ranke did not forget to add that the goal of his reveling in the rich discoveries of the documents was "the knowledge . . . of the God of our nations and of the world."[33]

III We know from Ranke's works and from the uneasy blurts in his correspondence that he did not advance far beyond this projected relationship between the actual multiplicity and the ideal coherence of his history during his initial Berlin period, which spanned the years between his appointment to the University of Berlin in the spring of 1825 and his return from Italy to participate in the counterrevolutionary politics of 1831. In addition to his persistence in the particularistic schema of tracing the plurality of southern European "princes and nations" through the sixteenth and seventeenth centuries and to his intensified need for the diffused archival records that would supply direct testimony to the extensive history he projected, during these years Ranke also exhibited a certain personal continuity with his Frankfurt temperament that helps to explain the inertia of his historical approach. It was this personal dimension, indeed, that gives the period its unity, despite its division into a Berlin residence of two and a half years and a lengthy research tour of some three and a half years physically away from Berlin, in Vienna and the archival centers of Italy, for he nurtured his personal connections with Berlin by correspondence and the cultivation of mutual acquaintances in Italy, and he continued to express in Italy the same kind of personal interests he had exhibited in Berlin. Certainly Ranke's Italian experience was marked by some noteworthy personal as well as historiographical reconsiderations that can be seen as preliminaries of his reorientation in the 1830s, but they are more intelligible if they are viewed as the concluding phase of his personal interaction with history than as a distinct phase with separate personal and historiographical parts.

When Ranke moved to Berlin and assumed the role of scholar-teacher in the university, his belief in the complementarity of historical writing and intellectual community led him to accom-modate himself to what there was of cultural life in the city. Berlin "society," hardly an object of European envy throughout the nineteenth century, boasted two circles of lively and sophisticated discussion during the 1820s, the salons of Rahel Varnhagen von Ense and of Bettina von Arnim, and, despite the half-amicable competition for adherents between the intellectual ladies who ran them, Ranke belonged to both. The two salons did share many qualities that appealed equally to the young historian. Both were "liberal" in the general, open, unorthodox, and spontaneous sense of the term. Both were romantic, again in the broad sense of an intellectual generation that adored Goethe, respected indis-criminately philosophical and literary geniuses of the age such as Hegel, Schelling, the Schlegels, the Grimms, the Humboldts—regardless of the internecine difference among them—and en-couraged spontaneity and unconventionality in both the tastes and the discourse of their participants. Both salons, finally, were led not only hospitably but actually by women of considerable charm, respectable social eminence, and unquestionable intellectual capacity in their own right: Rahel Varnhagen von Ense, neé Levin, was a sensitive intellectual Jewess closely attuned to her cultivated and progressive husband, the upwardly mobile Karl August Varnhagen von Ense, self-made aristocrat, retired diplomat, and amateur historian; Bettina von Arnim, sibling of the literary Brentanos and married into one of the great Prussian families, was a brilliant and willful hostess whose scintillating conversation of the 1820s presaged her emotional and shocking writing of the 30s and 40s.

Insofar as the salons shared fundamentals, and the personal relations between the Varnhagens and Bettina were cordial, there seemed to be little difficulty in Ranke's division of his attention and attendance between the two coteries, and to this extent indeed they could afford him complementary attractions. As a team—and so they were for Ranke—Rahel and Karl Varnhagen von Ense appealed to Ranke's intellect, satisfying both its moral and its utilitarian claims. Soon after his arrival in Berlin, Ranke declared his "principal and best acquaintance" to have become Karl Varnhagen von Ense, and he explained his "great pleasure in Varnhagen's conversation" by the latter's "pure and good intentions."[34] Rahel's evident moral integrity and her unflinching quest for truth struck resonant chords in Ranke's own prosaic strivings. Her didactic response to Ranke on the occasion of an Indian poem that she had received from him was at once sincere and ad hominem. "This Indian poem has awakened a thought in me ... about history, ... to wit, that there are two kinds of nations, the superior and the others; that superior are all those whose development rests on fantasy ... and relates no longer to needs, whose rational product is utility, nor to rationality, which makes us inclined to recognize limits. For is it not better to live in play and fantasy, where we can find nothing and no one who is wholly irrational, and thus to approach closer to reason than to settle ourselves in pure utility and purpose and thus to *reach* for fantasy and play? ... What do we want then, ultimately? Illumination! Because we *are* not enlightened and have to ask questions."[35] Such a convergence of literature and imagination upon history and knowledge was indubitably to Ranke's own taste, and it is no wonder that in his autobiography Ranke would retrospectively characterize his experience in the Varnhagen's salon in edificatory terms: "The acquaintanceship with men and ... women who had universal culture exercised great influence on my style."[36] The distinctive cast of the Varnhagen salon was not only expository but political. Karl Varnhagen himself was an unabashed Revolutionary Francophile, and, again retrospectively, Ranke testified that he had been inspired to his first authentic historical interest in the sources of the French Revolution at the Varnhagens, an inspiration that would bear fruit in the conservative later Ranke's surprisingly sympathetic understanding of the internal French conditions and motivations behind the Revolution.[37]

But it was characteristic of Ranke that he found the Varnhagens useful to his academic career in a more immediate way and that, as in the case of his Prussian loyalty, his attachment was founded on a blend of expediency and intellectual respect which met in the promotion of his historical scholarship. His first appreciation of Karl Varnhagen was connected with the latter's immediately preceding

enthusiastic review of Ranke's first book—a review in which
Varnhagen had recommended "leisure and research travel grants"
for a talent such as Ranke's (no wonder that Ranke would soon after
refer to him as "a man, so far as I can see, of the purest taste"). In
subsequent years both Varnhagen and his intimate friend Alexander von Humboldt would exercise themselves in Ranke's behalf to
secure him the requisite release and support from the Prussian
authorities.[38] Ranke responded not only by keeping in close
personal touch with Karl but also by "visiting diligently" with
Rahel in Karl's absence as long as Ranke was in Berlin, and by
maintaining a running correspondence with the pair after he had
left for Vienna and Italy. Despite his protestations of affection—
"How please I am by the idea that I shall again pull your bell, enter,
and enjoy your conversation after such a pilgrimage, for there I am
indeed at home"—and gratitude—"You care for my affairs more
carefully and better than I could myself: I wish that Heine were
here so that I could tell someone who feels the same way how I feel
about you"—it is clear that Ranke not only shared but even pushed
to excess the expediential component in his relationship with the
Varnhagens.[39] "Ranke," Rahel reported with some bitterness to her
husband, "came when he wanted and needed something," and
after asking favors from abroad Ranke himself ultimately had to
explain that "each of my requests has, as should be self-evident, the
tacit clause: if it causes you no great inconvenience." He disclaimed
an attitude of "superiority" in commissioning services from his
friends, even "should I not express my thanks in so many words,"
insisting rather that it was more an attitude of "complete brotherly
trust." But he admitted—and expressed "surprise" thereat—that
"Varnhagen has not felt the same way about it."[40]
    The fact was that for the lyrical, effusive side of his nature Ranke
had Bettina von Arnim and her salon. The tendency to take more
than he gave at the Varnhagens was compensated by his tendency to
give more than he took with Bettina. From his conduct in her group,
she could recommend him as "the liveliest . . . of fellows, Savigny's favorite conversationalist," an accolade he certainly did not
merit at the Varnhagens.[41] Ranke preferred the von Arnim salon,
first because it was more exclusively literary in its interests (Bettina
would not develop a concern for politics until the 1830s)—an emphasis that corresponded far more to Ranke's own and called forth

far more of his participation than did the considerable political dimension of the Varnhagens'— and second because he was more than a little infatuated with Bettina herself. Varnhagen remarked, rather nastily, anent Ranke's attentions to Bettina, that "he seems most pleasing to ladies whose men are absent," and it was certainly true that Ranke's connection was rather with Bettina to the exclusion of Achim von Arnim—indeed, that his connection had such running ardent, or at the least flirtatious, overtones as to be necessarily addressed exclusively to Bettina. She was a maddening, intriguing creature of extremes, impulsive, passionate, sensitive, unconfined, contradictory—to Ranke the very embodiment of the feminine principle. Once he compared her, scandalously, to "the Mother of God in beauty."[42] When he first met her, she impressed him as a kind of "Pythia" with her "flowing eloquence," and he was already struck with her oracular ambivalences: "She has grace and obstinacy, kindness and its opposite."[43] A year later he was still trying to grasp the mercurial personality of his sometime hostess and continuing correspondent: "This astonishing creature is, as it were, drawn into a sympathy with nature, although she really lives alone. She taps with her divining rod—with her ideas—often for a long time here and there, until she breaks through. Then her preaching is prophecy, and the fullness of life is born in her again. At the same time she is a splendid child, a tease beyond compare, delightfully mischievous and good-tempered." And with this exemplar of womanhood in mind he concluded that "in women there is a disordered, chaotic existence which, when it does not injure us, is not less attractive than perfect development."[44]

There is little doubt that, whether as examplar or individual, Bettina did attract Ranke strongly. His devotion was no secret: the Varnhagens commented on it; Bettina herself was well aware and spoke openly of it; and there was in Ranke's letters to her a mixture of reproach and insistence that is unmatched in his other correspondence but rings a familiar note to anyone acquainted with the language of a one-sided courtship. Soon after he left Berlin for Vienna and the south, he wrote to her wistfully: "Have you thought of your traveler from time to time? ... Only one thing is in my heart. I should like to know how you are.... It is now a year that I have known you.... Would our friendship not be still better if I had stayed at home? ... You must now miss me, ... but when I return my place will be kept for me. Won't it?'' A few months later, when the joy of archival research had seized him, Ranke joined it to his feeling for Bettina and asserted a modicum of independence therewith: ''I would wish very much to sit—not to lie, but to sit, and indeed on the sofa—at your feet soon again; but if only I should not have to return for it.... You will not believe what a pile of manuscripts, full of the most valuably knowledgeable things, awaits me.'' A year and a half afterward the degree of reproof was somewhat greater, but the longing continued unabated. ''Why do you want to be dead for me, when I know that you are well and go from time to time to Frau von Varnhagen and there get the idea, under duress, to write to me. A successor will soon be found for me, but I can never find another Frau von Arnim.'' When he was not writing to her in this vein, he was asking others to ''tell her something good about me.'' Well might the shrewd Rahel discern in the relationship between Bettina and Ranke that ''she gives him the nourishment he needs.''[45]

And yet, despite the variety of intellectual and emotional fare by which the youthful Ranke was being sustained in the Berlin cultural community of the 20s, there were unsettling aspects of it which stirred his discontent and ended by providing additional reasons for his growing personal dependence upon historical scholarship. Although it is not clear whether Ranke experienced directly the reservations about him which arose in Rahel from her salon keeper's jealousy of Ranke's preference for Bettina's—and then which arose in Karl because they had arisen in Rahel—it is clear that Ranke did experience directly other grounds for dissatisfaction with the Varnhagens' salon. His comparative indifference to the political themes which were staples of discussion at the Varnhagens might not have been damaging in itself, but it was intensified into inner withdrawal by the personification of these themes in the figure of Eduard Gans, Hegelian jurist who monopolized the conversation with his radical criticisms and political passions and reduced Ranke to the status of silent auditor.[46] Not surprisingly, toward the end of the decade it was to Karl von Varnhagen that Ranke admitted his awkwardness—that, in his words, ''I cannot claim to move about even for the span of a single evening in a salon . . . freely and with satisfaction.''[47]

As for Ranke's connection with Bettina von Arnim, in which the personal aspect came to outweigh the social, the emotional exercise he derived from it ultimately came to be frustrated by the doubts he had about its object and his relationship to her. We can only guess at the effect of the condescension toward her academic wooer and his infatuation which was publicly evinced by Bettina in the nicknames —such as "house pet" (*Haushammel*)—which she had for him.[48] But we do know that Ranke was generally aware of the critical dimension in Bettina's attitude toward him—"with Frau von Arnim, it seems to me, you will come without delay to my failings and my lacks."[49] We know too that Ranke was in himself of two minds about Bettina: certainly he was emotionally intrigued by what he took for her essentially feminine caprice, but he was also rationally aware of the moral and tasteful limits it entailed. Even at the beginning of their friendship when he wrote so admiringly of her "Pythian" eloquence, he added cautiously: "But who can believe everything she says?"[50] And in the 30s, after his ardor had cooled somewhat but before Bettina's politicization had led to a break between them, Ranke not only compared approximately simultaneous and analogous publications by Rahel and Bettina to Bettina's disadvantage but delivered a balanced judgment upon her in terms which he claimed were continuous with his personal experience with her a decade before. "In the third volume [of Bettina's *Goethes Briefwechsel mit einem Kind*] the general discussions of genius, love, beauty, and art . . . are precisely the tears or fantasies which I heard there so often in 1826 and 1827. The book is the whole person: just as lovable and spirited, but also just as designed despite all the claims to spontaneity and in its transports not without boredom."[51]

Ranke's notice of the disingenuous quality in Bettina's apparent impetuosity was a projection of an analogously fabricated quality in his relationship to her. The perceptive Rahel had recognized the prominence of this quality in the relationship. "He needs . . . to be seen as a suitor [*Kourmacher*], . . . and, as irritably prudish as Frau von Arnim . . . acts, she gives him occasion for it. He needs this exercise to enliven his leisure hours."[52] This contemporary observation of a tacitly shared affectation in Ranke's romantically phrased attachment to Bettina von Arnim gets impressionistic confirmation from the mannered language of his addresses to her. It was as if the young Ranke was playing a role—not feigning affection, which was genuine enough in its source, but holding it out before him where he could observe it, shape it, and direct it in accordance with his own wants and society's rules toward an appropriate *persona*. In any case, his relationship with Bettina von Arnim and her salon no more brought him a fundamental fulfillment or spiritual community than did the Varnhagens and theirs. The intermittent anguished refrain of his unbreached solitude sounded time and again from Berlin and from his southern research residences as it had from Frankfurt. "I experience the greatest pleasure from my progress in world history. For the rest I am completely alone. I am predestined to loneliness. Wherever I shall be, I shall be alone."[53] But there was a different note in the elegies of isolation that belong to this later period: Ranke now regularly connected them with his historical work. He associated his individual detachment with his archival research into particulars, and his dissatisfaction with his detachment—his yearning for fellowship—with the quest for historical totalities that would bring him an understanding and a kind of loving union with all humanity.

Thus the two sides of his personal posture became invested in the two levels of his historical endeavors, his individual self-satisfaction in the accomplishments of his particularistic archival research and his thwarted sociability in his frustrated quest for the unity of history. In his individualistic gear, he would write of the "just one idea" that came out of his "dry notes" in a whole day of documentary research, and declaim rhapsodically that "I have rarely felt as happy as now"; and it was in this context that he could boast of having written his first book in "an innocent passion for the event, the given."[54] But when he was in his dissatisfied gear, he would connect his complaint that he could "produce nothing but fragments" with his "predestination to loneliness," and he would assert autobiographically that "whoever seeks the truth of universal coherence, of God, and of the world will always despair, and in the despair lies the calling." At times he would then expressly reveal the bond between his personal quest for human fellowship and the union with humanity which he looked for in general history. "I am again lecturing on world history. Often my heart beats hard when I contemplate human things. Yet I cannot succeed with the presentation because I still have not yet entirely fathomed them."[55]

The society which Ranke cultivated during the 1820s when he was in Berlin and with which he maintained connections when he was out of town functioned as intermediary between his personal temperament and his professional endeavors. Each of the two salons he favored was linked for him, indeed, with a different set of his personal and professional concerns and helped to cement the association between them. His relations with the Varnhagens were tied to the achievements of his detailed researches through their forthright appreciation of his early works that were based on those researches, through the influence they exercised for the extension of his research facilities, and through the promotional expectations he correspondingly cherished toward them. Not surprisingly, therefore, his correspondence with them was full of reports on his cumulative progress and of his satisfaction with its particular results. His relations with Bettina von Arnim, on the other hand, were expressive of his striving to grasp transcendent truth through the coherence of worldly phenomena. The association of his unsatisfied longing for Bettina with his craving for historical totalities which were equally beyond his reach was not merely implied in the relationship. At times Ranke showed that he was explicitly aware of it. "It only goes well with me when I immerse myself completely in one thing or another," he wrote to her revealingly, "but not when I survey the whole and want to bridge the gaps. You are luckier. You paint for yourself a world as a whole from the whole."[56] A more precise statement of Ranke's historio-graphical orientation and a more direct testimony of its personal embodiment during the 1820s can scarcely be envisaged.

Aside from reinforcing the divergence between attainment and projection, the personal disposition of the young Ranke had one further historiographical result. The continued prominence of his aesthetic—and especially his literary—avocation during his early Berlin years found professional expression in the directed reading and observation that led ultimately to the main nonpolitical histories ever published by Ranke.[57] In October 1827 he indicated his intention to include "a chapter on literature and art" as an integral part of his planned *Princes and Nations of Southern Europe.* The volume on *The Ottoman Turks and the Spanish Monarchy* had just been published, and Ranke was thinking in terms of a second volume, on the states of Italy. He was just beginning the research leave obtained to further his work on the European origins of modern history, and his declaration of cultural-historical intent, like his subsequent reading of Italian poets and frequenting of Italian galleries with which he interspersed the long hours spent in libraries and archives excerpting documentary materials on the politics of the European states, was the joint product of his personal interest and his historical design. Certainly it was difficult to discern from his enthusiastic reports of his literary and artistic immersion whether it was hobby or profession in which he was indulging. His involvement with Italian painting had more of the hobby in it, and the manuscript which he completed in 1831, the year of his return to Berlin, he did not publish until 1878 (under the title *History of Italian Art*).

Ranke's *History of Italian Poetry,* on the other hand, which was not ready in manuscript until 1835, was published in 1837, presumably because its theme was so literally akin to the general topic he had set for the *Princes and Nations*: the change of "world epochs" between the Middle Ages and modern times. He selected for his subject matter the single literary tradition represented by the *Reali di Francia*—the saga of the conquest of Europe for Christianity—a widely known folk epic through which he could trace "the changes in method and taste" (*Art und Kunst*) that "gradually emerged" in the humanist treatment of medieval materials during the fifteenth and sixteenth centuries. Although Ranke did scatter aesthetic judgments of the sundry poetic versions of the tradition through his work, they tended ever to subserve general history—to illustrate "another world of ideas, a divergent form of expression, a different orbit and connection of those spiritual tendencies which rule all creation, another heaven (so to speak) and another earth."[58] His primary concern was to portray the leavening of the Christian, chivalric, episodic, archetypal, repetitive, fantastic, and populist features of the medieval romance by the naturalistic, individualizing, sensuous, dramatic, vital, coherent, and cerebral artwork of the classical Renaissance, with the purpose of showing how the intellectual and artistic instability generated by the tension between the two themes could be resolved only by the synthesis of classical humanism and renewed Christianity exemplified in Torquato Tasso.[59] In this approach, judgments of aesthetic form accompanied interpretations of intellectual content as complementary indicators of the "spiritual tendencies" appropriate to the successive ages of man: the shift from loosely strung modules to purposive composition in the structure of literary works was as meaningful as the shift from edifying piety to narrative realism in their content for Ranke's genetic understanding of the distinguishing features of modern man.

Reflecting the earlier date of its composition rather than the later date of its publication, Ranke's *History of Italian Art* was more internalized than its poetic counterpart, as befit its conception in the aesthetic atmosphere of the 1820s, but its theme was parallel, and it is best understood in the light of the connection with the general change in "spiritual tendencies" and "world epochs" that Ranke made explicit in the *History of Italian Poetry*. While these works were gestating in him, Ranke was entirely conscious of this linkage of the art forms through their common participation in a spiritual historical movement. "I have decided," he wrote from Rome in 1830, "that the course and development of modern art—naturally only since the end of the fifteenth century —correspond completely to poetry and the other forms of literature, and that as soon as the most important changes can be grasped with certain perception, one could approach a history of the internal existence of the nation."[60]

The work on art had as its theme the change from formlessness to form in the painting and the sculpture of a period initiated by Giotto and ending with Caravaggio—a change traced not as a matter of the artists' capability but as a matter of their "differing intentions." As in the case of poetry, the two keys to these intentions were the religious purpose and content of medieval art, which subordinated dynamic form to static symbol, and the increasing attention to the natural forms which were the media of the representation and gained increasing independence of their content and erstwhile purpose. But the theses of the two parallel works differed in significant degree: where the poetic development showed a persistent tensile relationship between the Christian spiritual tendency and the naturalistic spiritual tendency of which aesthetics was an integral part, the artistic development showed the domination of naturalistic form by technical considerations of color, light, and shadow, and the simple supersession of religious by formal art as two separate and incompatible modes of art. "Earlier men had had the idea without the form; now men had the form without the idea."[61] Ranke's *History of Italian Poetry* can be viewed as a product of his aesthetic interests in the 1820s. His *History of Italian Art* can be viewed as a product of his multiple commitments in the 1820s.

The two works on the history of Italian art and literature were short—essays, really—in contrast to the extended span of Ranke's political histories, but they were independent works, and this independence too was in contrast to his subsequent focus on politics. He would treat cultural subjects again, but always, in his own later terms, as "inseparably bound together with politics and war and with all the events which constitute the facts of history"— a formulation which in practice organized the consideration of art and literature within the history of states as their spiritual components.[62]

But it is important to realize that Ranke's mature focus on political history was a genuinely composite resolution of a prior plurality in his approach to history, and that an explicit formulation of this plurality, in direct contrast to his formulations of political focus, prefaced his separate work of literary history. "These days no one can casually believe that he knows a nation or an age if he has not considered, *besides* the actions which occur in state and church, in war and peace, also what can be said to be the more direct, the more unconditioned expressions of its spirit in literature and art."[63] The formulation, like the work it introduced, corresponded to the stage in Ranke's development when he had brought his personal interests into the realm of history but had not yet, either on a personal or a historiographical level, unified their multiple facets within that realm. The principle behind it was the parallelism which at once connected and distinguished the various branches of human activity. This principle, which inspired his aesthetic writing of the 30s, was first articulated in the university lectures on literary history that he gave in 1827, at the start of his short-lived professional concern with cultural history, and it

faithfully reflects the balance of practical diffusiveness and normative cohesiveness characterizing the Ranke of the 1820s. Arguing
that literature is related to life not as one great potency to another
but as an outer expression of life is to the spiritual ground of all
expressions, Ranke insisted that literature, like art, is "a part" of
life's "manifold appearance, like the rest of the life of humanity."
At this stage, then, Ranke's emphasis was on literature as a form of
human activity, in some ways superior to the other forms of
human activity, and on the history of literature as an authentic
branch of generic history. "A tour through literature is a tour
through history," for "literature encompasses a great part of
human knowledge and ability." Far from his later subordination
of it to political history, he now stressed the distinctive form of
literary history—the arbitrary, multifarious, and frequently unin-
fluential productions of its geniuses. "One can compare literature
with a forest, full of the most varied trees, plants, shrubs, and
fruits." If, moreover, literature is distinctive in this respect
vis-à-vis other kinds of history, it is superior to them in one other
crucial respect: literature has the advantage over the rest of life that
it is "indestructible," and that through it, therefore, we are "at
home in the particular and knowledgeable [*kundig*] in the general." Ranke's early addiction to literature, then, overlapped his
professional commitment to history, for he could find in literary
history the substantive interaction between particularity and
generality for which he could still only yearn in political history.[64]

Between his early celebration of aesthetic history as a compara-
tively advantageous form of generic "inner" history and his later
subsumption of literature and art under the state in an expanded
version of political history, Ranke developed a modulating attitude
which eased his transition from one phase to the other. This
attitude, which retained the separation of aesthetic and political
history but raised political history to an equivalent status by
aesthetizing it, is traceable back to the turn of the decade around
1830 and consequently must be recorded as part of Ranke's mental
equipment while he was composing his works on Italian art and
literature. In his university lectures of the early 30s he repeatedly
told his students that "we include both the inner and the outer"
sides of history; that one must attend not only to "the political
tendency" but also to art and literature, churches, economics, and

technology in modern history; and that, especially in contemporary history, politics itself is governed by principle and has "something ideal" about it.[65] The equivalence of political history which was the clear implication of these arguments he explicated in the article "On the Influence of Theory" which he published in 1832. While conceding the autonomy of "language and art" among "the great creations of humanity," Ranke put his emphasis upon showing the spiritual component of the state and consequently "the most intimate relationship" of politics with the disciplines governing language and the arts. "Eternally fresh and inexhaustible is genius, and the task will always be to immerse oneself in the object, be it a language or a work of art, and grasp its inner necessity; for it bears its own law within itself. . . . But states too are products of a creative genius, . . . and as they come from an original energy of the human spirit, they have their own laws of inner development."[66] From a parallel product the state would soon become for Ranke history's most accessible case, but not before the relationship between art and aesthetics had been built into the relationship between historical politics and the historical state.

The stage of decisive personal contribution to Ranke's historical commitment, a stage representing a kind of leading tone in the scale of his ascent toward the complete historian he would soon become, came to an effective end with his return to Berlin in 1831. His own growth and outer circumstances combined to transform the conditions under which the course of his private life essentially influenced his approach to history. The open disenchantment with Goethe as a reliable source of things Italian—a disenchantment stemming from Ranke's own Italian experience—had as its factual consequence a decisive breach in his relations with both of his fanatically pro-Goethean salons and as its symbolic consequence the end of the independent involvement with literature which had for so long complicated his commitment to history. The opposite responses of Karl Varnhagen von Ense and Ranke to the revolution of 1830—the one prorevolutionary and cosmopolitan, the other antirevolutionary and particularistic—confirmed the breach by bringing on the bitter, permanent, and hostile contempt of the liberal aristocrat for the conservative and "characterless" academician, a contempt whose effect was enhanced by accident.[67] The possible reconciliatory influence of Rahel, who did not share her husband's recoil against Ranke, was removed with her death in 1833. The possible persistence of Bettina von Arnim's hold was undermined when, after the death of her husband in 1831, she turned her interests and her passions to issues of liberal politics and social reform, a shift which put her under the increasing influence of Karl Varnhagen and in growing estrangement from Ranke. He continued to see Bettina occasionally during the 30s, but the old magic was gone. By the middle of the decade he was characterizing her bitterly as "a Circe who differs only in that she does not wait for someone to come within her reach but herself seeks her victim, entices him to her and confers favors on him—then tires of him and rejects him."[68] Bettina did not finally turn Ranke out until after their break on the issue of the brothers Grimm and academic freedom in 1830, but clearly the relationship did not play the same role in Ranke's life after his return to Berlin in 1831 that it had played before.

But undoubtedly it was Ranke's own integration, after the convergence of his interests in Italy and under the centripetal impact of political revolution in 1830 and 1831, that ended his personal distraction and its relevance to his historiographical resolution. Under the pressure of revolution, his personality jelled and his history was synthesized: the multiple and competing claims of life and history were replaced by the complementary duality of politics and history. Henceforward the company—both physical and epistolary—in which he moved seemed rather a function than a constituent of his scholarship. The fellowship was political, historical, and undemanding—Berlin "court society," the archconservative political general Edwin von Manteuffel, the historical buff Prince Maximilian of Bavaria, and assorted students and ex-students. "I am happy only when, while studying, I produce."[69] The dynamic of his historical production, and the political conditions of it, would now determine the inner and outer course of his life.

6
The Incomplete Historian
(1819–31)

Successively spawned but indelibly accumulated, these three factors—
Ranke's vocational loyalty to the state, his religious quest for
knowledge of the divinity immanent in man, and his personal
involvement with the intellectual options of his environment—
were the dominant conditions of his development into a historian
and then of the approach to history which characterized his first
professional works. We are now in a position to narrate this
development and epitomize this approach.

I   Ranke made his specific commitment to history soon after he
assumed his duties as a gymnasium teacher in Frankfurt am Oder.
When he left the University of Leipzig in 1818, after attaining his
doctorate with a (now lost) dissertation on Thucydides, it was as a
young man convinced of the sanctity of the academic vocation by
early nurture, profoundly committed to a questing religiosity by
avocation, and educated for a career as high school teacher of
classics with a sideline of literature and history and a penchant for
research. It was through the way station of ancient history, in
which Ranke developed a fervent interest associated with and
ultimately transcending his pedagogical work as a classicist, that
Ranke became a passionately committed historian. Although he

was himself never explicit about his conversion, it can be reconstructed from related things he was explicit about. Two convergent lines of consideration led him to modern history, and they led him in such a way as to make his commitment to this history absolutely necessary to him, as the only possible resolution of his indecisions and, henceforward, the key to his identity.

The first line was drawn by the direction of his spiritual concerns. In his last years at Leipzig he especially worried about the relations between the standard polar opposites, variously expressed as the infinite and the finite or the general and the particular, and he dreamed of "an ideal history, which represents the infinite in finitude," as the mode of their engagement—even if "such a history has hitherto seemed to be impossible." He saw in the dramatic sequence of events a way of representing "particularity ... according to strict logical principles." The ideal history's representation of the infinite in the finite "by discovering how it appears as an idea and as a whole" is "the intermediary" (*Mittelglied*) between poetry, which tries simply "to represent the infinite by the finite," and philosophy, which tries simply "to explain the finite by the infinite."[1] Theoretically, then, domains of religion, art, and philosophy on the one hand and the domain of history on the other were for Ranke already distinct, albeit not opposed; he was beginning to think of history as an autonomous field of knowledge.

Such intellectual considerations disposed the young Ranke toward history in general; a second, personal line of consideration, equally revealing of his age and of his distinctive place in it, attached him to modern history in particular. For Ranke combined distinctively three personal traits which were shared distributively by his contemporaries: he burned to be active, productive, creative, but rather through art than through deed; he grasped for what was definite, specific, palpable, certain, and had a passion for discovering new realities of this kind; and he was professionally ambitious. Hence he directed his attention to the past foundations of the present neither because of his direct concern for the political stability of the establishment (if we remember his sympathy during these Frankfurt years with the protesting patriotism of the Father Jahn stripe and his resentment of the establishment's persecution of his younger brother for participation in Jahn's movement), nor because of his direct concern with the historical bases of patriotic action (his sympathies extended neither to membership nor to action).[2] He directed his attention to history rather as a surrogate for such direct concerns, in part because he was averse to activism by temperament and in part because his combination of particularistic conservatism and patriotic nationalism was viable far more as a project for the past than as a program for the present. Further, he turned to the historical rather than belletristic evocation of the past not only because he could not stand the liberties which historical novelists like Walter Scott took with the facts but also because he simply found historical truth to be "more beautiful" than historical fiction.[3] The insatiable desire for the actual, as the progressive revelation of the infinite guises of the absolute, was a frequent ingredient of the romantic temperament—the justification of history in terms of it was a well-known argument of Friedrich Schlegel's, for example—but in Ranke's case it would go beyond parity with other forms of being and consistently turn him off any poetic or dramatic product that seemed to infringe upon history, for to history he assigned a monopoly of the past. In him the hankering for existence was connected with his passion for the unknown: the fact that something real was not known to have been real, together with the act of getting to know it, conferred upon this reality a value enhancing its intrinsic worth. "The known sources," he wrote early in his historical career, "are soon exhausted and help no one. What is important is either rare or unprinted."[4]

His urge to discovery, in turn, was rooted not only in the spiritual drive to grasp all the varieties of religious experience but in the most elemental ambition to work a virgin field, and it was this ambition that led him to seek his fortune in *modern* history. Despite his later contention that "political conditions" led him from ancient to modern history, during the early years of his historical research he admitted that his first works on modern history "are far from present politics and concern a world that has passed away," and his correspondence of the period stressed repeatedly how clear was the need and how great the opportunity for a historian of the modern period on the lines of Thucydides and Niebuhr for the ancient.[5] As he would cannily tell his publisher on one of the occasions when he was exulting in the new information he was mining from the sources of modern history, "without it one runs the danger of being superseded by an immediate successor."[6] The linkage between personal ambition and an academic career in modern history was long-lived in Ranke, and it is probably no anachronism to read some of the later evidence back into his initial decision. He would always be most attentive to pressing his demands for increases in salary and honors upon authorities in Berlin and in the other governments which bid for his academic services, and his personal satisfaction in these emoluments and perquisites was inextricably mixed with the scholarly requirements of multiarchival research in the modern history of Europe.

So Ranke committed himself to modern history as the confluence of his intellectual needs and his immediate drives. In the fall of 1818, only a few months after his arrival in Frankfurt, he was offering a course in the history of ancient Greece with the laudable historical aims, as he expressed them at the time, of "attaining a complete picture of its life in its graphic vitality, of learning how everything happened as it did [*also gekommen*], . . . [and] of progressing to the complete presentation [of Greece's original constitution] from the first memorials [*Denkmälern*]." In retrospect he later claimed that courses like this and like his history of ancient literature led him, by "an infinitely gentle transition, from philological and generic disciplinary [*allgemein-wissenschaftlichen*] studies, which included the historical, to the authentically historical," since his pedagogical interest in Greece at this time "was directed more to the understanding of great events and remained truer to the scholarship based on the factual [*das Faktische*]" than other classicists. But if the connection between classical philology and history was undeniable in Ranke and if his teaching did bring him closer to history, his course notes tell a somewhat different story of the limitation to which his conception of history was subjected as long as it was associated with classical antiquity. According to these notes, he retained the classicist's final goal of grasping the Greek "essence" by concentrating on the sources of its origins; he still posited, as the explicit religious end of historical knowledge, "the intuition of the eternal laws of the divine order" and "the complete fall of the partition" between past and present; and by the end of the year he was again, as at

Leipzig, despairing of a history wedded to the classics, admitting ruefully that a complete presentation of Greek constitutional history "is impossible for now," and relying for the later period of Greek history (as for the course he gave in 1819 in medieval history) on standard commentators more appropriate, in the words of a recent editor, to "the reader" than to "the scholar" of history.[7] By the fall of 1819 Ranke was confessing a desire to know modern history, and by the spring of 1820 he was announcing to his brother his intense interest in the historical transition from the middle ages to modern times—"how the empire and papacy died and a new life with a new breath blew in"—that was the theme of his first book and marked his beginning upon it.[8] By 1824 he was declaring lyrically: "I live in history and feel my soul blessed, satisfied, and content in it." By 1830 his commitment had hardened from an enjoyment into a necessity: "I know that I was born to do what I now do, that my life has no other purpose."[9]

But history was not, at the start, the solution of his problems: it was the arena for their solution. And we find indeed that for the first dozen years or so of his career as a historian Ranke wrestled with the same kind of problems as those with which he had struggled as a youth, but now in historical translation. His quest for the absolute turned into the priority he accorded to universal history, and his romantic exaltation of the individual as the absolute's manifold mode of expression was diverted by his practical embrace of the historian's craft into a spontaneous love of past facts for their own sake.

II Ranke professed equal attention to both universal and specific history during these years, and he was well aware that this was history on very different levels, entailing attention of very different types. He would repeatedly distinguish, in his progress reports to his brother, between the "two kinds of studies" in which he was engaged: "the idea of world history" (*Weltgeschichte*), which "has the greatest attraction for me"; and second, "for the rest," the particular archival concern of the moment.[10]

Ranke was no more definite about the meaning of world history than his predecessors had been or his posterity has been. For him—as for us—the idea combined the extensive reference to the past events of the world's peoples with the universal connotation of an integral human past appropriate to the unified nature of man's spirit; and he combined them usually without distinguishing between the two. Occasionally in the 20s and more frequently thereafter he would use literal terms for "universal history" (*Universalgeschichte* or *Universalhistorie*, depending on whether he was indicating the actuality or the discipline of history) when he meant to be more analytical about the notion of general or world history than his use of these terms admitted; but he usually succeeded on these occasions only in identifying the unreconciled components he included in the notion, and thus he merely tended to replace ambiguity with ambivalence.[11]

In the next stage of his career, after the revolution of 1830 and when he was in the midst of his most intensive theoretical activity, he would be much more self-conscious about the variety of meanings included in his idea of universal or world history, largely because he was becoming much more attentive to the idea of "coherence" (*Zusammenhang*) as an independent factor of universal history which could be applied to particular and general phenomena alike. But even then he would only add coherence to the other factors, and he persisted in the flexible employment of the terms themselves. Indeed, at least one of his constant foibles can be attributed to this confusion. His notorious limitation of world history to the history of western civilization and its Mediterranean cradle was traceable in good measure to this blurring of distinctions, since the coherent development which connoted world history in one of its senses he could find only in the west, and the historical-mindedness which he required in a culture for it to be susceptible to the historical discipline he could also find only in the west, with the consequence that world history in its extensive sense became in effect coterminous with the frontiers of western civilization. As we shall see, this limitation was already evident in Ranke's first historical works of the 1820s, but he would formulate it explicitly in his notes "on the scope of world history" in the early 30s. In this rationalization of his earlier, as of his later, historiographical practice, he excluded from the scope of world history not only primitive peoples who left no written documents but also peoples like the Indians and the Chinese because "they persist today in a state of nature"—that is, without change—and because they have "chronology" but no real history.[12]

The roots of Ranke's chronic confusions about world history lay in the young Ranke of the 1820s. In this period he usually applied no special term or analysis to universal history; he felt the lack both of the knowledge proper to the extensive world historian and of the understanding proper to the coherent universal historian; and he mixed both wants in his inchoate yearning for world history (*Weltgeschichte*) in general.[13] When the Ranke of the 1820s wrote of the "broadening" of his knowledge "about world history," or of "all the deeds and sufferings [of] our species" in "the tale of world history," or placed in apposition his imagination of "the new world history" and his cherishing of "my cosmopolitan wishes," he was thinking of world history in its extensive, variegated sense.[14] But when he wrote of world history as an "idea" which referred to "the course of human development" and "leads us closer to the knowledge of essential being," he was clearly thinking of it in its integrative universal sense.[15] It was this sense of world history especially that gave him the consciousness of the categorical difference between the particular history he was doing and the world history he dreamed of doing. Thus he was fully cognizant not merely of the difference in range but of the actual gap between the "holistic nature" (*das Ganze*) of world history and the "fragmentary nature" of what could be certainly known from the sources: he confessed to "despair" as the inevitable concomitant of the search for the first, and to his fear, concerning the second, that "I produce nothing but fragments" —that "the illumination of an obscure thing is all that I can hope for in life."[16]

The gap was more than a matter of general conceptual and emotional awareness. It was also operational, for he used different historical media for the two kinds of history: he lectured on universal history, and he wrote on specific history.[17] This division of function, glaring during his early career before he developed historical patterns which would bring the two types into conjunction, would persist as a seam in his work throughout his life. Early in his career, indeed, he even made a principle of the distinction, arguing in the fragment he entitled "The Idea of Universal History" (itself the draft of an introductory lecture) that, whereas written history was both an art and a science, "in lectures history can appear only as science" and, consequently, lectures must consider "the idea of universal history." In another introductory lecture he made this distinction between the written and oral media of history even more revealing, for his explicit formulations of it here explained why he did not hesitate to put into lectures the universal-historical dimension about which he always remained so cautious in his written scholarship. Repeatedly, he insisted that the historian's success in perceiving the objective coherence of universal history through methodical research was only a matter of time—"the idea has not yet attained its realization"—and he differentiated "lectures" from "historical works" precisely by the former's concern with "the inner growth" rather than "the achieved certainty" of a science, assigning to lectures, consequently, the responsibility for "pointing in the direction the science is to go." Consistent with this general prescription, the lectures on "contemporary history" which he gave soon after his arrival in Berlin he explicitly justified by "the persistence in our everyday life of the causes this history reveals to us," and he defined his purpose to be frankly the demonstration of "the connection" among the events associated with the French Revolution.[18]

Nor were Ranke's oral excursions into universal history limited to formal lectures in the classroom. Both of the later extended efforted which he devoted to universal history as such were orally delivered: the lectures to King Maximilian of Bavaria in 1854;[19] and his final *World History* (*Weltgeschichte*) itself, which was dictated to assistants from 1880, after Ranke had lost his sight and could neither read sources nor write. Scholars have traditionally felt less responsibility for the evanescent spoken word than for what they have fondly thought they have written for the ages, and Ranke's persistent association of universal history with the oral and soliloquizing modes, however unintentional (he did not make a point of it), betrayed his inability to apply the rigorous method and self-disciplined approach of his specific history to the level of universal history. Indeed, even with the oral medium his course on world history in Berlin during the 1820s was a failure from the point of view both of student interest and of his own feeling about the course.[20] It was not because he found instant integration in history that he was so committed to it.

What is clear from the unmediated tension of his early historical career—that is, until 1830—is that Ranke's subscription to both universal and particular truth was not simply the expression of a single dialectical religion or philosophy, such as it seemed both before and after his first historical phase, but rather the crystallization of the separate effects of two mutually independent urges within him. Normatively, in accordance with his spiritual priorities, he assigned primary value to universal history; actually, in response to his visceral impulses, he devoted himself primarily to the particulars of "fragmentary" documentary and archival history.

Ranke's early predilection for working on this kind of history, in conscious contrast to the universal history which he deemed more essential, stemmed from something other than a slowly ripening religiosity which recognized the hand of God in individual acts before it could recognize it in the collective pattern of individual acts. The new historian's passion for facts, sources, and archives stemmed even more basically from the elemental desire, prior to any religion or philosophy, of a lonely and inhibited man to possess the human Other—to vitalize and grasp the definite, certain identity of what existed inertly, indefinitely, and uncertainly without his touch. The facts of archival history satisfied this desire exactly: they were expressions of other real lives; the temporal distance between them and him shrouded them in the seductive mystery of exotic strangers; but they were approachable through the documents and they revealed themselves in the intimacy of his exclusive embrace.

There was indeed, as we have seen, a pronounced sexual quality in Ranke's relations with his sources, and it was a quality dramatically confirming the active presence within him of an elemental passion for appropriating the tangible things of this world that was in direct conflict with his transcendent religiosity. This earthy sexuality was categorically different from the "mystical-erotic tone" which some commentators have found in other contexts to be consistent with the religious integrity of Ranke's historical personality.[21] Whatever the validity of this thesis in those contexts, it does not apply to Ranke's intimacy with the palpable materials of his sources, for the unabashed libidinous language which he used about them reveals this intimacy to be a substitute for the physical drives he felt he must divert. This passionate but curiously bound man at the ripe age of twenty-seven could still claim virtuously that if "from time to time my soul has desired the love of a gentle maiden it has never desired a woman, for . . . I am determined not to pay the least attention to my body in this kind of affair." Later he would report an isolated passing affair euphemistically as an "analog of love," yearned in his young years for an interpersonal communion that always evaded him, and cherished in later life a fond but cool affection for the wife he married when he was almost fifty. Such a man could admit his "innocent desire [*Lust*] for the data," could write of facts in unpublished manuscripts as "so many princesses, possibly beautiful, all under a curse and needing to be saved," and could even demonstrate a surprising note of libidinous coyness in his response to the documents themselves. "The object of my love," he wrote of some Venetian manuscripts, "is a beautiful Italian, and I hope that together we shall produce a Romano-German prodigy." Even in his forties he could say of a closed archive that it "is still absolutely a virgin. I long for the moment I shall have access to her and make my declaration of love, whether she is pretty or not."[22]

As he aged, Ranke's documentary and archival analogies lost something of their particular sensual edge, but not the general physical associations of youthful vintage. In his sixties he made the connection himself. "I still study the archives with the greatest imaginable pleasure," he wrote. "There is some gleam of youth or rather of youthfulness in these studies, where one always learns something new and important, with the idea of communicating it to the world—a sentiment which makes one forget a little that one is getting old."[23] And a little later he resorted to a characteristic analogy, corrected for his advancing years, when he said of the "old papers" in which he "steeped" himself, "From these flowers—they actually seem very dried up but they have their scent—I draw honey."[24]

That these figures symbolized a basic and immediate impulse toward the tangible particulars of this world was confirmed by Ranke's firmly stated conviction that in their historical documentary forms he could attain secure possession of humans of whom he could not be sure in any other forms. Thus he could strive continuously in the realm of particular history for the historical "certainty" (*Evidenz*) which he knew could be "attained" only by the research into the "moments of modern times" revealed in "existing but unprinted and scattered reports, letters, and chronicles."[25] His repeated insistence upon this limited certainty and upon his effort to "grasp" (*fassen*, one of his favorite terms) this certainty patently had roots in him that were independent of his search for a higher truth.

Ranke could let himself go so uninhibitedly in his quest for the ascertainable particular realities of history because he was sure of their congruity with the general truths of human nature and was not yet seriously concerned with the connections between the two levels. He was aware of his current inability—during the 1820s—to make the connections, and he sporadically fretted about it, but he cherished at this stage two convictions about the general nature of humanity which encouraged him to think that the connection would in time come of itself from the accumulation of the reliable knowledge of specific events and institutions, newly acquired from the sources.

First, his memorable exaltation of the unique in history—that one learns how humanity "has lived . . . without any other object in view, just as one enjoys flowers without thinking of their classification"—must be placed in the context of his early composite view of human nature. "To grasp in their origin and structure all the acts and suffering of this wild and violent, this good, noble, and peaceful, this tainted and pure creation that we are"—to grasp these products, however unique in themselves, and to align them in the "course of events"—is to get at "world history" as "the core and essence of our species."[26] Although not yet clear about the pattern of world history, Ranke's view of a mixed human nature at this stage required, a priori, the accommodation of its universal qualities to a heterogeneous history and assumed that something in the temporal sequence would organize disparate events into a coherent development.

The second assumption which impelled Ranke to focus on particulars and retain confidence in their ultimate compatibility with a general meaning was his early notion that in history the relationship between the particular and the general took the form of the relationship between the person who acts and the circumstances which he did not make, which condition his action, and which embody "Providence, God, . . . the higher destiny of humanity." The corollary of this assumption was that in "great, dynamic periods," such as those on which he wrote in the 20s, "the precise research into the particulars" of "single actions" was more revealing than the network of conditions bearing upon the actions.[27] Ranke's initial translation of the absolute into the open-ended historical development of a multifarious human nature and into the historical context of free individual acts permitted him to develop his science of empirical history in the chrysalis of a comforting world order and to continue striving toward universals in history that would be compatible with this historical science of particular historical truths.

The historical writings which Ranke published during the 1820s constitute a record attesting both to the security he found in particular facts and to the persistent effort he made to overcome the limits of particularism in history.

III Ranke's historical publications of the 20s were all remarkable for the distance between the unified conceptions promised in their introductions and the detailed, motley political narratives which made up the body of the works. This relationship corresponded precisely to his privately expressed conviction that only world history was worth writing and only particular history was what he was writing.

His first work, the *Histories of the Latin and Teutonic Nations from 1494 to 1514* (1824), has rightly been known for the several chronological sets of royal descriptions, diplomatic negotiations, and military activities aligned like beads on separate strings of narration in conformity with the plural "histories" of the title; and for the famous purpose "to show what actually happened" (*zeigen, wie es eigentlich gewesen*), which has been associated ever since with this kind of factual research. It has also long been associated with its appendix, *On the Critique of Modern Historians*, which was published separately in the same year (1824) and whose explicit conjunction of the "intention only to transmit what happened" with the admission that "this book is a fragment on a fragment," with the reliance on primary sources—"the actors speak; documents, authentic and dubious, are present in masses" —and with the pervasive stress on conformity to the historical truth of particular facts as the supreme standard of criticism made it in reality the methodological extension of the *Histories* that it was designed to be.[28] But this dominant particularistic character of the *Histories* and its appendix tends to obscure the conceptual unity which Ranke set forth as the framework of both volumes and which bore an essential relationship to the distributive factuality so prominent in them. Insofar as there was a large discrepancy between the generality of the plan and the particularity of the achievement, it expressed and confirmed a tension that was fundamental to the Ranke of the period. As he projected it, this first historical work of his was to embody the epical dramatic form, the cosmic religious manifestations, the pan-human scope, and the literary cultural motifs that were continuous with his previous humanistic and theological inquiries into human destiny, but the diffractory nature of the historical medium frustrated the project. Not only did he break off at the year 1514 a work grandly designed to interweave the politics of the Renaissance and the religion of the Reformation because the documents went in too many "varied directions to be combined in a single presentation," but, even within the confines of the book he wrote, the generality of the approach and the specificity of the evidence tended to cancel each other out, leaving the ordering principles detached and the grasp of particular politics inchoate.[29] And insofar as the universal aim occasionally intruded upon the individualized presentation, it shed light upon what seemed otherwise inexplicably incongruous in that presentation.

Ranke's preface to his *Histories* was frankly dualistic. "The purpose of the historian depends on his point of view, and of this point of view here two kinds of things must be said," he began. The two kinds of things were the universality of his conception and the multiplicity of the content, and he varied the priority according to which of these points of view he was taking at the time. First he struck his universal keynote in decisive terms. From his point of view, he wrote, "the Latin and Germanic nations appear as a unity." Not only, moreover, did he see them as a unity in themselves, and not only did he deem them grounded in the "analogous concepts of a general Christianity [and] of the unity of Europe," but for him "the history of the cognate nations of either Germanic or Germanic-Latin descent is the core of all modern history." And he promised an introduction that would show "how these nations have developed in unity and in uniform [*gleichartig*] movement.'' In this context (and paragraph), even the frank characterization of the episodic contents of the book's main body—which he summarized in synoptic novelistic style—as ''histories,'' in the plural, which express ''the other side of the book's point of view,'' was modified by the unified goal those contents were intended to serve. For if the contents were ''only histories, not the history'' of the Germanic-Latin nations because they dealt with ''only a small part of the history of these nations,'' they also had a common factor—''the beginning of the modern''—and Ranke announced as his firm intention that ''this book seeks to grasp all these histories . . . of the Latin and Germanic nations in their unity.'' It was in this context (and paragraph) too that Ranke declared his principle of showing how history actually happened, and the context indicates that his contrast of this principle with the invalid assignment to history of the duty ''to judge the past, to instruct the present world for the benefit of future years'' was not simply the plea for the autonomy of history that it has been correctly reinterpreted (from the interpretation of literal objectivity) to be. It was also a declaration of belief in the unity of the past against the tendency of moralizing historians to break up the past into discrete acts which they could judge or from which they could draw lessons and analogies.[30] Since Ranke's principle has so often been applied to the isolation of unique events for understanding in their own respective terms, the original orientation in quite a different direction is worth noting for its future reference.

But then Ranke shifted gears from the concept to the actual method of his work. He specified primary sources—memoirs, diaries, embassy reports, and eyewitness accounts—to be the main bases of his research, sketched the restrictive conditions for the selective use of secondary commentaries, projected the separate and simultaneous publication of his volume on critical method, and from this perspective concluded with the flat assertion that ''strict representation of fact, as contingent and as homely as it may be, is undoubtedly the supreme law.'' Now ''the development of the unity and of the progress of events'' became merely ''a second law''—a proposition that testified not only to the secondary status of the generalizing aspect but also to its transmutation from an identifiable universal theme into the developmental connections within and between individual events whenever Ranke thought about history from his operational factual perspective.

General theme and logic of development were thus two sides of the same universal coin for the Ranke of the Restoration decade. He adumbrated both in his correspondence as in his prefaces of the 1820s without making the distinction between the individual locus of universal development and the general locus of universal theme, and without showing the capacity to translate the factors of either development or theme into historiographical practice that he would accomplish with approximate simultaneity in the decade of the 30s.

Characteristically for the earlier decade Ranke concluded his first preface with a confession of failure to combine the two dimensions of his approach—a public confession that was no pro forma ritual of modesty (that was not Ranke's style) but a reiteration of his private despair that is illuminated by it. The "noble ideal ... of entering into the situation itself [*die Begebenheit selbst beikommen*], in its human intelligibility [*Fasslichkeit*], its unity, its copiousness [*Fülle*]: ... I know how far I have remained from it. One tries, one strains, and at the end one has not attained it."[31]

The text of Ranke's *Histories* was true to the main categories of Ranke's prefatory promise, without the interaction of the categories that might have satisfied his ideal. He devoted the introduction to demonstrating the unity of the "six nationalities" formed in the Carolingian empire (the preponderantly Latin nations of France, Spain and Italy; and the preponderantly Germanic nations of Germany, England, and Scandinavia) by specifying the three great medieval "enterprises, which, stemming from the same spiritual foundation, form a progressive development of Latin and Germanic life from its origins to the present." These enterprises— the great migration (*Völkerwanderung*), the Crusades, and colonization—were themselves aligned in a continuous chain of succession; and "in the multiple happenings" that make up each "one can almost perceive the unity of a single, closed event" which produces "a common history" and therewith "binds nations in a closer unity." Taken together, "these enterprises are, however long the centuries through which they extend, common to all our nations; they join both, the periods and the peoples;

they are, so to speak, three emanations—[literally, exhalations, *Atemzüge*]—of this incomparable union."[32]

But in the main text that followed, the perceivable unities were the unity of place—the Italian arena that was the battlefield for the great powers—and of a dramatic style which ran parallel through the several blocks of narration. For the rest, the theme and the form of the history, unlike the analytical unity of the introduction, were dominated by the refractive tales of multilateral discords and confusion. Ranke's cast of characters featured the rulers of the three national powers—France, Spain, and the Hapsburg Austro-German empire—and the several Italian states embroiled in the peninsular conflict, and he brought them into his account, identified at their first entry on stage by a curt constitutional description of their position that was as close to historical analysis as he got in the body of the book, when his narrative required their appearance. Then he followed their roles separately until they became entangled in a many-sided struggle with one another.

In this context Ranke saw division and isolation everywhere, as befit the historian's exclusive focus on foreign relations and on the domestic discords that were their conditions or effects. When, in an exceptional departure from international politics, he raised the familiar issue of how there could be such a vital Florentine art under despotism, his characteristic answer was: "It comes from the antagonism of the ever-present . . . parties, from the vigilance of all human forces in conflict, from generally pervasive jealousy." On the occasion of a Venetian defeat, he asked philosophically: "what is it then that exalts and humbles nations?" And his only definite answer was that "around the nation that is striving to rise there are still other vital forces, which oppose its indefinite expansion." In this gear he even cut directly across the moral of the introduction. As he contemplated the start of the long Franco-Spanish rivalry in Italy, he sighed: "It is the life and fortune of the Germanic-Latin nations that they never attained unity." And at the very end of the book, when Ranke broke off with the defeat of the French party by the merged Austro-Spanish House of Hapsburg, he could only write fearfully that the two great opposing combinations "threatened" to become one, and he could view the apparent imminent consequence of European unification pejoratively as "the enclosure of Europe by the Spanish monarchy," thus satisfying negatively his prefatory pledge to finish with an insight into the coming "great disruption" (*Spaltung*) of Europe in the sixteenth century.[33]

This differentiation of introduction and main body of the *Histories* turned out to be not complementary, as Ranke intended it, but segregative. It was not the universal motif in the former but the deficiency in it that had a bearing upon the scattered, apparently inexplicable anachronisms in the latter. In the introduction Ranke candidly qualified the common medieval enterprises of the unified Latin-Germanic nations as "external enterprises," and he did not identify the internal spiritual unity which worked behind them.[34] Since these enterprises were conditioned by time and space, the unity they delivered to modern nations was only an original, formal unity of a common tradition. Thus Ranke had no persistent, substantive, and operative universal factor to account for in his history of the modern nations, either in the form of identifiable universal themes and institutions or in the form of developmental and causal principles for relations within and between individual events.

Into this historical vacuum was drawn, sporadically, precisely the old, uncritical kinds of explanatory and judgmental absolutes that Ranke could not abide in his particular research and that went so ill here with it: divine Providence and the imposed moral verdict on the past by the present. Ranke invoked God, as He had been traditionally invoked by historians, when he wished to place some causal link in the gap between events and their unexpected consequences—as in the gap between the squabbling of Spain with Portugal and the magnificent voyage of Columbus ("God willed that something wholly unexpected would emerge from these quarrels"), or in the gap between German military power at the time of Emperor Maximilian and his relative military impotence ("Had Maximilian collected this whole power in his hand, neither Europe nor Asia would have been able to resist him, but God ordained that it be used more for freedom than for suppression").[35]

Ranke levied his own judgments of good and evil, not, as he would do later, in terms of a constant and explicit moral law in history that made such a judgment an internal criticism of the historical agent, but in terms of an unhistorical judgment that filled the gap left by his narrow political focus within history. After painting a lively word portrait of Maximilian's personality and character, Ranke deliberately excluded it as an inappropriate parenthesis because, unlike Maximilian's attitudes toward "his public life," his "nature [Wesen] has little to do with the coherence [Zusammenhang] of history." For persons and situations in which public attitudes were not so coherent, Ranke sometimes filled this gap in coherence with his own unhistorical judgments on the "nature" of men. Thus of Italian princes in the late fifteenth century: "They consider cruelty and licentiousness to be permissible things. . . . There is nothing in them of the good qualities of human nature; they are unjust and know nothing of true kingship." Of the election of Pope Alexander IV: "Amid the general corruption it was indeed a general calamity and dishonorable for the whole human race." And of Pope Alexander VI: "A strong man, whose soul had become tainted through a long life by licentiousness, greed, and all the vices of the world—when he . . . suddenly saw himself half-divine, should he use this position for good or evil?"[36]

But it was for the rare occasions of his broader explanations that Ranke saved his most elaborate moralizing. To understand the position of the papacy at the time of Alexander VI's accession, he announced "the necessity of starting from a general reflection," and he proceeded to deliver a banal sermon on the ubiquitous human need of law and order for protection against oneself as against others and on the consequent "great danger"—especially exemplified in the institution of the papacy by "the Germanic-Christian nations when they were still unified"—of choosing "watchmen" who are not themselves watched. Again, when he raised the thorny question, so crucial to his entire book, of why a nation as powerfully influential for Europe as Italy was should fall under and remain under foreign domination, his answer progressed from the cryptic "God's judgments were upon Italy" in explanation of specific calamities to an openly labeled "moral reflection" on the general question. "Far be it from me to wish to cast judgment on the temperament of a great nation," he began, and then he went on to cast judgment on the temperament of the great Italian nation. It was not "incurably sick," he decided, "but certainly it suffered from serious diseases"—such as pederasty, syphilis, and, in a more general vein, the imitation first of "the shadow" rather than the substance of the ancients' virtues and then of their invaders' manners and literature. "The basis of imitation is always weakness," he intoned sententiously, substituting a timeless adage for the substantive unity of Latin-Germanic culture from which he started. "Alien customs forcefully took the upper hand."[37]

Even the appended *On the Critique of Modern Historians*, with its evident orientation toward the exaltation of factual accuracy, bore traces of a synthetic yearning that could not be historically realized. Not only did Ranke's own characterization of it as "a fragment" imply his continuing awareness of a larger whole, but he made it clear that his critique was motivated as much by the desire to bring order out of historiographical chaos and to go beyond the unreconstructed details of antiquarian history as to bring generalizing historians to account. The memorials of modern history are so multifarious as to be "frightening," he began. "They speak to us in a thousand voices; they show the most various natures; they are clothed in all colors. . . . The main question is— . . . by whom can we be taught?" And when he came, at the end of his survey, to specify areas for future research, he claimed that the most important work was to be done for Germany, where "the precise connection between general and German affairs has been proved."[38]

But despite these formal indications of Ranke's esteem for as yet unidentified universals in history, unquestionably the net weight of his first work was on the side of particular factuality. In the *Histories*, this weight was obvious in the discrepancy between the brief introduction and the discursive narrative of the body. In the *Critique* it was obvious from Ranke's continual overbalancing of general by particularistic principles in respect to historiographical practice. After admitting his work to be a fragment and indicating the general ideas "it should have had," Ranke entered a practical dementi of these in terms literally directed against the notion of "dominant ideas" (*leitenden Ideen*) which he would later find indispensable for historical explanation: "the path of dominant ideas is as dangerous as it is tempting: when one errs, one errs doubly and triply; even the truth becomes untruth by sub-sumption under an error." Correspondingly, he found the "more general writers neither adequate nor reliable," and even in the case of Germany, where he found the connection with general history valuable, he had to add: "What is the general history of Germany without a precise consideration of at least the more important [of the particular chronicles]?"

Most revealing along this line was the tie in Ranke's mind, revealed by the *Critique*, between general history and integrated history—that is, between the comprehensiveness of the framework around events and the rationality of the relations between events. His criticism of Guicciardini for being "more concerned with ground and conclusion than with fact" was obviously for him in the same class as his criticism of other sixteenth-century historians for being generalists. Indeed, he summed up his practice in a series of phrases that formalized the suprahistorical solution he had actually employed for both kinds of universals in the *Histories*: "Naked truth without adornment, solid research of the particular, and commend the rest to God."[39] Small wonder that the historical writing about which Ranke most bemoaned his limited fragmen-tary scope was also the writing in which the logic of his historical narration was weakest.

IV Ranke published two more historical works during the decade of the 1820s, and in them the preeminently pluralistic character of his early period continued to prevail, albeit with its particularistic antithesis to the universal in history softened and redefined by his attempts to find historical connections compatible with it. Indica-tive of the primary operational status of detailed research for Ranke was the focus of his attention, from 1825 to the end of the decade, on the sources rather than the concepts of his scholarship. During the winter of 1824/25, soon after the publication of the *Critique*, Ranke's attention was caught by a reference to the "Venetian Relations"—the manuscript corpus of contemporary reports by Venetian ambassadors throughout Europe in early-modern cen-turies—which would furnish the documentary core of his subse-quent history writing. At least for the rest of the decade Ranke's work seemed to be determined by the available records—primarily the Venetian sources but also other unpublished documentary collections to which Ranke's enthusiasm spread—rather than by a plan of coverage.

He did indeed begin to employ the Relations in an extended project which he first called *Politics and State Administration of the European States in the Sixteenth and Seventeenth Century* (*Politik und Staats-Verwaltung der europäischen Staaten im 16. und 17. Jahrhundert*) and then changed to the more flexible *Princes and Nations of Europe* (*Fürsten und Völker von Europa*). But he based the organization of the project on the Relations—and wound up with another fragment. Just as he took his notes from the Relations nation by nation, he planned his treatment nation by nation. The first volume, entitled *Princes and Nations of Southern Europe*, was intended to include the Ottoman Empire, Spain, and Italy; but he published it in 1827 as a first volume of a first volume, after he had written only the first two sections, because the Venetian reports for it were available in Berlin. The materials for Italy there did not suffice him, however, and the intended second volume on Italy was never published as such. Ranke was diverted from it from 1826 on by his attraction to concentrated research on papal history and then by his composition of *The Serbian Revolution,* and he would only publish scattered pieces of it, such as his three monographs on the history of Venice, his histories of Italian poetry and art, and a collection of Italian character sketches, seriatim throughout his life.[40]

The first volume of the *Princes and Nations of Southern Europe*, then, is the book that Ranke would publish in later editions under the title *The Ottoman Turks and the Spanish Monarchy in the Sixteenth and Seventeenth Centuries* (*Die Osmanen und die Spanische Monarchie im 16. und 17. Jahrhundert*)—the title by which it has since been generally known. His other work of the 20s was *The Serbian Revolution* (1829), and this too was essentially conditioned by its sources. In 1828 he went south on leave from Berlin, following the trail of the Relations and ancillary collections for early-modern European history, but the first published fruit of his trip was *The Serbian Revolution*, an excursion into contemporary eastern European history that was a spatial exception in an historian who always shunned the Slavs and had dismissed the Turks as unhistorical peoples (save for their Latin-Germanic components) and a temporal exception in an historian then steeped in the research of a "modern" history that by definition was closed by the age of revolutions. He wrote it, as the subtitle (*From Serbian Papers and Reports*) indicated, because a Serbian friend gave him the materials for it.[41]

Now Ranke's passion for the Venetian Relations, which bore *The Ottoman Turks and the Spanish Monarchy* as its first historical product, was no simple or irreducible drive, and the composite nature of the enthusiasm helps to explain the puzzling features about the work that was its initial effect. Certainly Ranke was the first to make widespread use of these documents, which had been only noticed by others, as historical sources which recovered the contemporaneity of the early-modern past, and certainly he experienced what he is widely reputed to have experienced—the pioneer's delight at being the first to perceive things previously unknown. In his first announcement to his publisher of his intention to base his work in modern history on them, he referred to the Relations in the particularistic terms which have usually been associated with scholarship in documentary sources, as "certain authentic manuscripts which contain unknown, indubitable, and most interesting reports," and more than forty years later he was still characterizing "the Venetian papers" as "then [in 1825] unused, almost unknown."[42] But as historical sources, the Relations also had three peculiar characteristics that transcended the reliable testimony to new facts so obviously important in Ranke's addiction: they spanned the whole of Europe and were thus relevant bases for general history in the comprehensive sense of the term; they concerned the area of domestic history, in which connections and coherent relationships loomed large, as well as the area of diplomatic history, in which the sequence of individual events predominated; and in their reports the descriptions of governmental and social structure elevated the analysis of connections and coherent relationships to the status of matters of fact.

Not only were these traits actually true of the Relations but Ranke was well aware that they were true. Indeed, Ranke was captivated by them as much because they seemed to satisfy his need for a bridge between world history and particular histories as because of the new detailed information of a reliable and contemporaneous kind they delivered. The comprehensive quality of the Relations was prominent in Ranke's first communicated reaction to them. In his first revelation of them to his publisher (June 1825) he declared his intention to use them for a work which "combines the high points of general history from Charles V up to and including the Thirty Years War," and six months later he was still declaring himself to be "attracted, in this preoccupation, by the prospects of a fundamentally new . . . researching of a great part of general history."[43] Ranke's actual use of the Relations proved to be somewhat more serious than his anticipation seemed to promise, but he did remain true to his expectation of their general employment. He would exploit the collection that he made during the next seven years continually in the histories of Germany, France, and England, as well as of southern Europe, that he wrote over the next half-century in his professed pursuit of an extensive universal history. And he would justify his use of the Relations not simply in terms of their reliability as sources—for he sometimes acknowledged their unevenness in this respect—but even more emphatically because they covered "the most important states in the world" and because they were the antidote to the "fragmentary and one-sided" quality of other archival documents.[44]

He expressed his appreciation of the Relations' synthetic attributes in the very first work based on them, *The Ottoman Turks and the Spanish Monarchy*, although this was a product of his history in its most particularistic phase. Here, in a preface devoted overwhelmingly to a description of the formation and location of the Venetian manuscript collections, the point of his few substantive remarks was to insist that these sources were indispensable to his prosecution of his theme because they, and they alone, could elucidate the coherence in internal history. His initial formulation of the theme was to pose the question: What produced the joint decline of the Ottoman Empire and the Spanish monarchy, a decline that successively defined the two main periods of modern history? The proposition from which his answer started was that "it happened primarily through internal development," and he proceeded to assert categorically that in contrast to the familiar published documents, which "are entirely concerned with the daily events of political or religious conflict," and on the basis of which "I would not even have undertaken my work," the Venetian Relations "instruct us about the gradual development of internal conditions, of peaceful existence." Because of them, the historian "not only researches particulars [*einzelnes*] more precisely but believes himself to have gained new and true perspectives on the whole [*das Ganze*]."⁴⁵

Unquestionably the special character of his new sources enabled Ranke to pose such general questions of his material and to attempt historical answers. *The Ottoman Turks and the Spanish Monarchy* was shot through with this kind of question, and not only was the divinity conspicuous by its absence from the answers, but the obiter dicta on human nature in which Ranke still occasionally indulged himself had the function rather of conferring a general resonance on specific historical explanations than of substituting suprahistorical explanations for them. Thus when he asked why the Turks submitted to the all-pervasive judgments of the patriarch of Constantinople, he observed: "So it is with human nature: whole nations can be governed by an error, and this error can serve for their best interest: seeds which propagate life can be preserved under this shell. . . . The ideas in which a man passes his daily life demand a spiritual finality (*Schlusspunkt*); they desire to be joined to the Almighty."⁴⁶ But he used this observation not to answer his specific question, which he satisfied by reference to distinctive qualities of Turkish religiosity, but to provide in his answer general coverage of the praiseworthy daily piety of the Turks and the salutary maintenance of nationality by the Greek priests as well as the "insanity" and the "terror" of patriarchal superstition. Again, he concluded his account of the ever-increasing levies of taxes by Spanish monarchs upon a people ever less able to pay with an Olympian remark that was designed rather to draw a general inference from the history than to explain it: "It is not blindness or ignorance that ruins men and states. . . ; but rather there is in them an impulse, favored by their nature and reinforced by custom, which they cannot resist and which drives them ever forward as long as they have a bit of force left. Divine is he who controls himself. Most men see their ruin before their eyes but they hasten to it anyway."⁴⁷

Such generalities were but the top layer of a whole hierarchy of historical generalizations which defined not only the outline but the organization of the book. The next level was occupied by the initial theme of the two nations' joint internal development from the foundation of hegemonial power to the condition of relative

impotence; this theme, summing up for Ranke the two main periods of modern history, prescribed that the temporal span of the
book be from 1540 to 1620, since this period summed up, in turn,
the transition of both nations from the heights of power (coinci-
dent with the start of their European hegemony) to the origins of
decline. The next lower level of generality was occupied by the
distinctive representative role of each of the two nations, a role
which Ranke formulated alternately in military-anthropological
and in political terms since he found the fundamental differentiation of European nations at the beginning of the modern era to
consist both in the contrast between the fortress pattern of warfare
practiced by the Germanic-Latin nations and the massed cavalry
pattern practiced by the rest, and in the contrast between the
oriental state whose prince is a despot and the western state whose
prince is limited by the privileges and rights of individuals and
associations. In both areas the Ottoman Turks were the representative leaders of the one set of nations and the Spanish monarchy was
the representative leader of the other.[48] These subthemes prescribed the separate treatment of each representative nation.

On the next level down, each of these representative nations had
its own characteristic general structure and its own general developmental tendency through the period. The power and energy of
the Turkish Empire was based on the military unity produced by
an integrated structure of universal slavery, feudal system, and an
unrestricted sovereign warlord; its developmental tendency was
toward the disruption of the unity and the attenuation of the
military disposition. The organization of the section on the
Ottoman Turks was determined by "our purpose . . . to show how
all this happened."[49] Spain, on the other hand, was structurally a
congeries of "territories" (not *Provinzen* but *Landschaften*) and
estates, with their own interests and rights, different from one
another and opposed in their particularity to the prince with
whom they were joined only through inheritance. The developmental tendency of this structure, again the obverse of the
Ottoman, was the triumph of the king and his councils—"a most
noteworthy spectacle for the domestic history of the European
states." This structure and development again prescribed the
internal organization of the Spanish section. "The purpose [of our
next investigation] is to bring to view the conflict between the

sovereign and the particular territories in the orbit of the monarchy, first the nature and intentions of the rulers, . . . then the
resistance they found in the chief provinces, how these rulers
conquered them—more or less— . . . and finally the economy
which they established and the condition in which the provinces
were placed.''[50] And true to this program the Spanish section was
topically organized, dealing successively with kings, the court, and
the estates for their respective policies on administration, taxes and
finances, and ''public conditions''—that is, the relations between
society and government—in the respective territories.

But under this apparent continuum of general organizing
concepts there were more fundamental divisive factors which made
Ranke classify this book as another pluralistic and fragmentary
work and which left him still uncomfortably aware of the gulf
between his ideal of universal history and his practice of particular
history. For its working title, he repeatedly used the distributive
''Commentaries on Modern History,'' and when he was finished
he confessed to its ''deficiency'' and ''inadequacy'' in terms that
betokened a generic dissatisfaction well beyond the awareness of
particular gaps. ''It contains much that is entirely new, that has
not previously been known in print, and yet that is worth
knowing,'' he wrote resignedly; and what troubled him most were
not the ''great gaps in particular matters'' and the ''incomplete
observations'' that were on the same plane as the achievement, but
rather the fact that ''what remains obscure is precisely that which
one wants most of all to illuminate''—a crucial failing which he
identified with the lack of ''a complete insight.''[51] Even when the
call for a second edition induced him to think and speak more
positively about the work, he characterized it as ''such an unsystematic and unscholastic book.''[52]

There were three features in Ranke's treatment of *The Ottoman
Turks and the Spanish Monarchy* which explain his persistent
uneasiness about its disjointedness despite the superficial integrity
of its conception and organization:

First, in Ranke's execution of his concept the Turkish Empire
and Spain were considered not only independently of other states
and nations but also separately from each other. The nominal
coverage of the cleft by the prefatory assertions of their joint
manifestation of political decline and their complementary repre-

sentation of political archetypes was not only inconsistent in itself but merely verbal in its historiographical effect. It led to a confusion, in the treatment, between the themes of decline and centralization; but more important, it did not prevent Ranke from writing his histories of the two nations additively, in two insulated sections, at the very same time as he was refusing a request to write a history of France on the grounds that "none of the European states can be presented separately from the others."[53] His awareness of the undesirable isolation into which he had cast the histories of the two countries was ultimately revealed in his appendage of a section on the international relations to the work in 1877. That the extension was a representative corrective and not simply an ad hoc enlargement was confirmed by his addition, two years later, of an analogous section on Turkey and Europe to his new edition of *The Serbian Revolution*, his other production of the late 1820s.

The second feature of Ranke's *Ottoman Turks and Spanish Monarchy* which undermined the overt integrity of its conception was the discrepancy between his approach and its content—that is, between the rational categories of his historiography and the escape of the actual history from those categories. His analysis of the Ottoman Turks, focused as it was on the shrinkage of the sultan's power, the detachment of the guard (*Janissaries*) and the church (*Ulemas*) from loyalty to him, and the rise of "both corporations" to de facto sovereignty, was by far the tighter and more unified of the two national sections, but Ranke made the Turks—and therewith his rational analysis of them—historically irrelevant by concluding that "through their religion the Islamic rulers, who constitute the state [and, except for one 'digression,' were the subjects of Ranke's analysis], are excluded from all real participation in the historical life of the human race." Since, moreover, this exclusion is based on their "unchangeable separation from the subject Christian population," it must apply as much to the Islamic past as to its present.[54]

The Spanish, on the other hand, were obviously historical, but their history did not bear the unity that the Turkish history did. In his introduction to the Spanish section, Ranke felt compelled to point out explicitly that "it is not only at the coherence of the whole that we are aiming," for "man fixes his eyes with lively curiosity above all on the particular.'' If he ostensibly proceeded to devote the history that followed to ''one question, the same for all territories''—to wit, how was the old corporate state undermined and a new centralized state founded?—he actually ''found it best to consider one territory after another'' for a full half of his history (the other half dealt with the kings and their central administration), because ''the territories are so different from one another'' and therefore the single monarchical power ''had very different results in the different territories.'' The differential element in Ranke's distributive consideration of the eight territories in question was intensified, moreover, by the historical character of the Spanish state as he saw it. Since the territories were joined only by the common hereditary right of the monarch, not only were their societies inherently variegated but these variegated societies were politically relevant. ''A prince can only promote; he cannot produce. He can indeed impede; yet he alone will never destroy.'' So wrote Ranke with particular reference to the history of Castile but in terms that were applicable to his diversified handling of all the territories. ''There appears a remarkable interaction between the government and the nation'' (i.e., the territorial society).[55] The results that Ranke registered covered all the possible variations in the relations of power and prosperity between the royal administration and the public institutions of the several corporate societies. Indeed, the book concluded on this note. The penultimate subchapter described the complete ''despotism'' of the king's viceroy in Milan. The final chapter ended the book with the contrasting picture of Dutch prosperity subsequent to the independence of the Netherlands from Spain.

The final divisive feature of *The Ottoman Turks and the Spanish Monarchy* was the subtlest but also the most revealing of all. ''Both the particular and the whole attract me extraordinarily,'' he wrote at this time. ''Happy is he who succeeds in understanding things simultaneously in the ground of their existence and in the fullness of their distinctive appearance.''[56] The fact was that he did present both aspects of history in his book but presented them juxtaposed— as he himself said, ''simultaneously''—and unreconciled. Ranke's habit here was to derive general questions from general categories and to seek out single nodal events wherewith to answer them. The result was, often enough, to leave a perceptible gap between the generality of the question and the particularity of the answer. On one rare occasion Ranke himself admitted the gap openly. After describing to his own satisfaction the hows and whens of corruption in the Turkish palace guard (most notably, the *Janissaries*), Ranke concluded with a confession of his inability to cross the gulf between such particular internal explanations and the question of general decay from which he started. "It is clear enough how it happened in the three sections of the guard. But . . . a state is such a tightly connected whole that the corruption which takes possession of any one part usually also seizes the others. It happens, without our being able to say precisely how it happens."[57]

Behind this gulf lay Ranke's incapacity, at this early stage of his career, to discover any large-scale historical process that could link particular events in a general development. A recent editor has characterized the original version of *The Ottoman Turks and the Spanish Monarchy* as "situational" and "static," admitting "dramatic tensions" but bereft of "the dynamic element" that would loom so large in the later Ranke.[58] Implied in this judgment is the recognition of Ranke's penchant for composing situations out of interpersonal characterization and definitive events rather than out of a continuous temporal process, and it should be accepted in conjunction with Ranke's tendency to select particularly transitional figures, actions, and periods—such as his basic choice of 1540–1620 for the span of his book—because it seemed to encapsulate a whole process within a single event.

This format traded on the ambiguity in Ranke's notion of universal history between the general element that inheres in any individual connection and the general element that connects all the members of a series. It thus enabled Ranke to use the local connections he found within or between particular periods and persons as explanations of the general relations which they were assumed to incorporate. But the effect of localizing connections in pivotal particular events was to factualize the connections and thus to reproduce the generic division between particular and universal history, which had differentiated between all facts on the one side and all connections on the other, in the relocated but persistent form of a division between particular facts and their connections on the one side and a general coherence on the other. Ranke's peculiar but crucial notion of "great facts" (*grosse*

Begebenheiten), to which he was addicted through his career, finds
its explanation here: the great fact is the fact which contains a
general connection within itself as the cement of its internal
identity. The schematism of *The Ottoman Turks and the Spanish
Monarchy* may be seen as the exaggerated scaffolding from which
Ranke built general associations into particular connections.

Ranke himself seems to have been aware that he had merely
displaced the gap he acknowledged between his ideal and his
performance; this awareness may well have entered into the
persistent dissatisfaction that outlasted the publication of *The
Ottoman Turks and the Spanish Monarchy*. In the introductory
lecture note, "The Scope of Universal History," which appears to
have been penned around this time, its characteristic stress on the
feasibility of "the research of the particular" and its equally
characteristic acknowledgment of "the dilemma" produced by the
impractical desirability of "knowing the life of man in its universality" were topped by a provisional recommendation that did not
claim to resolve the problem but displaced it in such a way as to
make possible the prosecution of historical operations like *The
Ottoman Turks and the Spanish Monarchy*. For in the note Ranke
recognized the internality of a single development to be a part of
universal history alongside the external relations of succession and
simultaneity, and he distinguished from the universal "in its full
scope," which cannot be reliably known, "the general tendency"
which is in "the great combination." This general tendency is
continuous with "the part and piece of the general" that "lives in
every detailed particular [*im Kleinsten*] and that can be known
in it." This latter guise of the universal—in the particular detail and
in the particular combination—was what Ranke urged historians to
pursue, "for the time being."[59]

We meet here an articulation of the approach with which we
should be familiar from Ranke's historical publications of the late
1820s: the introductory announcement of a universal process in
history as the ideal object of the historian's knowledge; the
admission—implied or explicit—of a hiatus between this desirable
object of knowledge and the truths which the historian can
authentically acquire through research; and the focus on the
specific connections within or between particular persons and
events to provide a practical model of the elusive universal. Both

the universal and the particular truths in history were becoming more negotiable for Ranke than they had been in the original confrontation of an absolute divinity above history with the shell of particular appearances which manifested it imperfectly and refractorily. But until he could identify in history a large-scale historical process that could link the extensive and the systematic senses of world history, the cleavage between the desirable and the operational would persist.

The Serbian Revolution, which was the first scholarly product of his documentary pursuit southward, may well be accounted a sport in the Rankean corpus by virtue of its subject and its method, but in terms of its conception and its organization it supported and confirmed the stage of imperfect integrity which he had reached in his approach to history by the closing years of the Restoration. The processed sources at Ranke's disposal (he could not read Serbian, and the documents were in German), the thread of continuity afforded by the theme of historical Christian influences upon an unchanging core of Slavic Serbia, and the automatic relevance conferred upon any event in the framework of revolution (a topic, let us recall, that Ranke accepted rather than chose)—these fortuitous features of the work certainly helped to minimize the evidence of Ranke's characteristic polarity in it.[60] Yet it did evince the familiar pattern of Ranke's approach. It was furnished with a general introduction which in broad strokes traced the medieval development of the Serb nationality as an alternation of influence by and reaction against the distinctive but related world-historical movements of eastern and western Christianity. It concluded with separate and static structural analyses of the dominant Turkish and subject Serb nations, analyses that were occasioned in the text by the disruption of Serbian integrity under the centrifugal pressures of outside world-forces and by Serbia's submission to the Turks in the early-modern age. These analyses were themselves connected by Ranke's general comparison of the Christian and Islamic faiths, and the comparison was in its turn solidified by the final unifying principle that the sundry differences between the two faiths were all reducible to the ''truth of the one faith . . . and the falsehood of the other.''[61] The main body of the book which followed on these introductory chapters exhibited Ranke's wonted change of pace: it was a detailed and circumstantial narrative account of the revolution.

Yet, despite the extraordinary circumstances and the familiar format which together seemed to assign *The Serbian Revolution* to a merely parenthetical function in Ranke's main development, it did signal a further stage in his growth. First, the schematic introduction, which featured the international role both of Christianity and of Christian political powers, furnished the occasion for Ranke's first explicit statement of his "doctrine of ideas" (the *Ideenlehre* so ubiquitous in discussions of the mature Ranke); and the context of the statement reveals that by it he not only adumbrated the doctrine of the state's spiritual essence that he would develop later but also was indicating the principle of intellectual universals in history that grew out of the preoccupations of his early career. "Ever since powers have been established on earth, endeavoring to realize, to represent, and to promote those *general* ideas which involve the destiny of the human race," he wrote in the decisive passage which introduced the Serbs' involvement with the expansive forces of universal Christendom, "it would seem that no nation is any longer allowed to develop itself by the unrestrained exercise of its own innate strength and genius. The progress of all development depends materially on the relation into which a newly emerging people enters with the nations already in a state of civilization."[62] Clearly, Ranke was feeling here for the large-scale connections in history that had hitherto eluded him, and not so clearly he sensed that these connections would originate in the realm of ideas—not God's ideas, which were knowable through discrete appearances, but human ideas, which would be knowable through the process of history.

The full integration of his synthetic ideal into his discriminate method would have to await his identification of the substantive connections between general development and particular events within the content of history itself. The first of these identifications would have as its components particular and general historiographical concerns continuous with his professional career of the 20s, but between the juxtaposition and the connection lay the external influence of an experienced revolution. Whether as stimulus or catalyst, the experience attended the first operational juncture of the general and the particular in Ranke's history.

7

The First Synthesis:
Revolution, Religion, and History
in the 1830s

The revolution of 1830 was actual in France, palpable in the smaller states of western Germany, and only potential in Prussia. Ranke himself was even further removed from the realities of the revolution, since he remained in Italy among his beloved manuscripts throughout 1830 and did not return to Berlin until March 1831. When, some nine months later, he was drawn into the orbit of the "revolution," it was as the reluctant editor of an officially inspired journal which was designed precisely to keep the French model out of Prussia both in its revolutionary and its counterrevolutionary forms and which was addressed to the distant spectators of this model, both partisan and uncommitted, in the Prussian governmental and social elite. Indeed, for the publisher Friedrich Perthes, who first proposed the idea of the journal, Ranke's appointment as editor was precisely the unwelcome signal that the enterprise would be, not a popular organ of public opinion in accordance with the original design, but just another academic periodical for "officials, specialists, and the upper political circles."[1]

Yet it was precisely this initial experience of revolution through so many filters that made Ranke susceptible to it and set the pattern for his reactions to such cataclysmic contemporary experiences throughout his life. From his perspective the striking events of his own time came through as articulations of organized, long-range tendencies rather than as immediate, raw, and unprocessed sensations. "I am terribly excited over the political events [in France]," he wrote from Venice in October 1830, "and am convinced that for our whole life long we shall be concerned with the things connected with them."[2] Contemporary political experience, indeed, in times of crisis assumed for him the shape not only of a processed contemporary history but of an especially integrated kind of contemporary history. At such times politics, thus mediated through contemporary history, became compatible with past history in a way that transcended the normal problem of their relations, and politics contributed to past history integrative themes that synthesized the manifold diversity of his normal researches into remote ages. The pattern, moreover, was not simply recurrent. Ranke did tend usually to slip back toward his regular posture of insulating past history from present politics and of stressing the multiplicity and variegation of historical life once the crises were over, but each turning point built a connection into his historiographical equipment that he would carry with him as a persistent assumption until the synthetic increment of the next crisis.

I   The revolution of 1830 was rendered appropriate for its historiographical role by Ranke's peripheral location in it and by the deliberate hybrid character of his journalistic function. The *Historisch-Politische Zeitschrift* which he edited was no misnomer, at least for him, since for the understanding of politics he proposed to adduce, over and above "contemporary general history," the "origin and development" of "present conditions."[3] This revolution became Ranke's first effective spur to bridge the gap between the normative universality and the operative particularity of his early historiography. For he saw in the specific events of the crisis an actual historical theme of continuing general revolution to which he must respond.

What was crucial about his response was that he reacted to the revolution more as a historian than as a man. Certainly with his ingrained conservative sensibilities he found it instinctively intolerable "that apprentices and urchins should want to govern us," but his two main reasons for opposing it were filtered through his historical categories: "to defend the actuality of our native development against the flood of alien demands stemming from ... presumptuous theories"; and to resist the "critically disorganizing force in these so-called new ideas" which was undermining the long work of history.[4] In a lecture of the early 1830s Ranke explicitly linked contemporary politics to his "idea of world history," asserting the incompatibility of the historical principle as such with either revolution or reaction. He excluded both from the historian's otherwise unqualified obligation to impartiality—"our task is not to judge error and truth but to penetrate to all parties' reasons for existence and to represent them with complete objectivity"—because both "eternal stagnation" and "the overthrow of the old as if it were a completely dead thing" destroyed the past and negated the very essence of history. As might have been expected from the conservative overbalance of his moderate politics, it was especially revolution that aroused his opposition. "History approves the principle of movement, but as evolution not revolution, and therefore history also recognizes the principle of resistance."[5]

As is indicated by the placement of his views on revolution in unprecedentedly extended (for him) theoretical discussions of historical principle, the impact of the revolution upon Ranke inspired him to synthesize his ideas about history. The first of his objections to the revolution led to his theory of individuality. The second led to his conscious allocation of complementary roles to individual and universal history in his historical practice.

II The classic formulation of Ranke's theory of historical individuality is Friedrich Meinecke's exposition of it in terms of "historism" (*Historismus*), and we must put this theory in its proper Rankean context—that is, in the context of the articles on "The Great Powers" and "Dialogue on Politics" which Ranke wrote from 1833 to 1836 for the *Historical Political Journal* and of his notes on "The Idea of Universal History" which date from the same period—before we can understand what is valid and what is deceptive in Meinecke's exclusive focus on the idea of individuality in Ranke's historism. Historism, in Meinecke's rendition of Ranke, posits history as the autonomous realm of knowledge inhabited by spontaneously developing individuals who manifest the fusion of

materiality and ideality into a principle independent of both—
"the real-spiritual principle" (*das Real-Geistige*), in Ranke's
awkward but telling phrase, "which suddenly appears in unforeseen originality and cannot be derived from any higher principle."[6] In Meinecke's historistic exposition, individuality, as the
unity of spirit and earth, is the primary reality of history, in explicit
opposition to generality, which thus becomes the principle of
other, nonhistorical kinds of knowledge; and even such apparently
general Rankean categories as the "tendency" or the "idea" of an
age are in this version instances of "the highest and most
comprehensive of all visible historical individualities."[7]

Meinecke's formulation points to an important truth about
Ranke's history, but it also contains an important distortion. The
important truth is that for Ranke intermediate positions, such as
history's place between nature and spirit in the corpus of knowledge, were not mere compromises or accommodations of higher
principles but were animated by primary principles of their own.
In his discussion of moderation (*juste milieu*) in the *Dialogue on
Politics,* Ranke distinguished precisely between the "negative
kind" of moderation, which is the balance between extremes and
which he rejected, and the "positive" kind, which "excludes . . .
the extremes . . . because it has a positive content of its own, its
natural innate tendency which above all else it must realize."[8] This
commitment to principled moderation, moreover, was more than
political—it ran through his most fundamental convictions. In
matters of religion, for example, he rejected not only the "fanati-
cism" of the orthodox and the "philistinism" of free thought but
also the "halfheartedness" (*Halbheit*) of compromise. As in
politics, he affirmed "the mutual approach of positive and
moderate souls in authentic—not indifferent—tolerance."[9]

Insofar, then, as the standard emphasis upon Ranke's notion of
historical individuality points up his commitment to history as the
realm in which new, independent forms of life and of knowledge
are generated by the interaction of otherwise antipodal principles,
it is correct. And insofar as it points up his commitment to the
multiplicity of unique individuals as *an* irreducible principle in
history, this standard emphasis is also correct. But insofar as it
argues for individuality—or more precisely for the hierarchy of
personal and collective individuals—as Ranke's exclusive historical

principle, on the ground that his antitheses of spirit and earth and of generality and particularity were resolved for him only in individuality, it distorts Ranke's working idea of history. For the fact is that Ranke never, not even in his history, reconciled these antitheses in such a monistic way. They reappeared both in his perception of the historical process and in his standards for the historian; their resolution not only in the theory but in his practice of history remained his most constant and pressing problem from the beginning to the end of his career. Ranke was a man who was passionately devoted to both sides in each of the great confrontations in the principles of life—to religion and to science, to spirit and to nature, to the particular and to the general—and he committed himself to history not because he could cancel the opposition of his principles there but because he could exercise all his principles there, logically opposed or no, without sacrificing his integrity. Certainly he was thinking of this refractive role for his history when he insisted on how "ridiculous" the idea was "that I lack philosophical or religious interest, . . . since it is precisely this and this alone which has driven me to history," and he insisted repeatedly that history "is not a denial but a fulfillment of philosophy."[10] Since "philosophy . . . always deals in the universal," something of this must rub off on history. Ranke subscribed indeed as much to the principle of historical universality as to the principle of historical individuality, for only from the coexistence of both the individual and the universal in history did he hope to fathom the tensile relation between life's great antimonies, the relation which was the only resolution of them accessible to man.

Hence Ranke was as open to philosophy when it was the way to unitary principles within the framework of history, as he was opposed to it when it was a rival structure of a priori knowledge outside the framework of history. Certainly there are good reasons, even apart from the slanted concern of his later interpreters with the individual rather than the universal side of the historical process, for misunderstanding Ranke on this score. His occasional theorizing about history would always retain the particularistic and individualistic emphasis of its incubation in the circumstances of the revolutionary 1830s, for he was not then theoretically able enough or later theoretically interested enough to make explicit the distinctions which were certainly implicit in the theory and which alone made it fit the whole range of his historical practice.[11]

But there is a whole intellectual dimension to this incubation that helps to explain the limitations of the theory just as the political dimension helps to explain what coherent force it had. Neither as an original quality of mind nor as a function of Ranke's growing relative indifference to the theory in contrast to the practice of history does the judgment of Ranke's theoretical incapacity suffice to explain the distortions of his own position that are in the historical theory he articulated during the early 30s. Judgment on the first count is subject to cavil, and on the second to anachronism. The fact is that Ranke was intensely interested in the theory of history now, as he would not be later, because he was concerned with establishing its credentials as an independent and fundamental sphere of knowledge as against the other independent and fundamental spheres of knowledge, and that the distortions of his theory stemmed not from any original inability in the medium but from the restraints imposed by the priority of history's external independence upon the language of its internal relations. Ranke's special tyrant, in his declaration of history's emancipation, was philosophy. His perception of the split between "the philosophical and historical tendencies" at the University of Berlin as a bitter academic struggle, "like two parties," undoubtedly helped to focus intellectual struggle in this direction, as did his need to settle his own debt to Fichte—his chief target during the 30s.[12] More important for Ranke's focus was his broad view of philosophy not simply as a speculative discipline dealing in general truths but as the approach covering all forms of knowledge directed to the assertion of and deductions from constant laws and principles. It stood, in short, for the whole mode of thought which he deemed not only antithetical to but subversive of his conception of history: later it would be called nomothetic and be attributed to the natural sciences.

But there was a final reason for Ranke's inimical focus on philosophy, and more than anything else it was this reason that led to the distorting of his historical theory: philosophy was the form of knowledge that was not only the chief rival to the historical form of knowledge but also the only model for the highest truths incumbent upon the historical form of knowledge. From the one perspective, "the way of philosophy" is "the way of abstraction" and "is indeed to be severed" from history, which is "the knowledge of the particular." From the other perspective, however, "history, in the sense of the whole circuit of world history which fills us with spiritual content, is not an antithesis but a fulfillment of philosophy," and the "conception of totality" is a requirement of "the historical principle."[13] It was precisely because the philosophy which Ranke rejected for history dealt in universal truths that Ranke could find neither the concepts nor the language to indicate the way to the universal truths which he accepted for history. Hence the imbalance, in his theoretical expositions, between the categorical assertion of the particularity which was philosophically respectable for history and the diffident uncertainty about universal truths which could not be asserted for history in a language attuned to philosophy without the submission of history to philosophy.

Ranke's notes of the early 30s on historical theory demonstrate clearly how his derivation of his theoretical concepts and language from the external relations of history and philosophy made these concepts and this language misfits for the internal relations of history and universal truths, thus blocking Ranke's path to understanding the problem of historical universality in the theoretical medium and promoting posterity's path to misunderstanding Ranke on this problem in this medium. In his manuscript "Idea of Universal History" Ranke established "the historical principle" as the unqualified principle of particularity against philosophy conceived not in the usual caricaturing terms of "abstraction" and "speculation" but as the authentic form of knowledge oriented to "the universal," "the process" (*Fortgang*), "the whole," "totality." In terms of their respective principles, the opposition is entire and unrelieved: "philosophy deals in the universal interest, history in the particular interest; philosophy grasps the process as the essential, . . . history turns to the particular by inclination; philosophy is always negating . . . , history sees the good and the beneficent in all that exists and seeks to grasp it." From this point of view, even the omnipresent Absolute does not qualify the historical principle of particularity or bridge its separation from the universal principle of philosophy. "While the philosopher . . . seeks the infinite in the process, in development, in totality, history knows an infinite in every existence." To safeguard historical particularity, indeed, Ranke even engaged in dubious logic to delimit the Absolute. "The inherence of the eternal in the particular need not be demonstrated—it is the religious ground which our historical effort assumes," he wrote in an evident attempt, later to be spelled out by Kierkegaard, to avoid any universal mediation in the approach to the Absolute. And he immediately followed this prescription with the argument on the opposite tack that "the historical effort" must not focus exclusively on the search for "that higher principle in appearance" because to do so would be "to assume rather than to perceive that principle." Nor was Ranke evasive about the point that motivated these qualifications of the Absolute, and overrode any problems in them: to conceive it otherwise "would approach too close to philosophy. . . . The appearance in and for itself is sanctified for what is in it."[14]

The definition of history in relation to what was not history was therefore the empirical inquiry into particular existence pure and simple. But when Ranke proceeded to the internal "requirements" of this historical principle, history as such became synonymous with universal history, and Ranke confronted the problem of filling the outer framework of particular history with a universal content without thereby philosophizing it. The result was a set of confusions stemming from his attempt to find historical equivalents for philosophical principles of integration. First, the relationship between the appearance and the Absolute in particular facts was articulated to juxtapose ill-assorted historical and philosophical methods, without further explanation, in a nominally single procedure: "the documentary, thorough . . . inquiry into the appearance itself," and "the grasp of its ultimate unity" through an act of "spiritual apperception." Second—and a stage further on the road to generalization—the relationship of "succession (*Aufeinanderfolge*) between various events," a "connection" (*Zusammenhang*) which is "sufficient for original research," is also "an inner connection of cause and effect" and thus partakes of "the causal nexus" (*Causalnexus*). Ranke gave but one "ground" to link succession and cause, and that was the inquiry into "real motives" through "research in the authentic document"—"pragmatism in our sense," as contrasted with the a priori pragmatism that assumes the chief motives (greed and power). Clearly, Ranke's appropriation of and focus on "pragmatism," which he defined as "the approach to history which derives effects from causes" and which he prescribed to be necessarily "based on the sources" (*urkundlich*), were designed to historicize and particularize the general philosophical category of causality. Open-ended motivational causality was the only kind that could align the general category with particular factual existence and give it the sanction of treatment by the historical method devised to treat that existence. "The inner connection of cause and effect . . . exists," he asserted, "and because it exists, we must seek it and we must know it."[15] What he did not assert was a status for any connection of cause and effect that went beyond the individual kind of existence signified by the documentary conversion of intentions into facts.

But when Ranke came to the inescapably universal "conception of totality," his makeshift translation broke down, laying bare the mechanics of his procedure. For he could not do without totality, but it was too irreducibly general and approximately philosophical for him to do anything satisfactory with it either. On the one hand, as an autonomous component of universal history the idea of "a Totality (*Total*), a Becoming (*Werden*), . . . a Flux (*Vergehn*) that transcends its embodiment both "in every moment" and in "the succession of particular moments" is "an idea to which we cannot refuse our attention." For example, "in the case of a people, the idea speaks to us not from all the particular moments in which it vitally expresses itself but from the whole of its development." But since, on the other hand, "it is only through precise research, step-by-step understanding, and entry into the documents that we accomplish anything, . . . we do not know much beyond this." "The farther we go toward totality, the harder it is to get at it. . . . We can wish only to grasp the causal nexus everywhere, but hardly to grasp the essence of totality." Indeed, he declared categorically, "I hold it to be impossible to solve the task of totality completely. God alone knows world history; we know the contradictions. Of its harmonies we can have only a presentiment" (*können wir nur ahnden*). But neither resignation nor intuition provided Ranke with a resolution for the problem of the irreducibly universal in history, however definitely he may have seemed to recommend them. Toward the end of the essay he burst out despite his previous argument, "Yet clearly for us a unity, a process, a development does exist" (*ist vorhanden*). Appending the brief marginal qualification that "it is to be narrated, not to be proved," he could then conclude that "we have now arrived at the task of philosophy by the historical path," thus validating within history precisely the same integrative concepts that he had denied to history in its external relations with philosophy. Small wonder that in these terms he could not find the way to them and that in this context he reiterated his well-known complaint: "How infinitely difficult it is with universal history!"[16]

Thus he could not at this time, in his first attempts at theorizing about history after the revolution of 1830, get beyond the block imposed by his use of philosophical concepts and language in a historical medium. His theoretical statements stressed particularity as the primary canon of history but elided the problem of reconciling this canon with the historian's function in grasping the general coherence of the historical process as a whole. He continued, for example, to exalt the distinctive identities of nations and states as objects of history but to insist that their "connection, which . . . must be the theme of any universal history, is dependent on the particular nature of each." And for the historical epistemology which sought to validate the historian's knowledge of general truths that was not reducible to his research into particulars, Ranke could not get beyond such vague and inconsistent formulations as the active injunction that somehow "historical science . . . should and could raise itself in its own way from the researching and consideration of the particular to a general view of affairs" and the passive injunction that "the historian should keep his eyes open for general truth [*das Allgemeine*], not by thinking it out beforehand like the philosopher but by letting himself be shown, during his consideration of the particular, the course which the development of the world has taken in general."[17] Since, moreover, he now denigrated the extensive concept of world history in principle because "too much of it is lost and unknown, . . . without any hope of ever being found," and affirmed "the spiritual content of world history" in terms of its "inner truth, necessity, and energy, in whose succession is an immeasurable progress," he ruled out the additive approach to universal history as a detour around his problem. History, like philosophy, "deduces the life of the spirit," but unlike philosophy does it by somehow "perceiving spirit in its appearance and development": Ranke's dilemma of facing the philosophical issue of unity with the unphilosophical instrument of particularity was unavoidable.[18]

Characteristically enough, it was only when he passed from thinking about history in the abstract to thinking about it in the concrete—when he passed, that is, from theorizing about history to inferring from history—that he first expressed confidence in the historian's capacity to acquire general truths about humanity and began to emphasize his primary responsibility to grasp the universal coherence which was the historical equivalent of these truths. Just as characteristically, the two kinds of occasions that evoked this positive development in him were the lectures he gave on contemporary history and on medieval culture. This coincidence demonstrated how the current post-revolutionary politics which he was experiencing and the historiographical discovery of Christianity as the viable agent of universal history in the book he was writing— *The History of the Popes*—joined to impel this development. He adumbrated the generalizing role of historical Christianity in the very lecture which he gave on the morrow of the revolution of 1830, for after he had revealed his theoretical doubts about the achievement of a universal history he proceeded to talk far more sanguinely about it in the different context of the substantive scope definitive of universal history. "The spread of Christianity over the German world has created the basis from which everything that has been great and noble in modern times has come," he said now in defining the actual scope of universal history. ". . . The whole orbit of world history fills us with spiritual substance— full of inner truth, necessity and energy, and in whose succession is an infinite progress in the midst of which we still stand. By the law governing the creature [man] he passes away, but the spiritual content which he has developed belongs to the realm of the eternal, the ideal. It also has an indestructible efficacy, once it has entered into that great, ever more substantial, and ever broader stream of spiritual life."[19]

In subsequent lectures during the 30s and the early 40s, while his scholarship was focused on religious history in his composition of the *History of the Popes* and the *German History in the Age of the Reformation*, Ranke confirmed this association of the spiritual component in history with the diachronic continuity and the synchronic universalism of history, and he stressed ever more emphatically his concomitant belief in progress as the corollary of this historically universal spirit. Although the argument was much more explicit in his lectures than in his scholarship, as befit the characteristic generalizing tendency of the one and the particularizing tendency of the other, it is an important argument for the understanding of Ranke and his historical scholarship, not only because it articulates the assumption behind the occasional and unexplained paeans to progress in his book on the German Reformation but also because it helps to qualify and to explain the later notorious antiprogressivism of his lectures *On the Epochs of Modern History*.[20]

After the bout of inconclusive abstract theorizing about history which was part of his direct involvement with the revolution of 1830, Ranke typically advanced his general remarks on the nature of history as introductions to his lectures dealing with church history in medieval and early modern times and with the contemporary history into which he converted his political experience of the early 30s. He continued in these contexts to distinguish between "the antiquarian method" of history, which "starts from the consideration of the particular, develops itself on externals, and seeks to establish . . . the factual," on the one hand, and "the philosophical method" of history, on the other, which "is concerned with knowledge of abstract connections in the concrete"; and he continued to find both unsatisfactory, since the one lacks "the integration of the whole" and the other is scientifically unreliable. But when he insisted on their distinctive historiographical juncture now, his emphasis was on the integrative component, stressing not merely its desirability but its possibility. He characterized "the presentation of the inner connection, the continuous development which joins what precedes irrevocably to what follows and so has progressed to the idea of constant perfectibility" as "a higher principle in history," vis-à-vis history "in its outer course," which is a mere "trivium."[21]

The grounds for this priority of values were that the spirit is universal and eternal, and that history could fulfill its supreme function of tracing the manifestations of spirit only by following the continuity and perceiving the totality of human things. In history

> the human spirit confronts itself and knows itself. Therefore history is immediately the life of the human spirit and at the same time the common property of the human race, which thereby possesses itself in its totality. Universal history . . . grows with the world: the human race reproduces itself in its history. . . . From the nature of spirit men have derived the necessity of development and have sought to prove this in history. Progress in the life of humanity reveals itself in the consideration of its totality. . . . History opens to us not the realm of fleeting appearance alone but also that of the eternal spirit. . . . The sphere of history is the realm of a spiritual existence which develops constantly. . . . Historical phenomena are of a very variegated nature, but always of a spiritual content, filled and determined by all the limits of their existence; in their succession is revealed . . . a great—more precisely, an inner—connection which constitutes the spiritual life of the human race. . . . Universal history concerns the past life of humanity in all its fullness and totality. . . . Only through history is the human race conscious of itself as a unity. . . . Only general history attends to all the sources of life.[22]

Nor was Ranke reticent about making the connection between this unifying function of spirit in history and the substantive commitments to religious and contemporary history which were then his chief professional and personal preoccupations. The church represented "a unity which provided a common basis for artistic and scientific culture" in the middle ages, he adjudged specifically, and then he drew the general conclusion that "the religious spirit is the most universal spirit. . . . The movement of religious ideas has largely contributed to the character of the modern world and its distinction from the Middle Ages."[23] "In contemporary times" analogously, he indicated in his introduction to his version of their history, "not only do all endeavors have an ideal content, but men are more conscious of this ideal content than they ever were before.'' Contemporary history, then, must deal less with ''dominant personalities'' than with ''a power in things and in the great interests from which men get their impetus.'' Hence the historian's task is to ''grasp the penetration of the real by the idea, . . . the integrity of the phenomena.''[24]

While Ranke still specified the distinctive historical attention to the contingencies of outer appearances, to ''the great freedom and variety'' of individual events, and to ''the research of the fact,'' he now subsumed the understanding of individual events and particular facts under the knowledge of the general connections in which they were involved. ''We know *what* has happened,'' he said in the mid-1830s, ''when we know the inner connection of things, the spirit of events, the *how?* . . . In events there is more than what appears on the surface; there is the content to be researched [*der erforschende Inhalt*], the idea.'' And it was in this context that he repeated: ''The purpose of universal history is the knowledge of the past life of the human race in its internal coherence.''[25] He even made explicit the contrast between his earlier appreciation of the individual event because it embodied an otherwise inaccessible general spirit and his current appreciation of the individual event because it contributed to the knowledge of a larger, accessible, general process of spirit. In his earlier abstract theorizing about history, he exalted ''every positive moment even if it does not have a great importance in general, . . . because it includes a modification of spiritual life in itself.'' But half a decade later he was recanting this independence of the historical individual. ''The individual moment . . . becomes important through the modification of the general spiritual substance without which it would not be and which represents itself in it. . . . In the succession of these spiritual substances there is an infinite progress of development.''[26]

Similarly, the prescription of historical objectivity—the stress on ''what really happened''—which he had earlier required of the approach to the particular facts of history, he now assigned to the historian's knowledge of general processes in history. It was in the context of affirming the historian's obligation to root all events in the progressive ''spiritual connection of existence'' that he now raised the issue of historical objectivity; and he resolved it, correspondingly, by postulating the objective and researchable reality of this connection. "There is . . . objectively a world-historical general development," he said at the end of the 30s. "It exists and therefore it must reveal itself to the simple, conscientious, and attentive procedure of research." Hence the historian can "give himself wholly to the object," and it is possible for him "to attain the perception of spiritual elements through mere research" because the general object "requires" such perception and the historian himself "is but an organ of the general spirit which realized itself through him." Consequently, when in the early 1840's he deliberately repeated the famous formula, which he had first announced under different auspices in the mid-20s, about the historian's obligation to look for "what really happened," he specified the obligation to mean the knowledge of general process rather than of discrete facts. "Only from a spiritually combined series of facts does the event result. Our task is thus to inquire into what really happened [*eigentlich geschehen ist*] in the series of facts . . . , in its sum."[27]

Ranke's endorsement of the idea of progress in this period was clearly tied to his discovery of the cumulative continuity of spirit in history. He cautioned now, as he would later, against the derivation of progress from "the postulates of logical categories," but his general view of progress was positive. "The axiom of the progress of the human race, . . . often misunderstood, has its truth," he declared, and in the lectures that he delivered from the early 30s to the early 40s he repeatedly affirmed this favorable orientation toward the idea. Time and again he associated "an infinite progress of human devlopment" with the spiritual continuity perceptible in historical succession until he finally made progress an indispensable criterion of historicity. "Only nations that are involved in a continuous spiritual progress are historical," he defined. "What is more, to be historical a nation must participate in the general spiritual development of humanity." And when Ranke came to balance his belief in the autonomy and the equivalence of each age with his belief in spiritual progress, he came down on the side of progress. "Not every age is more perfect than its predecessor, but each age has its task, its perfection, and a progress becomes visible from the unconscious to the conscious, from intuition [*Ahnung*] to knowledge, from presumption to knowledge, from nature to organized force."[28]

Since Ranke himself modified the abstract language of his historical theory when he turned, even in his most thoughtful moods, to history proper, it is clearly not by epitomizing the theory or by exalting its own particularistic emphasis into a full-blown theory of individuality that we can understand his approach to history. We must rather undertake a radical reformulation of the theory, in terms of its real implications, to get at what he really meant. If, then, we reformulate his theory of historistic individuality to articulate the unspoken differentiation between the cognate pairings of particularity/generality and individuality/universality —a differentiation obscured in Ranke's language and yet crucial for the theory—we shall understand how it could reject general principles in history but still provide for the possibility of the universal connectedness of history.

For Ranke, particulars were singular phenomena which were perceived as such by the historian, apart from any general connections. They were the basic units in historical research, necessary but insufficient for historical knowledge. Generalities, to the contrary, were abstract, classificatory, or formal principles which were, as such, extraneous to history and inconceivable by the historian. But in the historical process particulars were actually involved in general connections; when the particulars acted in the light of these connections they became individuals, both in history and for the historian. The general connections which, along with particularity, defined the historical individual derived not from general principles as such—since these did not exist for history— but from two hybrid general sources which do exist for history because they are capable of organizing particular phenomena without subsuming or canceling them. One source of the general connection which translates the particular phenomena of research into the individual realities of history is the absolute reality of God's spiritual unity, for any particular existence that acts and is viewed as an inimitable manifestation of this unity becomes itself an inimitable, vital, developing individual unity by virtue of what we may call its vertical connection with the One.

The other source of the general connections which define the individual is the universal pattern emergent from the interaction among particular existences which become individuals as the active participants in this pattern. Now in Ranke's overt theory of individuality his transitory political concern with the circumstantial particularity of historically sanctified individuals and institutions produced the appearance of an essential opposition between the individual and the universal principle in history that was congruent with the essential opposition between the particular and the general principle in historical method. Indeed, at this stage Ranke emphasized the priority of historical individuals for all connections—that is, the individual's exclusive embodiment of the absolute spirit and the individuals' continuing production of the universal pattern of relations among themselves. But this appearance of congruence—the congruence of the particular with the individual and of the general with the universal—was deceptive. Unlike particular phenomena, which by definition excluded general considerations, individual realities were, equally by definition, involved in universal connections. And unlike general principles, which corresponded to no historical reality, universal connections were themselves historical realities. Moreover, while universals in history were necessarily compatible with and related to historical individuals, they were also necessarily independent of them in principle, for without the countervailing autonomy of the universal connections in history, the particular component of historical individuality would have no limit and would therefore negate the principle of individuality itself. Thus the place was actually plotted and the need created, by the very theory of individuality, for the discovery of universal themes in the historical process. Just as particulars required a quasi generality to become individuals, generalities required a quasi particularity to become universal. If the historical individual was the generalized form of the particular, the historical universal was the particularized form of the general. As the absolute but unknowable spirit of God generates particular existence into individual reality, just so does the same absolute spirit particularize logical general ideas into operational universal principles. Since the absolute was ineffable and general principles were inapplicable, universals must be historical.

So Ranke's theory of historical individuality—and the doctrine of "historism" which has been derived from it—should be taken as but one side of his total approach to history, and its function in this total approach can be understood in the context of the conditions under which he developed it. When it is reconsidered in this context, two crucial but unheralded features of the theory emerge. First, despite the impression it makes of an antisystematic endorsement of an infinitely diffracted reality, Ranke's theory of historical individuality actually demonstrated the synthetic function which history filled in his thinking. He initially formulated the theory as the conservative obverse of the radical doctrine of general revolution, and the historical dimension that he perceived in the contemporary events of the turbulent early 1830s enabled him to elevate the fortuitous complex of existing political authorities into a pattern with universal validity. For the revolution of 1830 appeared to Ranke as an intersection of politics and history, in which the politics confirmed the sanctity of particular traditional institutions and urgently required their justification by universal principle, while history supplied this universal matrix to the particular manifold in the form of collective individualities, at once unique and continuous through time.

Second, this context of the theory of individuality demonstrates its clearly delimited role in Ranke's own attitude toward history. Because he viewed the revolutionary theme primarily in its universalizing aspect, he developed his counterrevolutionary theme of historical individuality primarily in its particularizing aspect. After he acknowledged, at the start of *The Great Powers* of 1833, his historical "urge to survey the whole [of modern history] from a detached viewpoint" and to open himself to the "intuition of their unity" which "arises spontaneously from the multiplicity of particular perceptions," he finished by making the "separation and independent development" of the several states, fortified by the centrifugal force of "the national principle," embody "the secret of world history" and thus serve as the conservative general counterpart to "the general movement" of democracy which would dominate or homogenize the individual states.[29]

In his *Dialogue on Politics* of 1836, analogously, he countered the invalid force of the abstract, universal, revolutionary "concept" with the valid relations of generality and particularity which he attributed to the states as collective individualities: "The formal is the general, the real is the particular," and in the independent states the general "forms are a secondary, subordinate element" vis-à-vis the particular "reality which fills them."[30] When Ranke was in this particularistic gear, he limited the universal level of history to individuals (persons and states) and their "mutual interaction and succession, their life, their decline, or their rejuvenation" as the general forms of the particular. It was precisely because of his political concern, at this stage, with attributing universal validity to individual realities in the historical process that his methodological precepts were slanted toward particularism. When the only two ways to general historical truth were to perceive "the particular fact (*das Besondere*) as bearing a general principle (*ein Allgemeines*) within itself" or to depend on the "spontaneous" emergence of a unified aspect from "the multiplicity of particular perceptions," general truths were obviously as subordinate in the method as universal developments were in the reality of history.[31]

III But his politically conditioned emphasis on individuality and particularity was only part of Ranke's reorientation after 1830. He retained the belief in an autonomous general reality, manifest in the normative priority of world history to particular histories, and he met the challenge to pull his ideas together by going beyond his theory of political individuality to take a giant step toward historical synthesis. This he did outside of theory in any form, through the actual identification of substantive universal themes within the historical process. In the context of his whole attitude toward history after 1830, practical as well as theoretical, it is clear that historical individualities and their interrelations were for him not so much universal as universalizable forms of the particular, for he also now worked out, separate from them but converging toward them, a universal historical process which was in effect the individualizable reality of general forms. He had long been aware, from the history of the continental European states, that in practice the study of no one particular state could produce general truth or, indeed, even itself "be presented separate from the other with any success,"[32] but only during the 1830s and apart from his individualizing theory did he come to perceive a European process that was something more integrally general than the international relations of individual states, and more concretely identifiable than the faith in inscrutable Providence.

Ranke's advance to the recognition of an authentic universal reality in the context and behind the development of individuals was conditioned by the condensation of his formerly nebulous approach to the composite nature of man. Where he had thought of man's mixed qualities and infinite varieties as articulate manifestations of an ineffable absolute, he now collapsed them into two engaged sides of a definite dialectical whole. The transcendence which he had seen as an undefined harmony composed of ''a thousand dissonances,'' creating ''world's divisions so strong'' that they inhibited him from carrying out his desire ''to consider a whole human development with love,'' became, as he later phrased it, in different contexts, a ''unity in twofold leadership,'' an ''action and reaction of minds'' which ''furthers the development'' of the human spirit, and a ''unity'' consisting in ''the higher . . . attitude'' which joined the opposing parties of a ''mutually recognized antithesis.''[33]

There were several partial indications, from 1831 on, that in the context of his own scholarly readiness for integration the centripetal pressure of the revolutionary situation was having a cohesive effect upon Ranke's practice of history. The first—and most tenuous—of these indications was the short book *On the Conspiracy against Venice in 1618* (*Über die Verschwörung gegen Venedig im Jahre 1618*) which he had written quickly between August and December of the revolutionary year 1830 and published in the following year. On the face of it the monograph continued his historiographical concerns of the previous decade and seemed to show little impact of contemporary events. It grew out of his immersion in the Venetian Relations, which supplied him with the authentic sources for correcting previous errors in an oft-told story and for simply ''distinguishing the true course of the matter.'' Hence he himself characterized it as ''a revisionist monograph'' on this ''in itself not very important subject,'' bringing as it did ''not even the knowledge of a great event or of significant conditions,'' and the body of the essay combined, as the Ranke of the 1820s had been wont to do, the virtues of methodological precision and of dramatic narration. His conclusions—that there had been a conspiracy but that it had not progressed very far toward execution and that the Venetians were correct about the fact of it but both in their history and in their historiography had exaggerated its danger out of all proportion to the fact—were appropriate to this specialized intention. In the preface to the new edition which he wrote almost half a century later (1878), moreover, he even recalled, faithful to his pattern of the 1820s, an ideal *manqué* of universal history—a general "history of Venice" that "would have plunged me into the center of the relations between east and west"—which was in contrast to the monographs on Venice he actually did write. In this retrospect he even emphasized the historical insulation of his Venetian monographs, arguing for their worthiness of attention despite "the disappearance from the face of the earth of the conditions of the Venetian Republic's existence and of the very possibility of a position like the one it held" since the period of the sixteenth and seventeenth centuries covered by his essays.[34]

And yet at the time of its first publication, in 1831, Ranke did evince a concern with the more general connections of his essay *On the Conspiracy against Venice in 1618* which not only belied his later impression of the conspiracy's historical insulation but showed a possible influence of the contemporary revolution he was experiencing. In his preface of this year he claimed the attention of his reader not because of the insulated temporal distance of his material but because of its relevance both to "European politics" and to "the existence of our society." Because for Ranke "events are evanescent, multifarious, and hard to grasp in their pattern," because they dominate "European politics," conferring on it these same qualities, and because they both "stem from" and "variously react back upon the very depths of the existence of our society," clearly the description of such a single event as the conspiracy against Venice, "characteristic" as it was for politics on the eve of the Thirty Years' War, was as close as he could get to European politics and society as such. Obviously for such a conception, an event can be joined to the larger stream of history only through analogy, and there are signs—however inconclusive in the absence of any explicit testimony from Ranke—that at some psychic level he was aware of an analogy between the conspiracy against Venice and what he was currently experiencing as an alien revolutionary threat against Germany. For the conspiracy he wrote of was fomented by hostile Spanish officials who planned the military overthrow of Venetian independence with the aid of

French mercenaries, and ultimately he divested it of any fortuitous character by rooting it "generally in the nature of the men of that period" and in "the conflicts [which] were coeval with states, inherent in their principles and in their world position." Even so did he conceive the revolutionary threat of 1830 from France, and it can hardly have been psychological coincidence that he first announced his little book to his publisher in a letter otherwise devoted to discussing the "coming frightful catastrophe" of revolution and especially to distinguishing the peace-loving Germans from the tumultuous French. He may thus have had the contemporary analogy very much in mind when he meaningfully recommended the little book to the crown prince of Prussia in pragmatic terms—"because many another famous conspiracy may well have a structure similar to this one."[35]

But there were other, more direct signs of the interaction between his contemporary experience and his professional history during this revolutionary period of the early 1830s. In 1834, he wrote (but did not publish) an essay on the Bosnian revolt of 1820–23 against Turkey, apparently on his own initiative and under the influence of the international revolutionary atmosphere. The theme of revolution enabled him to present a tableau of the relationship between the rulers and the ruled that was far more circumstantial and substantive than anything he had been able to do five years earlier in his Serbian book—the book in which the Bosnian essay was ultimately incorporated.[36] Again, between 1831 and 1834 he reorganized his courses at the university, instituting now the methodical pattern and general framework of the seminar which would prove so fruitful, and converting the alternation of universal and periodic lecture courses into the sequence of general courses in modern and contemporary history, each prefaced by a systematic prolegomenon, that would attract his largest student audiences after 1834.[37] During these same years, finally, it may be recalled that he was immersing himself in the purely intellectual side of the change to modernity with his compositions of the histories of Italian poetry and art that he would publish later.

But it was his discovery of a universal theme within history that gave him for the first time an authentic sense of a general process of human history, and it was with his immediately subsequent discovery of an individual theme historically complementary to universalism that Ranke's historical practice was at last fully integrated. The first discovery resulted in *The History of the Popes,* the second in *German History in the Era of the Reformation,* and the paradigm of Ranke's mature approach to history came out of the relations between the two.

8
The Complete Historian:
The Works of the Thirties

The universal theme which Ranke acknowledged during the 1830s to be
both temporally and essentially prior to the individual states of
Europe and which conferred substantive continuity upon their
relations was the historical role of Christianity. The connection
between the transcendent and the immanent God which he could
never make in his own Christianity he found spread out before him
in the interplay of spiritual independence and worldly engagement
which he found to be jointly inherent in the mission of the
Christian churches. It was thus in the framework of the *History
of the Popes,* his primary scholarly concern between 1826 and
1836, that he first gave historical substance to universal principle.
We can, indeed, trace his ever-increasing capacity to historicize the
universal level of reality in his changing attitudes toward history in
the context of this work.

I   Ranke began his study of the popes as a continuation of his studies
on the *Princes and Nations of Southern Europe* in the early-
modern period, and indeed early editions of the papal history were
published along with the previously composed history of *The
Ottoman Turks and the Spanish Monarchy in the Sixteenth and
Seventeenth Centuries* under the general title.[1] In the early stages

of the papal history, moreover, he classified this ongoing work, as he did the other components of his princes and nations, with the particular history on which he was working over against the world history to which he hoped they would somehow add up. When he wrote then about his papal research, it was the "remarkable gallery of characters"—that is, the individual popes, "the great men among them," the mixture of nobility and criminality in them, their limitation "by the situation in which they find themselves" —that he stressed.[2] But from 1830 his point of view began to shift. He acknowledged now, when reporting on the progress of his research in Rome, that "one comes to a point where development is no longer national but universal," and it was during the final stages of his writing on the popes that he exclaimed, hyperbolically but revealingly, that "nothing more can be written but universal history—all our studies strive to produce it." This universal history was "the general context" necessary for "the appearance of the particular in its full light," but it was also much more. It was "a kind of history" in its own right and on its own level, embodying the "ideal" which Ranke confessed he was trying to attain as he wrote the third and concluding volume of the work on the papacy: to show "the inner changes of the spiritual-earthly tendencies of the world as they appear from epoch to epoch, fight one another, conquer one another, and have ever broadened." It was, in other words, a universal history that has "a logic, vitality, and developmental grandeur" of its own.[3] The grand theme of the *History of the Popes* thus became the destiny of Christian universality in modern times, and with the focus on this theme Ranke translated the historiographical problem of meshing particular and general history, which he could not resolve abstractly, into the historical process wherein the attitudes and values of universal Christianity actually moved from their ecumenical locus in the medieval church and churchmen and were diffracted into the characteristic goals of the several modern states, a process which could be comprehended by standard historical methods because its particular subject matter was precisely the universal ideas and organization of individual persons and institutions.

If the *History of the Popes* thus helps to explain Ranke's intellectual development, the converse is also true: the essential points in the *History of the Popes* are illuminated by its place in

Ranke's intellectual development.[4] The general features of the work to which reference has already been made are themselves explained by their role for Ranke. The theme of the book—the refraction of the papacy's universal religious mission through the denser earthly media of personality, Roman politics, ecclesiastical abuses, and national interest into a congeries of individual Christianized states imbued with transcendent spirit—follows consistently from Ranke's striving to find actual agents and events which would realize his ideal of universal history. Similarly, the recurrent pattern of the work—the repeated dualities between spirit and flesh, morality and interests, religion and politics, world and nations, into which the material is characteristically organized—follows naturally from Ranke's need to have an ordering scheme which would connect the principle of unity embodied in "the common basis of the Christian faith" and articulated in "the fundamental ideas of a universal republic, as it were," with "so great an abundance and variety of events and modes of life . . . that we have to fear the impossibility of comprehending the whole under one view."[5] The organization of the work, too, with its initial focus on the papacy and its subsequent alternation of setting between the counter-reforming popes in Rome and the Counterreformation in the several nations of Europe is explicable by reference to Ranke's initial identification of the universal in history with the reality of the papal tradition and his subsequent pursuit of it in the universal aspects of national history. Finally, the apparent inconsistency of Ranke's persistent vacillation between the freedom of spirit, for which, "once . . . aroused, there is no presuming to prescribe the path it may pursue," and "the necessity of things," "the silent and often imperceptible, but invincible and ceaseless march of events" to which "all the purposes and efforts of humanity are subjected," becomes coherent as Ranke's resolution of the antinomy of liberty and necessity into an alternation in historical sequence.[6]

But in addition to these fundamental intersections of Ranke's history and historiography there are special puzzles in the *History of the Popes* for which our knowledge of its place in his development, at the turning point of theoretical dualism into historical synthesis, provides solutions. First, Ranke repeatedly resorts to absolute, suprahistorical causes and principles of interpretation which are surprising in view of his scientific reputation but understandable in view of what he was actually trying to do in the 1830s. When he characterizes historical movements in terms of "community in the one true God" (*Gemeinschaft in dem Einen wahren Gott*), or of "the plans of God in His government of the world"; when he refers events to causes in the permanent traits of human nature, sometimes its pliancy ("inexhaustible is the plasticity of human nature") and at other times its constancy ("there is invariably opposed to [absolute dominion in Europe] a vigorous resistance, having its origin in the deepest springs of life"); when he indulges in timeless maxims ("fortune ebbs and flows; the man remains the same") for the ultimate satisfaction in explanations; when he proudly announces his discovery of "one of the universal laws of social life" but tentatively assures us that he does not thereby "pass beyond the province of history"; on all these occasions Ranke was clearly engaged in his great effort to translate his beliefs in absolute principles into the realities of universal history.[7] In his later works, where historicization is complete, the principled scaffolding was no longer in evidence, but by the same token neither was Ranke's reaching for ultimate motives and causes. Relevant causes, like relevant universals, were limited to what sufficed to account for the temporal sequence of men's actions.

Second, Ranke intermittently elided the related canons of impartial description and historical empathy which he espoused in principle, which are otherwise such prominent and admirable features of his book, and of which, as a Protestant historian of the papacy, he was expressly, defiantly, and justifiably proud.[8] His sporadic partiality for Protestants (especially German) and against Catholics was both overt and covert. Overt instances of his partiality can be found in his testimonial to the religious reformation of Catholic corruption as "one of the most characteristic and successful tendencies of the human spirit, ... opening it to the freedom of a new and different progress"; in his categorical identification of German Protestantism with "the undying merit of having ... rediscovered the true religion" (*die wahre Religion*); in his slanted comparison of Luther and Loyola; and in the even sharper contrast, within seventeenth-century Catholicism, between the Jansenists he revered and the Jesuits he deplored. The last of these preferences was obviously connected in Ranke's mind with the propinquity of heretical Jansenism to the Protestant attitude and with the entrenched position of the Jesuits in the Catholic church, but it also showed that the ground of his inequitable treatment, when he slipped into it, was not so much sectarian as religious and moral: his commitment to a pure spirituality, transcendental in origin and integral in practice, vis-à-vis his suspicion of an engaged religiosity, mixed and compromising with the carnal things of this world. But more important than these striking—but isolated—examples of partisanship is a covert bias in the *History of the Popes*, for it is a running line that is both harder to detect and closer to the main theme of the work. The main theme is the relationship between religion and politics within both the Catholic and the Protestant camps; and although Ranke is superb in explaining events as products of the shifting proportions of religious conviction and political interests in both camps, his tendency is to stress the priority of religious conviction among the Protestants and the ever-growing priority of political considerations among the Catholics.[9]

The explanation of this exceptional partiality in the *History of the Popes* is connected with the reason for Ranke's third kind of violation of his own principles—the moral judgments which he scatters through the work in apparent contradiction of his own famous dictum that his history did not assume "the task of judging the past." The fact is that he used ethical criteria in his characterization of individual popes (e.g., of Pius V, "this union of upright purpose, elevation of mind, austerity, and devout religious feeling, with morose bigotry, rancorous hatred, and sanguinary eagerness in persecution") and of whole institutions (e.g., of the Roman Curia, "egoists to the very core").[10] These moral judgments of Ranke's obviously could and did coincide with his partisanship, since his partisanship had a moral as well as a religious base, but in principle they were independent of it. More frequent than his partisan moral judgments were his balanced moral judgments, and he himself righteously declared that to show in the same group "the dignity, the seriousness, and the religious zeal" on the one hand and "the wordly aspect, ambition, avarice, dissimulation, and craft" on the other was to have "a clear and unprejudiced view" and "an exact perception of the whole subject."[11] Thus Ranke did impose moral judgments upon his historical subjects, partially when he measured their acts and their characters by his generation's standards—the degree in which they were "consonant with our notions of right"—rather than by theirs, and impartially when he measured his historical agents by the standards which he felt were common to their generation and to his.

These apparent discrepancies, both partisan and moralistic, from Ranke's own scholarly prescriptions are explicable ultimately by the inherent tension between his requirement of historical empathy for every position and his requirement of a critical approach to every testimony of every position, for the first requirement postulated the understanding of the position in its own terms and the second postulated a standard of criticism outside those terms. But the implications of this tension, which the mature Ranke would later cover with his ethic of the historian's self-denying responsibility (the historiographical ethic defining the truth of every past in terms of its immunity from interpolations of the present), can be clarified by considering the stage of Ranke's development at the time of the *Popes'* composition. Ranke always felt that impartiality in the historian was "no kind of indifference," and that truth for the historian comported with both moral judgment and with a higher partisanship. He must "recognize only the great and worthy and never neglect the eternal ideas which condition the spiritual life of mankind," for "in history sanctity [*das Heilige*] must triumph over vulgarity and evil."[12] What was invalid was for the historian either to import the particular divisions and values of his present into the past or to accept the particular divisions and values of the past. What was valid was for him to use the universal truths common to past and present alike as the criteria of the truth of the past, and it was precisely in the *History of the Popes* that Ranke first identified the form taken by the eternal truths within history and applied them literally to the historical judgment of the past.

The final surprise afforded by the *History of the Popes* to those whose expectations have been nourished on the familiar caricature of the political and narrative Ranke is the analytical power of the social and intellectual descriptions. The social history includes explanations of the religious wars in the terms of the interests and attitudes of the articulate classes (clergy, nobility, lower aristocracy, burghers) which have become staples of historical interpretation, but it also transcends this familiar scheme. In his dissection of early-modern Roman society, Ranke, though never losing sight of papal politics, plunges into a sociological analysis of the elite classes and then goes beyond them to reconstruct the activities and the demography of hitherto anonymous masses.[13] The achievement was not fortuitous, for in his next book (on the German Reformation) he would present an even more penetrating delineation of the south German peasantry, and it should be comprehensible to us who are familiar with Ranke's notion, emergent around this time, that the state was but the historical crystallization of humanity in modern times, and that it was the movement of the entire society which eventuated in it and continued through it.

Even more spectacular, because more pervasive, is the role of intellectual and cultural history in the *History of the Popes*. The explicit sections devoted to discursive doctrine, literature, music, and the plastic arts are impressive enough for their sophistication, for their smooth balance of description and interpretation, and for their versatile attention both to the distinctive forms which were peculiar to each medium and to the common tendencies which aligned all the media under the general characteristics of their age.[14] But over and above the specific intellectual chapters, the recurrent theme of the book as a whole provokes the illuminating realization that Ranke actually conceived the *History of the Popes* as a work of intellectual history. For the great "march of events," or "inevitable necessity," or "tendency of the times," as he optionally labels the overriding connection in history, turns out to be composed of "ideas that . . . , once widely diffused, assume an irresistible force of coercion," in the form of "the force of public opinion," or "profound religious conviction," or of "an ideal of a forthcoming advancement of society" which accompanies the rise of any power "into universal influence." For "theories . . . reproduce the moral import and significance of facts, which are then presented in the light of a universal and effectual truth, as deduced from reason or religion and as a result arrived at by reflection."[15] Thus the universal truth which Ranke had located in the true religion he now historicized by turning it into the stream of equally universal ideas governing the development of humanity.

The ostensibly scientific and political Ranke, then, leaves us with the intriguing thought that the only scientific universal history is intellectual history.

II Under the influence of the juncture between his open-ended particular research and a historically relevant general revolution after 1830, then, Ranke made his first identification of a universal history whose very substance consisted in its relations with the individualizing power of men. As articulated in the *History of the Popes,* the essential pattern of this kind of history was duality, in comparison with the unity that he asserted to be the principle of the pure world history on which he lectured and the multiplicity that he asserted to be the principle of the purely political history on which he wrote. In his new hybrid history, human diversity and human universality were redefined in terms of their actual encounters and were organized into the pervasive conflict of earthly individuals about common overriding spiritual issues. Whether it was the incessant struggle between self-centered material interests and universal ideals within each man and each institution or the repeated struggles of powerful political and social groups for the direction of a common transcendent cause, Ranke's spotlight in this kind of history was ever on the continuing interaction of men's worldly divisions and man's universal spirit. The whole structure of his work on the popes was built around a continuing series of real conflicts on the alternative means of realizing general ends: the claims of the papal states versus the requirements of the papal international ministry for the guarantee of Catholic spiritual independence; papal arms and diplomacy versus ecclesiastical world monarchy for the safeguarding of the papal international ministry; Protestant repression versus Catholic reform for the preservation of the ecclesiastical world monarchy; political and social interests versus religious conviction in the line-up of the two world churches. In this structure the universal issues and individual agents of history met not only during each moment of historical time, but also in the developmental sequence from the preeminence of the politically influential universal church to the preeminence of the ecclesiastically supported individual states.

When, therefore, Ranke wrote, as he did in the early 1830s, of the modern national states as supreme individualities in which power and spirit merged, the doctrine should be qualified by his view of a historical process which identified the spiritual component as the deposit of Christian universality. But the *History of the Popes* worked out only one side of this process. It followed the diffraction of Christianity from the perspective of its universal institution. What it did not show was the other aspect of the process—the way in which individual nations appropriated this universal spirit. The exhibition of this process was the function of Ranke's next work, *German History in the Age of the Reformation,* which he began in 1836, the same year as the publication of the last volume of the *Popes,* and which can be considered its complement.

The dual origins of *German History in the Age of the Reformation (Deutsche Geschichte im Zeitalter der Reformation)* demonstrate the combination of linkage to and displacement of the universal theme embodied in the *History of the Popes*—the combination which is the key to the structure and thesis of the new work. There has been scholarly dispute about the relative proportions of his interest in Germany and in the Reformation which inspired Ranke's book. As long as it takes the form of weighing his old concern for religion, whose touchstone was the Reformation history embodied in Ranke's Luther fragment of 1817, against his new concern with politics, which was triggered by the revolution of 1830, the debate must probably remain inconclusive.[16] If, however, Ranke's approach is conceived not in terms of the primacy of religion or politics as such but in the historicized terms of a religious thematic universality continuous with the *Popes* and a political individuality associated with his visceral feelings for his native land and its imperial past, then the two roots of the work become compatible in themselves. They are characteristic of a Ranke whose original approach to history in general was impelled, as we have seen, by precisely such a combination of belief in a transcendent unity and passion for particular realities.[17]

One line of thinking that led him to the *German History in the*

Age of the Reformation was continuous with the generalizing historical mentality that was emerging ever more strongly from his work on the *Popes*. While he was still working on the latter part of his papal history, in February 1835, he admitted that "a development similar to the Catholics took place with the Protestants," and he indicated then that only practical reasons of length and complexity prevented him from having treated the Protestants in the first part of the *Popes*, which depicted the general movement ushering in the modern era: "It would have carried me too far in both the research and the presentation." He made explicit, moreover, the association in his mind of the missing Protestant movement with universal history, for it was in this context of indicating the desirability of including the Protestant Reformation that Ranke made his categorical declaration: "I am ever more confirmed in the opinion that in the final analysis nothing other than universal history [*Universalgeschichte*] can be written."[18] In his lectures of the very same period, moreover, Ranke was beginning to justify identifiable historical epochs in terms of the seamless general continuum that had constituted his prior notion of the historical process. There are no "discontinuous divisions" (*Abschnitte*) of history, he argued, but "from the entirety of previous history to some extent certain points erupt and are produced as results of the whole." Such a crystallized point is "a great epoch," which "denotes the identity of the content in the strivings of a period."[19] Certainly Ranke was prepared to treat the Reformation historically as a great epoch which focused universal history.

But Ranke did not embark upon his work until he had an impulse from quite a different root: his spontaneous and distinctive sympathy for his own Germany and its history. Back in 1826 at the very beginning of his researches on the *Popes*, Ranke explicitly expressed his preference for writing a German rather than a papal history—"I am only sorry that I do not come around very much to the Germans, whom I would really much, much rather treat"— and grounded it on the internal empathy he could have only for German history in particular. "I was born for German history and not for Italian [*welsche*], which in the last analysis I cannot understand as well as the German."[20] His first publication from the documentary materials of his Italian journey, moreover, was a treatise on sixteenth-century Germany which he subtitled "Fragment from Reflections on German History" and which appeared in the first volume of his *Historisch-Politische Zeitschrift* during 1832. Significantly, he chose a point of view that was consciously "German and political" rather than "universal and theological," and the subject matter that he chose in conformity with this point of view was the dissolution of German unity by the "centrifugal elements" of the post-Reformation generation through "accidental circumstances, avoidable mistakes."[21]

Obviously his feeling for German history weighed on the particularizing side of Ranke's historical motivation, and consistently with it the event that triggered his decision to write a German history was his discovery of an appropriate archival cache, unleashing the kind of enthusiasm for detailed authentic truth with which he had always associated documentary research. During September 1835, as he was about to wind up his work on the *Popes*, he found the official records of the German Reichstag in the municipal archives of the old imperial city of Frankfurt am Main. He described them characteristically as "a sea of manuscripts promising the most splendid discoveries"—discoveries which "contain a significant number of still unknown facts that throw new light on the history of the [German] Empire especially at the end of the fifteenth and the beginning of the sixteenth centuries" and "which really should make it necessary for me to devote a few years to German history."[22]

Conformably to this root of the work, the preface which appeared with the first volume in 1839 stressed the persistence and the preeminence of Ranke's intention to write a constitutional history of the German Reichstag—"I long had in mind the idea of dedicating my industry and energy to so important an object"— and he devoted most of the brief prolegomenon to a catalogue of the relevant manuscript collections in sundry German archives to which, starting from Frankfurt, the pursuit of this worthy national purpose had led him. In this context the truncated treatment of the Reformation in "the first part of my history of the popes" was not accountable, as he had indicated before his discovery of the archives, to a practical defect of universal history but to his "hope of being able to dedicate more thorough researches on another occasion to this, our most important patriotic [*vaterländischen*] event." From this point of view, the genus of what Ranke was writing was German history, and the Reformation was "an event of such intensive spiritual content and at the same time externally of such global impact" that it would be the "main focus" (*Mittelpunkt*) of this German history.[23] In the university lectures on German history which he was giving during his composition of the book, he elaborated on this national point of view. "Each nation," he said, "has a particular spirit, breathed in by God, through which it is what it is and which its duty is to develop in accordance with ... the ideal." Nations, therefore, are "ideas of the divine spirit" which are not mere means but "the essential basis of spirit." While all national history is important, moreover, German history is the most important of all, both because the German nation, "always unconquered," is "the mother" of the rest and because German history, without a geographical or political center, "must always be considered a national whole." Hence German historians should strive "to provide body for an otherwise vague national consciousness, to reveal the content of German history, and to experience the effective, vital spirit of the nation in it."[24]

Ranke's express emphasis on the national root of his history faithfully reflected its substance: its sources and its framework were German, and the Reformation was treated primarily for its political effects within the empire. But to understand both Ranke's purpose and execution aright, this national emphasis should be construed in apposition rather than opposition to his universal theme. There is ample evidence that Ranke so construed it. For he was explicitly intent upon unifying themes within the nation, and these were connected, in the structure of his thinking, with unifying themes that transcended the nation. He found the constitutional history of the Reichstag important because there "the unity of the nation found its vital expression," and we know from his first historical work, the *Critique of Modern Historians*, that he had long thought of the German Empire as the meeting ground of general and particular history.[25] The same lectures which justified German history as a species of national history while he was writing *German History in the Age of the Reformation* made explicit the association he felt between the national and world history in general and between the unities of German and universal history in particular. National history, he rationalized, is simply one way of doing world history. When national history is studied with an eye to the divine spirit that is in it, said Ranke, it "leads to the complex of world history; it is another dimension, but the same substance, the same world." Especially German history, which "has the outstanding characteristic of traversing all the centuries in unbroken continuity, of filling the great ages or of affecting them through its universal influence" so that "everything joins itself to German history," is therefore "of universal-historical importance."[26]

Similarly, he justified the Reformation historiographically not only in terms of its intrinsic interest and external influence but also in terms of the coherence it supplied. It would have to be the main focus, he wrote, "if I wanted to make a book out of my work," and he even limited his archival research for fear of "losing, over a long stretch of time, the unity of thought which had risen up to me from previous studies."[27] The reference was probably to the papal history and its theme, but for Ranke's awareness of the universal component of the Reformation we can rely on testimony that is more solid than such cryptic indications and even than his collateral definition of an epoch as a point on the line of universal historical development. "If the great development of the Reformation is to be understood," he wrote to his English translator in 1841, "people must be at the pains [sic] to study the conditions of Germany at that time, without which it could never have been accomplished. This includes an appreciation of the whole history of that period which reacted upon the conditions of Germany."[28] In expounding his idea of an age or an epoch, Ranke was careful to identify it rather with a confluence of ideas than with a period of years. The Reformation for him was the movement at the dawn of the modern era in which universal and national principles intersected and the universal religious principle began its historical transformation into the spiritual component of the individual nation.

Ranke said as much, using these very terms, in the introduction, where he was wont to state the general themes of his histories. He wrote of the fundamental conflict between "nationality," which "moves within its natural limits preestablished by the independence of its neighbors," and "religion," which "strives eternally to be universal," since nationality is associated with the state, which "asserts a particular principle of an equally spiritual nature" with "its own inner necessity . . . and claim to unlimited freedom," while religion produces the "church with its farther-reaching forms which embrace various nations." It "strives to subject the principle of the state to itself," and ultimately it produces too "universal religion . . . as a great tradition handed down from people to people." Not only did this statement of the conflict match religion and politics as polar historical principles of universality and individuality, but Ranke's discussion of them took place on two corresponding historical levels.

From his point of view in this book, Ranke's basic position was to observe the conflict from within the nation which he now conceived to be its main locus, since any "great nation worthy of the name is unthinkable if its political life is not inspired and exalted by religious ideas and if it is not continuously concerned with developing these religious ideas and bringing them to a generally binding and public expression." Hence the struggle between universal religion and individual nationality is within the nation itself, because nations require both a spiritual basis in transcendent religious principle and the capacity "to examine critically the content of the spirit originally implanted in them." But then, when he discussed the issue itself, Ranke momentarily but revealingly, shifted his position to one well above the national arena: "From the nature of this opposition there emerges the realization of what a great theme [*Moment*] for all human existence lies therein." On this level it entails the irresoluble conflict between, on the one side, a universal religious truth which needs an independent "freedom of national development" for its own vitality and yet must fight this antithetical particular principle and, on the other, the particular national state which needs the independence of the religious principle "to remind it continuously of the origin and end of the earthly life, of the right of its neighbors, and of the community of all nations" and yet must fight this antithetical universal principle for the preservation of its own integrity. On this level, then, "the truth is that the life of the spirit—certainly in its depths and in its activity always self-identical, one and the same—yet embodies itself in both state and church, which rub against each other in the most various changes, penetrate each other, or also try to discard and exclude each other and yet never collapse. Neither can ever overpower the other—at least it has not come to this in our western nations.''

Then Ranke glided imperceptibly from this principled analysis of organized religious and nationalized states to the discussion of ecclesiastical and political history, conformably to his belief that only history could grasp the kaleidoscopic relations between polar principles. ''Hence it is that the combination of church history and political history permits either one to appear in its true light, and only this combination can perhaps lead to a presentiment [*Ahnung*] of the deeper life from which they both come.'' And now it was from this universal perspective that he justified the choice of Germany as his historical object, for though this combination of church and political history has its locus ''in all nations,'' it is ''particularly clear in the German nation, which has concerned itself most continuously and most independently of all the nations with ecclesiastical and religious affairs.''[29]

Clearly, universal, patriotic, and scholarly motives converged to make Germany Ranke's first test case for his pursuit of the forms taken by the persistent confrontation of universal theme and particular existence in the modern era of national individuality. Original Protestantism supplied the new form of universal religion; the empire provided the renewed political identity of nation and state; the confessional and territorial parties (including the Hapsburg emperor, as distinguished from the empire) were the subjects and the objects of the documentary facts that associated clerico-political particularism with historiographical particularity.

Ranke's decision to concentrate on Germany in the Reformation as both a section of national history, in which the particular facts assumed an automatic patriotic importance, and as the national counterpart of the *History of the Popes,* in which particular facts were selected for their participation in universal themes, was obviously easier of conception than of execution. To interpret *German History in the Age of the Reformation* in terms of his attempt to resolve this problem—the problem of determining the forms taken by historical univerals in an individual nation whose history is knowable by particularistic methods—reveals facets of the book that are obscured by such of its obvious features as the constant movement of focus from religion to national politics to international relations and back again, the shift of preeminent attention from religion to politics (both constitutional and international) within this cycle of interest as the book wore on, the frequent recourse to general dicta on the nature of men and history, and his obvious particular bias in favor of Protestant reformers, both religious and political, over Catholic resisters, both ecclesiastical and temporal. That a persistent thematic structure should be sought through and under these overt attributes is indicated by the discovery of an increasing emphasis on general principles as well as on politics (in comparison with religion) in the sequence of lectures on the German Reformation which Ranke gave in the very years he was composing his book on the subject.[30] The combination of generality and politics is certainly odd in view of the particularistic content of internal Reformation politics and Ranke's particularistic method of researching the events of international politics, and it is one that provokes structural analysis.

The pattern that runs through *German History in the Age of the Reformation* is the presentation of each historical strand and of each relationship between historical strands as homologously two-faced, showing now a particular and then a general side, tending to find integrity only in the assessment of its alternating expressions by the constant standard of the national German individuality, but yet at the same time reaching for a higher integrity through the incorporation of the national standard in a historically demonstrable universal process. Let us first consider Ranke's religious theme. He followed Luther's development step by step, noting seriatim his arrival at religious and ecclesiastical positions he had not held before, and yet he could also view the religious progress of the reformer from his need of God to the "fullness of conviction" "inherent in the laws of the eternal world order" and thus produced by universal necessity. He characterized the consolidation of Lutheran doctrine as following a direction "at the same time more individual and more universal." He attributed the spread of Protestantism on the one hand to Luther's own will, since "in a determined will there always lies a power of carrying minds along with it" and since, as he asserted in another context, "such is the state of human affairs that ... only an overwhelming force and a firm will can lay down tenable foundations"; but, on the other hand, he also attributed this same success to "the course of things" and "the necessity of things" which caused "the force of the Protestants' principle to advance all by itself, without any assistance from the Protestants."[31]

The recurrent point of reference which organized Ranke's picture of Protestantism, reconciling the spontaneous and determined facets of its development, was its "representation of the spirit of the German nation." First he showed how Luther's message responded to the need of the nation for religious renovation and acquired the support of the nation. Then, after the consolidation of Lutheranism in the Protestant party, Ranke equated Protestantism itself with German nationality. "Apart from any doctrinal preference, from the purely historical point of view, it seems to me that [the triumph of the Protestant system in all Germany] would have been the best thing for the national development of Germany. The reforming movement had come from the deepest and most distinctive spiritual impulses of the nation. . . . The fundamental strivings which now featured the lives of the German Protestants gave a fulfilling content to the national consciousness." In certain contexts, indeed, Ranke frankly recognized the distinctively particular aspect of the Reformation's association with the German nation. After the rise of Zwingli, Lutheranism and Zwinglianism together made up the Reformation in Germany, and the difference between them lay "not merely in the different conceptions of dogma" but "in the origins of the two-sided movement, in the political and ecclesiastical conditions from which they took their respective departures." Ranke concluded by giving his blessing to these "distinctive roots" and "particular forms," since they gave "a new steadfastness and inner force to the general principle of the Reformation."[32]

But if Ranke's identification of Protestantism with German nationality thus provided him with a way of historicizing the conflict of religious principles, and enabled him thereby to make a historical theme of other-worldly religion and incidentally to justify his Lutheran bias on patriotic grounds, still he did not find this characterization adequate to either purpose. He insisted repeatedly on the universal side of the Reformation as a facet independent of its national embodiment not only in its Lutheran root but in its permanent Protestant organization as well. On this facet the religious movement of the Reformation had both a

universal source in the Christian world-religion and a universal
destination in its contribution to the progress of the human race.
"Apart from all the more particular provisions of Protestant
dogma, . . . the epitome of the religious movement lies in the
maturation of the spirit of Christianity, which had lain latent in
the depths of the Germanic nature, to the consciousness of its
essence [Selbst], independent of all accidental forms; in its return
to its origin—to those records in which the eternal covenant of
God with the human race is directly proclaimed." "It was
necessary to bring again to the light of day the core of religion
which had been hidden under the multifarious cover of accidental
forms," and "the German spirit succeeded in . . . procuring a
legal validity for the inner truth of Christianity." To do this, "the
Reformers" adhered not only to "the purity of the Gospel" but to
the universal tradition embodied in "the culture and the learning
of Latin Christianity."[33]

So great, moreover, was Ranke's need to establish an ultimate
foundation for his overt thread of German national development
that he planted it in a notion of universal spiritual progress which,
as an abstract proposition, he had denied in his theoretical
disquisitions of the early 1830s and would deny again after the
revolution of 1848; and he made Protestantism the connecting link
between the national and the universal levels of development. The
movement "to draw religious conviction from the purest and
earliest sources and to free civil life from the encumbrance of a
restrictive and monopolistic spiritual institution," he wrote, was
"an enterprise of the greatest importance and prospect for the
progress of the human race, but first it had to establish itself in
Germany." The German Protestants, he went on, "represented a
new stage in the culture of the whole Germanic-Latin west . . . ;
Europe could not and would not do without their help" against
the "barbaric enemy" (i.e., the Turks) of that culture. And he
concluded that the Reformation, as "the product of the distinctive
German genius that entered creatively into the realms of the
self-conscious spirit for the first time, . . . expanded the vital
elements of the traditional culture by breathing into it a fresh
spirit which strove for real knowledge and thereby itself became an
essential part of the universal-historical progress which connects
centuries and nations with one another."[34] Clearly, if the Protes-

tant sympathies of Ranke the man called forth a universal grounding of the German Reformation from the historian, it was also true that the historian's quest for a demonstrable universal history in modern times exalted the role of Protestantism in the origin of that age.

Ranke's depiction of Catholicism was the obverse of his Protestant portrait. It too was Janus-faced, showing now a particular and now a universal side; it too had an inadequate constant in its relationship to German nationality; and it too revealed a historiographical requirement as well as a religious bias in the two-sided presentation of it. The particularistic aspect of his approach to Catholicism was associated with both his religious and his patriotic antipathies to it. He attributed the multifarious "accidental forms" that encrusted the true life of religion to the development of Roman Catholicism, which he thus explicitly castigated for "the ever more rigidly and obtusely growing particularism of its dogmas and rituals," markedly in contrast to its "claim of universal validity for all races and ages," and for this development he laid special blame on the papacy, which he debited above all for "the accidents of Christianity's recent external forms."[35] When he was in this vein he measured Roman Catholicism, on the national scale that was his constant historical barometer, by the specifically un-German character of the papacy, which was opposed in Germany from "the very depths of the national life," and by the similar character of the emperor Charles V, frequent papal ally who himself "had no concept of the workings of the German spirit" and "was alien to its nature."[36]

But Ranke did not rest content with this picture. It was shaken in part by the developing history of the Reformation: the growth of a princely Catholic party in Germany with policies independent of the papacy and the analogous maturation of Charles V undermined the particular monolithic view from which he had started. But these factors were explicable by the Catholic princely emulation of Protestant ecclesiastical autonomy and reform—Catholic reforms were "mere analogies to the movements named for Luther"—and by the impact of Charles's international embroilments on the elaboration of his German policy: certainly Ranke gave full scope to both explanations.[37] The alternative approach to Catholicism which he advanced in contrast to his own particularistic and national perspective on it was the product not of any such historical revision but of an opposite, universal point of view. When Ranke adopted this universal stance, Catholicism became a demonstrable theme in world history, at once the counterpart and the predecessor of the Protestant Reformation. The "secularization" (*Verweltlichung*), which from his particularist perspective he had deemed the root of the Catholic excrescences upon the true faith, became from the universal perspective one of the two "opposed world views" (*Weltansichten*) which contended against each other in the sixteenth century. On this level, the Catholic established order "was fundamentally the same military-sacerdotal state which had been formed in the eighth and ninth centuries, and it had remained ever the same in its fundamentals—in the mixture of its basic components—despite any changes which might have occurred in the interim." "For in the totality of the established order [*des Bestehenden*], once it has been established, everything is connected and mutually supportive." Hence from this angle Roman Catholicism was viewed not as an externalized and degenerate form of Christianity but as a "system of ideas, . . . by its nature simultaneously political and religious," standing for "the formal unity of western Christianity" under a joint "spiritual-worldly authority."[38] Catholicism in this sense represented the universal principle in all of its integrative senses—as a "community embracing heaven and earth," as an authority combining religion and politics, and as a "hierarchical power" which, whether under papal or imperial supremacy, rules all of western life from a single center.[39]

Ranke's Catholic universalism, like his Protestantism, was itself two-sided, serving both a synchronic and diachronic function. On the one hand, as one of the opposing general ideas in the sixteenth-century, Catholic principle provided a fundamental cohesion for the resistance to the vital expansion of spiritual Protestantism. Thus Catholic "ideas of formal unity," even if "no longer predominant," were yet still present "in the existing conditions and in the opinions of men," and on this perspective the Catholic view "of ruling the whole worldly and spiritual life of nations" was only "one-sided." Now Catholicism manifested a fundamental principle not only on the world stage but even for the German nation as well. From this point of view Catholicism was not the alien and anachronistic power it was from the particular-istic perspective but rather an essential component of the dif-fracted "national idea." "Happy are the times when a single national idea seizes all minds because it satisfies all; but here this was not the case." The synthetic function of principled Cathol-icism became transparent in Ranke's explicit linkage of Luther's two main opponents—the papacy and the religious radicals—by virtue of their common subscription to the connection of heaven and earth, of "the highest idea and the whole civil life."[40] Clearly Ranke had come a long way historiographically from the collegiate years of his early Luther fragment, when he had thought that only the recalcitrance of the outer phenomenal husk inhibited the diffusion of spirit. What he practised now was a kind of historical synecdoche wherein a holistic movement was conceived as a thematic part of a total situation.

What guaranteed the universal aspect of Catholicism in its partisan sixteenth-century stance was its developmental function in western history. The partiality of its role during the Reformation was rooted in the generality of its existence in the prior period: it was "the system of ideas on which medieval Europe was based," and since "it is always important in the change of periods that . . . the essential results at which past generations have arrived are transmitted from one century to the next," medieval universalism persisted into the origins of the modern age. "The idea of the undivided unity of Christendom, which had domi-nated minds for so many centuries, could not possibly become at once so ineffective as not to find a later resonance." The Catholic resistance to Protestantism stemmed indeed not from some atavis-tic attitudes but from the whole hierarchical order of society, headed by the pope and the emperor as its two universal masters and "too deeply intertwined in public law" for its effects to be considered matters of mere individual "caprice."[41] Hence the same historical process that caused the main—Lutheran—line of the Protestant Reformation to bear the original universal purity of western Christianity into the beginnings of the modern period perpetuated the equally but heterologously universal structure of medieval Catholicism in the same period as its antithesis.

The other major focus of Ranke's work—alongside religion—was the politics of the German Empire, and here Ranke's pervasive pattern of a dual perspective, moving between particular and general angles of vision and incompletely mediated by the common criterion of nationality, was entirely overt. He started from the rival plans of princes and emperor for national constitutional reform at the beginning of the sixteenth century, with the princely project emerging from an excess of particularism and the emperor's (first Maximilian's and then Charles's) from the requirements of international politics. With the frustration of both plans by the conflict organized around the religious Reformation, the disjunction continued but was relocated. Now the nation was represented only by the princely estate, which was incorporated for this function in its expanding Protestant party, while the emperor became simply the chief conduit for the impact of international relations upon the German nation. During the period from the Diet of Speyer in 1526 to the final religious war of 1553, the political history of the Reformation alternated between internal German constitutional politics, featuring the particular princes, and pan-European international politics made both actively and passively relevant to the domestic German constitutional struggle by the emperor Charles's universal commitments. It was a time "in which all general and German relationships intersected," when "our German history became at the same time general history."[42] By the end of the period "the interests of the emperor and of the German nation had separated for ever," while this same nation continued to "see gladly its princes take leadership over it."[43]

But the end of the particular-general interplay also meant the end of the German Reformation. The settlement at Augsburg in 1555 was made possible, in Ranke's version, by the exclusion of both the universal factors—religion and international politics—(including the emperor) from "the territorial conflicts in Germany" with which they had been connected. The German constitution which emerged was "largely of a princely [ständischer] character," and precisely for that reason it was a constitution that conferred only "a certain unity," resting on "both of the opposing [princely] parties and on their relationship to each other" and incapable of preventing "the most particularistic development of this territorial factor in the immediate future." The constitutional settlement did preserve a measure of national tradition, order, and peace, but the subsequent development both of German culture and of territorial politics would take place "under the changing influence of different world-relationships than those which have been considered here."[44] Without the universal facet, in short, no development and no history.

Not only, moreover, did Ranke's two major themes—religion and politics—each have a double aspect, but their relations to each other did too. Here the formal duality in the work became the substantive historical pattern dominating the progression of the whole book. The one continuous issue underlying the struggle between Protestantism and Catholicism (as well as of Lutherans and Zwinglians and of Lutherans and radicals within Protestantism), as Ranke presented it, was the merger of religion and politics in Catholicism (and in the Zwinglians and the radicals) as against their separation in Lutheran Protestantism. For Luther himself this separation was presented as a deliberate and fundamental response, for the sake of religious purity, to the corruption of spirit which he associated with its politicization both without and within the movement for religious reform; for his princely followers the separation was manifest in the wonted religious motivation of their actions in despite of or indifference to their political interests as contrasted with the persistent political conditioning of Catholic attitudes and deeds.

To this extent the dualism of a good separation versus an evil interpenetration of religion and politics repeated the point that Ranke had made more briefly in his *History of the Popes*. But *German History in the Age of the Reformation* evinced a second aspect of the relationship that cast it in a quite different light. For Ranke also saw the tension between separation and merger in the relationship between religion and politics as a feature within the history of Lutheran Protestantism itself, and in this context they were the alternating causes which produced historical movement rather than moral antitheses culminating in historical success or failure. The origins of the Reformation lay in the principled independence of the movement for religious reform from the movement of national political protest. But the consolidation of the Reformation lay in the "union of the most vital interests"—including that "of the worldly power"—with the Lutheran movement and in the "strong support" furnished by them to it.[45]

Again, if Germany's role in the age of Reformation was focused on
its religious development and if the fulfillment of this role lay with
the Protestant princes who defended transcendent true religion
against defilement by worldly interests or power, still the universal
significance of the age lay in the coincidence of the religious
development with global dominion by the Latin-Germanic nations
—"one of the greatest combinations [*Kombinationen*] of world
history"—and in the event German Protestantism itself not only
became rooted in the empire through the influence of international relations but was itself generalized beyond the national
boundaries to become a factor in international politics.[46]

If, indeed, Ranke could maintain in general that "religious
opinion . . . possessed a broad independence in and for itself
[and] was powerful enough to realize itself at times in precise
contradiction with what the political situation seemed to require,"
he could assert just as definitely that "a union of the political and
religious opposition was needed to smash the spiritual-worldly
authority" of Catholicism.[47] Thus he could implicitly favor both
the distinction between religion and politics in the imperial
behavior of the Protestant princes—usually in the form of the
priority of their religion over their politics but occasionally in their
deliberate choice of patriotic politics over the interests of their
religion—and the connection of religion and politics in the spread
of Protestantism through the German principalities.[48]

The kind of conjunction that Ranke obviously rejected and
against which he adduced the historical force of separation was
itself historical: the unitary amalgam of religion and politics which
was actually embodied in Catholic historical agents. The kind of
conjunction he favored was historiographical, characterized by an
external relationship visible rather to the historian than to the
historical agent. Hence, when he approved the conjunction, he
would characterize it in terms of a temporal juxtaposition or of a
complementarity acknowledged to have been unperceived by the
Protestants themselves. "It is a remarkable coincidence" that at
the start of the Reformation the religious and the princely political
movements should have arisen at the same time.[49] Again, despite
their contemporary hostility, Ranke adjudged Lutheranism, with
its purely religious principle, and Zwinglianism, with its "politi-
cal-religious principle," to "belong together and complement

each other reciprocally."⁵⁰ And in the final resolution of the long spiritual and constitutional conflict at Augsburg in 1555, the German princes separated the political from the religious factor in the integral sense of their former union, but the "spiritual" and the "worldly" agreements were connected in the "complementary" sense, and "both together formed a new stage in the development of the empire."⁵¹ Indeed, the alternation of the antithetical and the complementary relations between religion and politics was the running theme making for the continuity of the whole work. Ranke could epitomize the theme by declaring that the spiritual struggle of the Lutheran Protestants was "the most essential part" of the worldwide politico-religious enterprise against "the unity" of Catholic Christianity but that it reflected as well as opposed this unity. He concluded with a salute to coherent historiography: "it would be a mistake to believe that the Protestants . . . were conscious of these general relationships."⁵²

The duality of historical perspectives which pervaded *German History in the Age of the Reformation* was not only a function of Ranke's wonted antithesis of spiritual principle to earthly appearances nor even only of his more recent appreciation of the opposition of religiopolitical principles to each other: he also grounded the duality in a fundamental division between the universal propositions about human behavior to which he subscribed. For Ranke was just as willing as he had been in the *History of the Popes* to assert general laws of human nature which served as axioms for the historical arguments they supported; but now each of these laws was more categorical, and together they were distinctly bipolar in their effect (although Ranke himself did not bring them into direct confrontation). On the occasions when he felt moved to give an ultimate explanation for the various resistances to unitary movements, whether to early Protestantism or to the later imperialism of Charles V, Ranke resorted to the inherent divisiveness and bellicosity of human kind. Because "it does not lie in the nature of man to content himself with a moderate gain" or because "the severest and most variegated struggles" which accompany the assertion of any opposition to the established order "is grounded deep in the nature of human affairs," Ranke concluded with the categorical proposition that "the more strenuously one tries to impress one's will or opinion on the world, the more strongly will the spontaneous forces rise to fight against him."[53]

But at other times, when Ranke was positing a final reason for the harmonious organization of multifarious wills and interests or for the strict limits which the Reformation drew on radical dissent, his laws of human nature and behavior asserted the necessity of unity and order. In these contexts the "firm will" which otherwise provoked proportional counteraction and conflict was an essential force in "the laying of durable foundations" and the production of "new institutions"; it "always has a power of carrying other minds along with it." The assumption on which Ranke predicated such a generalizing role for individual will and effort was the underlying cohesiveness of human nature not only as a norm but as a fundamental reality even admitting the integrative notion of progress. In this vein Ranke saw in conflict not a fruitful law of life but a threat of chaos and anarchy, "for everyone and everything is enmeshed in the total pattern of the established order," and the success of radical opposition to this order would have meant "the end of all steady development according to the laws ultimately prescribed to the human race." Such "uniform progress [*der gleichartige Fortschritt*] of culture and power," indeed, forms "the common basis" making for the modern "unity of Christianity" under the divisions of religious confession.[54]

For men in history Ranke would not resolve, on principle, the internal contradiction in a general truth which asserted the primacy both of conflict and of order in the human condition, but he did resolve it for the historian. He resolved it, moreover, on synchronic as well as the diachronic axis of human reality, just as he maintained the disjunction for man as such on both axes. From the point of view of living men, "authentic activity in every present moment is exclusively a matter of the proper treatment of what is immediately at hand, of the good cause that one has, and of the moral force which one invests . . ., and [therefore] the value of man depends on his self-determination and his effectiveness." But to such active men "the forces which condition the course of world history"—"general relationships"—are not only qualitatively different but essentially unknowable. They are "a divine mystery, as it were." But these general forces are no mystery to the historian, for "we can perceive from the distance of centuries the great combinations which inhere in things."[55]

Again, from the point of view of living men the temporal pattern of human reality must necessarily remain secret, both because such men cannot foresee the generalized results of their own individual actions and because the long-range temporal organization of variety transcends the experience of any single living generation. In this context, "how far do divine destinies surpass human ideas and plans!" But the divergence between individual effort and general disposition does not hold for historians, for they can connect such incongruities, which may be simultaneously incompatible, along the time line. "We may say that ages succeed one another precisely so that there may happen in all of them combined what is possible in no particular one of them—so that the whole fullness of the spiritual life inspired in the human race by the divinity may come to light in the course of the centuries." Under this historiographical principle the incongruity between "the progress of the human spirit in tranquil constancy" and "a general movement in which minds feel, as it were, the limits of custom and strive to overcome them"—the very incongruity which made for irreconcilable conflict for men in the Reformation—became intellectually harmonious as a sequence of historical periods.[56]

III Ranke's historiographical resolution of his twin dilemmas—the disjunction between general and particular phenomena and the antinomy of unity and plenitude within general principle itself—presumed the historically knowable character of general principle, and we find that he did in fact acknowledge this presumption. For it was precisely in the context of his two pivotal works, on the papacy and on the German Reformation, which developed a demonstrable, historical, universal theme in its general and its national setting respectively that, in a rare display of confidence, he categorically asserted the general process of history to be empirically ascertainable. In the introductory notes for the lecture course on modern history which he gave during 1832-33, at a time when he was writing the *History of the Popes* and in special connection with his teaching of Reformation history, he acknowledged the complementary assumptions behind the twin academic preoccupations of his postrevolutionary period by posing the criteria of valid inquiry into "the individual event" and into "the whole" as two equivalent aspects of the historical enterprise. The formula with which he emerged—that "our task is to present the characteristic, the essential in the individual, and the coherence, the connection in the whole" was not itself surprising in view of his dual concerns in the preceding decade. What was surprising was not only the implication now that both levels were equally accessible to the practicing historian, but even more the methodological reversal which signified the new concreteness of Ranke's direct engagement with universals in history. "Intuition [*Anschauung*] and research [*Forschung*]," he prescribed as the "rites" of historical understanding. "Intuition into the particular phenomena of our science [?]; research into their connection."[57] By the end of the decade, while he was still writing in high gear on the *German History in the Age of the Reformation*, he could homogenize his whole historical method and list under the rubric "Historical Research" four continuous steps leading from the most particular to the most universal level of history. "Exact knowledge: 1. of particular forces [*Momente*], 2. of their personal motivation, 3. of their interaction—of the whole working of personalities, and of their reciprocal influences—4. of the universal coherence. The ultimate result is sympathy, empathy with the All [*Mitgefühl, Mitwissenschaft des Alls*]."[58]

Ranke's internalization of general principle within the individual states and nations of modern history through the media of premodern universal history and Reformation national history essentially modifies the particularistic exegesis of his historicist doctrine, but certainly the result was still to leave universal history without a demonstrable empirical embodiment in modern times. For the *German History in the Age of the Reformation* concluded, as had the *History of the Popes*, with the emphatic declaration that religion had supplied a universal spiritual dimension to the states and nations of Europe during the transition to modernity at the cost of its own universality, and that the modern development of these states and nations would consequently have to proceed under the aegis of a universal dimension that was other than religion. On the world-historical level Ranke noted that the homogeneity of

"European culture and power has taken the place of ecclesiastical unity" in composing the modern "unity of Christendom." And when he turned to elaborate the same theme on the national level in the concluding chapter of his book, he started from the historical generalization that the religious Reformation "derived from the totality of a great spiritual movement" that transcended it, and he proceeded to show that this movement would not again rise to a universal level until "the German spirit" would take the form of a literary culture based on classical humanism and natural science progressing under the auspices of "a political development which made possible the slow maturation of general life." Not until then—that is, until the middle of the eighteenth century— "could the original projects of the age of Reformation be achieved," originating as they did in the larger movement of the human spirit and adhering as they did "to the vital forces of general and national history."[59]

Hence Ranke emerged from the revolutionary 1830s with a commitment to a knowable universal component in modern history that was rooted in identified premodern antecedents and that was compatible with the particular varieties of modern multistate politics. The conviction of a manageable universality would continue to enhance the particularism of his method and of his modern material by organizing its results in the light of political individuality, but so long as a modern general theme remained unidentified the balance between universality and particularity in the political behavior of the individual states and nations of Europe would be weighted on the side of particularity. It would take other convulsions to substantiate Ranke's new-found historical integrity. But subsequent breakthroughs to union are always easier than the first, and Ranke would ultimately find a secular universal pattern in history on the model of the religious and distinctively modern in its incidence. The discovery would be staggered, and it would turn out that, as is so often the case, the process of getting there would be more fruitful than the actual attainment of the goal. Yet the goal illuminates the path that leads to it, and it behooves us to follow Ranke through both of the stages leading him to the literal universal history that he had always coveted.

9
Conservative Retrenchment and Patriotic History in the Forties

The pattern which Ranke had established after the revolution of 1830 for the resolution of his personal, philosophical, and religious antinomies—the identification of a vital unity in the actual substance of the historical process from the clues offered by the translation of his own experience into contemporary history—was confirmed in his subsequent development. For each of the successive convulsive events through which he would live defined general themes that were continuous from the present into the past and reinforced the universal dimension in his history. The revolution of 1848 supplied a modern substance for his unifying historical dialectic to replace the anachronistic religious motif, and the German unification of 1870 brought him an even tighter unity, transcending dialectic and triggering his final integration of specialized research into general history.

Each of these unsettling experiences was preceded by a longer period of quiescence, signifying at once a relapse from the tensile unity which he had achieved as a result of the last upheaval and a preparation of the issue which would be his prism for observing and understanding the next. Each of these preliminary periods functioned, then, both as challenge and as condition for Ranke's next breakthrough into an intellectually and emotionally satisfying synthesis, and each of these periods also functioned to register the indelible residue of the previous breakthrough in the form of a great historical work or set of historical works.

I   The years from 1840-47 constituted such a period of placidity for Ranke, marking an interval of scholarly relaxation between the eventful decade of the 1830s and the shattering direct experience of revolution in 1848 and its aftermath. Not for him was the mounting excitement of the early 1840s. Rather did he settle into a political, professional, and personal life-style made up of political conservatism, scholarly dedication, and individual autonomy. The political conservatism was itself largely a compound of political indifference and academic accommodation, and it worked to release the historian to a full concentration on his individual historical writing and teaching—in that order of priority. His endeavors were crystallized in the continuation of the *German History in the Age of the Reformation,* initiated during the previous decade, and above all in the *Nine Books of Prussian History (Neun Bücher Preussischer Geschichte),* which was his primary scholarly enterprise of the new decade and which he published in 1847. This work carried on the political motif which, in the form of state building, Ranke's epochal masterpieces of the 1830s had adumbrated as the universal theme appropriate to modern history, but in the relaxed circumstances of the 1840s his elaboration of the theme was unbalanced on the side of narrow patriotism in scope and particularistic factuality in method.

Such was the background that conditioned his reception of what was to him the cataclysmic outbreak of revolution in 1848, and it goes far to explain the impact of the revolution upon his historiography—an impact that once more drove him to find synthesis in history. The impact can be traced through his political memoranda of 1848-51, wherein he turned revolutionary experience into contemporary history, and finally through his private lectures of 1854 *On the Epochs of Modern History (Über die Epochen der neueren Geschichte),* wherein he settled his historiographical accounts with the revolution by integrating it, as contemporary history, into world history and reinterpreting the general historical process in the light of it.

Here, then, is the scenario of the second act of Ranke's drive to realize the dramatic unities in history. But as all historians know (and Ranke himself would have agreed), synopses are useful in history only for identifying the relevant personae, deeds, and circumstances. Only the story itself can show how they interacted to produce what happened, and this "how" is what history is all about. Let us proceed, then, to fill in the connections among the background, the events, the psyche, and the productions sketched in the foregoing outline of Ranke's first decade of settled maturity.

II With the turn of decades several events, of different kinds, conspired to bring a change in Ranke's circumstances and his attitudes. The accession of a new king, Frederick William IV, in 1840 brought a new promise and a new atmosphere to the generality of the Prussian educated elite—a promise and atmosphere that the king himself soon belied—but to Ranke it brought something at once special and characteristic of the period he was about to enter. He had known Frederick William personally ever since he had struck up an acquaintanceship with the crown prince as fellow traveling companions in Venice during 1828, and both men had maintained the tie in the interim, sustaining it by Ranke's demonstrations of antirevolutionary monarchical loyalty from the one side and by the princely exhibitions of admiration and respect for the historian's publications from the other. Ranke himself testified that with Frederick William's accession "the horizon in Berlin changed completely," and henceforward he could rest content with the knowledge that the throne of his adopted country was occupied by the man who, as he recalled later, not only fought for "the positive and the historical" in general but "always remained my gracious lord and patron."[1]

Nor was this patronage slow to take tangible form: in 1841 the king designated him official historiographer of the Prussian state, a post whose roots in the early-modern position of court historiographer helped to orient Ranke toward the parochial political focus of his scholarship in the following decade. Frederick William's accession tightened Ranke's ties to the regime at this time, too, through the early appointment of the historian's friends to high governmental office: Johan Albrecht Eichhorn, the foreign office department head who was named minister of education in

1840; and Friedrich Karl Savigny, the renowned Roman legal historian and Prussian privy councillor, who became minister of justice in 1842. With Savigny, Ranke had long associated as a fellow historian and Berlin professor, and the persistence of the bond through Savigny's elevation helped to personalize Ranke's connection with the regime. But it was especially through Eichhorn, whose function brought him more directly within Ranke's ken, that the historian made his accommodation. In the gossip of the time he was regarded, indeed, as Eichhorn's man—the minister's "loyal attendant"—because of his usually unquestioning submission to the educational and cultural policies of this bureaucratic chief. Well might Ranke greet Frederick William's assumption of power and his immediate promotion of Eichhorn with the exclamation that "these days I have the feeling that this state is a family."[2] This feeling was reinforced, after Ranke's marriage in 1843, by the intimacy between the Rankes and the Edwin von Manteuffels. Von Manteuffel, the officer who would become an influential army general and royal adviser, was already adjutant to Prince Albert of Prussia, and through this connection Ranke himself came to know the prince.[3]

The same period witnessed changes, too, in Ranke's more immediately personal circumstances. Early in 1840 his connection with Bettina von Arnim and her circle, which had persisted through the 30s despite the loss of its earlier warmth, was abruptly terminated by the violent quarrel between Bettina and Ranke on the occasion of his defense of the conservatives' opposition to the proconstitutional heroes of the Göttingen Seven—the Grimm brothers—whose cause Bettina vociferously championed. Bettina forbade him to "come across my threshold again," and thenceforward counted him among her enemies.[4] The break was permanent because the Grimm incident simply activated a persistent divergence of political temperament between the erstwhile friends. It was in the context of Bettina's enthusiasm for the cause of "constitution, freedom of the press, reason, and light" and her justified alignment of the historian with the other side that she was reported to "reject Ranke completely."[5]

Ranke would frequent the gatherings of Berlin court society during the ensuing decade—he could be met, for example, at the parties of Heinrich von Bülow, the Prussian foreign minister—but

the company here was mannered and shallow, and Ranke participated only formally in it.[6] What did replace the social activities of
the available bachelor was the stable routine of family life into
which he entered with his marriage to a British lady (Clara Graves,
an Irish Protestant) in October 1843 and the birth of a son a year
later. Ranke's own explanation of his decision to get married—"I
was alarmed by the way of life [Wesen] of several old bachelors
whom I had met shortly before"—faithfully conveys the intent to
settle down which lay behind the decision and which helps to
explain the confluence now of his regularized private life with his
wholehearted commitment to the Prussian establishment in politics and to the profession of historical scholarship. For some time
before his marriage there were signs of Ranke's hankering for a
more stable life-style. Early in 1842 Ferdinand Ranke, Leopold's
second younger brother, became director of the Friedrich-Wilhelm-
Gymnasium in Berlin, where he remained until his death in
1876. The personal intimacy of the two brothers during these
years contributed to the pacific personal environment which was
beginning to surround Leopold, for unlike the ardent and provocative Heinrich, Ferdinand was a placid and relaxing influence.
Leopold characterized him as a man who "lived his life consistently [in einem Zug]," and he testified that in the thirty-five
years of their companionship in Berlin "there had never been a
quarrel between us."[7] Unquestionably, Leopold was now properly
disposed for this kind of influence. When he first considered the
possibility of bringing Ferdinand to Berlin, he wrote with unwonted contentment about Prussia: "It is a blessing and a
necessity for me to belong to a state with whose intentions I in
general agree."[8] The connection between this desirable solidity
and the institution of marriage was called to Leopold's attention
by the wedding of his youngest brother, Ernst, late in 1842.
Leopold greeted the prospect with the envious congratulation:
"You . . . will now do something that I have never succeeded in
doing." And he related the coming nuptials directly to Ernst's
even life-style: "I have so often noticed with pleasure that your life
attains its ends so regularly, in proper stages, without deviation—I
perceive this again."[9] Immediately before his own marriage, he
wrote correspondingly to his bride-to-be: "Generally, sweet Clara,

I flatter myself with the prospect of quietness and a peaceful love.''[10]

From the beginning, Leopold Ranke deliberately made his altered personal orientation relevant to his interests as a productive historian, and this relevance endows both his marriage and his family life as a husband and father with a meaning that transcends biography. At first he deemed the connection to be antithetical, and as long as he held this concept of the relationship between life and work, he resisted marriage and family, however attracted he might otherwise be by the idea of them. At the time of brother Ernst's marriage—and scarcely more than a year before his own— Leopold was totally occupied with the composition of the last volume of his *German History in the Age of the Reformation,* with the preparation of a new course for the next term at the university, and with the scramble for an hour here and there simply to think a bit, and these preoccupations had led him to declare defiantly: ''I now believe that God has definitely destined me for celibacy—it is almost impossible for me even to attend a wedding.''[11]

He was soon to change his mind, and it was a change of academic scene and circumstances that induced the shift. We need not accept the literal testimony of Alexander von Humboldt's malicious comment about the newly-wed to an English correspondent—that ''our historian, Ranke, since he has espoused a virgin of the Thames, has given up our language, without having made much progress in yours''[12]—to grasp the cosmopolitan implication in the sudden resolve of the forty-seven-year-old historian to become a family man, but this implication itself needs circumstantial definition. He met his Irish bride-to-be in Paris during July 1843 and married her in England less than three months later. The places attest to Ranke's inner withdrawal from the social life of Berlin, but the time suggests a further-reaching implication. When Ranke visited Paris (at the invitation of Adolphe Thiers, an admirer of the *History of the Popes*), he had just finished writing the *German History in the Age of the Reformation* and was between books. He went with the intention of repairing ''the gap in my general historical training'' which stemmed from his want of ''firsthand acquaintance with the great nations'' of modern history and with the aim of thus ''realizing the idea of a general comprehension [*Umfassung*] which I had held for so long."[13]

Ranke's choice of a wife was thus consonant with the persistence of his historical universalism, but even more indicative was the coincidence of his courtship and marriage with a period when he was reassessing his relations with fundamentals of his craft. Clearly a term off in Paris, away from his classes and at loose ends in his scholarship, jogged him out of his personal inertia, and his turn to the history of his adopted Prussia from this new perspective made a standardized private life and a dedicated professional vocation now seem compatible in a way that had not been true before. Henceforward he was eager "to prove that my marital status does not inhibit my literary activity."[14]

The marriage, which would last for twenty-seven compatible years until the death of his wife and would yield three children, in many ways fulfilled the function which Ranke originally seemed to mark out for it. Far from diverting him from his scholarly endeavors, it provided him with the routinization of his personal concerns that established a secure base for his historical writing and indeed enabled him to channel his passions to it. For Ranke proved to be a solicitous husband and an attentive father, qualities that focused his anxieties continuously upon his ailing wife and evoked his "paternal conscience" as well as affection for his children but that did not prevent him from departing on lengthy research trips, from waxing more enthusiastic about his work than about his family, or from taking note of his wife's "little love reproaches" wherein she evidently registered her resentment at the limits of his love.[15] He explicitly connected the two facets of his life, moreover, by using his family as a captive audience for his stories about his scholarly finds and about the titled notables with whom his honorific historiographical status brought him into contact. To this extent, the record confirms the manifest picture of a Ranke who organized his private life in such a way as to absorb his problematical personal drives and to create a respectable foundation for the untrammeled pursuit of historical scholarship.

A collage of typical sentiments from his faithful correspondence to his wife makes this relationship clear. "I hope with all my heart to find you and the children in perfect or at least passable health." "You do not write what the doctor says about your condition." "I enjoy with you the pleasure of the children: kiss them from their papa." "Clouds lie over my soul as long as I hear of the family problems at home," but "this cloud is now dispersed and I can now continue my work, which holds me with the same interest as it always has, without pressing fears." "My work is long but not dull; it always gives me the greatest pleasure." "I am as eager about it as ever." "If you will give me a little longer leave, I should still go on here [in London, doing research for his *English History*], looking for new material. . . . But if it is necessary, I will come, as soon as you tell me to." "In the meantime I have experienced much that I must tell you about when I come home."[16]

But a closer inquiry into Ranke's attitude toward his wife and family indicates the presence also of a more positive contribution of his personal to his professional arrangements. For time and time again he gave expression to a devotion that went far beyond the level of emotion appropriate to a convenient marital tie and a proper paternal pride. When he referred to himself as a Faust who had acquired a Helen; when he called his wife "the beloved friend of my life [*die geliebte Freundin meines Lebens*], wailing time and time again, "how I long to be with you," that "you have no idea how much I wish to have you here," that "my whole soul desires that you be well, for your well-being is also mine"; when he cried out, at the prospect of his wife's death, that "I would be completely alone" and, after she died, that "among us and in us she will live forever"; and when he greeted the birth of his firstborn with the genuine wonderment that "to me the first entrance of a human creature into this world has never come so close . . . —it is a miracle, both of God and of nature": in all of these many outbursts he went beyond the modalities of his status and the formulas of a prudential existence to disclose a genuine, direct encounter of self and life.[17] For Ranke his relations with wife and family were so many immediate experiences of the great events affecting humanity, and they lent depth to his reexperiencing of these events in history. If the functional dimension of his private life exhibited the influence of his historical profession upon his personal existence, this paradigmatic dimension of his private life demonstrated the influence of his personal existence upon his profession of history. In his own mind, clearly, the first effect of his new life-style was to create an atmosphere in which he suspended his open-ended quest for the larger community and dwelt upon the individuality of the small cognate group. "So now I spend most of my evenings in quiet domestic seclusion," he wrote early in his married life, "whereas I used to go from one party to another."[18] His was a domesticity that refracted rather than excluded the world. It was no mere coincidence that as long as his wife lived and his family was intact Ranke concentrated confidently on patriotic and national history as the foci of the general human past.

Ranke's attitude toward himself, his profession, and his government during these years before the revolution was consonant with these changes in his circumstances. He tended to withdraw his essential self from all those external connections—literature, academic community, and politics—which had generalized his existence and to place supreme value on his privacy as a person and his individuality as a writer. The tone which he struck in a diary entry on the occasion of an excursion from Paris to Honfleur during July 1843 was undoubtedly hyperbolic but it did reveal the onset of a renewed inner isolation. He noted "the profound solitude, simplicity" of the place, "thanked God for leading me here," and then confessed: "But I suffered pain the whole day long, as if I had separated myself from friendship and from hope."[19]

Unlike his youthful complaint, however, the new loneliness was balanced by no compensatory attachment to the literature of his own age, for it no longer fulfilled for him the function of joining him to the general ideas of humanity. "What distinguishes the present state of literature is that it depends so little on the general concern for truth and intelligence [*Einsicht*]. Previously, great convictions were common and on the basis of them men strove onward. Now everything fades away. Whoever gets on in the world expresses the opinion of a party and finds approval there. It is itself no longer debated, as it should be. Historical judgments waver this way and that."[20] He even found a new reason now for repelling Goethe, a reason consonant in an essential respect with his rejection of his own literary generation. It was about Goethe's "later things" that he now complained, and found them unsatisfactory because they presented "literature as literature, as something independent, fabricated. . . . It is as if there were nothing else in the world but literature and a little art.''[21] What alienated him, again, was obviously the access to the fundamental issues of humanity which he had found in genuine aesthetic creation and which he now missed in an insulated literature.

The mature Ranke was, in general, diminishingly involved with questions of religion, either personally or historiographically. It is all the more revealing, therefore, to find that, from the beginning of his reorientation at the end of the 1830s until well into the next decade, not only was he still articulate about Christian doctrine but his exegesis of that doctrine bespoke his need to find an ultimate ground for his current individualizing bent of mind. The private musings on religion which he noted in his diary for the period addressed themselves repeatedly to the relations between God and distributive humanity and to formulations which placed the authority of divinity behind the personality, the actions, and the freedom of individual man. ''The mystery of Christianity,'' he wrote, ''is that the Universal, the Divine has at the same time the analogy of personality with mankind.'' Hence not only does ''the personality of the authentic man'' require ''the consciousness of God'' for its own existence but, ''since one can be conscious only of one's person, one can perceive the divine element only in oneself.''[22] When he turned again to the doctrine of sin, which he had defined during the 30s in universal terms as ''the violation of the eternal law implanted in us and responsible for our existence'' —a violation which is a ''general spirit . . . provoked in personality, in ourselves''—he now reconsidered it in individualized terms as dependence on ''the soul, considering itself as a Self— which is certainly a degree of perfection—and finding its innermost core interrogated about the offence it has perpetrated,'' and he paired with it a concept of ''redemption'' which ''was required for belief in personality and immortality of the soul.''[23] Where he had defined conscience as ''consciousness of the rule,'' he now defined ''good'' as ''that which the good man does,'' and he contended that the good man not be judged by the idea of it but rather that ''judgment must conform to his deed.''[24] Freedom, finally, he now thought of explicitly as ''individual freedom,'' and in this context he deemed it to consist no longer in the conformity to a higher order or general principle but rather in the distributive effect of division and conflict. It is "opposition" (*Gegensatz*) that "makes individual freedom possible."[25]

Whether the application of this univocally individualized view of Christianity to himself was the cause or effect of his doctrinal view we do not know. But we do know that he assuredly made such application, and he made it to himself in his capacity as a producing scholar. "Sometimes," he exulted, on the occasion of reporting on some successful archival discoveries, "it seems to me as if a destiny, a fate, is at work. I do not think that it is arrogance to cherish this opinion. What would providence be if it did not also interest itself in individual men! That we are thought by an eternal thought, that we do not pass away like a falling leaf in the autumn, that we belong to the essence of things, is the sum of all religion."[26]

This principled disposition toward privacy and toward a personal, almost aesthetic approach to the historian's art explains his settlement into a chronic indifference toward the corporate life of academia and into a more transitory passivity in his relations with government. The two attitudes were connected, not only in their quality, but also more directly since Ranke's deliberate noninvolvement in university affairs was a condition of his casual attitude toward the academic policy of the government. Of his institutional nonparticipation there is abundant evidence, but there is less clarity about its cause.[27] Certainly his own contemporary view of the university in the 1840s as a place where he felt "the resistance of a bogus political [*after-politischen*] and negative religious spirit" helps to explain his abstention,[28] but even more telling was the circumstance that, both for his primary professional interest in his own historical research and writing and for his primary personal interest in his own dignity, his direct relations with the government were vital, and intermediaries were equivalent to intruders—a circumstance which favored his accommodation to the one and his neglect of the others.

And well might he think so. He was never popular with his colleagues at the university; his faculty—the philosophical—still bore the disparaged cachet of a pre-professional general studies program and had minimal influence within the university; and his own promotion to full professor in 1834 had been put through by cabinet order, without consultation of his faculty and against the opposition of the university. By the 1840s he had begun his custom of nonattendance at faculty meetings: he had learned to look rather to the government than to the university for his honors and perquisites as well as for the subsidizing of his research.

Ranke's usual docility in his relations with the government, like his customary corporate indifference, were in this period thus a function of his privatization. This basis of his governmental as of his academic politics, ordinarily unobtrusive for obvious reasons of inadmissibility, became manifest on the rare occasions when he was not politically docile or academically indifferent—occasions when he felt his own rights as a writer or as a teacher to be threatened. When Eichhorn, the minister of education, issued an order which overruled the faculty's right to set its own schedule of examinations, Ranke joined his colleagues on the philosophical faculty in their formal protest, despite his friendship with the minister.[29] And, in a more serious case of academic freedom, when the government instituted proceedings in the university designed to expel the liberal historian, Karl Nauwerck, from the faculty, Ranke joined a majority of his colleagues in asserting the principle of academic freedom against the government-sponsored action by the university. Justifying his stand by his finding that even Nauwerck's politics "keep on a scientific level" and that the accused professor has thus "formally kept within his duly assigned competence," Ranke proceeded to endorse the standard argument for intellectual liberty within the academic community. "Who will set himself up as the possessor of the truth? His doctrines, as I understand them, appear to me to be very false, very objectionable, but I cannot fight them with other means than he himself uses."[30]

It was in the Nauwerck case too that the residual character of his political conservatism in this period emerged. After defending his colleague against repressive action by the university, Ranke did approve the possibility of such action directly by the government itself. "In my opinion," he wrote, "the tutelary [*aufsehende*] power of the state applies here . . . , the capacity to intervene where the existing laws do not literally suffice." "It is," he concluded in comfortable ear-plugged fashion, "a part of the executive power in which we have no share."[31] That this privatized conservatism represented not an ad hoc declaration but a persistent attitude of Ranke's in the years before the revolution of 1848 is indicated by the similar sentiment that was attributed to him as his response to a question about the capricious general censorship policy of the governmental leaders he befriended and revered: "The answer was: he will never talk of these things. 'Leave me alone; I want to hear nothing; histories are what concern me.' "[32]

III Accompanying these changes in his personal and political circumstances and cradled in the insulation from general professional and political connections which was promoted by these changes was the analogous shift in Ranke's approach to history.[33] By the end of the 30s the first part of the *German History in the Age of the Reformation* had been published and its total conception already set. By early 1843 the writing was completed. From it Ranke could go in two directions: he could pursue into modern times the universal theme which he had traced through Reformation Germany, at the dawn of modern history; or he could resume his patriotic stance and follow the political fortunes of a German principality which embodied the national spirit in the modern period. Not only was he uncertain of his way at the time but it was a signal mark of his dilemma that even in retrospect he was indecisive about the reasons for his final choice of the path he took.

The externals of the story seem clear enough. He went to Paris with a scholarly project appropriate to his expansive self-educational intention: he would resume in a serious way the study of the French Revolution with which he had toyed at the behest of the Varnhagens almost twenty years earlier. But once in Paris his habit of being guided to his subjects by the available reliable sources reasserted itself: he decided that the materials at the National Archives were inadequate for a history of the French Revolution, but he did find reports of the French ambassador at the court of Frederick the Great which could serve as the nucleus of a Prussian history during his reign.[34] Now it would seem clear, a priori, that a historian who discovers more suitable materials for a Prussian than for a French history in the French national archives must be working from a definite perspective—especially since that same historian did find a suitably manageable subject in the universal aspects of the French Revolution much later when his perspective had changed.[35]

The fact is that the evidence for Ranke's internal state of mind during this period essentially modifies the implications of the external sequence and must be invoked to supplement it. The issue is important because it entails the hierarchy of motives that went not only into Ranke's *Prussian History* but into the histories of all his postsynthetic periods until the last one.[36] The implication of the outer story is that Ranke sought essentially to continue his universal theme but was diverted by his passion for the sources. The implication of his internal testimony for the same period is that his shift to a particularistic subject matter was deep-seated and betokened a priority over, albeit not an exclusion of, his universal historical concerns. It betokened a state of mind that conditioned, antedated and prepared his tendentious judgment of the Parisian sources, since the kind of French source which he deemed inadequate was the detailed, factual, political document homologous with his historical interest in the Prussian state.[37]

The evidence in Ranke's lectures, his correspondence, and the first edition of the *Prussian History* itself shows that his readiness for the writing of Prussian history was independent of any urge to develop the universal or national themes of his earlier work and that, as a native history whose details were ipso facto important, it was associated with his reversion to particularism in historical method. From the vantage point offered by this testimony, even the evolutionary coherence premised by Ranke's later formulation of his theme as the rise of Brandenburg Prussia was an interpolation holding more for the *Prussian History*'s second edition of 1874 than for the original edition of 1846. Both Ranke's contemporary commentary and the first edition of the work referred rather to the insularity than the resonance of patriotic Prussian history and satisfied the requirement of universality, not through the connectedness of development, but by subsuming universal history in its extensive sense of international relations under the particularistic historical method.

Ranke's whole approach to history during the prerevolutionary 40s was consistent with his total commitment to the facts of congenial history. He speculated much less than in the preceding

decade on the theory of history or on universal history—to judge
by the paucity of published remarks and of the extant unpublished
notes on the subject—and on the few occasions when he did he
ventured only with diffidence and with doubt beyond the internality of particular truths, while yet recognizing the necessity to
venture beyond them. He inserted into the *Prussian History* itself a
brief digression in which he prescribed "the development of the
positive [*das Positive*] to a generally valid truth" to be the task of
the nineteenth century, but his own diary and lecture notes reveal
the renewal of his uncertainty about how to do this—that is, to
proceed beyond "the positive"—for history.[38] The entries in his
diary on this subject for this period asserted the primacy of "a
return to the most original report," and in terms of this primary
principle all the external relations of history—the involvement of
the historian with his present, the rewriting of history by each
generation, and the framing of historical interpretations—were at
once inevitable and questionable. The dependence of historical
judgments on the standards of the age that does the judging Ranke
asserted as a universal proposition that should be somehow resisted
by immersion in original research, while he acknowledged both
the present involvement of the historian and the historian's
necessity to arrive at historical interpretations on the basis of
historical actuality in the form of questions about their relationship to the same specific historiographical activity. "But in general
would one study it [the most original report] without the impulse
of the present?" And again: "But how and when does interpretation get modeled on [history as the image of time]?"[39]

A brief introduction to a lecture on universal history of the same
vintage was somewhat more positive in its formulation, but it
made essentially the same point of limiting the general connections of history to what the historian brings to its particular objects.
Declaring both the merely factual approach and the (Fichtean/
Hegelian) philosophical approach to universal history to be equally
inadequate—the first because it is "external" and slights the
"purpose" as well as the "inner connection" of events, the second
because it slights "the truth of individual consciousness"—
Ranke's own answer here to the problem of universal history, the
problem of penetrating "the inner core of the magnificent
substance [*Stoff*] of history," was to raise the necessity of making
history in the "subjective" sense of knowledge (*Historie*) "coin-

cide" with history in its "objective" sense of "what happened" (*Geschichte*). This answer was obviously analogous to the desperate answer he proposed to the questions he raised around the same time in his diary—that authentic history (*Historie*) could come only from the historian's somehow "raising himself to pure intuition [*Anschauung*]" and embodying it "in the purest kind of representation [*Darstellung*]."[40] Both in the lecture and in the diary, Ranke's notion of universalism in history was reduced to general categories in the historian's method of treating documentary history. These categories were the theoretical analogues of the sympathy he brought to the facts of his *Prussian History* and testified both to his continuing concern for something more than the particular facts of history and his temporary settlement for general principles of method that were tailored to those facts.

The university lectures on modern history which Ranke gave in the later years of the 40s, while he was finishing the *Prussian History*, reveals the shift in his orientation since the universal preoccupations of the previous decade. He now saw his contemporary age as an era of dissolution, standing for "conflict and convulsion" vis-à-vis the "construction and consolidation" of the early-modern period. Even more impressively, he found the great problem of the age to be not the need for reintegration which might be expected from his diagnosis but "whether and how individual existence should and can be maintained."[41] The lectures demonstrated unmistakably, moreover, that this individualizing attitude was rubbing off on his approach to history. For when he recurred to his old concern for the definition of universal history, he acknowledged, as he had in the 30s, the viability of the historian's obligation to "raise himself above the individual" by "perceiving the generally effective, concurrent powers which . . . fill individual minds with general spiritual impulses"—in short, to know "this general truth [*dieses Allgemeine*] that transcends the particular"—but he now insisted that this level of history was inadequate to the understanding of "the evolution of spirit," and he put his emphasis on the contribution of individuals to the development of the general powers, "independently of human progress." Thus, he concluded, "the self-referring event" as well as "the associated movement of the spirit" is required for world history.[42]

Hence during the 40s Ranke was influenced by and contributed to the broadly diffused current of opinion which attributed a general mission to Prussia through that state's national role in Germany. Just before he set off for Paris, he reported with approval the opinion that his *German History in the Age of the Reformation* "is the first part of a Prussian history," and he promised the king that in Paris "I shall not for a single day forget the idea of the fatherland [i.e., Prussia] in its world relations." After his return from Paris he testified repeatedly that "after the king named me Historiographer of the Prussian State I resolved to dedicate my modest forces to native [*vaterländischen*] history as soon and as much as the other duties of my position permitted."[43] The first edition of the book, published in 1847, reflected nicely the combination of predominant particularity and subordinate universalism that went into it: the nine books were concerned overwhelmingly with Frederick the Great and only briefly with his predecessors, as befit Ranke's discovery of local materials, but he justified the focus too with a general argument reminiscent of the individualized universalism of his early essay on *The Great Powers*. Europe in the early eighteenth century, he began, was dominated by "four great powers, . . . related to one another like so many worlds [*Weltkörper*] which described their own orbits according to inherent laws," and his book would concentrate on the few short years—from the accession of Frederick the Great in 1740 to the end of the second Silesian War in 1748—in which Prussia filled a vacuum to become another "great European independency."[44]

Clearly, Ranke had not forgotten the general theme of "European power and culture" which he had adumbrated as the modern equivalent of universal Christianity in history, but there had been an obvious break in his development, and he was approaching it from a pluralistic point of view and with a strictly contextual function. The rest of the preface was dominated by a methodological and documentary discussion of the charm and challenge of writing on so articulate a hero as Frederick the Great. "Who has not felt or heard expressed the wish to obtain for once more detailed and thorough information on Prussian history and especially on Frederick II than he himself has given?" The difficulties he now recounted were those of the plethora of documents and the opacity of the specific political issues. The ideal to which he aspired was "to consider events . . . with as objective a perception as possible." It is hardly surprising that, writing from this particularistic perspective, Ranke started the story of his researches in Berlin and came to Paris only subsequently, as one in a series of non-Prussian archives he visited in order "not to limit myself to a single point of view."[45] It is hardly surprising either that Ranke's own summary of his achievement in the book was along this same line of methodological performance on historical facts. The summary was indeed one of his most memorable statements on his scientific method, and it should be remembered in the specific context of his *Prussian History.* "My purpose," he wrote to Frederick William IV in the letter accompanying the second volume, "was . . . to raise myself above the gossip which surrounds the living and easily fixes itself for posterity as accepted tradition; to find the right track among the actors' thousandfold expressions, which often seem to contradict one another, to plunge myself into it, to say the unvarnished truth, to write documented and informed history."[46] Of universal coherence, totality, or theme, not a word.

That the specific emphases and general omissions in the original preface and in Ranke's contemporary remarks reflected a meaningful attitude rather than an automatic adaptation to an inflexible subject matter becomes irrefutable when they are contrasted with Ranke's orientation in his preface to the second edition, written in 1874 under very different auspices. Now he explicitly denied the adequacy of "a mere territorial history," and asserting the peculiarity of Prussia to consist in its not being itself "a national power of age-old legitimacy," affirmed the continuous connection between Prussian growth and the international constellation throughout the territory's whole history. His whole point in the book, therefore, was to present the "reciprocal connection" between "these two elements, the universal-historical and the territorial," and to solve this problem not only did he promise to focus on "the forces of historical becoming in its unexpected but yet regular development" but he concluded the preface with a methodological defense of "general views" (*allgemeiner Ansichten*) in history. "The vital forces of a general development must also be able to form the object of research."[47]

The body of the book itself followed the main lines of the

original preface. It began with the assertion of a decisive break between the national—*gemeindeutscher*—convictions of the Reformation princes and the princely particularist reality of the early-modern period which "reserved the question of whether the remembered unity of the nation could be reestablished ... to a distant future," and the bulk of it was devoted to the consistent demonstration that "the nature of Frederick's spirit" cooperated with "the necessity of things" to "assign the Prussian state ... its particular and self-reliant position," at once "victorious on its own account [*für sich*] and vanquished in its German policy [*im Reiche*]."[48] Ranke's conclusion, moreover, was that even as a policy (expressed mainly in Prussian designs on Saxony), the national dimension of Prussia's position was inessential. Frederick considered himself to be "a German prince almost by accident, a European prince by nature," and the Prussian state itself, to whose "conditions of preservation the prince completely subjected himself," "tore itself loose" both from "its historical basis" in the "imperial principality" and from the confessional Protestantism associated with it to become a continental state, "bearing its necessity in its own existence," taking account only of "inner need" for its domestic policies and justifying this standard "by the independence abroad which it asserted."[49]

Ranke's approach to his material was conformable to the particularity of his thesis. His focus was on the activities, ideas, and character—that is, on the "genius," as Ranke termed it—of the individual Hohenzollern rulers, notably Frederick the Great but also even the creator of the institutions with which Frederick worked, Frederick William I. Not only did the historian keep a constant eye on these princes as a matter of historiographical fact, but he stressed their role in the history of their state as a matter of historical interpretation. Frederick William I's institutional establishments were not "the necessary realization of the original idea" of the Prussian state but the work of "an energetic spirit who perceived the general purpose—that of opposing a self-reliant, invulnerable state to powerful neighbors—in a definite way—and who recognized the means of attaining it with the insight of genius."[50] As for Frederick the Great, Ranke used the opposite argument with the same individualistic result: precisely because Frederick William I had given the Prussian state a "definite stamp and character," through an "organization of state" which "no successor could question or make free with," the task was to apply the system to actual achievements and for this only "a very energetic spirit," with "gifts of genius," was called for. In his interpretation of Frederick, consequently, he stressed the individual internality and isolation both of decision and of idea. Frederick "considered difficult questions only by himself alone," summarized Ranke. "His decisions were taken in the depths of his spirit [*Gemütes*] and then remained ever firm." Frederick's own ultimate conviction, moreover, was "that the purpose of the world consists in individual happiness" (*individuellen Glücke*). Ranke even grounded these historical facts of individuality in an ultimate principle of politics—"if monarchy is to be a truth, . . . the supreme will must direct itself only to the nature of things"—and in the ultimate principle of human nature—"What makes man but the inner impulse and force of his moral self?"[51]

So prevalent was Ranke's particularistic thesis and individualistic agency in his *Prussian History* that the universal motifs he wove into it were cast in forms compatible with particularity and individuality, which thus became the frameworks within which universality historically appeared. Thus the "necessity of things," which constituted at once the limits and the materials of Frederick's actions and ideas, was ultimately articulated in the narrative sequence of Prussian international relations, which comprised most of the book and posed Prussia's universal involvement in a serial dimension amenable to Ranke's particularistic methodology and intimately bound to the perspective of his individual agents. The other fundamental universal motif invoked by Ranke was the intellectual "standpoint" of the eighteenth century—"a great transformation of views" in which "the human spirit tore free from domination by religious ideas," since the dogmatic divisions of the Christian religion frustrated its aspiration "to be universal," and which itself therefore now constituted a "world-historical force." Ranke presented this motif, however, not in itself but in the context of Frederick's "convictions." The Enlightenment, therefore, was recognized as a fundamental stage in the history of humanity, but it was presented in the version that Frederick took it to be. "His own standpoint . . . was the standpoint of the century and every day became more so." The domestication of the

universal intellectual motif in Ranke's *Prussian History* was epitomized in his summary of the "three powerful forces" that made
up the whole core of the Prussian state: "the established order, the
ideas of the century, and the independent spirit of the prince who
combined both." Frederick's entire achievement, indeed, was to
"unite the strict political order inherited from his father with his
own innate cultural endeavors, an achievement through which the
contradiction between militarism and the tendencies of the centuries was mediated."[52]

As the far-flung components which Ranke read into the thinking and the activity of his historical agents indicate, the methodological key to his work was sympathy. Certainly he applied his
usual critical approach to the sources, correcting the less reliable by
the more authentic, but the purpose of the criticism tended now
rather to find understanding than to cast verdicts of invalidity.
Thus, after noting generously that, in his history of the Silesian
war, Frederick "still stood too close to things for an objective
conception, but the immediately fresh recollection in every word
lends the work all the more value," Ranke concluded by revealing
his rule of internal reconstruction: "We are far from passing
judgment on the great king . . .; he writes always as the king. His
conduct and his attitude express his own standpoint."[53] The
objectivity which he promised in his preface thus turned out to
consist not in the revisionist judgments of a uniform criticism but
in the impartial re-creations of an all-sided sympathy. What
balanced his congenial portrait of Prussia and its rulers was the
equally understanding, but much briefer, attitude toward the
Austrian situation in general and the Hapsburg Maria Theresa in
particular.

It was this homogenized mildness in Ranke's approach at this
time that earned his *Prussian History* the immediate qualified
reception it had from conservatives, liberals, and nationalists
alike—from all those, that is, who bemoaned the absence of a
variable criticism or a definite thesis favorable to their own cause.[54]
In general, the negative comments testify more to the historiographical views of the reviewers than of the reviewed, but
there was one feature of the adverse judgments that did reveal
inadvertently an implicit correlation in Ranke's book. Whether
they took his claim to objectivity at face value and accused him of

carrying it too far, or whether, more sophisticatedly like Varn-hagen von Ense, they called his claim "to write as objectively as possible without consideration of present inclinations or aversions . . . only a phrase" since his very omission of anything "that intrudes on present life" is itself a product of conservative influence that "gives on the whole an erroneous picture of Prussian conditions"[55]—in either case Ranke's critics glimpsed the connection that he had made between the particularism of patriotic history, the particularity of factual historiography, and the preference for sympathy over judgment in the critical approach to the past. Ranke himself as much as admitted the connection when he made one of his rare confessions and even rarer justifications of the historian's involvement in specific reference to his *Prussian History*: "I do not deny that I display a lively sympathy with the event I describe—the rise of this state—but without such sympathy a book of this kind could not be written."[56]

With this renewed imbalance between the individual and the universal in the substance of history and between the particular and the general in its method, reinforced now by a new imbalance between sympathy and judgment in his approach to history, Ranke's attitude toward history was once more open to the convulsive influence of experience. This the revolution of 1848 provided.

10
The Second Synthesis:
Revolution, Politics, and History
at Mid-Century

Unlike the revolution of 1830, which had impinged on Ranke only belatedly as an observer from afar and as a responder to a potentiality, the revolution of 1848 was an immediate experience that had a shattering impact. It broke into his own city and country; it directly affected those on the throne and in the king's councils whom he considered his friends; and until the months just prior to the outbreak of the revolution his political passivity had left him unprepared for the storm. He had indeed observed the working of French and British constitutionalism in the early 40s, and he had taken note of the Greek revolution in 1843 and the Polish uprising in 1846; but until the approximate coincidence of his responses to the Swiss civil war and to the Prussian United Diet in 1847, he hardly seemed involved in the politics of his day. True, he made reference in 1845 to "elements with whom some day a serious conflict impends," to "the rabble's increased preponderance, clamor, and self-confidence," and to his own fear that "sometimes the business can appear dangerous," but the remark was made casually to his brother en passant, was probably triggered by the temporary unrest in the hungry Berlin of the mid-40s, and in any case remained an isolated expression of his general need for order rather than the revelation of any serious political commitment.[1]

What struck him in the Swiss turmoil was the connection between religious division, which had concerned him continuously, and politics, and he concluded from the Swiss lesson of a political "radicalism" triumphant by virtue of a religiously divided conservatism that "one could say: it was precisely the same in all Europe."[2] He followed with close attention the agitation for and then the meetings of the Prussian United Diet during the first half of 1847, but was rather disgusted than upset by it. There were two reasons for the moderation of this his first real political immersion since the revolution of 1830, reasons why the United Diet prepared him for his reception of the revolution that followed while not really cushioning the shock of it. First, he still cherished in 1847 something of a contempt for domestic politics as such that kept him above the conflict. He held that in general "the spirit of youth is corrupted to the core by political machinations." And he confessed himself to be "but little edified by the deliberations of the Assembly of Estates" in particular, both because in all the parties he found "politics [*das Politische*] one-sidedly doctrinaire," referring to theories and principles which inhibit the crucial matter of their "execution" (*Ausführung*), and because he saw in the meeting of the estates an irresoluble set of oppositions—between government and liberals, monarchy and constitutionalists, aristocracy and bureaucracy—which could lead to no decisive result. "I am entirely displeased with the Estates, who begin again the old dispute which cannot be settled. They can fight about it until Judgment Day."[3] He might be displeased with the bickering, but he was also relieved at the frustration of the liberal opposition which it entailed.

But it was the second reason for Ranke's restraint about the United Diet, despite his keen interest in it, that more clearly foreshadowed his ultimate response to the revolution that would follow: he turned it into history. It was, indeed, the effect of these contemporary events upon history that troubled him the most. "But these things touch [*ergreifen*] history [*Historie*], correct it," he wrote in connection with the events at the United Diet of which he so heartily disapproved. "They have even made me uneasy for a few days."[4] And well they might in this context, for from the beginning of his recorded interest in the affair he rooted it in the contemporary history of the nineteenth century. Not only did he trace the specific occasion for the convocation of the United Diet back to the early promises and legislation of Frederick William III, but he used it as the historical lever wherewith to sketch a thematic history of the century in terms of the recurrent conflict between "the liberal principle—that is, . . . that subjects in one form or another be brought into participation in the state—and monarchy" and of the equally recurrent "natural tendency" for "an alliance between monarchy and liberal principles." Clearly, Ranke was on the way to the identification of a universal theme of modern history. But he was not at full comprehension yet. The coexistence of the disjunctive and conjunctive themes led him at this stage simply to the acceptance of the United Diet, with all its confused squabbling, as "inevitable," "a necessary evil," incorporating a tendency which "should be so carried through that no damage is suffered." And his final word on the United Diet was "the historical conclusion" (*das Historische*) that it embodied the triumph of "the nobleman," culminating the "great importance that had been accorded him since 1815," and that it also demonstrated the noble's "political incapacity," since he sold out the monarchy to "traditional liberalism." In this final historical verdict, the United Diet, through its dominant nobility, did not manifest but only "prepared" "general revolution" (*Umsturz*).[5]

The general revolution, when it did break out in March 1848, struck Ranke as something different in kind. As he himself admitted not long afterward, in a lecture of 1850: "Two years ago there was a sudden turn [*Umschwung*] of events that nobody anticipated." Certainly his immediate response to it was visceral and not historical. That his reaction to it changed from personal outrage to historical reflection is well known and so is the role of the revolution in crystallizing Ranke's positive political and social views.[6] But what may not be so well known is the effect that the revolution itself had on his approach to history and the converse meaning that the historical mold in which he subsequently cast the revolution had for his politics.

With all due subtraction for the unfriendliness of the source, the intensity of the shock which the outburst of actual revolution in Berlin visited upon Ranke and his utter distraction in the face of it are visible in the graphic word portrait that his erstwhile patron, Varnhagen von Ense, drew of him during the "March days":

Ranke has completely lost his mind. He laments and rages, holds everything to be lost forever, believes in the complete decline of the civilized world, and in a barbarism of unbridled violence such as has never existed before. (The fool wants to be a historian!) "Scoundrels have custody of the king, the mob rules according to its caprices, all morality and religion are gone!" (On account of Eichhorn and Savigny?) He would like to flee but does not know where!—Cowardice, how widespread it is![7]

What seems authentic in this report—for it is confirmed by the little we have from Ranke's own pen at the time—is the immediacy of the experienced catastrophe, an immediacy which inundated for the time being those wonted categories with which the historian was used to view his life. His diary and his letters from 1848 revealed a reception of the revolutionary events in raw social, personal, and moral terms that had little to do with his customary historicopolitical view of things. It was because his good friend Edwin von Manteuffel became Frederick William IV's adjutant in 1848, he admitted later, that "we all assumed the role of immediate participants in the movement of that day."[8] In March and again in August he characterized the revolution in the volcanic language of elemental direct action: "From the depths of European society a power rushes forth to overturn or dominate society . . .—bearer of the financial and mercantile movement, the factory population. . . . The whole order of things on which the further development of mankind depends is threatened by anarchic powers. . . . Here we are still in continuous unrest and disorder, and how could order ever come out of base subversion?" It was not by pure happenstance, obviously, that he juxtaposed social chaos with a cholera epidemic to point out the perilousness of Berlin for family living. Even the memoranda on the current situation which he submitted to Frederick William IV through von Manteuffel showed, despite their presumably professional format, the same demoniacal social approach to the mass movement in what Ranke admitted were those "rather desperate moments" of spring and summer 1848. "'Manual workers and day laborers, in city and countryside, have suddenly gained a share in the state power which they did not expect, so that through joining the extreme party they could hope for a liberation from all by which they felt oppressed, and perhaps for more.'' Thus "the radical world . . . calls the appetites of the unpropertied into the struggle.'' The net result, as might be expected from the Ranke of this period, was that "all central Europe has fallen into anarchy or a condition bordering on anarchy.''[9]

Even when he seemed more analytical about contemporary events in this period, he could view them only as monstrosities—unreal, personally alien, and vicious. He contrasted the ideas of the revolution to his youthful sympathies for the nationalism of Father Jahn—themselves "immature" and reverent of "leaders ensnared by superficial politics and misunderstood history''—for the purpose of giving personal expression to the moral obloquy and the hyperillusions of the current revolution. "How different things look now! Our pure ideas have been replaced by the madness of the red republic. . . . Nationality now is only an externally fabricated phantom; at its core it is only the negation of everything effective that has ever formed nations. One would like to cry, or laugh, when one sees the unity of the Holy Roman Empire associated by the upstarts [den Unberufenen] with the delusion of popular sovereignty.'' At this same time the Frankfurt National Assembly was appearing to him, analogously, as a purely "literary effort.'' "They all assembled, accomplished nothing, and only tore at each other.''[10] In his memoranda of this period to the king he did adduce once more, as in 1847, the recurrent risings of "the revolutionary spirit" since 1815, but he dehistoricized the movement of 1848 by stressing its character as an "unforeseen uprising" and he depoliticized it by attributing its origins to a group of outsiders in Paris—"a coalition of the emigrés of all nations, of native and foreign manual laborers [Handwerkern] and some literary people''—and then insisting that its spread to Prussia and Austria "came from outside''—i.e., from Paris. "For is there not also an invasion of foreign ideas?'' And he called for "a well-considered, well-prepared restoration.''[11] During the revolution itself, moreover, he justified his decision to give a course on ancient history in language that ran counter to his usual defence of the historian's capacity to present contemporary history validly and impartially. In a lecture of 1848 he acknowledged that "the turbulent movement of the age directs minds to the interests and issues of the present" and seems to make the history of its genesis "advisable," but now he admitted that because of this very movement "the quiet contemplation that is necessary to science would suffer," and he announced his preference for ancient history.[12]

But once the revolutionary wave had crested and the restoration of control by the authorities was an established fact, Ranke's perspective on the revolution changed. It was not only that with the passing of the threat to everything he held dear he became less panicky and more rational; it was that he could assess the meaning of the revolution only after it had passed because it had to become a part of history before he could endow it with roots, essentiality, and duration. Shortly after the events of 1848 he was viewing them as part of the age of revolution "which will henceforth be discerned in history" just like the "age of the crusades," for "our age gets its character" from the revolution and the resistance to it. Consequently, he no longer received revolution like a frightful convulsion, on the order of a natural catastrophe, but as the fundamental tendency of contemporary history. "We are born in it," he said of the age of revolution, "and it will outlast us all." Now (in 1850) he justified "didactic history" as especially useful for modern times because it communicated the genesis of the present, and he argued not only that the parties in the contemporary conflict "have a historical origin which bears them and limits them" but that the analogous conflict of the earlier centuries "we find [again] in modern history struggling constantly toward higher stages of existence." He insisted that the revolutionaries and the counterrevolutionaries alike were "unhistorical" in their refusal to recognize the ineradicability and the indispensability of both the new and the old Europe to the fundamentals of the contemporary age of revolution, and a year later he was noting contentedly, along the same lines, that "the new ideas and ambitions," like the resistance to them, were products of historical Europe itself. In his terms, they "come from the profound necessity of the inner course of things"; hence not only "can the new never completely replace the old" but also "for many centuries no event has occurred which has affected a general

revolution [*Umsturz*]. The western world has withstood the greatest, the most dangerous, storms.''[13]

The historization of contemporary political experience, moreover, also brought Ranke's admission of the converse—that contemporary political experience was relevant to history. Thus he
maintained that it was possible to study the revolution of 1789
only after the experience of 1848, for "the events we experienced
destroy many illusions and make clear the inner nature of the
impulses and tendencies of that time. . . . Recent developments
cast light on the historical event.''[14]

The political memoranda which Ranke wrote for Manteuffel
between the end of October 1848, when Ranke's version of
"public order" was reestablished, and January 1851, when the
reverberations of the revolution finally subsided, were composed
with this sense of the revolution's historical relevance. They were
not themselves historical documents but were rather political
analyses that cast the revolutionary situation in a sufficiently
historical mold to enable the revolution to exercise an important
effect on Ranke's general view of history. Ranke's reconsideration
of the revolution, then, did not cancel his original convulsive
response to the cataclysm, but translated it into terms that once
more crystallized Ranke's latent universal strivings and established
the relationship between monarchical stability and democratic
revolution as the general theme of modern history.

The role of history in the memoranda was thus a delicate one.
Ranke neither affirmed nor denied—but he also did not neglect to
mention—Manteuffel's position that Ranke's historical training
made him "also capable of seeing present things as they are, of
knowing their true posture." Similarly, he did not hesitate to
convey his ideas on the kind of issue which he expressly admitted
"lies beyond my competence," but the clear implication of this
stipulation was that other parts of his analysis did not lie beyond
his historically based competence.[15] Conformably to this ambiguity about the place of history in his political reflections, the
substance of his memoranda demonstrated an approach that
differed from his original response to the revolution by adding an
historical factor, but it was a historical factor that was largely
implicit. Ranke's basic position in these memoranda was that the
monarchy could save itself and the Prussian state only by stripping

the policies of constitutionalism and national unification of their revolutionary aspects and adapting them to itself. His fundamental ground for this position was that "it appears as a matter of necessity, which it is," and this necessity he defined in the historically conditioned terms of the age's demands and the anachronism of the alternatives. He asserted the "restoration of the old" to be impossible: "The storms of today must be met with the institutions of today." A constitution must be adopted because "constitutionalism must be viewed without love or hatred, as a form in which men now wish to live." The king must proceed to a policy of German unification with the exclusion of Austria because unlike "the old self-contained Frederician Prussia," the new Prussia cannot persist as such and because the Germanic Confederation, based on a constitutionalism "in the old Germanic sense," was "torn down by the current of ideas" bearing toward a more modern and more authentic unity. "In the present state of the world," he concluded from this perspective, "a people which is convinced of the justice and urgency of certain demands can hardly be governed any longer when its leaders hinder their satisfaction." Thus "it is for us, after so many centuries, to realize . . . the great ideas which our fathers had but without the talent to carry them out."[16]

There was, in addition to this location of the revolutionary situation in the context of a contemporary historical age, a second historical aspect of Ranke's memoranda. Although he justified his championship of monarchical Prussia essentially by its capacity to maintain order—"that the stronger should be given laws by the weaker runs counter to the nature of things; only a moderate influence of the stronger power can control anarchy and restore a viable order"—there was a historical dimension in this defense. For the main bastion of Prussian power, in Ranke's analysis, at once the bulwark against revolution and the fulcrum of reestablished authority, was the Prussian army—"the only really existing army in Germany"—and its defining characteristic was its historicity. "It is a tree from an old root. . . . The other troops have no such history." The Prussian monarchy as such, moreover, represents "historically grown sovereignty" against "revolutionary sovereignty" or "popular sovereignty," which "negates the past."[17]

So much for the contribution of history to the politics of the memoranda. More important for Ranke was the contribution of the revolutionary experience, as recast in the politics of the memoranda, to his notions of history. The clue to this contribution is offered by his treatment of the French influence and of the Frankfurt Assembly, which had figured so largely in his early convulsion by the revolution. The original notes of abhorrence and unreality were still present, however muted, for he still felt that "events in France have determined the course of affairs in Germany," infusing the "German spirit" with an alien "something superficial and fanatical," and he still rejected the Frankfurt Assembly for its "union of constitutional ideas with destructive tendencies" and for its impotent reliance on "the word" in "the realm of shadows." But now he also recognized a positive function for each of these factors—the function of triggering the development toward unity. The revolutionary movement which was initiated from France was "promoted extraordinarily by the need for a greater unity, at once ideal and intensely real." The Frankfurt Assembly, moreover, performed "an undeniable service for the maintenance of order" by proposing the idea of a German emperor, by "entering the sphere of reality" to offer the throne to "the mightiest prince," and thus "tightening the union of the nation."[18]

The keynote of national unity that Ranke sounded here spoke more for his unity than for his nationalism. "Man lives on general ideas which nourish the spirit, whether it depends on them or produces them," he wrote, revealing the concrete universal behind his national emphasis. "This spirit needs the fatherland as it needs religion." By placing both the conservative and the revolutionary forces in their historical contexts he could see the events of the revolution triggering a political integration that went far beyond the issues of national unification and that bestowed its integrated categories on the interpretation of modern history. From Frederick William's grant, in response to the revolution, of a constitution to Prussia and from his agreement with the traditional princes on a representative German constitution, Ranke expected the resolution of historic divisions most characteristic of the revolutionary age. Such a policy most obviously meant an end to the conflict of "absolute monarchy" and "absolute democracy": "A real understanding is only now possible.'' Indeed, with the actual institution of the Prussian constitution this resolution has been attained: ''The feeling for the dynasty and the latter's pacific attitude joined everything together.'' The new Prussian constitution contains much ''which recalls its revolutionary point of departure, but the principles of the monarchy and the military state are saved in it.'' Even the revolutionary movement now ''acknowledges the chief principles of the old state which it would have lifted from its hinges.'' Through the monarchical constitution, moreover, a solution was found even for the internal uncertainty, extending beyond Germany and coeval with recent history itself, of sovereigns and their bureaucracies between their attraction and their opposition to the constitutional principle. The idea of an imperial constitution was equally cohesive. However revolutionary in its origin, ''the German Empire [*Kaisertum*] is by its nature conservative. . . . What a prospect is offered for bringing power again into harmony with the ideas of the nation. . . . The idea of the empire falls like a ray of light on this chaos.''[19]

Such a coherent view of the contemporary German situation raised a parallel integrating idea into Ranke's historical consciousness. He learned from direct experience the centrality of the state for historical life. After the revolution of 1830 he had recognized the spiritual component of the state's power in abstract principle, interpreting it in practice conformably with his doctrine of individuality as the vital force behind the rich and fruitful variety of political forms, and as late as 1847 he was asking the question ''whether the state was actually the Universal [*das Allgemeine*]'' and raising as a problem for ''investigation, whether the spiritual life of a great nation can flourish under complete unity.''[20] Through the revolution of 1848 he found the affirmative answer to these questions in the actual unity of spirit and power manifested by the monarchical constitution and the national empire. The constitutional system ''hovers between'' the opposed systems of monarchy and republic, and when attached to monarchy it ''maintains the protective principle and rejects the destructive forever.'' The imperial ''harmony'' between power and the idea of the nation realizes the ''association of all conservative elements in the idea of freedom and order.''

Through its merger of national constitution and power the state thus becomes the unifying locus for the relationship of spirit and appearance in modern times. It provides the central organization, moreover, for social as well as for spiritual factors in history. Ranke's much-remarked expressions of social concern in his memoranda—his acknowledgment that "the great masses . . . have a claim on the state for their livelihood" and his recommendation that "the state should organize labor and perhaps recognize the right to work"—were designed primarily to exclude the social interests of these masses from political and consequently from historical relevance. The masses "have no real political interest," he argued, and the state's responsibility for their social welfare is connected to the one political interest it has in them—to keep them bound to the state in view of their military service. But the consequent right of the "manual workers" to this paternalistic social service, which is valid, is to be categorically distinguished from their claim to political rights, which is not. The political defusing of this elemental social force which Ranke feared so deeply is a clear enough tactic on the face of it. But what should also be clear is that this lesson of the revolution confirmed Ranke in his understanding that the state, and its history, was the thread of what was unified or unifiable in modern life, and that divisive and heterogeneous social elements could have no active role in it. Indeed, his notice, in his political memoranda, of "the recent association of a social tendency with the concept of popular sovereignty" furnished him with a revealing reason for excluding the concept of popular sovereignty from the new constitutions: the infusion of the social tendency into the political concept "puts everything in doubt."[21]

His diary notes of the period, where obviously the factor of counterrevolutionary tactics did not come into play, demonstrated the conviction behind his social recommendations—that the social problem essentially was a matter of politics and could be interpreted therefore in the light of the main political theme of modern history. In these notes he deemed "a revolution of property" to be a potential "constitutional" act of popular sovereignty, and he associated this social revolution with the hegemony of the Prussian provinces over "the idea" of the Prussian state through the common political principle of one man-one vote. In general history he aligned "communist ideas" with the "political opposition'' which was connected with religion down through the seventeenth century, and he aligned it now, in the nineteenth, with the sequel of religion in history, "the idea of national sovereignty." But if Ranke thus saw the social problem to be contributory to the main theses of history, he saw the idea of the state, in its turn, to be at the very heart of it. For this idea "has its justification in the historical necessity from which it has come," and through this "historical right" it is rooted in "divine right," which is itself "that-which-has-become-historical" (*das Historisch-geworden-sein*).[22] This political confrontation therefore constituted for Ranke the primary theme of modern history, and he conceived both social and religious issues to be now ancillary to it.

Ranke's lecture courses during the revolutionary years reflected precisely the even balance of universal and national history which was appropriate to the modernized political version of his general theme in history. In this format he was explicit about the connection of his old and new themes, for in a course on contemporary history he argued that the origins of the present were to be found in the medieval struggle of nationalities toward a stable unity, and in this context he insisted that "the rival political tendencies of our own time have a historical root which bears them but also limits them."[23]

Consonant with the revolution's production of an incomplete unity, his interpretation of history in his teaching now took equal account of universal coherence and national individuality. Thus he justified his reversion to ancient history in general and Roman history in particular as an indirect way of doing universal history, appropriate to the present stage of this history. "Since a new world-historical movement has entered our globe," he said, "the most ancient things touch the most modern and are instructive for them. . . . We look both for world history, which we have wholly in mind, and for ancient history, which we mean to consider first." It was at this point, in a lecture of 1848, that he broached the idea to which he would recur later, when he would be blending universal and national history for publication—that the task of world history in its coherent sense was to trace the self-conscious idea of human unity itself in the history of the discrete nations. "It is almost the most important object of historical research to see how mankind's consciousness of its unity—the concept of humanity—was formed, developed, and spread. It is not that this concept of humanity destroys nationalities and distinctions, . . . but the existence of an individual modern nation cannot be conceived except in contact with general ideas. The chief task of world history is thus to present the origins of this spirit, which floats above all nations, and to present too its relationship to them."[24]

Nor did he shrink from open statements of the desired balance. "Only when we set ourselves to learn to know individual events . . . will we perceive the ideas [of humanity] in their entire fullness. On the other hand, only when we raise ourselves to a view of the whole can we hope to grasp the individual which in its principle and its life participates in the life of the whole. . . . To know and to understand world history is one of the greatest tasks of the human spirit. . . . It can come only from an understanding of all the parts." Under the aegis of revolution, then, Ranke revealed that his rehabilitation of particularity in history was now complementary rather than antithetical to his fixed faith in the general coherence of the human past. The balance in his historiography ran precisely parallel to the incomplete unity of his contemporary political experience, which conditioned it. He again identified the pursuit of world history with "the plan of God in the world," and although he still maintained that it was an unattainable ideal, it was no longer in principle but only on currently practical grounds that he thought it unattainable. "Let no one object that it is a part of divine knowledge for which we strive: divine knowledge is truth; all science strives for it. . . . The ideal is unattainable for the simple reason that the means for it are wanting."[25]

The major result of the revolution for Ranke's approach to history was thus the identification of the modern universal theme which gave historical substance to the unified life of the state and insured the magnetic attraction of the state for the significant life of humanity. This theme, a secularized expression of Ranke's habitual overbalanced duality, was the worldwide conflict between conservative monarchy and revolutionary democracy in which both sides had ineradicable historical roots but of which the predominance of monarchy was the teleological end, however illogical such a postulation was for him. "The convictions of men seem once more to favor the notion that the progressive development of the world is connected with monarchical institutions,'' he wrote about the fundamental conflict between these institutions and republican popular sovereignty.[26] His histories of the postrevolutionary period would make a central theme of modern dualism while their author yearned for the true universalism of its conservative resolution.

I   The decade following the revolution of 1848, like its predecessor of the 1830s, witnessed Ranke's ascent to the height of his productive powers. Once more he was able to find coherent historical expression for both the generalizing and the particularizing demands of his nature. He articulated a mix of universal theme and individual agent in a series of memorable historical works which, along with the *History of the Popes* and *German History in the Age of the Reformation,* gave most satisfaction to their author and have procured the highest rating, of all his publications, with posterity. In 1854 he delivered the series of private lectures "on the world-historical epochs of modern times" which was posthumously published as *On the Epochs of Modern History (Über die Epochen der neueren Geschichte)* and has been called one of the "basic works" (*Grundschriften*) of nineteenth-century German historiography.[27] In 1852 and 1859, respectively, he published the first volumes of his *French History, Especially in the Sixteenth and Seventeenth Centuries,* and of his *English History, Especially in the Seventeenth Century,* two of the rare national histories by an alien historian that have enjoyed general respect and an impressive longevity. Not only does the distribution of these two radically different kinds of historical works—off-the-cuff thematic lectures on universal history and precise, archivally researched narratives of national history—in the same period testify to the blend of disparate elements in Ranke's approach to history, but each type itself incorporated the amalgam. The mix was so fruitful because Ranke now had a substance for his historical universals and a form for his historical individuals that made them mutually complementary for the actuality of modern history and equally accessible to scientific historical method.

To pursue our concern with the meaning that history had for Ranke we must inquire into the role played by the conditions of the postrevolutionary period and by Ranke's reaction to them in his approach to the history he then wrote, and we must examine that history to define in the light of that experience the new stage of harmony he had reached in relating historical generality to historical particularity. Since this postrevolutionary period, like his last, also produced a rash of Ranke's most quotable and quoted propositions about history, our inquiry should contribute, as a byproduct, a contextual understanding of these historical maxims.

The first question to be asked, obviously, is: what part—if any—did the revolution and its results have in Ranke's decision to undertake the works he did during the decade that followed?

The answer is not quite so obvious. Not only the proposal of the lectures that eventuated in *On the Epochs of Modern History* but even the general scope and character of the lectures came not from Ranke but from King Maximilian II of Bavaria. The immediate occasion of it, moreover, was not politics but the king's previous offer of a professorship at the University of Munich, which Ranke rejected in 1853 and for which the king considered the lecture series to substitute. Insofar as the invitation took Ranke's own position into account, it referred rather to his long-established views than to any relevance of contemporary events. Ranke had just refused to give a semester-long series of public lectures at the University of Munich precisely because the format was "new and unusual," and the new invitation made explicit reference to Ranke's familiar "system"—known to the king presumably through his long acquaintance (since 1831) with the historian's lectures and conversations on modern history—as the expected basis of the newly proposed series. What is desired, wrote Wilhelm von Doenniges on the king's behalf, "is a short or compressed survey of the changing ideas in the various centuries of the history of the Christian era. . . . It must, if I understand the king aright, seem to be an extract from your system, so that the chief sections, the leading ideas and actions, predominate therein and the facts are added to them only for example and brief exposition."[28]

The venture into the national histories of France and England was Ranke's own idea, but to it too a long pedigree can be assigned. As far back as 1826 he accepted an offer to write a history of England for a series on the *History of the European States*

(*Europäische Staatengeschichte*), and although in the event the pressure of other scholarly commitments made it impossible for him to carry the project through, he had gone so far as to compose an outline for the book and he repeatedly expressed his "enthusiasm" at the prospect of it. The background of the French history is not so definite, but what there is of it also points to a long gestation. He had been invited to write the volume on France during the same year (1826), and despite having turned it down in favor of the English option he was still including "French studies" along with English and German some three years later in the range of history he contemplated working on. Certainly both France and England were integral parts of the original plan of 1825 for his own work "on the politics and state-administration of the European states" in the sixteenth and seventeenth centuries, and we have already noticed his claim that in 1843 only his feeling about the inadequacy of the sources kept him from writing a history of the revolution in France—a ground that assuredly did not hold for the early-modern period.[29] In his memoirs he would explicitly recall "falling back on the collections which I had made in Italy" and embarking on his French history for his old scholarly reason—because of "the conflict of the documentary reports with accepted opinions"—and as a withdrawal from "the unrest which I saw before my eyes."[30]

There is little doubt, then, that professional and scholarly links existed between the directions that Ranke's historical writing took in the 1850s and projects that antedated the circumstances of that decade and the persistent effects, therefore, of the prior revolution of 1848. Yet those circumstances and that revolution were necessary conditions of Ranke's decisions to undertake the historical projects in question during the decade in question, and it was in significant measure because he did undertake them during this decade that they assumed the character they did. Certainly Maximilian's offer of a Munich professorship and his proposal of the private lectures were grounded in the king's long-lived admiration of the historian's scholarship and in his ambition to make Bavaria a stonghold of the new scientific history, but the specific proposal of the lectures took the form it did because of more current royal concerns.

Maximilian had come to the throne amid the storms of March

1848, and his inauguration had lent new urgency to his unease with the divisions of his age, his uncertainty about their future, and his indecision about what he should do about them. From the time of the new king's accession, Ranke had tendered him a running stream of political advice, to keep him in their mutually held version of the trias idea that would elevate Bavaria to the status of moderator in the conflict between Austria and Prussia, and by 1853 Maximilian was broadening his request for counsel to the broader issues of the political and religious ideological rifts in western culture. In that year he had consulted with the aging philosopher Schelling on the future of ''world-shaking ideas,'' and his next step was to chart their projection by consulting Ranke about their direction from the past and present.[31]

As for the historian, it was noteworthy that he accepted the invitation in this format—private lectures to the king on leading themes in general history—after he had refused an academic forum. What made Ranke's role in the business even more positive was his decision to accept the invitation for himself when the king, fearing still another refusal, had requested only the recommendation of a Rankean student.[32] In a way Ranke was prepared for this situation in which he could adapt his history to the needs of his age. Early in 1852 Ranke had written to King Maximilian, with obvious reference to the postrevolutionary present, about ''the serious responsibility of history in times of religious and political divisions,'' and he spelled out this responsibility as a blend of scientific detachment and edificatory involvement that could only be realized on the heights of a universal history. ''In what does history's scientific vocation consist, but in not allowing itself to be captured by these divisions and yet not to lapse into indifference; to seek the truth . . . ; to recognize only the great and the worthy; never to neglect the eternal ideas which articulate the spiritual life of mankind. In history too the Holy [das Heilige], . . . should triumph over what is vulgar and evil.''[33] True to his word, Ranke's lectures to the king some two and a half years later mixed precept and analysis. The first was triggered by the turmoil of the period, the second by the knowledge of history in its long sweep from the distant past, and the bridge between the two by the universal themes that connected past and present. The initiative for such a history may not have been Ranke's own, but certainly it was congenial to him. "I have never," he wrote ecstatically to his wife in the midst of the lecture series, "enjoyed my history so wholeheartedly and completely as here." Soon after he had finished these lectures and the historical discussion with Maximilian which they instigated, Ranke made it very clear that this congenial history was a history infiltrated by the present and continuous with it. Announcing that "a dark peril hovers over Germany and Europe" and referring ominously to the prevalent "fear of a social convulsion," Ranke admitted to the king the intimate connection between these contemporary concerns and the kind of history they had recently shared: "I must confess for my own part that I have not thought through and worked out remote history as often as I have the part of history about which we last spoke."[34] And when, some eight years later, he delivered to the king a lecture on the contemporary situation that would serve as an epilogue to his previous lectures *On the Epochs of Modern History*, Ranke bluntly asserted the reciprocal interaction of past and present for the general historian: the persistence of the past in the present at once provided ordering principles from history for understanding that present and guided the historian from interest in the present to knowledge of the past. "The commotions which now convulse the world are not as confused as they seem at first glance: they are all joined to the past; the attention of the historian can even be stimulated by how the unresolved conflicts of the past centuries again rise before our eyes. . . . Everywhere the present is permeated by the struggles and oppositions of the past."[35]

Ranke's national histories of the period are noted for their paeans to historical objectivity, but curiously enough Ranke himself admitted the crucial role of the revolution in turning his attention to them. In this as in so many other points his reminiscences were inconsistent, a quality which often enough reflected his divided mind at the time being recollected. In apparent opposition to his remembered alignment of the French and English histories with his "falling back on" (*zurückgreifen*) ancient history, with the "resumption of the whole body of my historical studies," and "not so much with the events of the day," Ranke also recalled, with equal definiteness, the linkage of these same national histories (and also the last part of the *Prussian History,* completed in 1848) with these same revolutionary events of the day. ''The Revolution of 1848 introduced a new epoch. . . . Who could avoid participating in it with his whole soul? I steadfastly held out against every appeal to speak out. I felt it more important to bring to light the great historical phenomena that stemmed from the same kind of conflicts: the development of the Prussian state, the formation of French power, and finally the history of the seventeenth century in England.''[36]

What connected these two variant accounts of motivation for the national histories, just as for the lectures *On the Epochs of Modern History,* was the idea of universal history: it was an idea that stretched far back into Ranke's past and that was at the same time activated for modern times by the persistent results of the revolution. Despite their national content Ranke was insistent upon the universalism of his approach to these histories, and he was equally insistent on connecting this historical universalism with the great general political themes of his present: ''You know that I study all this not as the history of France, or of England, but as general European, as world history, in which one epoch joins on to the other,'' he wrote to his political confidant, von Manteuffel, as he was completing his *English History,* and he proceeded to develop a continuous survey from the seventeenth-century histories of England and France to the great conflict between liberalism and monarchy which he saw governing the current destinies of all Europe. Ranke concluded, moreover, with the admission that Manteuffel's reported political mission to Austria—besides Prussia, Ranke's other hope for defense of conservative monarchy in Europe—was the impetus for his excursion into universal history: ''You will notice that I consider your mission in the light of world history.''[37]

Nor was the connection merely retrospective. In the preface to the *French History* which he wrote in 1852, he stipulated that of the two kinds of history which ''great nations and states'' have, ''national'' and ''world-historical,'' his was of the second type, and he specified that what made it so was its concern with ''the general commotions'' which ''for a long time have arisen chiefly in France.''[38] Toward the end of the same decade he made an analogous connection during his research and in his preface for the *English History.* When he was doing research in England during 1857, he expressed his admiration of the Whig historian George

Babington Macaulay, especially for "the way in which he explains the present through the past," and he confessed his commitment to the same connection in its converse sense as well. "My studies have led me here to England, where I simultaneously try to elucidate the past from old papers and to get to know the present through the most various possible circles. Here, if anywhere, the one is explained by the other."[39] In the preface and introduction to the first volume of the *English History,* which he published some two years later, Ranke left no doubt that he was writing from the perspective of universal history and that this perspective was what made the interaction between the present and the past historiographically valid. Declaring his intention to write on English history in the epoch "which has had the most penetrating influence on the development of humanity," he characterized this history as "a world-dominating [*weltbeherrschende*] historical region," comparable to those "mountain masses by which the plains that are covered with human settlements are dominated." Ranke set his English account explicitly in that development of "universal history" (*Universalgeschichte*) which "relocated the political and spiritual life of the world" from the Mediterranean to the Atlantic and thereby made the western nations what they have been "ever since, the chief workshops of the general spirit of the human race—of its state-forming, idea-producing, nature-controlling activity." And he made it clear that the central strand of this universal activity in its English manifestation was the political theme that stretched continuously from the seventeenth century to the present. For it was in the seventeenth century that the parliamentary power triumphed in England and came into conflict with the absolute monarchy that had emerged during the same epoch in France. "Between these different tendencies, which comprehended opposite poles, European life has moved ever since."[40]

II But if Ranke's politicized theme of universal history admitted his present concerns into participation in the gestation of the history he wrote during the decade and a half after the revolution of 1848, this establishment of contemporary relevance only raises a further question. Since this was the very period in which he made some of his most famous, because categorical, pronouncements on the necessary objectivity of the historian, and since this was also the period in which he expressed himself most confidently about the compatibility of general and particular history, we must ask: What was the mental attitude that now permitted him to affirm positively relationships which had given him such trouble in the past? Because general history tended to be correlated for him at this stage with the connection of the present to the historical process, and particular history tended to be correlated with the historian's claim to methodical objectivity, a single attitude is involved in the two relationships. The question becomes: What was Ranke's attitude to his present, and to the factors of universal history which it contained, that made them reconcilable with his persisting affirmation of the historian's duty to write the objective history of individual formations?

The answer is that Ranke became vitally and constantly interested in the politics of this period and that his sense of its profound and essential divisions set the tone for his whole mental orientation, since they furnished a versatile prism for his general outlook and were accessible to historical extension. Depending on his angle of approach, he could see the conflicting parties as the complementary aspects of a fundamental unity in which everyone, including the historian, was involved, or as irreducibly plural and incommensurable entities which grounded the principle of individuality, including that of the historian. By and large, he tended to shift his angle on the divisions of his age from the first to the second of these approaches as the years moved him gradually away from the centripetal experience of the revolution. He gave expression to his unitary feeling for contemporary conflict in 1852, when he raised the question of "another revolution" coming from "dynamic France," and in this context he gave a constructive interpretation of Austro-Prussian dualism as the German form of common defense against "revolutionary storms": "It [the Austro-Prussian dualism] has something necessary about it.... The opposition is a fundamental factor in German life and, rightly understood, makes both states strong. What it weakens is the all too various kinds of friction in disputed areas . . .: unity lies in the higher political attitude. Alliance is not sameness or merger, but mutually recognized contrast" (*Gegensatz*).[41] That Ranke's notion of "necessary" existence related now rather to the pattern than to the facts of life was clear from his notebook entries of the same vintage. "The government of a state must command only what is necessary," he jotted down, "because then it touches God-on-earth." But this God-on-earth can be grasped "only through the moral world-order." For in the relationship of rules to life, "not everything is absorbed by the 'nature of the thing'" (*Sache*): required too is "the eternity and truth of ideas."[42]

From this perspective Ranke tended to take a thematic view of European and German politics: he stressed the connection of foreign with internal policy and interpreted both in terms of the polar schema he had developed from his revolutionary gloss on universal history. In 1852 he was still maintaining that "we wish to govern the old Europe through principles and forms." Moreover, he was still specifying these principles to be monarchy and the constitutional system based on national sovereignty, and he was still calling for their conjunction. "My doctrine is that it is necessary for both these tendencies, which cannot maintain themselves separately, to be united through the idea of the state."[43] In the Crimean crisis of the mid-50s he buttressed his advocacy of Prussian neutrality first by internalizing and polarizing Austrian policy into a preparation for "civil war in Germany" and then by simplifying the Franco-Austrian rapprochement into "a coalition between liberal and ultramontane tendencies"—"the two elements hostile to the independence of the German states because they try to subject these states to general political theories or spiritual powers." Thus "the present external conflict is also an internal one . . .: theory against theory, tendency against tendency."[44]

It was when he was looking at his political environment from this holistic set that Ranke was aware of the general connections between past and present. "I am astonished at how many echoes of the endeavors of our present age are to be found in the Reichstag records of the fifteenth century," he testified in proposing the analogical significance of his remote research, and he was even more conscious of relevance in his feeling for recent history. "It is an epoch," he wrote about the early-nineteenth-century revelations in the correspondence of Baron vom Stein, "which instructs us step by step, which enlightens and explains our point of view year by year. We were all 1805 constitutionalists. We see here the kind of spirit that learns from things. . . . Would that it were put into practice. And so does this spirit once more pass us by."[45]

But when he was convinced of the irresolubility of the current political conflicts—and he was increasingly so convinced as the 50s wore on into the 60s and the European, German, and internal rivalries all sharpened apace, each on its own level—Ranke tended to emphasize the ineluctable plurality of political things and to withdraw into his historical self as an independent individual outside them. A new tone became audible in his analyses of the implications of the Austro-Italian war between 1859 and 1861 and of the constitutional conflict in Prussia from the same period. Now he emphasized the centrifugal factors in the situation—the separation of the former liberal allies, France and England, with France now representing militarism and England democracy; the rivalry of France and Austria as "the two great military monarchies in the world"; Prussia's vacillation among her sympathy for Austria, her external tendency toward a French alliance, and her internal tendency toward the emulation of England to the despite of her own army.

Hence the lecture on contemporary history which he presented to King Maximilian in 1862 had a much more multiform and open-ended cast to it than the previous decade's historical series which it presumably continued. He still focused on the connection of past and present conflict as the hallmark of the contemporary age, but now he saw this conflict as an ultimate expression of diversity rather than as two sides of a unified theme. "Men try to sum up their conflict under the fashionable concepts of progress or regress, liberalism and absolutism," he said in deprecatory terms that applied to his own recent counterrevolutionary self as much as to others, "but these are much too narrow. Everywhere there are vital forces which struggle with one another." And he went on to summarize the general history of Europe since 1830 in a narrative of events that highlighted the internal limits and varieties of the partisans in the main liberal-conservative rivalry. He concluded by acknowledging that the liberal powers (England and France) "have put their stamp on the world's dominant movements," but he followed this acknowledgment with the countervailing recognition in general of persistent and "inherent fundamental differences" that "maintain the world's balance of power" and, in the particular Prussian case, of the incompatibility of constitutionalism with "the principle which the state may not give up if it wishes to continue to exist" (i.e., "the military autonomy of the Crown").[46]

Small wonder that he drew from such a picture the general inference that "our vacillation is not simply personal but lies deep in the situation itself." He tended now to conclude either with an unanswered question—"Will a power be formed here which strikes a direction appropriate to our general and particular [i.e., European and domestic] interests?"—or with a recommendation to avoid conflict by withdrawal. "My advice to him" (King Maximilian II of Bavaria), he summarized, "was always to keep away from the opposed tendencies . . . and govern his country well."[47]

More important, Ranke applied the same conclusion to himself as an historian from the same present premises. Looking about him in 1862, he observed not only that "the present world presents the sight of a polarity of historical ideas" but that the polarized ideas varied with the different states, and from this variety he culled the lesson of detachment: "Is it not advisable not to get passionate about it? Not to accept one system for all instances?" And a little later he spelled out the meaning of these rhetorical questions unmistakably: "We have fallen into a period when the great oppositions in which the age and the century move touch and oppress everyone, whoever he is. In this situation one must see only to his own self; then the rest becomes rather indifferent." Nor did he withhold the assumption of ultimate disharmony that was at the basis of this retreat. "Whatever one may do, one will never reconcile opinions: there is nothing for it but to go one's own way and do what one holds to be right."[48] He explicitly aligned this irreducible multiplicity of political forces and consequent detachment of the historian, moreover, with the particularistic fragmentation of the historical process. "Who would want to say at every point what is right and what is wrong?" he asked after insisting on the ubiquitous variety of history's competing vital forces, and, consistently with his titling his lecture "A Moment of Time," he went on: "If one indulges one's sympathies one would only obscure one's perception. Our purpose can only be to understand the age, to apprehend the countenance of the passing moment, the today which will no longer be such tomorrow but which will have produced that which then is."[49]

Now these two attitudes toward the political constellation of his present age—one that entailed universal history as its luminous unitary root and the other that excluded the historian from any efficacy in the present because the multiplicity of history merely repeated the multiplicity of politics—manifested not so much an essential change in Ranke's mentality as a shift in the approach to the same conception induced by the different light thrown on it by moving circumstances. The shift from the unitary to the pluralistic emphasis may have been important in itself for the preparation of the intellectual need that would be filled by Ranke's final synthesis following the German unification of 1871, but for Ranke's ideas about history and for the history that he wrote in the period between the revolution and the unification its importance was only to reveal patently the inherent ambivalence of his views about his postrevolutionary world. Within the same lecture of 1862 and in reference to the same historically conditioned, contemporary situation, for example, he could emphasize the infinite variety of the "vital forces which struggle with one another everywhere" or the homogeneity of "the great antagonism in which the world is caught up," depending on whether he was arguing in his detached or his committed role.[50]

Hence what he said, during this whole period between the revolution and the unification, about the relationship of history to the contemporary political world always applied to but one of the aspects he recognized in this world, and this relationship should always be qualified by the subliminal effect of the other aspect. When taken in this qualified sense, Ranke's statements on historical objectivity which resound throughout the period acquire a new meaning. Through the mediation of an ambivalent present which both contained and shunned universal history, Ranke's assertions of historiographical detachment and objectivity became as applicable now to universal history as they ever had been to the particular facts of critical history, and therewith universal history achieved scientific respectability for him. For though Ranke thought of the connection of history with the present and its detachment from the present alternatively, he thought of the relationship between universal and individual history conjunctively. The two apparently opposite modes of thought were themselves connected: it was because Ranke's intermittent stance of detachment was itself a reaction to his present and to this extent a function of that present that the relationship between historical detachment, with its implications for individuality in history, and historical involvement, with its implications for universality in history, could, as the relationship between two functions of his present situation, take the historiographical form of the complementarity of individual and universal history. Consequently, the standards possible for individual history could now hold for universal history as well.

Thus almost every one of Ranke's arguments for historical objectivity in this period can be countered by another in the same context for historical involvement. Because they were in the same context, the explanation of the apparent discrepancy is not a change of mind or perspective but rather the Janus-faced role of universal history as common denominator. In two letters which Ranke wrote to the same recipient—Franz Pfistermeister, Frederick William IV's secretary—within the span of three weeks, Ranke advocated both points of the apparent disjunction. He recommended the collection of historical documents because it "would not only be of historical importance but also offer a certain political interest" based on Ranke's own admitted experience of the "similarities" between past and present. At the same time he warned against "the danger ... in the close relationship of historical to political questions," advising the dedication of the planned *Historische Zeitschrift* to the "historical motif" in contradistinction to the political. Relevant to this apparent discrepancy was Ranke's immediately adjoined counsel that the scope of the *Historische Zeitschrift* in the field of modern history should extend beyond Germany and be comprehensive, thus equipping the quality of universality with the capacity both to involve past knowledge with present political concerns and to detach past knowledge from present political concerns.[51]

Analogously, in the same letter to his student the historian Georg Waitz, during the troubled year of 1863, Ranke both hoped "not to be touched by public affairs," since "studies follow their own principle and arm the soul against the influences of the moment," and proposed "a meeting of impartial men, knowledgeable in the past as well as in the present, to consider how the miseries of our fatherland are to be overcome."[52] Again, the apparent divergence of the propositions obscured their common denominator of an iridescent contemporary situation whose universal issue—monarchy versus revolution—in one light invited participation in its resolution and in another discouraged participation because of the fragmentation of its national and intraconservative divisions.

Ranke's position on the involvement of the historian thus vacillated with the shifts of his perspective from the universal confrontation which engaged all men and the multifarious particularism of the several parties which stimulated only the detached study of their historical roots and analogues.[53] For his attitude to history, his vacillation was less important than the approach to his own age that made it psychically tolerable—than, that is, his dialectical insight into the compatibility of universality in theme and individuality in the theme's disputants for contemporary history.

III For the rationale of this connection between Ranke's self-abnegatory assertions of historical objectivity and his present-minded involvement in universal history we must look, in this postrevolutionary period, to the historical works in which he displayed both. Of these, the general lectures which were posthumously published under the title *On the Epochs of Modern History* are especially appropriate, for here he espoused both positions categorically and simultaneously, thereby exposing the grounds of their compatibility with explicit clarity. The national histories which he wrote during this era incorporated the same positions and the same problem of concordance in a more subtle and more professionalized form. These we shall reserve for separate consideration (see chapter 11 below).

On the Epochs of Modern History leaves little doubt of Ranke's commitment to both sides of what are usually considered historiographical alternatives. These lectures have become most famous, indeed, for their epigrammatic restatement of the historicist focus on unique individuality and particularistic incoherence which he first formulated in the analogous postrevolutionary years of the 1830s. Three points along this line are associated with *On the Epochs:* the argument for the equivalence and incommensurability of the various ages of history and against the idea of progress between the ages; the related argument for "dominant tendencies" rather than "dominant ideas" within each age; and the inference of historical objectivity which Ranke himself drew from these arguments. Ranke's expression for the ultimate individuality of each historical era and for the historian's consequent obligation to lend himself wholly to its values is one of the two best-known descriptions in the Rankean canon: "Each age is immediate to God, and its value depends not on what comes out of it but in its own existence, in its very self. Therewith the consideration of history, and especially of individual life in history, gets its entirely distinctive charm, since by it every epoch must be viewed as something valuable in itself and as entirely worthy of consideration. The historian has thus to direct his main attention in the first instance to how men have thought and lived in a certain period, and then he will find that apart from certain unchangeable and eternal main ideas—for example the moral—every epoch has its particular tendency and its own ideal. . . . All generations of mankind appear equally justified before God, and so too must the historian regard the matter."[54]

The argument against progress in history was the counterpart of this stress on historical discontinuity: Ranke rejected the idea both in its version of "a universal controlling will," which promoted the development of humanity from above, and its version of "a trait of human spiritual nature," which impelled affairs to an inevitable end from within—because in either version the idea abridged man's actual freedom to create at any moment in time, because it violated the integrity of each historical era by imposing the standards of a successor upon it, and because the historical record gave no evidentiary support to the idea of progress. Ranke left no doubt that his denial of progress was in the service of his principle of individuality. He admitted progress "in the realm of material interests" and he admitted "an extensive progress" in quantitative diffusion "in the moral realm," but he rejected progress in the "moral respect" that mattered to him most—the morality that comprehended "the productions of genius in art, poetry, science, and state—because "moral force always depends on individuality and individual development" (*Ausbildung*).[55] Thus for Ranke the equivalent individuality of each epoch in human history was bound up with the spontaneous individuality of the spiritual events that gave each age its historical character.

Ranke's argument for "dominant tendencies" was obviously designed to bring universal history into line with this doctrine of objectivistic individuality. "The chief object of history," wrote Ranke in this context, "is to analyze the large-scale tendencies of the centuries and to unroll the large-scale history of humanity, which is precisely the complex of these various tendencies." These tendencies form such an undefinable complex because they differ with different ages and are so particularly and empirically conditioned that "they can only be described but cannot in the last instance be summed up in a concept." It is precisely because an "idea" can "have a life of its own" spanning the individual productions of men, whereas a "tendency" is "always a definite particular direction which predominates and causes other tendencies to recede," that "dominant tendencies" rather than "dominant ideas" are the proper objects of history. The relationship among these dominant tendencies of the various ages—the relationship which constitutes the history of humanity—is therefore not a linear or developmental progress but what we might call a varietal progress, that is, the progressive revelation of the separate but equal strands of man's multifarious activity which rotates around an undiscoverable axis. "[Authentic] progress depends on the expression in each period of a certain movement of the human spirit which emphasizes now one and now the other tendency and manifests itself in this tendency distinctively. . . . From the standpoint of the divine idea, if I may dare to take it, I can only think that humanity contains within itself an infinite variety of developments which appear one by one, in accordance with laws which are unknown to us and are more mysterious, vaster than one usually thinks, and far removed from any end."[56]

Consistent with this individualized, panoramic view of history, Ranke made an explicit point of the historian's necessary objectivity in his approach to it. During the discussion following the introductory lecture in which he expounded this view of history, he was driven by the persistent questioning of King Maximilian to concede the "probability" of "inner moral progress" in the presumptive adoption of "the idea of humanity" by all mankind and the "religious necessity" of thinking Christianity destined to become the "universal religion," but Ranke insisted that he could speak so as a man and as a Christian but not as a historian. These ideas of moral and religious progress can neither be "proved by history" nor be made "the principle of history." "Our task is to adhere only to the object" (*uns bloss an das Objekt zu halten*).[57] Presumably Ranke himself was not satisfied with this casual distinction between the man and the historian, for in a letter to the king some five years later he recalled the discussion and developed his view of historical objectivity and its limits in the somewhat different terms of distinguishing between the past on the one side and the present and future on the other. Reaffirming his position that "the historian must strive for objectivity" regardless of "personal limitation" and that "the ideal of historical training would consist in making the Subject able to make itself purely into an organ of the Object, that is, of science itself, without being hindered by the natural or fortuitous limits of human existence from recognizing and presenting the complete truth," Ranke now admitted the claims of subjectivity not as a matter of personal belief versus historical evidence but as a matter of time dimensions that did not entail the past, even if such subjective judgments were made by a historian. "But when one must, as Your Majesty commands, express his opinion about things of the present or the future, then must subjectivity once more come into the foreground."[58]

Ranke's acknowledgment of his own pliability in the face of royal importunities reveals the temperamental side of his apparently inconsistent concessions to a belief in integrated human progress, but the form of it indicates a more fundamental unease with the implications of his theoretical statements on the negative relationship between past and present in history. It would have been odd, indeed, had Ranke committed himself wholly to the antiprogressive position which he now asserted so decisively in theory, for, as we have seen,[59] during the 30s and 40s he had been equally bent on asserting the opposite—that is, on asserting the continuity of human progress in general history. It should not be too surprising, then, to find a certain consistency among the different vintages of lectures on general history and to discern a progressivism in the substantive lectures *On the Epochs of Modern History* that is reminiscent of the commitment to progress in the cognate lectures of the past. What requires explanation is not the apparently incongruous concessions to progress in the substantive sections of *On the Epochs of Modern History*, for Ranke had been thinking in these terms for a long time. What requires explanation, rather, is the sudden emergence of a categorical antiprogressivism that had been previously subdued.

Two reasons can be adduced for this emergence. First, within theory itself an occasion had arisen for Ranke to develop his arguments against the philosophical ideas of progress, arguments which he had adumbrated just after the revolution of 1830. Second, the conversion of his experience of the revolution of 1848 into contemporary history altered his approach to the continuous historical process in which the contemporary age marked the last period. The first of these reasons, relevant to Ranke's theoretical postulates, should be discussed now, in the context of the introduction of *On the Epochs of Modern History*. The second, which is relevant to Ranke's substantive view of general history and reveals the actual balance and compatibility of his antiprogressive and progressive stances, should have its discussion reserved until after the depiction of the historical process which it helps to explain.

As was so often the case with Ranke's doctrinal pronouncements on the nature of history, his programmatic assertions of individuality and objectivity during the 50s assumed a particular reference which invalidated their literal application to the general history that he actually composed. These pronouncements were segregated in a conceptual prolegomenon to his historical lectures and in the principled discussions that he held with King Maximilian at the beginning and at the end of the series; and they pertained more to Ranke's formal refutation of the philosophical ideas of an inevitable and teleological progress imposed on world history by contemporary metaphysical idealism than to the structure of his history itself.

These theoretical discussions which framed *On the Epochs of Modern History* emerged indeed from the last of Ranke's direct confrontations with his era's philosophies of history. The historian was now particularly troubled by the apparent susceptibility of King Maximilian, his friend and political counselee, to the later Schelling's "positive philosophy" because this philosophy did not actually make its claimed transition from knowledge to being and carried "categories of reason" over into areas which, like history, are "beyond reason"; because it imposed on human history the progressive pattern of God's existential self-development to the ultimate union of the universe with the will of God; because it assigned "the monarch" the task of making the state into a means for the realization of the "kingdom of God"; and because this perspective of Schelling's was a mere "individual insight," without general validity and commanding no consensus.[60] So Ranke now closed out Schelling just as he had closed out Hegel twenty years earlier, dredging up an analogous theory to meet an analogous challenge—that is, asserting the autonomous plurality of history against the imposition of an alien and a priori unity.

But implicitly, unacknowledgedly, osmotically, Ranke absorbed into the structure of his history something of the progressive coherence he denied in principle. Whether because Schelling's was the most recent and therefore the most dangerous of the philosophical threats to the independence of history or because it was the most emphatically theosophical and eschatological, it was rather in the Hegelian than in the Schellingian form that the continuity of universal process crept ever more insistently into Ranke's historical work from the 1850s onward. This is not to say that Ranke consciously changed his views on Hegel—he still endorsed, en passant, a contemporary's view of Hegel as a philosopher who started from the wrong point of departure and "developed himself into a kind of anti-Christ"—but, as the cases of even such notorious Hegel baiters as Kierkegaard and Nietzsche show, nineteenth-century culture's commitment to both individuality and its transcendence was so strong that the Hegelian mode of connecting them ultimately infiltrated even those who overtly rejected him.[61] Since this was true of so many who remained hostile to Hegel, it applied all the more to someone like Ranke, whose increasingly benign neglect of the philosopher was signalized by the historian's relieved remark, at the very time that he was taking note of Schelling's new phase, that even in its practical application the Hegelian system was "outworn."[62]

Hence the pluralistic theory in Ranke's theoretical prolegomena and glosses for *On the Epochs of Modern History* should be interpreted in the light of the monistic structure internal to the history itself. When it is viewed in this light, indeed, even the theory can be seen to contain qualifications, otherwise obscure, which confirm such a reinterpretation. For Ranke left hints in the theoretical statements themselves which betrayed his belief in a progressive connection between the ages leading to the present, with this connection defined negatively as something that was not the closed and logically conceivable process postulated by the philosophers and that was culturally limited to the western—i.e., Romano-Germanic—community about which he wrote. Thus when he declared the idea of progress to be "inapplicable to the connection of the centuries in general," he hastened to stipulate the specific reference for which he designed this principle by adding immediately that "this means: one should not be able to say that one century is ancillary [*dienstbar*] to another."[63]

Again, according to the original stenograph of the relevant doctrinal exposition, Ranke added a significant qualification to his statement on the immediacy and inherent value of each epoch to God which was separated from it in the famous version of the published transcript. "Each epoch is immediate to God," reads the declaration in its original format," and its value depends not on what comes out of it but in its own existence, in its very self, but this does not exclude that something different comes out of it." And he followed up this qualification with the prescription that the second task of the historian—the first is to determine the distinctive way men lived and thought in a particular period—is "to observe the difference between successive epochs and to treat the internal necessity of the succession without directly asserting that the latter ages lead the earlier in all branches of human activity. It is natural, however, that where one epoch produced something good, something good issued from it into other epochs. Progress cannot be denied, but I should not like to say that it moves in a straight line. It is rather more like a stream which makes its own course in its own way."[64] Nor did Ranke fail to specify that this kind of progressive connection linked past and present for the western culture that was his historical concern. For he made this connection categorically in the same letter which contained his equally categorical distinction between the necessity of the historian's objectivity toward the past and the permissibility of his own subjectivity toward the present and future. "Hitherto spiritual development has always progressed in the western nations, despite the greatest hindrances—why should it not still continue?'' he wrote, pulling together in one context what he had put asunder in another. And then, as if to specify this different, open-ended context, he added: "For the end is still far from attainment and the spiritual path perhaps infinite."[65]

Thus the distinctiveness of the dominant tendencies in each age, the equivalent independence of historical periods from one another, and the unreserved investment of the historian in the past object were all designed to avoid the *subordination* of the past to the present and the future; they were not designed to adumbrate a history in which there was no *connection* between the past and the present/future. Yet these indefinite theoretical principles bore a relation to the definite general history they introduced. Once more we are faced with the necessity of getting behind the philosophically distorted literal references of Ranke's language to a more authentic meaning of his principles for his history. For what seems at first view a blatant contradiction between the pluralistic principles he espoused and the coherent history he wrote, turns out, upon examination, to be a reasonable relationship between his generalizations about history and the perspective he had reached on the actual process of universal history. Hence the reexamination of the relationship is most appropriately done in terms of the pattern of universal history to be found in his substantive lectures *On the Epochs of Modern History*.

Three basic patterns in the structure of *On the Epochs* were pertinent to the general historical propositions which prefaced it as its "main concepts" (*Hauptbegriffe*): it explicitly postulated the coherence of past and present in the culture of the west; it repeatedly asserted the unifying theme of dualistic struggle for monistic domination as the constant sinew of universal history, linking past and present; and it identified the contemporary conflict of monarchy and popular sovereignty as the present version of the homologous past conflict between church and state.

1. In framing his lectures, Ranke hit upon a simple device that enabled him to move freely back and forth among the centuries of western history, including his very own present, without violating his principle of individuality: he merely conceived all the centuries from the ancient Romans to his own times to be a single period, defined precisely by the historical homogeneity between past and present. Thus at the very start he justified beginning with ancient

Rome because it was included in "our era," in contrast to "a wholly remote age" which "exercises only an indirect influence on our present" and "would lead to alien things." He did not hesitate to make direct connections between the Roman centuries and his own. He concluded that the German tribal invasions of the late Roman Empire produced, "through the mixture of Germanic and Roman elements, a new world for itself on which the whole development of our own conditions down to contemporary times rests." This meeting of Roman state and German kingship, moreover, produced not only the common basis of the contemporary age but also the basic principles of its conflict. For the Roman idea stood for centralized administration and the Germanic idea for aristocratic personality, and "all this is joined to the present age. The tendency of the present age is to do away with personality and to reestablish the absolute state, which operates automatically. There is here something analogous to the old Roman state, as the resistance to it is to the Germanic state.... If the general ideas of the state would attain complete dominance in Germany so that nothing remained of personality and heredity, it would lead to the republic and later to communism. If, on the other hand, the Germanic state would develop so far that personal rights were everything, then public affairs would become the common property of private individuals.... These two ideas constituted the conflict. Between both these things one lives now."[66] If, as Ranke always claimed, a knowledge of history illuminated the understanding of the present, these explicit invocations of his own age in his consideration of the Roman past show that his postrevolutionary understanding of the present clarified his organization of his historical knowledge.

2. As the Roman example indicates, the constant thread that ran from the structure of the ancient age through to the structure of Ranke's contemporary period was the pulsating alternation of affirmed unity and the duel of polarized parties for a reaffirmed unity. There is little doubt that the medium for this continuous structure of the human past and present was what Ranke thought of as universal history. He described his experience in delivering the lectures in terms consonant with his earlier visions of such history: he referred to them as "my rhapsodies" and, as if to stress the generality of his survey, boasted that "I have not the trace of a

book by me.''⁶⁷ The lectures themselves were apparently more discursive and illustrative than the tightening of the ultimately published transcript has led posterity to realize, but still Ranke was held to the general consideration of dominant tendencies even in his original delivery not only by the dogged persistence of his royal audience but more importantly by the substantive universality of the historical tendencies he discerned. For though he found the recurrent hegemonial unities in western culture preceded and succeeded just as recurrently by the profound divisions of contending elements, he viewed these divisions themselves holistically, both because the opposing elements themselves added up to a unity and because through a historical synecdoche each of the opposing elements aspired to hegemonial unity. Thus ''the chief event'' of the first century A.D. was the unification of the oriental-Greek with Latin culture in the west. This ''immense unity'' then ''dissolved into two halves, one Greek and the other Latin. Yet the whole was still a unity.'' Next, during the early age of the Roman Empire, ''one meets the phenomenon that something general [*das Allgemeine*] gradually develops from the particular [*dem Partikulären*],'' thereby creating ''an unprecedentedly great unity.'' But the Romans themselves could not ''propagate the world-historical ideas and culture which had developed in the Roman Empire,'' and ''if we place ourselves at the world-historical point of view,'' the victorious struggle of the Germans in the west and the Arabs in the east with the Romans produced the ''marvelous global concatenation [*Weltverkettung*] that diffused the Roman achievements. Through the Germans, especially, ''the Christian world-religion first became the religion of all nations,'' and the German kingship, which began as the party representing personality and heredity against the Roman idea of the state, subsequently ''allied itself with the Roman ideas of constitution and administration,'' so that ''both principles are united in German kingship.''⁶⁸

The next age—the age of medieval Europe—manifested the same pattern of unity through division even more explicitly, since the pattern here was fleshed out in the bidirectional relations of the worldly and spiritual powers. First, in the Carolingian period ''a tight union between pope and kingdom, between the worldly and the spiritual power'' created ''a different world in the west.

Everything was united, but in twofold leadership, spiritual and worldly. . . . In unity there remained division." This unidualism eventuated, characteristically, in the resolution of its inherent tension through the monolithic triumph of the papacy. Although the papacy thus achieved its domination not by a linear "development" but "by conflict and warfare," it organized rivalry into hierarchy and established a unity that was total. Now the spiritual principle prevailed over worldly relationships. . . . This unification of religion and dominion, of priesthood and knighthood, of poetry and art formed a splendid but oppressive whole, articulated like a Gothic cathedral, at whose head the high priest stood and governed all." It was in the context of this triumph, moreover, that Ranke asserted the essential unity of western culture: "One of the grandest ideas that I have thought to myself . . . is that the complex of the Christian nations of Europe is to be considered as one whole—as one state as it were."[69]

But equally characteristic was the decomposition of this unity. "It lay in the nature of the thing that a different epoch followed upon this hierarchical one." It was an epoch (comprising the fourteenth and fifteenth centuries) of "general dissolution," brought on by the separation of the Germanic from the Roman components of "the European community," the assertion of independence by "the worldly power," and the disruption of papal hegemony, "which was based on unity," by "the opposition of the various nationalities." This age of "general decentralization," of "chaos," was itself then resolved into the bipartite period of Protestant versus Catholic religious politics, grounded in the twin development of territorial sovereignty and of religious reform. The limits upon the Protestant drive for unified dominion over the Christian world of the west ultimately made not merely for duality but for multiplicity, for these limits included both internal Protestant divisiveness and opposition by the several Catholic sovereigns. Hence the climax of the Reformation era was the disorder of the Thirty Years' War, and there followed the inauguration of a new era—that of the "great powers"—in which "the human spirit" again took a new turn, this time toward the secular organization of life on the basis of "a great territory."[70]

But however new literally, the century of the great secular powers (covering from the middle of the seventeenth to the middle

of the eighteenth century) had, in Ranke's presentation, a structure hardly different in kind from the other periods of world
history. For it too demonstrated elements of unity, duality, and
multiplicity, and although Ranke did not make a point of their
linkage he presented them as a historical succession. The France
of Louis XIV epitomized "the old Romano-Germanic state, but in
completely monarchical form." Then, with the revolution of
1688, "a wholly different principle"—the parliamentary—attained to power in England and constituted the only significant
opposition to the monarchical principle in France. Finally, the
growth of the other three great powers—Russia, Austria, and
Prussia—between the end of the seventeenth century and the
middle of the eighteenth loosened this system into the constellation of "five independent powers which were all based on
somewhat different principles. . . . In this epoch they were never
united; they always moved autonomously in accordance with their
own inner drive, for this is the nature of a great power."[71] At this
stage Ranke had caught up to the individualized conception of the
historical modern states which he had expounded during the 30s,
and it was a signal indication of the development in his synthetic
approach to history that he now transcended this conception by
appending his unified idea of contemporary history to it. He no
longer hypostatized the several great powers to be ultimate
individualities, but rather, in line with the whole pattern of his
lectures, made them another in the repeated uncrystallized pre-
ludes to unification in history. "But this was not yet the last word
of world history," he now wrote in concluding his section on the
great powers. "There still came the age in which we live—the
eighth, the revolutionary, age."[72]

3. Having thus integrated his contemporary times into history as
the revolutionary age, Ranke identified in this age the universal
historical theme that could serve him as the secular substantive
successor to the Christianity of the medieval and Reformation eras.
It was, moreover, in the context of this universal discovery that
Ranke affirmed a notion of ecumenical spiritual progress transcending the limits which his alternative pluralized approach to
history had placed upon it. The circumstances in which he
announced this discovery indicated that universalism had become
for him an optional perspective on all history rather than a limited

interpretation of specific themes dominating definite periods within history. For his announcement came not in the lecture itself but in the discussion following his lecture on contemporary history, and there was a perceptible difference in approach to the same material between the discursive style of the lecture and the general inference which Ranke drew from it in response to questions about "the dominant tendency" it implied. According to the lecture, the revolutionary principle of popular sovereignty was born outside the European orbit, in America, and when the "opposition of principles" represented by the American war against Britain was imported into Europe with the French Revolution of 1789, it had the effect not of polarizing but of refracting the European scene into a spectrum of several political principles, each associated with its own individual nation. But even here Ranke implied his belief in a rational order of things at least as a historically based possibility, when he adjudged this contemporary polymorphous situation to be "a frightful ferment" of "principles acting, reacting, and agitating against one another" and when he concluded with a projection of this implied standard, supported by the unitary pattern in the whole of his previous lectures, into the future: "But this [ferment] is not the final word, because everything is based on the profound ground of European history. So it can perhaps be believed that there will again be rational construction out of the past, where rational conditions have ever emerged from the greatest agitations and perils."[73]

But then, in response to the urgent request by Maximilian for the formulation of "the dominant tendency of our century," Ranke shifted his point of view and relocated his unitary projection from the future into the historical present. He now exalted "the confrontation of the two principles, monarchy and popular sovereignty," to the status of a dominant tendency "around which all other oppositions cluster," and he aligned this parent confrontation with "the infinite development of material forces and the very versatile development of the natural sciences" as the motor of the "boundless progress" in which "the human spirit is engaged." Having generalized his contemporary political duality by cultural association, Ranke proceeded to identify it as the equivalent successor of Christian universalism. He took up once more his stipulation of a historical place for such a successor—"the Romano-

Germanic spirit transcends the form of the church and, free and un-confined, diffuses itself as culture throughout the whole world''[74] —and explicitly named the political theme of the revolutionary era as the church's worthy replacement. "Just as the struggle between the spiritual and the worldly power contributed so much to the development of European Christianity, so is this also the case with the present struggle between monarchy and national sovereignty.'' Not only did he see the contemporary political struggle, just as he had the older ecclesiastical conflict, in general terms as the embodiment of *''a* mighty movement, *a* great life force,'' but he went beyond this aggregative parallel to discern in both the religious and political polarities alike the capability for a genuine reconciliation of opposites that would at once unify and preserve them. "On the opposition of the particular and general [*des Besonderen und Allgemeinen*] all European history is based,'' he declared in a penultimate context, and he went on to assign to the church in medieval times and to the prince in contemporary times the homologous mission of mediating between the particular rights of personality and the general idea of political sovereignty.[75]

This distinctive character of the universal structure that Ranke discovered in history helps to explain how his acknowledgment of a coherent world history that included the historian's present age could be congruent with his apparently inconsistent limitation of authentic history to an objective perception of a discontinuous past. That this combination, which he confronted directly in his later letter to King Maximilian,[76] was no fluke was indicated by his similar juxtaposition of two apparently conflicting ideas of progress in the concluding discussion of the lectures themselves. On the one hand, he saluted the "enormous force'' unleashed by both the popular revolutionary and the monarchical counterrevolutionary movements, acknowledged it to be "entirely unprecedented''— "the earlier world had no idea of all these things''—and ac-counted it to the infinite progress of the human spirit. Whereas he had used the parochical scope of western—i.e., Romano-Germanic —progress vis-à-vis the "barbarization'' of the eastern cultures in the Middle Ages as an argument against "the general progress of the human race,'' he argued for this general progress when he came to the contemporary era precisely because of the "subjuga-tion of all the other elements that are in the world by the spirit of western Christianity''—that is, by "the Romano-Germanic spirit.'' But, as if to demonstrate that this position represented a perspective rather than a supersession, Ranke was careful to follow this admission of a new "progress in humanity" with a repetition of his principled rejection of progress in morality and intelligence because both were rooted in "personality" and hence were randomly individualized in their historical appearances.[77]

Ranke's association here of historical discontinuity and individuality with personality affords the key to the countervailing role of continuity and generality in his approach to history. For personality, as we have seen, was for him the characteristic expression of the principle of particularity throughout western history, and his invocation of it in his argument against progress emphasizes all the more the function of generality in his argument for progress. The human progress registered in the contemporary age consisted, for him, precisely in the generalization of the Romano-Germanic spirit—that is, in the development of the western tendency to "world domination" from a medieval idea to a current reality—and this progress was driven by the universal cultural and political themes within Romano-Germanic history, thus effecting at long last a union of the coherent and extensive meanings of universal history.

With this union the universal theme of Ranke's Romano-Germanic culture became coextensive with the theme of human history as such, and Ranke's attribution of continuity to this theme, manifested in his endorsement of its progress, posited a common historical humanity which opened his own way to the integral understanding of the past. The political duality of his own age gave him the clue to the structural duality in all of western history, and since this universal theme of duality consisted entirely in the dialectical relationship between the particular and the general, it was precisely the continuity of this theme from the past into the present that made possible the historian's access to the autonomous personalities of particular men and ages in the past which must otherwise lie beyond his own individuality. Ranke's new vociferous assurance about the historian's objectivity in his approach to an individualized past was thus predicated on its unspoken connection with an actual historical theme which linked him to that past via a single process. Individuality and continuity or objectivity and involvement, like spiritual and worldly power or monarchy and national sovereignty, were antitheses that were indispensable to each other.

Perhaps it was because he had left his attitude toward progress so duplicit and the relationship of progress to the other fundamental issues of history so unresolved in these lectures to King Maximilian that Ranke returned to the problem in the very next year (1855) and devoted a special lecture in his course on medieval history to "The Concept of Progress in History." Here he repeated the arguments for and against progress which he had made the previous year—i.e., acknowledging progress as the extension of religion, morality, and good literary form and denying both uniform and intensive progress—but whereas in the earlier format he had grudgingly admitted the modicum of progress as an inessential qualification of his primarily antiprogressive position and had connected the concept with no important historical principle, he now posed the positive and negative sides of progress as an equilibrium and related it to the more fundamental issue of coherence in history. "But should this concept, which gives an inner impetus to life and a satisfaction to the generations of man, be rejected in general?" he asked, and the whole tone of his discussion was to negate the negation.[78]

What rehabilitated progress for Ranke in this context was his definition of it in terms of its distinction from other kinds of connection, with which it could be combined, rather than in terms of its distinction from individuality, to which it must in principle be ever antithetical. Thus what he set up against the progressive connection, defined as the kind of connection whose unity lies in the end toward which things move—that is, in the gradual construction of the present—was the more generic historical connection which contains both the progressive movements and "the future-building forces stemming from the past." This generic connection, then, is itself "a great movement of world-historical development which can be grasped only in its general outlines. To grasp it, one must take his stand not in the present moment, but over all. All ages together constitute historical humanity."[79]

When he repeated now that "each generation stands in an immediate relationship to God and has its value in its own existence,'' this famous celebration of historical equivalence was in the service not only of individual variety but also of a generic connectedness that was more than progress but included it. Within each period, ''the attitude of minds is what constitutes the harmony of the world at every moment; therein everything is connected and is mutually conditioning.'' Across the periods, ''all things are permeated with a common movement which constitutes the unbroken connection. What endures—that which is exalted above all ages—and the progress that goes through the ages are in continuous contact and constitute each age. In their succession there lies, if not an unconditional necessity, at least an indissoluble connection that is held tightly together by the nexus of cause and effect.'' Hence individuality and universal coherence in this large sense including progress are compatible in a way that individuality and progress itself are not. ''If one wants to know historical humanity one must attend both to the infinite variety of life which fills the centuries and the course of the great changes in which it moves. . . . Let us regard both the life of each epoch and the connection of them all.''[80]

And lest there be any misunderstanding, Ranke devoted another lecture shortly thereafter to spelling out in transparent terms this relationship of complementary opposition between the historical approach to particularity and the properly conceived historical approach to generality. He was careful first to establish the independence of general history, claiming that the ''general truth'' at which world history aims is something ''different'' from the documentary ''criticism of the particular'' which assures ''the reliability of modern history'' and different too from any ''combination of all the particulars'' which yields only ''a collection of reports.'' This distinctive general truth in history is not only irreducible but viable, and Ranke included ''the progress of culture'' among the factors that made general historical truths both autonomous and knowable as ''large conditions . . . independent of individual personalities.'' But then, after affirming so categorically the autonomy of coherent general history, Ranke was equally explicit in his insistence on not merely the compatibility but even the necessary interaction of general truths, when correctly conceived as so many ''invisible powers'' bearing on the individual, and particular facts in history. ''Only there must be no contradiction between factual history and the general interpretation [*Auffassung*] of the epoch. One must interpret the other. . . . The criticism of the particular belongs to the knowledge of the whole: each complements the other.''[81]

So did the shocking disruption of 1848 as a revolutionary political experience become an influence toward the recognition and accommodation of opposites when it passed into contemporary history. With this harmonious balance of individuality and universality in history, Ranke composed the great works that would take up the next two climactic decades of his professional life.

11
The Mature Historian:
World History in National Perspective
(1852–68)

Just as Ranke had viewed the universal Christian theme alternately from
unitary and national points of view (in the *History of the Popes*
and *German History in the Age of the Reformation* respectively)
during the productive period following on the revolution of 1830,
so in the period after the revolution of 1848 he analogously
accompanied the general history of the "world-historical" political
theme of modern history (in the lectures *On the Epochs of Modern
History*) with the view of this same theme from the national
perspectives of France and England in the early-modern age. His
focus was on the histories of these two nations in the period of
world history between the Reformation and the French Revolution, when France and England were the chief representatives of
the state-building that constituted for Ranke the characteristic
activity of the epoch that he called modern (and we call early-
modern) history. Thus what Germany was to universal history in
the Reformation, France and England were to universal history
thereafter, until the French Revolution of 1789 ushered in a new
epoch of world history. Ranke took all of the 50s and most of the
60s for the composition of these two national histories (the last
volume of the English history was published coincidentally with
the Austro-Prussian War of 1866, a year which thus marked a

significant change in the postures of Ranke and Prussia alike). The lectures he gave during this period show both his continual concern for establishing a positive relationship between national and universal history and the grounds of his professional preference during these years for approaching universal through national history rather than the converse option, which he had essayed but not published in his lectures to King Maximilian.[1]

In his lectures Ranke distinguished between two kinds of overlapping histories: a universal history which "... has general developments as its object—a cosmopolitan content, so to speak—" in which "everything particular does not disappear"; and "a particular history of each nation, in which general truth has a widespread role without constituting the particular history." Although he stipulated the compatibility of the two approaches— "between human history and national history there is a distinction but no conflict—the history of the world depends on their cooperation"—he stressed the priority of the national approach not only for modern history as such but even for the modern stage of universal history. For in the universal history of the premodern period "the great world movements . . . were produced by the different nations seriatim, each from its side. . . . One of them accomplished the work every time and thereby achieved a preponderant influence on the others. In a word: universal history is composed of the great actions of the various nations. . . . All these great actions of the nations are always the results of their own life." Hence "the connection of national histories with world history" from this perspective consisted in "the large forces of world history depending on the impulses which come from the individual nations."[2]

Ranke himself pointed out the similarity of Germany's universal role in the Reformation to France's and England's in the subsequent epoch, acknowledging only those distinctions which enhanced the general representative character of the French and English histories. He differentiated the "native history" of one's own country from the "national histories" of the other great Western nations in order to exclude "the content that concerns us immediately" from the universal contribution of the great events which is the object of national history.[3] Further, he stressed "the diversely segmented nationality," "the variety of conditions and

political institutions,'' that had distinctively featured German
history since the Reformation, as against the characteristic claims of
the French and English nationalities to the general validity of their
particular achievements.[4] Thus did the French and English cases
offer the historically most revealing individual embodiments of
political transition during early-modern times between the universal Christianity of the Middle Ages and the Reformation to the
universal confrontation of monarchy and revolution in the contemporary age.

In both the French and the English histories, then, as in the
German History, the national locus offered a historical process in
which individual events and agents had in fact a universal
resonance and in which, therefore, the method which Ranke had
designed for the precise researching of particular historical truths
became ipso facto appropriate to the discovery of general historical
truths—but now applicable to the whole of modern history and
not just its origins. Well might he define, in the appendix of his
French History, the "new direction" of historical studies in freshly
confident terms that asserted the continuity of the two kinds of
historical truths and demanded the same scientific standards for
both: "Through the precise establishment of the particular we
seek to prepare the way to the understanding of the general. . . .
Our aim is . . . the knowledge of the particular and the general; the
presentation of both with complete objectivity; simultaneously the
re-creation and the philosophy of what happened" (*des Ge-
schehenen*).[5] It behooves us to see how he accomplished this
long-postulated linkage.

I   The body of the *French History* shows that, as was his wont, the
fulcrum of his achievement consisted in the relocation of the
antitheses in his principles of history to the substance of history in
which they were stereoptically related. Certainly his statements of
historical principle in the book supported his proclaimed "new
direction" by affirming the scientific validity of both the particular
and the general levels of history, but they affirmed it merely by
juxtaposition, asserting seriatim one or the other side of what was
supposed to be bilateral without indicating any logic of their
coexistence. Thus he both repeated his familiar goal of producing
objective knowledge about particular facts and supplemented this

canon of the critical method by adding his intention of producing a comprehensive contribution of universal significance. "It would be enough for me if I could believe that through original and reliable reports I have attained the perception of what is objective in the large facts, beyond the mutual accusations of contemporaries and the often limited conception of later historians," he wrote modestly; but he added immediately, and without transition, the more grandiloquent claim that he had "sought to elucidate what was important for world history" (*das welthistorisch Wichtige*).[6]

Consistent with this duality of methodological intention, he intermixed two kinds of methodological principles in the work itself. On the one hand, he now declared the priority of the scientific over the artistic component in history, and he appended both a penultimate volume on the critical discussion of sources, as he was wont to do in support of his facts and in the disputation of others', and a final volume of edited correspondence from a German observer of French affairs under Louis XIV—the Duchess of Orleans—whose admitted alienation from all things French and whose "exclusive German-ness" made Ranke's acknowledgment of scholarly dependence upon her testimony an indication of his own external, skeptical approach. But on the other hand he also developed the methodological tenet that "the scientific contribution" of history to truth requires not so much the correction of errors in detail as the transcendence of one-sidedness in presentation, the rediscovery of "the divine or the God-related in human nature," and the recognition of the "address to the ennobling movements of the human soul."[7]

Similarly the obiter dicta on the nature of the historical process which he scattered through the *French History* showed a fairly even balance between statements declaring the individual and discontinuous qualities of events to be the essence of history and other statements declaring the concatenation of events to be the essence of the historical process, but only in rare and isolated instances did the one kind of statement take cognizance of the other. On the one side, Ranke argued for the independence of detached events, for the irreducible variety in history that followed from this independence, and against the efficacy of ideas that claimed to link the events. "In the various forms of the event lies history," he wrote to justify his "moment-by-moment consideration of the course of events." Not only is "historical science" wrong when it "claims to demonstrate the unbroken continuity of a growth once begun," but "the European world is composed of elements of original diversity from whose inner opposition and struggle the changes in the historical epochs develop." The essence of this original variety inheres in the superior effective power of peculiar circumstances over associative concepts for the life of historical forces. "Great historical phenomena cannot be explained by the constitutional concepts to which they correspond; they are based rather on the vital forces which become effective under definite circumstances independent of them. They bear the character of the moment in which they arose.... The development of earthly powers is ruled by their own constellations." And as if to underline the ultimately contingent character of the singular "large events" on which he had the development of France and of Europe so often turn, he would figuratively attribute them to a divine destiny beyond the mesh of human designs. "But what are human calculations? Divine destiny laughs at them," he concluded from the untimely and scheme-shattering deaths of Pope Gregory XIV and Alexander Farnese in the late sixteenth century. The invocation of divine destiny in this context obviously entailed the exclusion of that other familiar analogical device, the invocation of nature for its implication of continuous growth, and we find indeed that when Ranke was engaged in an open narrative, featuring the sovereignty and plurality of unpredictable events, he would draw the moral that "the institutions of states do not grow like the products of nature."[8]

But on other occasions, when he was inferring general propositions from the connections in his account, Ranke would maintain the essentiality, and at times even the primacy, not of the discrete events and their distinctive identities but of the total pattern they formed. Not only did he avow the centrality of such connections in the history of the whole Romano-Germanic world, but he warned that in principle the historian distorts history by detaching individual components from their collective pattern. "Our attention will be directed to the relations which these men of such varied origins struck with one another," he promised at the end of his introductory chapter on the ethnic roots of the French nation, and he proceeded on the conviction that in the modern period as "from time immemorial there was a profound internal coherence [*Zusammenhang*] in European life; movements of apparently local origin export their analogues to distant regions." From his summary characterization of Richelieu's various policies—"how indivisibly these things interlocked"—Ranke concluded that an authentic historical judgment could only be levied on their totality. "The placid consideration of posterity may choose which of these things pleases them and which not; time and history produced them together." Nor did he shrink from attributing an integral rather than a merely aggregative unity to these policies. "Everything was mutually conditioned, everything hung together . . . ; over the vast arena one idea prevailed and it embraced the world."[9]

Just as decisively, indeed, as he had subordinated connective ideas to distinguishing circumstances in some contexts, Ranke exalted the coherent power of ideas in others. Here he would point out the centripetal force of ideas in resolving the conflicts of opposing parties, whether by furnishing a common matrix whereby unified partisans could achieve victory or by furnishing the common grounds for a larger compromise. "Every power is moved by the inherent drive of the ideas lying at its base," and consistently with this principle he attributed political triumphs to such "a weapon" as "the concept of absolute monarchy," "the principles on which the French community was based," "the idea of the Gallican church," "the one-sided direction taken by the dominant ideas of the French state," for "the superiority of the idea that possesses the power—politics—plays a decisive role in the great affairs of the world." This efficacy of ideas, moreover, was a function of their essentially cohesive cogency, as the summary analysis of the strength of Louis XIV's France showed: this strength went beyond mere force and consisted in the "cheerful attachment" of all classes to the monarchy, grounded in their common subscription to "the great ideas of the unity of the nation, of a pervasive legal order, and of a glorious position in the world." And even on those historical occasions which witness the prevalence of no single force, it is still the conjunctive power of the idea that provides the explanation of the result. "In great moments a general conviction is formed which sets a certain limit to the conflict and exercises, as it were, a higher and moderating power."[10]

So even-handed was Ranke in his allocation of historical truth to the principles of both particular and general history that he did not hesitate to cover larger developments as well as unique events with the dignifying mantle of divinity. He balanced his individualistic exegesis of "divine destiny" (*das göttliche Geschick*) with the equally pious notion of a "world order based on moral laws which have never yet been violated without calling down revenge on those who violate them." He deemed this moral world order to be an integral part of "the religious idea," the part responsible for "the principles of morality that are at the basis of all culture and human society," and his general interpretation of the whole movement culminating in the religious strife of the sixteenth century was epitomized in his judgment that the world order and its moral principles had been separated out from religion and neglected, to the consequent benefit of religious particularism. When he was concerned with such collective actions, his attitude toward nature changed predictably along with his attitude toward the role of the divinity in history. Where he was careful to deny any natural analogy to the free political development of the state, he invoked it for the constant ethnic characteristics of the nation. The "mighty and instinctive force of the spirit" which "is always arising from the heart" of the French nation apart from or even against the dominant forms of European life "breaks through the sphere of legality from century to century almost, as it were, with the force of nature."[11] When he was in this gear, Ranke could well entertain the idea of a quasi-natural as well as a divine moral order of man.

Now this principled double vision of Ranke's was hardly new for him, although the bifurcation of its objects may have been more definite than previously. But what really distinguished these propositions from their antecedents in his experience was the integral view of the actual historical process he was covering, for the content of his *French History* merged the two levels and hence mediated between the apparently antithetical formulations of principle that took off from one side or the other of the composite content. Ranke attained in historical practice the unity he did not even attempt in historical principle through two courses: through

the concrete method whereby he organized the empirically ascertained variety of particular circumstances and individual acts
into a rationally comprehensible pattern of general results; and
through the clearly identified theme whereby the monarchical
development of an independent and individually distinct France
in actual fact represented the universal political tendency of the
entire Romano-German culture between the ages of medieval
Christianity and contemporary revolution.

Ranke himself gave a true abstract of the organizing method he
used in the *French History* when he distinguished between the
individual freedom which must be attributed to every historical act
in the doing and the generally integrated character of the necessity
which must be attributed to such acts in their results, but
postulated their mutual engagement. "What belongs to free
decision when one is trying it becomes irrevocable, independent of
any human will in its effects, a link in the chain of general
necessities as soon as it has been done, and it dominates the
following period."[12] Ranke combined these two modes of being in
historical practice by habitually denying the existence of prior
deliberate projects to his historical agents in favor of a limited,
vague, or internally divided mental orientation and then showing
the expansion, crystallization, and rationalization of this original
orientation, through voluntary acts and inimitable circumstances,
into a series of events and a set of related policies linked in an a
posteriori rational unity.

This schema was eased for Ranke by his capacity for focusing
general political movements upon the developing personalities of
the great—kings, ministers, regents, generals, and the leaders of
the disloyal opposition—for this incorporation permitted him to
combine the momentary freedom of individual decisions with the
larger and longer-range interests of the institutional objects of
those decisions. The intertwining of the personal and the political
was for Ranke a consciously held postulate which was entirely
conformable to the actuality of the history he was treating. For the
leaders of the French state from Francis I through Louis XIV, from
Sully through Colbert, Ranke sought repeatedly to show that in
each of these individual persons "the idea of an independent,
self-reliant state, which he bore in himself, was realized," that
"the personal self was the epitome of the general interest," until

the historian could exclaim at one point: "How intermingled at this moment again were the personal interests of great men and public affairs."[13] It was as a result of this continuing historiographical experience with personality-centered national history that Ranke penned his famous definition of historical biography— i.e., "the historical personality"—in the critical volume on sources which he appended to his *English History*. His characterization there of "what is historical in persons," vis-à-vis what is private in them, holds for his approach to the French as well as to the English history. "The more profoundly general relations are grasped, the more they are developed in the conflicts of the time and in view of the questions at issue, the more do they penetrate the individual life and impart a new, distinctive value to it."[14]

With this postulate of what we may call the incorporated personality, and with its corollary that fundamental policies and lasting political institutions are made by "the combination of circumstances which no one controls and certain great personalities," Ranke proceeded to unroll the historical development of French politics from the early sixteenth century to the eve of the Revolution. He wrote it as a linked series of dramatic narratives, organized around the interplay of limiting conditions, qualified free choices, and contingent events in spurring or frustrating the actions of successive political leaders and interspersed with choral reviews of the total resultant situations which set the limiting conditions for the next generation of political leaders. To assure the continuity of this pattern, Ranke found in each leader the same combination of indefinite character and susceptibility to circumstances, and he assessed the general result of each leader's work by the same criterion derived from the emergent general model of Romano-Germanic monarchy. Thus, however different the specific goals and general results of such an assortment of chiefs as Catherine de Medici, Henry Guise, Henry IV, Philip II, Richelieu, Mazarin, and Louis XIV may have been, what they shared, in the reiterated form of Ranke's portrayals, was a reputation either for long-range general designs or for thoroughgoing opportunism of the moment, which he rejected for them equally, and an actual intermediate posture which he accepted for them equally—the inchoate and indefinite desire for the consolidation of monarchical authority developing gradually into a coherent mesh of policies through its step-by-step definition under the influence of its response to the pressure of circumstances. Thus he redefined the attribute of "an inner duplicity" (*Zweizüngigkeit*) for Catherine de Medici to denote a morally neutral and flexible character "whose need and nature it is to have two strings to its bow so as to be able to fall back on the other if the first does not succeed," in order then to follow her endeavors on behalf of her family's power as an open process, favoring the different parties successively according to the conditions and the opportunities. Yet this empathetic and sequential account added up to the final judgment that Catherine committed a "great political crime" by involving "the sanctity" of the monarchical dignity in partisan revenge and private interests.[15]

Again, he redefined the concept of "universal monarchy" from world dominion to the looser idea of European "hegemony" (*Übergewicht*) in order to underline the absence of definite designs for conquest on the part first of the Spanish rulers and then of Louis XIV. To Louis especially Ranke extended a graduated treatment that articulated explicitly what was sometimes elided in his consideration of less central figures. Ranke took two initial positions which in combination guaranteed both a dramatic plurality of possibilities at every moment and an overall unity of theme: Louis' indefinite desire to assert himself in terms of the general monarchical tradition he had inherited from Francis I, Henry IV, and Richelieu and which he had learned from Mazarin; and the composite character of the Bourbon monarchy, in which "the force of the monarchical idea was held to be necessary in the lower groups not much less than it was desired by the highest groups of the country," and thus stemmed as much from the voluntary action of the society as from the compulsory power of the king.[16] Hence the aim of Louis XIV's policy should be ascertained "according to the content of the facts and the direction which is perceivable in actions," and by these empirical standards it developed from amorphous plurality to explicit uniformity under the continuing absorption of experience. The early Louis, concerned primarily for "the security of his realm," was rightly seen not as a conqueror but as "the commander of a fortress who, to maintain it and to make it formidable, extends its attacks over its frontiers on all sides." Thus several possibilities "hovered before him in more or less clear contours," and, together with "the organization he formed around him," he sought simply "to try his forces in new enterprises,'' as these were made appropriate to this vague purpose by circumstances. His whole organization, "feeling its superiority in the world, craved movement and activity and let the occasion for it depend on where it found resistance.''[17]

But the policies of the later Louis, in Ranke's presentation of him, were at once more comprehensive and more one-sided: what made these inconsistent qualities rationally compatible was that the policies became both more definite and more integrated; what made the combination historically understandable was the new discrepancy between the definite dimensions of his expanded ends and the limitation of his means and the new universal opposition that was aroused against him thereby. In his foreign policy Louis now wanted to be "master of Europe and to secure this power in his dynasty for all time.'' In domestic policy Louis proceeded from the earlier convergence of the several social and religious elements to the application of "the uniformity principle'' (*Uniformitäts-princip*) by his "one-sided will.'' The result was general in both a positive and a negative direction: "There was so tight an inter-weaving of all interests that the detachment of a single one was unthinkable,'' but by the same token "the ideas of men tore loose from the state of Louis XIV in every branch.'' Louis's achievement, then, was "of universal-historical significance''—it could be assessed as a general model. "People had learned what the exertion of the nation could accomplish under the Romano-Germanic monarchy . . . ; but people had also experienced that in the final analysis it did not attain its goal.''[18]

At the beginning and end of each unfolding narrative sequence Ranke thus touched base at his unifying theme, and it was this substantive historical theme that more than any other historio-graphical factor mediated between his individual and universal interests and permitted the application of the standards of the one to the materials of the other. For Ranke's theme was that national monarchy, albeit tied by its very nature to its independence in a plurality of states, yet was the phenomenal form of western culture's Romano-Germanic monarchy in the modern period, and that France was the primary manifestation of this connection between the individual state and the universal model in the early-modern section of that period. In his *French History*, then, Ranke resumed his thesis which he had adumbrated in his

Reformation history—that power and culture, associated under the primacy of the state, superseded Christianity as the universal tendency of modernity, and he sought to show precisely how that supersession took place, what was generic about the absolute monarchical form of the territorial state, and how the instability of this form prepared the way for the overtly universal revolution that was the substantive historical theme of the contemporary age.

The connection between the schema of the *French History* and Ranke's long-rooted desire to give a historical definition to the modern political stage of western culture was an explicit one. Ranke expressly marked the demise of the religiously conditioned culture of the sixteenth century—"a culture which contained all the vital elements of the past centuries in itself and was soon to be buried in a general ruin"—and just as explicitly marked the politics of state sovereignty as the dominant factor in the succession culture. "The whole life of the modern centuries," he wrote in the general conclusion to his treatment of Louis XIV's monarchy, "is based on the indissoluble unity of these forces" which make up "the constitution of the new states" and "upon the continuously effective internal opposition to them," and he proved the point—at least for himself—by describing French literature as a cultural component of political power. He found that for the sixteenth century "the condition of literature corresponded to the condition of the state," and that in the seventeenth century French literature not only was essentially conditioned by its base in the French state and society rather than by its own autonomous movement but served the political function of providing "the whole French community" (*Gemeinwesen*) with "a feeling of the unconditional value of the principles on which it rested" and thereby of sustaining its "intention to attain superiority over the world for the concept on which it was based."[19]

The book's most prominent thematic concern was with the mode in which this succession from religion to politics as the primary organizing principle of human endeavor took place. Like most successions, this mode combined rejection and absorption. Ranke's history was devoted to the empirical account of the winding but generally upward course of the French monarchy's struggle against the independent Catholic and Protestant principles and to analytical pursuit of the French monarchy's progressive incorporation, in appropriately politicized forms, of the religious element as an integral component of the state. In his account of supersession by rejection Ranke showed the protagonists of ecclesiastical supremacy against monarchical sovereignty to represent a persistence of the solidary hierarchical principle signifying the union of spiritual and temporal powers dominant in the Middle Ages, but he showed emphatically too that in the modern period this meant the alliance of universal religion with particularistic politics. "The concept of the indivisibility of the spiritual and worldly power had given the centuries of the Middle Ages their character: modern times begins with its being questioned and opposed," he wrote bluntly. "For the formation of the state, with which the centuries have been concerned ever since, ... the renunciation of the concept of general Christianity was a necessary step." Both the Catholic and the Protestant parties continued to espouse the predominance of universal religion—the Catholics through the hierarchical claims of the papacy and the Spanish ambitions for Catholic universal monarchy on the medieval imperial model, the Protestants through their claim to "restore what was generally valid [*das Allgemeingültige*] in religious doctrine"—but the Catholic Church in France was also one of the "great corporations" whose factionalism threatened "the inner unity of the state," while both the Catholic and the Protestant parties joined aristocratic allies whose preference for "personal relations" over "communal interests" helped to align these parties with "the particular individuals" (*Einzelnen*) who so often made "the state the playground of their connections and enmities with one another." Whether the alliance of religious party and aristocracy was considered to be an example of "the political danger of alliance with someone of opposite principles," as Ranke did consider it in reference to the Protestants, or was considered to be a case where "the religious factor embraced and excused everything and covered every contradiction," as Ranke did consider it in reference to the Catholics, he associated outmoded Christian universalism with particularism and disorder. Hence the French monarchy's struggle against the ecclesiastical parties was not antiuniversalist but antiparticularist. The monarchy represented not only the collective unity of the nation against the corporate "independencies" and their anti-French foreign associates but the emergent universal order. With the provisional resolution of the religious conflict through the supremacy of the royal right of legitimate succession under Henry IV, "its universal day [*Welttag*] dawned" for the Bourbon monarchy which he founded. "The comprehension of an equilibrium of both parties within itself gave the Bourbon French monarchy in this epoch a universal relation to everything that lived and was powerful in Europe."[20]

What consolidated the claim of monarchy to be the political heir of universal Christianity as the dominant general principle in the history of western humanity was its perpetuation of the religious motif under its own auspices. Especially did the regimes of the two great cardinal-ministers, Richelieu and Mazarin, offer Ranke the opportunity to make this rational inference from the empirical evidence, for after dwelling on "the most energetic zeal" with which they "destroyed particular interests" and "promoted general interests" and on the intensity with which they "lived only in the ideas of unity and political power," Ranke concluded with the assertion of "a certain affinity of principle" between the Catholic hierarchy and absolute monarchy. "Both carried a certain spiritual enthusiasm over into the administration of the state. Richelieu fought for the doctrine of indefeasible royal rights with a rigor which had hitherto been devoted only to religious ideas. He created a religion of the monarchy, as it were; Mazarin embraced it. Around this standard their supporters gathered." Louis XIV completed their work in this respect, for through his continuing attachment to the Gallican principle he equipped his state with a compliant religious arm that could produce uniformity within and universal claims abroad. Thus, Louis's opposition to the attacks from Rome and his suppression of the Protestant confession were two actions which corresponded to each other and complemented each other, for the latter "was the common action of the state as it had been formed by the union of the [*Gallican*] clergy and the crown and by the identity of their interests," and the former—the decisions against the pope and for the rights of the king—stemmed from an analogous union of church and monarchy, now in competition with the papal hierarchy for domination of general Catholicism. The Gallican church would raise the declaration of Gallican liberties on which it had resolved jointly with the king "to the status of a general norm, and . . . would even make it the basis for the reestablishment of Catholicism in the whole world." Well might Ranke account "the connection with the church," along with the concept of sovereignty and the aristocratic authority of the "feudal system," to be an essential component not only of the Bourbon monarchy but of all modern states. Their aim, like Louis's, was for "monarchy to exhibit the totality of the spiritual power in itself."[21]

But the supersession of universal Christianity by hegemonial monarchy did not in itself suffice to demonstrate Ranke's thesis that this monarchy represented an equivalent general theme for the modern period. For however spiritualized it may have become and however unifying its mission may have been with respect to the corporate institutions and private interests it joined to itself, the French monarchy still remained a national phenomenon and as such partook of the self-regarding individuality characteristic of the nation and thereby of the modern state. "This French community was a world unto itself; it presumed to suffice for the decision of all great and general questions." Louis XIV was a consistent representative of this distinctive national community, for "he applied to others a form corresponding simply to the French order of things." The exclusive "one-sidedness" wherein he arrogated to himself the imposition of a uniformity consonant with his own view of political unity and the interests of his own dynasty was a personal analogue of this national individuality. "In his relations with others the prince lived exclusively through the execution of his own idea."[22] Hence the connection between the modern politics of territorial monarchy and the universal historical theme it was supposed to constitute could not be assumed: it had to be forged. Three tried-and-true devices were available to Ranke—devices which he had already put to use in associating German national history with the universal Christian tradition during the Reformation—and now he used them all to make the French the most revealing manifestation of a universal political history in the early-modern period.

The first link between France and world history was subsumptive. The "Romano-Germanic state" was a general phenomenon coeval with the foundation of western culture, and the French monarchy was the true microcosm of it which pioneered its development in the modern age. Thus the struggle between king and estates, the constitutional form taken by the French religious wars in the late sixteenth century, was the early-modern expression of a general pattern: "These are precisely the opponents who eternally strive against each other in European monarchies." Reconstructed France went beyond the reflection of the pattern to the development of it. "In the French monarchy of Louis XIV all the elements of the Romano-Germanic state are still vital"— sovereignty from Rome, the religious connection from Catholicism, aristocratic authority from the Germanic kingdoms, nobles, incorporated commoners, provinces, capital city, peasantry—but whereas in the Romano-Germanic state these elements "for long lived in manifold conflict with one another," in this French monarchy "their strife, their independent dealings, were at an end," for all were controlled and promoted as parts of a whole. The structural organization that Louis imparted to the French monarchy became literally an international model: "All the princes who have made a name for themselves as absolute rulers have followed his example."[23]

The second link between France and world history was empirical. The events of the French civil war and then of its absolute regimes showed an actual linkage of internal interests and international politics. Until almost the middle of the seventeenth century this linkage was one which, on the model of Spain and the Catholic League, aligned domestic parties with foreign powers and made the triumph of monarchical authority over all parties within France of universal significance because it entailed the assertion of national independence abroad and hence the ultimate defeat of the Catholic Spanish attempt to perpetuate religiopolitical universalism of the medieval type. Henceforward the pope "had to recognize the independence of the worldly power and of the fundamental conditions of state life." But from the time of Mazarin on, French internationalism turned from successful defense against universal monarchy to ambitious initiative for universal hegemony—a shift that marked "one of the greatest changes that ever occurred in Europe and in the position of a great state." Persuaded of the priority of international over domestic concerns and utiliz-

262 · THE HISTORY

ing the power accruing to the Crown from its foreign wars for the consolidation of its authority at home, Mazarin made "the military principle" an essential component of the French monarchy, and thenceforward the extension of absolute power at home went hand in hand with geographical expansion abroad in quest of an ever-new "still greater position in the world" (*Weltstellung*). Louis XIV and his agents sought international preponderance for the same reason as they sought internal uniformity—"to try their forces in new enterprises"—and their initial successes along both lines made the history of the French monarchy politically congruent with the history of Europe. Thus France followed in the succession of the medieval popes and the sixteenth-century Hapsburgs as a "predominant" (*vorwaltender*) power aiming at "universal hegemony," and when France came to threaten "the general freedom of Europe," it brought about "another world conflict" which introduced a new system of states.[24] Thus the connection between national French and general European (including colonial) history was for Ranke a matter not of the historian's perception but of ascertainable historical fact.

The third link between France and world history was structural. The most common substantives of historical import in Ranke's *French History* were "opposition" (*Gegensatz*) and its plural "opposing parties" (*Gegensätze*), terms whose prevalence signified the correlation between the constant and pervasive structure of French history and the structure he found dominant in every age of universal human history from the classical era to his own contemporary period. Occasionally the conflicts which made up the stuff of his French history were multilateral and indicated a particular time of confusion and disorder, but in the main they were bipolar, like his view of human conflict in the large, and as in his larger view they expressed the controlled kind of human variety that is focused on homologous universal issues. In his structure of French as of universal history, moreover, the recurrent duality of the opposing parties on universal issues was pulled through its historical movement by the ever-present possibility of their unification. Thus the myriad oppositions and conflicts which crowd the pages of the *French History* are assimilable to the abstract archetype, set up early in the book, of an "eternal struggle" and its resolution. "From the concept of hereditary monarchy and the absolute power of the state one would come to general servitude; from the concept of corporation and of individual freedom to the republic or to elective monarchy. On the counteraction of both principles and on their reciprocal limitation rest our states." If this archetype is elaborated in the sense of subsequently added corollaries which make "great oppositions . . . bring forth general changes," which make diversity indispensable to "the continuity of a free historical development," and which spell out the primary mechanism of the historical movement to consist in the alternation between the "indissoluble union" and the "internal opposition" of sovereignty, church, and aristocratic autonomy in the state, then we have a Rankean model which accounts in universal terms for the opposition between king and corporate estates as the issue of absolute versus limited government, for the degeneration of this opposition into one between royalists and a coalition of corporatists and populace as the issue of political revolution, and for the alignment of the church on one side or another of either opposition to give a religious color to these issues.[25]

These are precisely the kinds of oppositions which constitute the empirical bulk of the *French History*, and in view of the underlying structure it is hardly surprising to find that Ranke distributes isomorphic conflicts across the historiographical spectrum from the most parochial French to the world arenas. Thus the French nation exhibits two apposite sets of constant antitheses: construction of dominant European tendencies versus deviation from them; and "presence of mind" leading to discovery of order amidst confusion versus the "restless mobility" leading to the kind of "conversion characterized . . . by the word 'revolution.' " Mediating between this purely national pattern of divisions, which underlay the turning-points in the running domestic battle between the royal and the corporate parties in France, and the world arena of hegemonial power and the resistance to it was the series of religious conflicts from the civil wars of the sixteenth century through the Huguenot controversy of the late seventeenth to the rivalry between Jesuits and Gallicans in the eighteenth. The ecclesiastical and doctrinal parties to these conflicts tended to parcel themselves out between the royal and the corporate parties and thus to confirm the main line of political division in internal French history, but this religious increment also had the effect of creating a common bond between domestic parties and their counterparts abroad and thus of internationalizing internal opposition. "That the sympathies of the Protestants, in opposition to the absolute monarchy which was united with strict Catholicism, turned to the forms of limited monarchy or of republican constitution was an enduring event," concluded Ranke after he had covered the revocation of the Edict of Nantes. "When one considers the position of the world—the nature of this monarchy which granted no peace for long and the energy of the opponents which it encountered—it could not be doubted that a great conflict must again ensue." By this "great conflict," of course, Ranke was referring to the global level of polarized forces and principles, manifest first in the general "clash of tendencies"—"the most fundamental clash in the Europe of the time," involving "oppositions extending over the whole [seventeenth century] between monarch and republic, mercantilism and free trade, exclusive Catholicism and Protestant toleration, modern official classicism and modern freedom of the press"—pitting France first against the Netherlands and then against the English as the heirs of the Dutch in this international duel.[26] But France always.

Overlapping the predication of the monarchical state to be the modern successor of medieval Christianity as the unifying force in human history and overlapping too the linked devices for associating French politics with general history, Ranke invoked the issue of revolution as a final recurrent theme lending a universal coherence and relevance to his empirical history. Ostensibly, as we have just seen, the revolutionary theme, with its associated concepts of popular sovereignty and the republic, was part of his generic dualistic archetype, occupying the place of a radical variant in the corporate and ecclesiastical opposition to royal political authority; and true to this apparent inclusion of popular revolution in the primary set of traditional rivalries among king, church, and estates in early-modern times Ranke linked revolutionary and republican ideas with the old corporations at sundry points in his narrative. He associated both French aristocracy and Holland with ideas of "the republic"; he deemed Catholic corporate, ecclesiastical, and popular ideas in the French religious wars to be "all connected in a single Catholic-liberal system," a deliberately anomalous characterization designed to evoke the revolutionary connotations he found in the liberalism of his own day; and he found that the late sixteenth-century Huguenot theories of popular sovereignty not only "deviated . . . far from the ideas on which the Romano-Germanic states are based" but spawned programs which "have an analogy with what was later effected by the Revolution."[27]

Such specific formulations hint at a seam in Ranke's thinking which militated against his mere subsumption of the revolutionary theme under the traditional opposition between king and estates and its religious associations of medieval vintage. The fact was that his repeated adversion to the theme of revolution stemmed from a modern concern that was independent in principle from the traditional conflicts so prominent in his work, and the later sections of his book were based on this distinction, thereby introducing overtly into his scholarly history the contemporary political preoccupations which he had already filtered through his scheme of universal history. The categories under which he interpreted the crucial conflicts of early-modern times were thus composite: concepts rooted in the medieval past and concepts interpolated back from their mature development in the contemporary age of revolution met in his interpretation of these conflicts. From a position almost midway through his history, indeed, Ranke frankly revealed the dual perspective he adopted in his *French History*: "We stand in the midst of the centuries: we hear, as it were, the various ages raising their voices. Alongside the hierarchical past, the roaring of a democratic future. Between them wavered the then-present" (*die damalige Gegenwart*).[28]

The telic dimension was responsible for the special adumbrative tone which Ranke imparted to his discussion of revolutionary movements even in the early part of his book, when he considered such movements only as extensions of old corporate struggles against the crown, and this dimension naturally grew stronger as he moved with the French centuries toward the Revolution. The two final books, which he devoted to eighteenth-century France from the death of Louis XIV through the reign of Louis XV, were dominated by the impending revolution, and to insure the connection between the monarchical old regime and the revolution of 1789 he added, as an appended "conclusion," a reprint of his old article on the Assembly of Notables in 1787.[29] In his consideration of eighteenth-century France he now identified the rise of an independent revolutionary movement in literature— whereas "the literature of the seventeenth century attached itself to the ideas predominant in the great institutions of the state and the church and developed its world view on that basis, the literature of the eighteenth century turned away from them"[30]— and in its context he now treated the renewal of the traditional conflicts between king and corporations and between the spiritual and the worldly powers as a "suddenly irreconcilable conflict of the principles on which the state was founded," making for "a general ferment [*Gährung*].... All elements of life and thought prepared themselves for a general convulsion." And to leave no doubt that the familiar struggles of the old parties which continued to occupy the center of the historical stage constituted not so much another, more desperate chapter of an opposition rooted in the past as a prologue to a new kind of struggle identifiable from the future, Ranke claimed to mark "the introduction of the idea of popular sovereignty into the heart of the French state" in the midst of the revived strife between crown and corporate church during the reign of Louis XV, through the transition from the prescriptive "right of the monarchy with its positive limits" to "the idea of the absolute state with its irrefutable force" in the royalist position itself—a judgment whose retrospective basis was patent in Ranke's admission that "this idea still found little acceptance at that time."[31]

Undoubtedly the customary divisions among the old authorities continued to occupy the center of Ranke's stage from his account of the French middle ages at the beginning straight through to his account of the prerevolutionary Assembly of Notables at the end, giving cumulative support to his theme of the internal duality, the resulting historical mobility, and the ultimate political instability of early-modern monarchy. But his recurrent invocation of an autonomous revolutionary motif with a future reference added to this theme a dimension usually obscured by the dramatic narrative of the intrastate conflicts: vis-à-vis the revolutionary "idea of the sovereign nation," all the historic authorities together comprised a unity of early-modern monarchy transcending their internal oppositions. This dimension was the basis of the implicit supertheme of Ranke's *French History*—implicit in that it was assumed throughout and stated only at the very end. The one-sided development of the French monarchy in the direction of a centralizing and leveling sovereignty secured the universal early-modern predominance of the monarchical state in its dualistic, internally riven form. Consequently, the revolutionary demise of the French monarchy may have betokened the historical end of monarchy in this schizoid form which it took in actuality, but not of monarchy in the alternative synthesized form which it had given the world as a repeated possibility. Hence Ranke could conclude his account of the dissolution of the French "old monarchy" with a peroration on the continued efficacy of monarchy in his own revolutionary age—and thus on the present relevance of its early-modern history—that was only superficially paradoxical.

An age began in which the old monarchy appeared to be completely destroyed: the flood of the revolution, victorious in France and destructive of church and state, poured over Europe. But it has not yet come so far. The tendencies of the revolution have not been eliminated, but just as little have they triumphed completely. The historical developments of the old Europe and especially of France could not be crushed or even subjugated. The life force of the old ideas has not only resisted but has exercised a powerful counterimpact. Through action and reaction a new world-era has been introduced.[32]

It was the general monarchical concept hypostatized by France rather than the actual absolute Roman monarchy realized in France during the early-modern period that would persist, in Ranke's view, into his own age. Between the two lay the opposing actuality of a "Germanic" style of monarchy—exalting the aristocratic, personal, and tolerant side of the monarchical state—which had developed contrapuntally during the same early-modern period and approached the postrevolutionary requirement of a synthesized monarchy much more nearly than did the Romanized French version. For the early-modern period this Germanic complement of the French monarchy lay in the history of England, and here, consequently, was the locus of Ranke's other great postrevolutionary scholarly endeavor.

II   Ranke had long been ambivalent about England and its history, and
this in two different ways. Both equivocations contributed to the
status of his *English History* as the companion study of the *French
History* for his fruitfully ambiguous attempt to read universal
history in a national setting. He saw England both as a "Germanic" nation that was akin to his own Teutonic nationality and
as one of the several European nations that were alien to him as a
German national and whose history was an integral part of general
or world history. Again, he saw England politically both as an
example of undeviating constitutional continuity, "broken by no
modern revolution" and commendable as a model to his royal
friends, and as the dominant international embodiment, along
with France, of the contemporary liberalism which was the principle of the revolutionary party as opposed to the conservative
monarchy.[33] These turned out to be historically fruitful ambiguities, for they enabled Ranke to set the English up as the heirs of the
religiously reformed German Empire who politicized the principle
of Protestant national independence for which the Reformation
had stood and who bore it as a universal European principle
against hegemonial France in the early-modern period. Where
France represented the homologous principles of absolutist uniformity and general revolution, England represented an antithetical set of heterologous principles—to wit, vital diversity and
historical continuity. The essential schema of the *English History*
lay in Ranke's dual demonstration of the developing unity behind
the recurrent internal divisions in early-modern England and of
the developing universalism, however paradoxical in political
logic, which its assertion of insular national independence effected
in actual history. Clearly the predication of France and England as
the rival champions of opposite constitutional principles in the
same centuries called for parallel approaches to the histories of the
two countries, but the substantive difference in the political
principles which the two nations respectively represented made for
an equally substantive difference in the historical themes which
exhibited the universal connections of individual events. Where
French individuals acted for a homogenized French nation in the
name of an explicit Catholic and revolutionary universalism,
English individuals acted for one or another of the parties of a
heterogeneous British nation in the name of factional religious and

political principles which only conjointly constituted a generalizable unity. The elucidation of such a distributive, vis-à-vis the French collective, universal obviously required a different kind of historical patterning. To the restatement of the particularistic and objective historical approach which the two histories shared in historical theory, Ranke added for the English case an unprecedentedly integral demonstration of how the variety, the individuality, and the local rootedness which he prized so highly in the structure of humanity could become the constituents of the supremely valid universal principle in history.

There can be little doubt that Ranke meant to apply the same rigorous method of detailed scholarship to his English history as to his French. The *English History*, indeed, is the source of some of his most memorialized statements on the ideal of the historian's objectivity and on the commitment to original sources, to political events, and to detachment of the past from the present as the ingredients of that objectivity. "I have wished," he wrote quotably in the midst of the book, "to extinguish my own self, as it were, and to allow only things to speak and to allow the mighty forces to appear which in the course of the centuries have arisen and grown alongside and across one another." Expressly denying himself the right to take a judgmental stance on the model of the criminal courts, he summed up the historian's proper credo in another of his self-denying ordinances: "We have only to do with the contemplation of the event."[34]

Behind these statements of historiographical principle lay his restatements of valid procedure. In the critical appendix which he added to this as to the others of his scholarly works he indicated that it was only his generation's addiction to "the original memorials of the past" that made it possible for the historian "to surmount handed-down traditions . . . and to see the past with his own eyes, so to speak, as if it were the present." In this programmatic statement he made it clear, moreover, that for modern history this "archival research" is directed primarily to "the field of political events, on which descriptive history operates." The goal of the historian then received one of those repeatable formulations of factual objectivity that characteristically followed from the address of his scientific method to this kind of historical object: "It all hangs together: critical study of authentic

sources; impartial conception; objective description—the aim is
the presentation of the complete truth. Here I set up an ideal
about which I may be told that it cannot be realized. Such is the
case: the idea is infinite, the execution by its very nature
limited.''[35]

But the implications of Ranke's position went beyond this paean
to a norm of factual objectivity that was vitiated only by the
unavoidable but undesirable limitations of fallible human nature.
He associated it with a general warning against contemporary
history, which he later specified in his critique of Bishop Gilbert
Burnet's *History of My Own Time*, alleging indeed the factual
distortions, delusions, and ignorance of "anyone who wants to write
the history of his own time"—that "most extensive, most ambitious, and yet most perilous undertaking which can be dared by
an author concerned with the truth"—but also adducing the
inevitable partiality which afflicts an observer in the midst of the
actions he describes. Even his much-cited extension of this warning
to any influence of the present upon the historian was now based
not only upon the optional fallacy of partisan judgment but also
upon the inevitable threat of partial contemporaneous involvement to the historian's responsibility for understanding in their
integrity "ideas and projects which transcend what is applicable in
their local place and time." For "the muse of history has the
broadest spiritual horizon and the courage of her conviction," he
set down as the premise of his injunction, "but it is thoroughly
conscientious in the formation of that conviction and, it can be
said, jealous in its service. To introduce the interests of the present
into the work of the historian usually has the effect of inhibiting its
free fulfillment."[36]

Now partisanship is different from partiality, and the human
limits stemming from a predisposition toward prejudice, which is
controllable, different from the human limits stemming from the
necessary localization of the contemporary observer in place and
time, which is not. Ranke registered these differences without
acknowledging them, and his confusion of the two kinds of
presentism enabled him to endow the practicing historian—i.e.,
Ranke himself—with the option of overcoming his partiality as
well as his partisanship through the recognition of the universal
connections in history. Thus he could extend the historian's

discretionary capacity for avoiding prejudice to his selective capacity for perceiving general processes in history, and thereby he could resolve for himself the implicit conflict between his commitments both to the disjunction between past and present and to the telic conjunction of past and present. He mixed the intellectual standard of "comprehensiveness" in with the scientific criterion of accuracy, and he argued that "the real nature of conditions appear in their true light only through their results" to show that the retrospective connectedness of history was a remedy for the discrepancy between a particularized past and the historian's differently particularized present as much as for the "errors" and the "deformities" of the historian's commitment to his present.[37]

The relationship between impartiality and universality which he implied in the text of the *English History* Ranke made much more explicit in the lectures he gave during the period of its composition. Here he drew no categorical distinction between the past and the present, arguing for the validity of contemporary history on the ground that the historian is as capable of impartiality for this as for any other historical era and demonstrating thereby that the issue of historical impartiality for him was not so much a matter of past versus present as of one-sided particularity versus concrete universality. Thus Ranke argued not only against the point of view that "the study of history is directed to the past" but also against the associated view that it seeks "the truth of the facts, . . . represented as objective truth." He made his argument by associating the problem of distortion with the partisanship of the historian, that is, with "the influences of transitory personal interests and opinions" on him; by asserting that in this respect there was no difference in kind between contemporary and past history, since "historical impartiality does not depend . . . on the closeness or distance of its objects" and "the difference of contemporary history from remote history . . . is only a matter of degree"; and by insisting that the remedy for it in the histories of both "our own times" and older ages, apart from the moral character of the historian, was to raise his point of view above the particular perspective and identify the historical object with a more general truth. The historian "must gain an independent point of view from which the objective truth, a general view, opens out more and more." Ranke habitually defined impartiality in terms of "historical objective truth," and he tended increasingly to defend his belief in such truth with references to the general connectedness of history.[38]

Hence the amalgam of particular and general history in the *English History* sustained the combination of sympathy and impartiality in his historical method. Already in his preface Ranke indicated that his *English History* would carry this amalgam to an unprecedented coalescence which would make the exacting standards of particular historical truths applicable ipso facto to the discovery of general truths in history. He made, to be sure, his familiar reference to the "clash of the general [*des Allgemeinen*] and the particular [*des Besonderen*]," in which the general represents "the large . . . movements stemming almost inevitably from earlier times" and "conditioning change . . . and decisions in general," and the particular represents "the orientation and energy of individuals," but he now put this confrontation in a context which looked to its practical resolution in the English case. The English history with which he was concerned "forms a world-dominant historical region," he wrote, "where it develops separately, according to its own inner impulse, as well as where it directly intersects with general events," and it was here to drive home his point that in the English past the particular and general historical truths were two sides of the same events, that he delivered his oft-quoted maxim: "Everything is universal and individual spiritual life."[39] Beyond his earlier histories, in which he identified the explicitly universal themes born by individual agents, whether papal, Protestant, or French, Ranke now undertook to demonstrate the universal resonance of an English development that was individuated in its intent.

The pattern of Ranke's book thus exhibited his wonted dualistic structure, but now with both parts accounted for more equally and integrated more tightly than ever before by the substance of what was distinctive in English history. On the one hand he repeatedly resorted to "destiny," "historical necessity," "impossibility," "natural limits," "the force of things," "the progress" or "course" "of events," and even "the logic of circumstances" to characterize the general forces which often explained the motivation or effects of individual persons and nations. This destiny or necessity was now entirely intrahistorical: it consisted of the projection into every historical present of the past "currents of general tendencies" with "a force which overshadows the best-planned political arrangements," or of the all-embracing framework established by the "international system of the west, whose life penetrates and determines the history of every individual nation."[40]

But on at least as many occasions, again in his customary way, Ranke would refer to the supervening spontaneity and intractable distinctiveness of individual persons and nations and to the consequently irreducible particularity of events for his explanations. Thus he could adduce the personality differences of James II and William III for the interpretation of their divergent destinies, structural differences between England and France for the interpretation of their running conflict, and "the turn of events" for the indication of the moment when "the events [which] have been irrevocably prepared by the past ... then develop themselves by their own impulses."[41] And as he had formulas for the explanatory force of historical necessity and the western system, so also did he concoct epigrammatic propositions for their contraries. "The effects of the sundry forces of the world are not so sharply defined that there does not remain something completely individual [*Individuelles*], which embraces a tendency contrary to the dominant one and is able to make a place for it." And in reference to the European system and its constituent individual states: "The life and destiny of Europe consist in the fact that its great general conflicts are ever being breached by the particular conflicts of the divers states."[42]

Here again, obviously, was Ranke's familiar duality between necessity and freedom, and just as well-tried was its anchorage in the general pattern of duality, or "opposition" (*Gegensatz*), which pervaded the *English History* as it had done the other great books of his postrevolutionary periods. For Ranke the connection between the antinomy of freedom/necessity and the prevalence of conflict in history was an explicit one, and it provided him with a fundamental grounding of such conflicts. "As highly as one must value the fact that the objective ideas which are linked with the culture of the human race get general respect and expression," he declared early in the *English History*, "yet spiritual life rests not so much on a credulous and submissive acceptance of them as on a free, subjectively mediatory, and thus also restrictive appropriation of them which is inconceivable without struggle and opposition.'' Hence once more he saw opposition and division as basic to the history and even the nature of man. "Western nations and empires have arisen in constant assimilation and rejection, in ever renewed conflicts for their future, and in an unceasing struggle with opposed elements which threaten them with destruction,'' he began, and he proceeded indeed to write English history primarily in terms of oppositions both persistent and successive. In the conflicts between state and church, Protestantism and Catholicism, Puritanism and Anglicanism, popular sovereignty and divine right of kings, parliament and monarch, England and France, he found the vitality of history, to be sure, but he also saw in them so many phenomenal expressions of a fundamental "schism" (*Zwiespalt*) under which "European life has been formed and developed''; so many "natural forces which create but also destroy''; so many "pitiless . . . great powers who fight for possession of the world''; so many "mighty movements without definite limits or fixed ends, rooted in the seething and divided depths of society." "In the great conflicts of the world,'' he concluded, "the outcome usually depends on those general antipathies which take hold of people and carry them away.''[43]

But however familiar the pattern, this polarized structure of human reality worked out differently in the English from any other national past, and because of this substantive difference it came to play an unprecedented historiographical role in the *English History*: whereas in the French, and even the German, past, something incomplete and penultimate always adhered to the pattern of duality, which was transcended by constant strivings and intermittent realizations of uniformity, in English history this duality was so continuous and inherent that it was itself an essential component of national and finally also of international unity. English history was of universal significance in the early-modern period precisely because it represented the general type which preserved division as against the French representation of the general type which abolished division. Thus he could summarize this great confrontation of universal systems in precisely these terms: "The one of these two great political bodies represented the combined Germanic and Romanic monarchy in its fullest unity of development. . . . Religion and culture, war and state, external and internal affairs, alike showed a unity in which one will was dominant—a will which at the same time was in harmony with the ideas of the nation. In this absolute subordination of all lay the unity and strength of the French monarchy. . . . In England, on the contrary, the authority of the highest power was closely attached to the resolutions of Parliament, . . . which were reached only by means of continual opposition and party strife. . . . That such a constitutional and Protestant power . . . took the lead in restraining and subduing the dominant European power—this it is that has given modern times their special character.''[44] Nor was Ranke any less explicit in attributing to this polarized England an alternative kind of unity: ''the most varied conceptions of the world and of life, of the state and of religion assert themselves alongside one another, . . . in ceaseless antagonism, not without passionate transport—but in which a higher community exists.''[45]

Hence the immanent design of Ranke's *English History* was to present a distinctive kind of universality, one which anticipated the inner harmony between unity and diversity that he would have liked to see realized in his own time. To be sure, he showed that ''even insular England,'' like all the other nations, belongs ''to the general community of the peoples of the west, derives its particular existence from it without being able ever to break loose from it, . . . feels constantly the effect of tendencies general in Europe and influences them in turn.'' He showed too, again as he already had with other states, that as England was a permanent ''member of the Romano-Germanic family of nations that formed the western world,'' its internal development was inextricably bound up with the international relations of Europe and thereby with the universal history of humanity. Thus he exhibited his characteristic alternation of internal policy and international relations as the discursive presentation of their real interaction seriatim through Britain's early-modern history until the climactic conjuncture of parliamentary revolution and the Grand Alliance toward the end of the seventeenth century led him frankly to align the English case under a general principle of national-universal congruence. ''Parliamentary tendencies in England had the advantage and the good fortune to enter into alliance with the general interests of Europe. Every power which has ever attained to independent life in Europe has had to win its position while thus participating in the conflict of general interests, and has had to prove itself indispensable to the European commonwealth. It depended on the victory or defeat of parliamentary principle whether there should be a balance of power between states and religions, and consequently whether there should be personal independence of the individual or not."[46]

But over and above the generic formal pattern of connecting particular and general relations, the distinctive contents of British history as he saw them gave Ranke the opportunity to bring the connection to new levels of integration. Four aspects of these contents served this purpose: its Germanic roots, its triadic political structure (England, Scotland, and Ireland), its persistent Protestant commitment, and its parliamentary constitution.

The Teutonic origins of English history, dating from the Anglo-Saxon conquest of the island, established a superiority of Teutons over Celts which first permitted "Germanic ideas to be expressed in their complete purity, purer than in the Germanies themselves," and, fed by the intervening compatible infusions of Protestantism, national separatism, religious toleration, and political diversity, developed into "the most powerful of the Germanic kingdoms" by the end of the seventeenth century.[47] For Ranke, England was the early-modern successor of the Reformation German Empire as the leading representative of the generic Romano-Germanic monarchy of the west on its Germanic side. England now carried Teutonic politics onto the world stage in opposition to the Romanic emphasis of the French.

The special relationship of Scotland and Ireland to England from the time of the Stuarts concerned Ranke not only because of the specific roles played by the Scots and the Irish in the great turning points of English politics but even more because the recurrent efforts that were mounted from England for "the unification of the three kingdoms" mediated between the insularity of English developments and the generality of their influence. Thus the Stuarts were led into their international Catholic alignment by their attempts to unite the three kingdoms under their monarchical authority. Cromwell's subjection of the three realms and his association of them "in common enterprises," however temporary, not only forms "in the succession of British events . . . one of the great links through which the whole historical development is held together" but also was one of the means through which Cromwell from his English base asserted for "Protestantism an independent position among the powers of the world." William of Orange, finally, extended the specifically English revolution of 1688 to Scotland and Ireland, and in the process generalized its sectarian base into the policies of religious toleration for which Britain would become universally significant.[48]

Despite, or rather precisely because of, the parochialism of the Anglican establishment, English Protestantism served Ranke in two different ways for the demonstration of the universal resonance inherent in England's very specificity. First, the existence of a generic Protestantism over and above its particular division into Anglican and Presbyterian parties was palpable in its surfacing at such turning points as the Restoration and the Glorious Revolution and in its collective hostility to universal Catholicism. The varieties of the English Protestant confessions indeed contributed to the general historical impact of English Protestantism, since its establishmentarian and Presbyterian churches and its radical sects were so many representatives at home of kindred movements abroad. In any case the anti-Catholic policies of the English kings from the Middle Ages through the Tudors, resumed in the proceedings of Cromwell and William III, "made common cause with the great reforming movement which was spreading over the world." It was largely through the Protestant religious component in British politics that intra-English conflict "lost its insular character; it became involved in the great religious and political conflict which [in the seventeenth century] divided Europe, and appears as an essential part of it." By the end of the seventeenth century England was not only participating in but leading the victorious side in this conflict, and it was the Protestant as much as the constitutional character of Great Britain, just as it was the Catholic as well as the absolutist character of its hegemonial adversary, that made these nations representative of universal movements.[49]

But secondly Ranke found a universal role even in the most distinctive aspects of English religiosity. These aspects were essentially two: the persistence of religious considerations in English politics and the union of the Anglican establishment with the whole constitution and not simply the monarchical head of the realm. The two aspects were connected with each other. "The ecclesiastical element appears at every step in English history. As the relation of Protestantism to Catholicism dominated the course of all foreign affairs, so the relation to each other of the two Protestant confessions . . . dominated the course of all domestic affairs." Both the sign and the guarantee of this religious persistence were marked by the entrenchment of Protestantism, in the form of the Anglican establishment and Nonconformist toleration, in the constitution. Thus the Restoration Parliament "established for all times the parliamentary and Protestant character of the English constitution. . . . The ecclesiastical reformation had been carried out in Germany by the princes: in England it was associated with parliamentary rights; for it was sanctioned by the laws." Hence more than in any other of his histories Ranke repeatedly attributed the crucial movements in his *English History* to "the combination of religious and political opinions," lent full weight to both elements alike, and thus made England an especially typical representative of "the close connection between state and church amidst a continuing clash of these principles" which he considered to be one of the two "characteristic factors making the Romano-Germanic nations a great indivisible community that appears as a unity in the world." The constitutional enshrinement of the religious motif in British politics, moreover, was a literal historical expression of Christianity's integration into the state, the process which he saw at the universal heart of modern history. In the combination of "opposition and cooperation" by English Anglicans and Presbyterians he saw the paradigm on which the whole "subsequent history of England depended," and in the particular presence in England of religious questions at "the very core of the political" he saw the paradigm of all modern politics. For "are they not still there today even if there is less consciousness of them?"[50]

The fourth thread running through Ranke's *English History* was the parliamentary constitution itself, and undoubtedly he found in it the most prominent and forceful generalizing theme of all. For this constitution made into undeniable fact historical desiderata which were incompatible in logic. In Ranke's version, it united conflict and harmony in synchronic relations, and it united constancy and change in diachronic relations. The first union was necessary for the reconciliation of individual autonomy with universal process which made up the substance of history; the second was necessary for the reconciliation of continuity and innovation which was required for the very possibility of history. Ranke gave full recognition to the special character of the English constitutional development—he deemed it "in harmony with the insular separation of Britain from the European continent"[51]—but by reason of its unifying functions within the English constitution the parliamentary nature of this constitution became at the same time a universal force in the life of western civilization.

The centrality of the politicoconstitutional theme in Ranke's *English History* is indubitable. Not only was the prominent religious theme ancillary to it—both the Anglican establishment and the Presbyterian Nonconformists were defined by their association with the political constitution of Britain—but Ranke's infrequent adversions to the society and literature of the realm were patterned on it. "The English church never forgot for a moment," he wrote of restored Anglicanism, "how closely it was jointed to the parliamentary system—albeit certainly in accordance with the course of English history in which the monarchy also had an important position.... Church and constitution were most tightly interlaced." Nor did he hesitate to articulate the parallel between the English culture and politics of the time along similar lines. "As in the state so in literature: severance and rivalry—and yet not merely the individual struggling of minds. One almost sees with one's eyes how two ages separate from each other."[52]

The parliamentary focus of this English constitution did more than thus dominate the national history—it linked the English constitution to universal history as well, bestowing upon this constitution a distinctively generic role in the world. As a rule, on the universal level Ranke attributed to the national constitutions of the Old Regime only the most formal representation of general principle. The "characteristic factor" which, alongside the relationship between state and church, made a unified and indivisible community out of the "Romano-Germanic nations" was, according to him, "the monarchical-corporate constitution of each individual country and the internal opposition to which it gave rise," and from this global point of view he adjudged the conflict between monarch and estates, like the struggle between religious and political tendencies and like the interaction of "independent nationalities within . . . an ideal rather than an existent unity," to be the typical activities on which "the characteristic life of the west" as a whole was based.[53] In the running battle between monarchy and Parliament (in the narrow sense of the houses of Parliament), England was certainly representative of this fissiparous life, but not distinctively so. What was distinctive about the synchronic relations in the English constitution and at the same time representative in reality of the constitutional unity that was merely ideal in generic western life was the fundamental collaboration of the parties which were in daily struggle.

Time and again Ranke stressed the indispensability of both hereditary monarchy and independent Parliament to the British constitution, and time and again he stressed the underlying unity which not merely moderated but harnessed the power of their divided energies. Thus in general, "on the unification of the national powers, king and Parliament, rests the omnipotence of the legislative power, which defines the character of modern England." More particularly, "the solution of the contradiction" between the extensive monarchical powers and the equally extensive parliamentary rights under Queen Elizabeth was that, despite all their clashes, "Queen and Parliament were allies in the general issues of the country and the world." In the Glorious Revolution, "King, Lords, and Commons formed a single great party," and in the worldwide historical struggle that followed "the English government, in spite of its internal quarrels, maintained itself in the form of its original establishment." Hence Ranke could summarize English political development in terms which supplied a rationale for his flexible use of "Parliament" to characterize both the corporate representation against the monarch and the constitutional sovereign that included the monarch: "The vital elements of the culture which comprised the kingdom acted in free, and often opposed, movements, which were therefore all the more forceful and versatile for that," and yet the individual and corporate independencies "were far from inhibiting a unified development of power." The universal conclusion which Ranke drew from this English constitutional pattern of unity amid diversity was a proposition on the integrative function of monarchy that betrayed a connection of his national history with the investment in the worldwide struggle of his own time. In contrast to the subordination of the sovereign power to party influence "in republican constitutions," Ranke wrote in a concluding formulation of the standards set by the English constitution under its best monarchs: "the advantage of monarchy consists chiefly in this, that it has the task and the natural impulse to keep its eye on the collective interests above all party considerations."[54] Precisely this, as his history was designed to show, was the role of the hereditary monarch within the traditional parliamentary constitution, and precisely this was the aspect of early-modern English history that could serve as a general proposition for the modern age.

Ranke's view of the English parliamentary constitution enabled him not only to span discrepancies across political space but also to weave constants and happenings together through historical time. He had both a political and an historiographical interest in such a diachronic connection. Politically, he had an interest in showing that the indubitable trend toward the constitutional limitation of the monarch by the power of the parliamentary commons was itself limited by the constant efficacy of historical tradition. Historiographically, he had an interest in showing a cohesive theme running through the vagaries of individual events, both to depict the "connectedness" he always found indispensable to universal history and to exhibit a continuously relevant past amid the spontaneous changes necessarily involved in every free act. Ranke's parliamentary constitution could perform these roles because it possessed, in his judgment, the faculty of remaining basically the same through all its novel adaptations to changing conditions. "It is at once the charm and the difficulty of this history," he noted in general during his account of the Civil War, "to perceive the autonomous movements which rise to prominence in the Britannic realms in the most varied forms but always in connection with old-historical developments and are engaged in a life-and-death struggle with one another," and in his exposition he repeatedly characterized not only the crises but also the great settlements of English history either as the literal "maintenance of the parliamentary constitution on its old basis" or at least as the establishment of constitutional forms "analogous to the old."[55] The reason for such constitutional longevity was at once spiritual and actual. The Protectorate could not last without a recognizable parliament; the Restoration was driven by the temperamental need for a hereditary monarch. These were examples of the fundamental fact that "in the historical elements of the state there lived an inner force which could not be stifled by any violence."[56] The British Empire of the eighteenth century, he concluded hyperbolically, was "the product of a history all of one piece from the moment of the first Germanic settlement in Britain to the foundation of maritime supremacy in both hemispheres. Through long centuries a consistently active national spirit [*Volksgeist*], which repelled everything alien and absorbed only what was analogous to itself, worked on the great structure which now represented the west most powerfully in distant nations."[57]

In this epitome of the constitutional constancy in his history, Ranke neglected to take into account the factor of innovation which was equally crucial to his account. For in this account he recognized that cyclical conflicts and mere restorations militated against both the indubitable constitutional change from monarchical to parliamentary preeminence which he found essential in English history and the freedom of individual action which he found essential in any history. Ranke denied, to be sure, any direct connection between the English constitutional development and the revolutionary movement of his own century, which he traced back to the French Revolution of 1789, for he rejected the idea that popular sovereignty was the basis of the English constitution in any of its historical stages. But he did admit an indirect connection between the two, and he stressed an innovative aspect of the English development that was independent of popular revolution.

Ranke traced the origin of the modern idea of popular sovereignty to the Puritan revolution, and although he aligned it with "tendencies that had been conquered," he also acknowledged its historical influence as a precedent for the great worldwide revolution of popular sovereignty that would come out of France. He found the ideas—interchangeable in his parlance—of "national sovereignty" and "popular sovereignty" in both the Long Parliament and the religious radicalism that rose to political ascendency in Scotland and Protectorate England, and he identified the revolutionism of his own time as their progeny. "It was in itself an event of incalculable resonance," he wrote about the espousal of popular sovereignty by the Long Parliament, "that an idea which arose in the realm of philosophical abstractions, after it had been seized by a powerful and armed party, obtained acceptance in the ruling parliamentary body of a great nation. There is no single political idea which has had an impact like popular sovereignty during the course of the recent centuries. At times repressed and only influencing opinions, but then breaking out again and openly acknowledged, never realized and always intrusive, it is the ever active ferment of the modern world." Nor was this tendency of merely evanescent import. "There were, so to speak, two different worlds in England," wrote Ranke toward the end of the Protectorate, "of which one clung to the institutions of the past and the other strove toward an unknown future." Then, in a thinly veiled allusion to the precedent set for the great French Revolution by the strenuous parliamentary opposition to the later Stuarts, Ranke mused: "Who could have had a presentiment that the events in England would one day react back upon France?" But the most striking line of descent was through the Americans, who realized the idea of revolutionary national sovereignty by basing themselves on the "Old-English institutions" which had remained recessive in the mother country. "Then followed, spurred by the parliamentary system and its effects favorable to the expansion of power and still more by the idea of national sovereignty and of equality which was realized in America, the French Revolution which . . . seemed as if it had to lead to an analogous transformation of the other nations and which attempted to convulse the previous state-system in general."[58]

More essential than such isolated precedents to revolution was Ranke's acknowledgment that the British constitution had to change with the times. Thus the recall of the old constitution under the Restoration meant at the same time the revival of the same old conflicts between Crown and Parliament. Clarendon's "historical merit" was to "join the new England . . . to the old," but "it contradicted the spirit of the time, the nation, and the king himself to continue leading wholly in the old way." The Glorious Revolution did not involve popular sovereignty, but it did extend the rights of Parliament and restrict the royal prerogative vis-à-vis the traditional constitution and, at least through the enactment of the freedom of the press that was part of the revolutionary settlement, fostered a change that "belongs generally to that system of thoughts, views, and institutions then opening new paths for the world." Indeed, Ranke would even conclude the main body of his history on this note: "Since ... the English Parliament rose to definite predominance over British affairs and decisive influence in the affairs of Europe, the element of innovation, previously repressed and vigorously represented in it, also attained a universal significance. The conflict between the ideas of 1640 [i.e., of the Puritan revolution] and those of 1660 [i.e., of the Restoration] became a general question for the nations of Europe."[59]

The synchronic political and diachronic historical functions of the parliamentary constitution combined in Ranke's presentation to produce an erratic but perceptible convergence from ostensive division to an ever more tangible unity within the bifurcated but nationally defined English system of government. With his ancillary generalizing themes—the Germanic, the Britannic, and the religious—organized around this blend of progressive synthesis and continuing diversity in the primary constitutional process, Ranke was enabled to resolve more integrally than ever before the two related historiographical problems that had plagued him from the beginning of his career: the relationship between the free individual agent of history and the general patterns of human development which conditioned the motives and the effects of his actions; and the relationship between the unpredictable individual event which provided the open drama of history and the universal tendency which provided its intelligibility.

On the first count, Ranke spanned the distance between individual agent and general pattern by attributing actual universal ideas or actual participation in universal interests to persons engaged in the English constitutional process. "Spiritually vital men are motivated more by general ideas than by particular interests," he opined toward the beginning of the book, and in the applications of the principle which followed seriatim throughout the work the relationship between the general and the personal in individuals was clearly a continuity that made general views actual rather than an antithesis that relegated them to an ideal. Thus he warned against the distortion of motives that is the result of interpreting "the connection of personal purposes . . . with an enterprise of general importance" in terms of personal interest alone. "The historian is astonished when, upon closer examination of the deliberations, he meets factors which have a certain importance in themselves." These factors, often enough, were universals with which individuals associated themselves. "The greatest thing that can happen to man," he generalized from the case of Queen Elizabeth, "is to defend the universal cause in one's own. Personal existence thereby expands to a world-historical force." He added, characteristically, that "the personal and the universal cause was simultaneously an English one." The cause was sometimes the deliberate appropriation of a universal idea, for now Ranke acknowledged the historical efficacy of such ideas across the ages: "Men and things change, but the ideas captured in words and writing can rise above this change and have an impact upon the most distant ages." But even more characteristic of Ranke's procedure in this respect was his investment of individuals with a universal nature through their perception of a general situation or their conscious role in a general movement. Thus he adumbrated "the future combinations of international affairs in the minds of statesmen who were aware of the general world situation," and he attributed deliberate universalism above all to William of Orange, "an international nature" and for that very reason Ranke's special hero. William's case showed that "the effect which a man can produce on the world" often depends "on the position he assumes and can assert in the conflict of the forces which contend with one another for the control of the general life of which they form a part." Thus he became the "condottiere of parliamentary ideas in the European struggle" and the "representative . . . of the idea of the balance of power, which is necessary to the existence of the states of Europe."[60] When, then, Ranke set forth the historiographical principle that "it cannot only be the business of history to show how far great personalities have attained or failed to attain the ideals which hover over human life, but it is almost more concerned to ascertain how far the universal interests, in whose midst important men appear, have been advanced by them," he was not so much announcing an abstract prescription for historical biography as drawing an inference from the actual involvement of his favorite characters in the *English History*.[61]

The second of Ranke's historiographical solutions—the integration of trends and events—was implicit rather than overt. He tended to explain conflict by the general tendency or the cumulative necessity of things and to employ dramatic description for the climactic and contingent events which betokened the resolution of the conflict. Time and again he would introduce a decisive confrontation or series of confrontations with the announcement that their issue—"what form the Britannic realm would take"— was "incalculable" and "lay in profound obscurity." The reason, quite simply, was that the great constitutional questions were decided "in consequence of events which gave one side or the other preponderance." At times Ranke would provide these decisive resolutions with such nominal and unsupported explanatory phrases as the "power of public opinion," the authoritative weight of popular "antipathy," the power of a popular "movement," the prevalence of a "general wish" and the attribution of "convictions" to the ubiquitous but indefinite "everybody" (*man*). But essentially for such occasions description itself was the only appropriate explanation, for "great constitutional issues . . . can be decided only as a result of events through which one side or the other triumphs."[62]

In the presentation of his historical agents, then, Ranke blended the representation of conflict situations in thematic terms with the description of events in narrative terms, attaching the universal views of his agents to the narrative as ingredients of the drama. Once achieved, the resolution would then enter into the redefinition of the narrowing thematic duality for the next generation. The interpenetration of dialectical analysis and synthetic narrative marked the high point in Ranke's professional self-integration. History finally did what he had always meant for it to do.

III It was fitting that Ranke should have registered the achievement of his practical historiography in a theoretical note which finally focused on the junction rather than the disjunction between particular research and general coherence; which formally admitted the relevance of the present to the connectedness of the historical process; and which projected an architectonic structure of history as a regular and interlocking hierarchy reaching from local to universal history, with each level pointing beyond itself to its context on the next higher lever. Embodied in an unpublished fragment, as was his wont with his ruminations on the theory of history after his articular flurry of the early 30s, this statement dated from the 60s—the decade that marked the completion of his French and English histories. Admitting still that "history does not have the unity of a philosophical system," that its "greatest attraction" is its concern with the expressions of human freedom, and that "nothing exists entirely in the reality of something else," yet his emphasis now was on history's "inner connections of its own." Despite his usual obeisance to the juxtaposition of freedom as a condition of every "new emerging activity" and necessity as its "basis" in the past, and despite his insistence on the disparity of epochs resulting from their clash, he also maintained that history's inner connection "penetrates everywhere," including the juncture of past and present. "What developed in the past constitutes the connection with what is emerging in the present." As a "discipline," "universal history" deals with these connections. It "differs from specialized research in that universal history, while investigating the particular, never loses sight of the complete whole, on which it is working." But like the object of specialized research, the connection between past and present which is the object of universal history is a valid material for historical method. "It existed in a particular way and could be no other. It too is a proper object of knowledge."[63]

But if Ranke merged fact and coherence here in his theory as he had in his practice of history, he also revealed that he still had unfinished historiographical business. For in this fragment, as in his earlier programmatic notes, he mixed the extensive meaning of universal history in with its intensive meaning, and in its extensive sense his program for history remained unrealized. For if universal history as a discipline studies the connectedness of history, universal history as a process deals with the whole range of the human past, "the sequence of centuries, each with its unique essence, all linked together, from the very beginning to the present day." In this sense, "universal history comprehends the past life of mankind, not in its particular relations and trends, but in its fullness and totality." The integrated relation that exists between fact and connection in the intensive sense of universal history pertains to the extensive sense as well, but now amended for the substitution of a quantified larger context for the logic of coherence.

> The study of particulars, even of a single detail, has its value. . . . But this specialized study too will always be related to a larger context; even local history will be related to the history of a whole country, a biography to an epoch of national or universal history. But all of these epochs . . . belong to the entire whole which we call universal history. The study of these epochs in a wider context is of a correspondingly greater value. The final goal—not yet attained—always remains the conception and composition of a history of mankind.[64]

"The universal" in this plenary sense remained for Ranke "the type of knowledge that everyone desires," but it remained necessarily abortive for him as contrasted with the practicability of universals in the qualitative sense of historical coherence. For in this sense "we are agreed . . . that the critical method, objective research, and synthetic construction can and must go together," whereas the combination of a *plenary* history which "would include a solidly rooted understanding of the entire history of man" with "the dictates of exact research" is and must be merely "an ideal goal."[65]

Like his hard-won integrity, this final dissatisfaction too was a true reflection of his experience as a practicing historian. The fruitful interplay of research and conception which dominated the main body of the *English History* did not apply either to its eighteenth-century epilogue or to its projection into Ranke's contemporary world of the nineteenth century. Consequently a gap, of which Ranke was himself well aware, existed between the history of the early-modern national states which was the focus of his history and the universal conflict between monarchy and revolution which was the theme of his nineteenth-century experience. The England which had been *the* Germanic representative of the monarchical-constitutional principle in the seventeenth century had ceased to be it in the succeeding period. The persistence of religious motives which had guaranteed the spiritual vitality of the English state faded in the eighteenth century as "religious considerations gradually fell into the background in contrast to political ones." With the onset of the revolutionary era, "the Whiggish spirit" proceeded to enact the reforms "that were peremptorily demanded by the spirit of the century," with the consequence that "the parliamentary-Protestant constitution," while not subverted, was "essentially modified" and possibly "impaired." In any case, Ranke concluded, England was no longer the national agent of world history. For the eighteenth century, "a history focused only on England does not lead to a satisfying and convincing result. Still less would it be the case for the times that followed, where the impulse of actions stemmed more from general relationships than from the internal sequence of the English development, much as this affected them."[66]

England, in short, did not bear the universal motif that could overcome the revolutionary-counterrevolutionary opposition of nineteenth-century contemporary history, and, until such an historical agent was found, universal history in the sense of the coherent history of mankind could not be written. In the years that surrounded the German unification of 1870, the discovery of the contemporary agent would spark the conception and the actual composition of a truly universal world history.

12
The Third Synthesis:
World History in German Perspective
(1867-79)

The last volume of Ranke's *English History* appeared in 1868, and despite his evident satisfaction with the work signs were not wanting during the latter years of this decade and the early years of the next that he was internally ready for still another turning point in his life and career and that he was open to external events as the occasions of it. Before 1870 there were indications of an inner unease; after 1870 there were indications of its resolution. Between the two states of mind lay a German unification which Ranke did not endorse in the political process of its achievement but which he did approve after its attainment and its consequent entrance into the realm of contemporary history. And, as usual, the experience that meant a rupture in his political life became the medium of a development in his history.

By the late 1860s Ranke was a septuagenarian, he lived amid a politics of force and of revolutionary implications which made him fearful, and he was finishing a book which he predicted (erroneously, as it turned out) "is my last archival work."[1] On all three of these grounds—personal, political, and professional—he was ready for a change. But their effects were convergent rather than parallel. His personal discomforts would remain with him henceforward, and his political uncertainties would be settled only with continuing internal reservations under the influence of changing external circumstances: but both intimate unease and political wariness would combine to goad the tensions of his historical writing to their final resolution.

I   Ever since his attainment of emotional security with his marriage back in 1843, Ranke had found acceptable vents for his passions and had indulged only sporadically in his bouts of discontent, but now, as he aged perceptibly and his family broke up around him, a mood of chronic gentle sadness settled over him. He let slip the kind of blurted confessions redolent of an old man who helplessly feels himself losing control and even comprehension of the stormy currents which flow about him. Earlier in the decade of the 60s he had already begun to refer to himself as an old man, and then he began to show the nostalgia, the revived religious interest, and the slightly bewildered passivity which so often accompany this consciousness. He returned to his old homestead in his native Wiehe and wrote movingly of the ''homely, local, and domestic emotions'' with which he again lived there. ''I do not forget how old I am and will see to it that our name keeps at least a local duration for the future generation.''² Such nostalgic hearkenings back to native environs and ''the family history'' would remain, surfacing occasionally and fed by the renewed plaints of loneliness following upon the deaths of those particularly close to him in the family.³ When he reviewed the course of his life on an anniversary of his wife's death, he came to the resigned conclusion that ''it has not gone entirely well for me, but it has gone tolerably.''⁴

He was bereft now too of the communication which his teaching had brought him, and bereft of it in a particularly traumatic way. In terms of student appeal his classes had been going badly for some years, but the end of his pedagogical career struck a note low even against this backdrop: he had to call off his last lecture course in 1871 because of sparse attendance, a faithful sign of his personal alienation from his immediate academic society. Confirmatory of this withdrawal was his avocational escape into his own isolated worlds. He took ''particular pleasure'' in ''going back to the ancient classics.'' He deliberately unearthed books and essays from his early student and teaching years "so that old age and youth directly coincide." And he studiously immersed himself in his work as "not only, in accordance with my motto, *voluptas,* but the very essence of life itself." What he wrote about the reading and discussion of the Greek classics held for this whole gamut of attitudes through which he diverted himself from his troublesome environment: "These hours raised me out of the orbit of views which dominate the modern world into higher and, as it were, purer regions."[5]

Mentions of the deity had never been wholly absent from Ranke's mind or his writing, but now they assumed an unwonted prominence as desperate invocations of an ultimate recourse from the mysteries and resistances of living—a recourse that even included, for the sake of psychic satisfaction, an intellectual acceptance of ecclesiastical institutions to which he could not subscribe. In the late 60s he wrote that he "was struck more than ever by how flesh and spirit hang together," but now he approached the connection no longer so much to know God through worldly appearance as to find rest in the divinity for the unsettling opaqueness of this appearance. "One must experience everything in order to understand, or rather to know that one does not understand. . . . It is all a mystery, marriage and birth, life and death; behind and with sensory appearance appears the Divine, as in the Lord's Supper." "Without an absorption in divine things," he wrote around the same time and along the same line, "man is a shadow on earth, passing through in the haze" (*Nebel*). Consequently, he would tell both his brother and his king a bit later that their destinies were accountable to "the finger of Providence." He would confess, indeed, that for him "the faith in Providence is the sum of all faith. I cling to it unshakably."[6] With this sense of dependence, it was not surprising that he expressed an unaccustomed deference to the dogmatic and ecclesiastical organization of the Protestant evangelical church. As early as the mid-60s he declared his advocacy of "the positive view" in the debate about the historical Christ, because it maintained "the evangelical principle," with its corollary of a "deep, unquestioning, and simple faith in the Gospel." When his son was ordained a minister in the Evangelical Church shortly before the end of the decade, Ranke obviously approved and showed sympathetic understanding of the clerical order. Although he still could not himself subscribe to the formula of the ordination, he admitted that "it contains the mystery which one must acknowledge without seeking grounds for it. It is so rigorous that I cannot conceive how a clergyman can bring himself to tear himself away from it or teach the contrary of it. One must overturn the church before one can change ecclesiastical theology; for the latter is completely determined by the former. My Otto is destined for it by nature, as it were, and is prepared to maintain it."[7] Only a short time before, he had revealed a predisposition which undoubtedly bulked large in his new appreciation of organized churches: he climaxed a deprecatory description of the uncongenially mobile political situation with a declaration of trust in the viability of the "establishment" (des einmal Gegründeten) and grounded this trust simply in the ultimate proposition: "I believe in the old God."[8]

II   It was in politics, indeed, that Ranke found the most focused source of his distress, and it was correspondingly from politics that the chief impulse toward his inner pacification would come. The fact was that the victory of the Prussian monarchy, under Bismarck's leadership, over the hated Prussian liberals, with their revolutionary implications for Ranke, restored his interest in politics but also intensified his feeling of impotence about it. "General affairs," he wrote during 1867 in reference to Prussian politics in northern Germany, "move in a way that we can neither foresee nor control. . . . An imperious necessity reigns over everything. There is no way out, either to the right or to the left, for everything is settled." And as late as October 1869 he was asking rhetorically: "Is the actual situation not this, that since the Peace of Prague we have fallen into a labyrinth which exits into an abyss?"[9]

But—and this is important for understanding the impact which the unification would have upon him—Ranke's feeling of helplessness about the politics of his day was the result neither of a fundamental hostility to what was happening nor of indifference toward an indecisive conflict. It reflected rather his own divided attitude toward that politics: he approved of the achievements while reprobating the means of attaining them. Hence he was engagé at the same time as he condemned himself to passivity—a perfect recipe for the translation of political experience into history. "With continuing reluctance I yet also feel sympathy with the course of events," he wrote frankly in 1867 on the very occasion that he complained of the "imperiously" determined course of these events. "From my own perspective I follow the situation with great interest as it unfolds."[10]

Thus he hoped for a good result from the Reichstag of the North German Confederation although, as he ruefully told his political crony, the archconservative Edwin von Manteuffel, "the idea was neither yours nor mine." And again: "There is something imposing in the deliberations of the Reichstag. I should not like to participate in them at any price, for my personal conviction cannot tolerate it. . . . The actual result is in any case acceptable. You may believe that there are people who even admire it."[11]

What Ranke welcomed in the political developments between 1866 and 1870 were "the initiative" of the Prussian king ("the hereditary Germanic prince"), the persistence in Prussia of the "military state" (i.e., of "the military principle at the heart of the state"), the primacy of foreign policy in the Prussian relations with Denmark and Austria, the resolution of the Austro-Prussian dualism in favor of Prussia and therewith the Prussian assumption of the defense of "the German fatherland." What he rejected were specifically such violations of "the old state" as the disappearance of Hanover and the creation of federal ministries, and generally the contradiction of "wishing to combine the old monarchy and its tradition with the constitutional system, . . . to wage a political war in the old style with a national army"—a contradiction that resulted in the anomalous subordination of the triumphant military conservatives to the "destructive" democratic faction they had beaten. "We used the victory to deny the principles on which we are based." So he welcomed the hegemony of the Prussian monarchy over northern Germany abroad and the liberal opposition at home; he deplored "the mixing of the [Prussian] State and the [North German] Confederation," the "rapprochement with democracy to make the Confederation strong," and the failure to "reject the Roman parvenu [Napoleon III]."[12]

This pattern of his response struck deep, for it was continuous with the feeling he now had about the meaning of his whole life. "What a change," he observed about the Rhine while recalling his other solitary walking trip along its shores far back in 1817. "My whole life in between: the ideas which I cherished at that time now well-nigh carried out, certainly in another way: the end of my life near."[13] In life the ideas he had cherished from literature, religion, and philosophy he would carry out in history; in politics the legitimist and national ideas which he had cherished were being carried out through a pact with the revolutionary devil, and ultimately they too would be detoured through history.

The lectures on contemporary history which Ranke delivered in the late 1860s showed how his ambivalent attitude toward his own times—primarily but not exclusively its politics—helped to condition an altered approach to history which led him to focus on post-Reformation Germany as an especially universal species of national history. His assessments of his own age were desperately divided. On the one hand, he admitted that what he called "the successes of the events of 1859 and 1866" entered prominently into his judgments on the positive side, for "the national interests—that is, the consolidation of the states, the assertion of their power—set themselves against the cosmopolitan interests of revolution," and, through its association with nationality, hereditary monarchy has compromised with revolution in the direction of constitutionalism. The forces of revolution, for their part, have equally moderated their claims toward constitutionalism, and through the continuous connection of internal movement to foreign relations—thereby to "the development of the state as such"—the chief factors of contemporary life stand in a viable relationship to one another. From this positive perspective, then, "the characteristic feature of the modern world is . . . the combination of the power of the state with the free development of the individual."[14]

But there was another, much more unsettling side to Ranke's contemporary attitude. From this perspective, "everything moves in incessant upheavals and transactions," and "we stand in the midst of an agitation of minds and interests" mended only by shaky concessions. "All contemporary history consists in the [three-cornered] struggle among the traditional state powers, the liberal tendency, and the revolutionary principle—a continuing conflict of all the vital elements" that is connected with "the conflict of the great powers, which can be seen as the chief product of modern history." From this point of view, then, not only in politics but in contemporary culture as a whole there are no longer any dominant convictions, with the result that individuals are isolated in society and particulars are exalted in the sciences. "In the ubiquitous conflict everyone stands for himself. . . . All sciences are involved in a process of change in which every generally valid truth is doubted and the particular is sought. . . . Conditions have attained no stable form." When he was on this tack, Ranke saw only unsolved problems where on the other tack he saw harmonizing moderation. Thus the connection of the traditional powers with the idea of nationality which from the first point of view has earned "the principle of hereditary monarchy general recognition as an indispensable form of the state," raises, from the other point of view, "the chief question of the day: How far is it to extend?" Ranke's ambivalence was appropriate to a political situation characterized by actual struggle and projected resolution, and to a cultural situation characterized by actual specialization and normative generalization. He welcomed the middling course that could harmonize parties, but he felt distinctly uncomfortable with a moderation that was piecemeal, expedient, and under duress, rather than principled and controlled. But he reacted differently to the two kinds of situations. About politics he could do nothing but wait uneasily: "Present conditions are too unsteady, still too much in the hands of the practical politicians, to be treated by historians." But history was a part of the cultural situation: about this he could and did do something.[15]

The feelings about the historical discipline which Ranke expressed in his lectures during the late 60s approximately paralleled his sentiments about politics and precisely mirrored his cognate sentiments about contemporary culture. He still, as he had so often in the past, characterized a universal history that would be at once extensive and coherent as "an unrealized ideal," but now he laid responsibility for the frustration of the ideal general history squarely on "the current condition of research as presently pursued," for the historian now "contents himself with research in the particular." Such was the passion for specialization and particularization, according to Ranke, that even general histories of individual nations or of particular epochs "are no longer being written." In some measure Ranke reluctantly accepted this uncongenial historiographical condition, partly because he felt compelled to submit to this restraining tide—"historical science is not ripe for the reconstruction of universal history on new bases"—and in part because he himself appreciated the value of particular research by reason of its credibility and of the "universal significance" to be found even within an historical particular. But Ranke was also disposed to counter this current and to present general history in a viable format, however much he was aware that "there could appear to be contradiction between renouncing the presentation of the general truth in the whole scope of history" and holding that "the scientific spirit . . . cannot neglect the prosecution of works aiming at and forming a notion of the general history of the human race." What was decisive for his attitude during this period was the main ground for his persistence in the study of universal history: it was not so much because he thought it "desirable" and because "the human spirit strives constantly, by its very nature, to grasp general truth," as he always had thought, but because he was now convinced that general processes necessarily existed in history and that individuals were inevitably involved in them. "We should consider the history of humanity to be a great, tightly integrated whole," he said. " . . . In the final analysis everything is interwoven with everything else, . . . for man lives only in community" (*Gemeinschaft*).[16]

Ranke had long felt the power of the connections among human phenomena, but never had he been so strongly convinced that all human phenomena were connected in historical actuality. Because of the synchronic connections among men, the coherent history of whole epochs became in his view unavoidable. "Chronicle becomes history when it appears in its connectedness; hence we have no choice but the separate treatment of the large and even the smaller epochs. . . . General truth too enters into phenomena by encompassing the particular. . . . The individual life stands under the influence of the general situation of the world. . . . A test for the perceptions of general knowledge is that they first make factual data comprehensible." But he found even this synchronic kind of generality an inadequate representation of the universal processes in which humanity was implicated. These processes extend across the epochs both for essentially human and for empirically historical reasons. Essentially, it is because what is valuable in human life endures across the ages. "General life is the eternally victorious and the continuously persistent. There cannot be separate sections of it, but only stages of development. . . . These stages appear in the epochs of general history and they can be distinguished from one another, but they all have the innermost common connection and they pass into one another." He proceeded to specify this diachronic coherence by indicating the substantive connections that link the epochs of western history and especially insisting on the relevance of medieval universal themes to both early-modern and contemporary history. "The great thing about the study of history," he said in general, "is that it combines the remotest epochs with the most recent." Thus medieval, early-modern, and contemporary history "are all continuations of one another, although each bears a distinctive character." Thus too "the complex of western nations which have preponderant power and culture" was "the chief product of modern history," "a creation of the great history of the Middle Ages," and a prominent feature of contemporary history. The religious conflict which came out of the Middle Ages and the Reformation subsequently "converted itself into a conflict of philosophy against theology . . . , through which there was aroused a general movement taking a development hostile to positive religion and rising to predominance in the history of the century of revolution." The nineteenth century, finally—this century of revolution—refers to past ages by its very character, for one of its most prominent features is its historical-mindedness: "it takes account again of the past and the positive." "The previous development of the European culture and nations was not broken off" even by the revolution, and, in the form of the association between the forces of revolution and the relationships of the traditional states, "historical factors" are part and parcel of the contemporary age.[17]

Ranke not only acknowledged the discordant requirements of his era and of his own perception in the approach to history; he sought to reconcile them in the writing of history. His point of departure had to be particularistic in method and individualistic in object, for he admitted these as conditions imposed by contemporary standards of research and by the analogous resonance of contemporary individualism in politics. But his goal remained universal history. "Only from the manifold is general truth composed, as individuals are more than ever called to participation in the state," he said, associating a pair of superficially ill-assorted categories. His solution, both for the organization of individual variety into general process and for the relating of historiographical and political categories, was to turn once more to German history, but now in the modern and contemporary periods when the starting point had to be particularism and the theme had to be Germany's universal involvement. In 1866 he offered a course on "Contemporary German History in Connection with General History," and he characterized his aim as "the description of the great struggle which encompassed the world from the German point of view," for "it is a struggle of two world powers, both in ideal and real opposition."[18] Thus did Ranke associate German history with one of the two sides in the homologous political and cultural divisions that so unsettled him in the frustrating years after the north-German but before the all-German unification.

The German unification of 1870 resolved Ranke's inner conflict: he accepted it not only as a political decision but as a turning point which marked the opening of a truly integrated modern epoch. Certainly the actual mode of the unification went far to pacify him, for it fulfilled his specifications in four important ways: it was, after all, "the happy moment" when "the general-German idea" (*die gemeindeutsche Idee*) which he had always represented was realized; the occasion was a military triumph over Napoleonic—i.e., revolutionary—France; the Imperial Crown was in fact "constituted exclusively by the princes," as he required; the power of the Crown over the army and finances—those twin "pillars of the monarchical state"—remained intact in the Prussianized Germany.[19] But he also filtered the unification through his own categories, and in these molds the event became acceptable as an inevitable fact of contemporary history despite the continued peril from the dilution of Prussian institutions. Two of these categories especially were conducive to his historicizing of the political experience: he perceived the unification to be necessarily implicated in the temporal succession of events; and he conceived the unification to be linked with—indeed to be the denouement of—the universal theme dominant in all of modern history. The lecture which he prepared just after the victories of 1870 revealed clearly the universal-historical considerations he associated with the German triumph. ''The great world event in the midst of which we live and which makes the year 1870 an epoch, is noteworthy for recalling to mind the earlier centuries in which similar conflicts raged and prepared for the conflicts of the present time.'' But when he looked to the early-modern past, it was not the conflict as such that riveted his attention. As befit the denouement of 1870, he promised to ''pay special attention to the German events. . . . For Germany was always the center of the endeavors of all the world.''[20]

When Ranke wrote and talked of the German unification, he tended to think of it not as the object of deliberate policy but as the product of a historical necessity about which there was little choice. ''For what purpose is the empire necessary?'' he asked, contemplating the event from the near vantage point of New Year's Eve 1872. And he answered: ''Yet I think that it was necessary; it formed itself in the struggle against France without our assistance, so it must be kept.'' Closer to the occurrence itself he told the Emperor William I in similar terms that the imperial crown had come to him ''in consequence of great events, through an ineluctable interconnection of things which an historian greets with happy congratulations.'' In the conversations which he held with Thiers during 1870 he attributed German war aims to the collapse of the middle kingdom after the dissolution of the Franco-German Carolingian Empire, to the seizures of Louis XIV, and to the inescapable but unidentified ''course of events'' (*Verlauf* or *Gang der Ereignisse*). Such a judgment of the unification obviously made it both acceptable and historical—acceptable, indeed, because it was historical.[21]

Alongside this formal view of the unification and its war, he set forth an idea of their historical meaning which lent it substance. From this substantive historical point of view the Prussian victory over France was the decisive event and the unification derived its meaning from it as its logical consequence. The Prussian victory was a historical event in two related senses. First, the victorious side itself represented the historical against the antihistorical principle. This conviction, in itself, went back to the appreciation for the conservative maintenance of historical institutions which he had developed after the revolution of 1830. But now he associated this appreciation with a concrete view of the Prussian role in the modern historical process, and this second dimension of the historicity of the Prussian triumph conferred a definable identity upon the historical principle it represented. Second, then, Prussia's defeat of France on behalf of Germany signified the resolution of the struggle between monarchy and revolution which, with antecedents in the early-modern period and a precedent in the Middle Ages, became the dominant theme in the history of the world since the French Revolution of 1789.

In Ranke's view, then, behind the events of 1870 and 1871 there ran a continuum of factors ranging from the particular interests of the Prussian state to the universal role of Germany in the world, and history was the matrix of this continuum. "In everything that we are experiencing," he mused retrospectively toward the end of the 70s, "a historical—I shall not say necessity—but consecution [*Folgerichtigkeit*] can be perceived." Before the unification he had written generally of Prussia as "the state in whose preservation almost most of all the connection of the past with the present and future is represented" and vaguely of "our mission in the world," but only with the war of unification did he get the two motifs together.[22] He saw the events of 1870 and 1871 both as "the realization of the Prussian-German idea" stemming from Frederick the Great and as the fulfillment of the "great mission assigned to the Prussian State" of having to combat "first the idea of universal empire [i.e., of the Bonapartes] and then the attempt at the universal republic." Both of these meanings—the particular Prussian and the universal-human alike—were essentially historical. The Prussian-German idea explicitly conferred on the new empire "a great significance referring to the earlier past." What raised the Prussian mission of fighting hegemonial empire and universal republic above the old struggle of "nation against nation" is that "we have at least the advantage of fighting for the institutions bound up with the historical development of the world." Between the two, connecting the two levels of conflict, was the German nation, with its distinctive historical needs and qualities representing humanity. For what distinguishes Germany from its western neighbors, Ranke insisted after the unification, was its striving "for a connection between the unity necessary for defense and the variety of the respective goals of the territories,'' and this striving could only succeed ''when we uphold ideas which have come to us from the past and maintain the national life in constant vitality through the union of the particular with the general.''[23]

Ultimately Ranke put the three factors together into a single process. In an epitome of the unification which he wrote shortly before his death he began with ''the necessity of freeing the Prussian state from the pressure which its foreign relations imposed on it'' as ''the idea from which the political movement took its start''; then proceeded to characterize the formation of the empire as an automatic result of the Prussian struggle against Austria and France in the service of its independence (''then it happened by itself, as it were, that the Prussian monarchy expanded to the German Empire''); and concluded by defining ''the whole of the transformation which was accomplished'' in terms of national organizations ''which must conform to what has become the authoritative constitutional idea in the European states generally'' and must be circumscribed ''by the idea of the encompassment and development of all forces.''[24] With this Bismarkian settlement a fact both in Europe and in Ranke's mind, his former diffidence in the face of the political situation gave way to a feeling of security. ''The self-confidence which the great decisive events have evoked in Germans generally communicates itself spontaneously to every one,'' he wrote gratefully to Bismarck.[25] Even the constitutionalism upon which he continued to look askance as late as 1871 for its incompatibility with hereditary monarchy he came to accept as a necessary part of the historical resolution which would attach the people to the monarch.[26] Thus he now could maintain that *as a historian* it was best to be a monarchist tempered by the republicanism that monarchy fought. ''The most popular and perhaps the most effective historians live on the dividing line between republic and monarchy, nourished by the productions of the former and unrestricted by the latter when it has entered the stage wherein it absorbs the general culture,'' he wrote in his diary during the late 70s, and he concluded with the consistent admission that ''my sympathies have long been for monarchy, . . . but I have never adhered to any specific and narrowly limited form of monarchy.''[27]

That it was indeed the historical integration of the unification into the schema of universal history that lay behind this acceptance was clear from the transcendent attitude he finally took toward even the threatening politics of the imperial period. "In the midst of the fortuitous disorder of the day the fundamental course of things can still be perceived; the fundamental relations are what make men." And he explicitly associated this grand view of politics with "the separation of the fortuitous, the transitory, from the constant [*dem Bleibenden*] in the *World History*" he was publishing at the very time of the political observation.[28]

With this supercession of the conflicts marking the revolutionary era by a constitutional monarchy on the German model, Ranke finally had possession of a *terminus ad quem* of universal history, and from its definitive merger of national individuality and universal meaning he could confidently move from patriotic to world history, applying a compatible blend of particular and general principles of method to both levels alike.

III   Ranke had turned his scholarly attention back to German history even before the unification of 1870. As the composition of his *English History* was drawing to a close in the later years of the eventful preceding decade he began to think in terms of what he himself admitted to be national history—i.e., the history of the historian's own country.[29] In October 1865 he accepted a testimonial that he had "never lost sight of native [*vaterländische*] history" on the somewhat disingenuous grounds that in writing histories of the popes, the French, and the English between the sixteenth and the eighteenth centuries "I have perhaps contributed something that was decisive for our fatherland," since in these centuries "German history can be . . . conceived only as a part of general history."[30] A year and a half later he was asserting directly that the discipline of history differs from "the universal equivalence [*Gleichgeltung*] of . . . the exact sciences" in that "it possesses, like poetry even if not in the same degree, an inherent national streak. German historical writing belongs with the elements which comprise the whole German nation and condition its national feeling." From this intensifying awareness of the national point of view that was built into his historiographical enterprise it was a short step to resuming a national topic, and when he sent the final volume of his *English History* to the Prussian King William I a year later, he announced that he now had "his hands free for other works whose object [*Gegenstand*] Your Majesty once deigned to assign me"—an assignment which Ranke identified, in another reference, as a "summons [*Aufforderung*] to dedicate my powers once more to native [*vaterländischen*] history.[31]

Ranke was always wont to embroil his royal patrons in the instigation of his historical writings—he usually mentioned the involvement to document his pragmatic assertion of the close association of the Prussian monarchy with German scholarship[32]— and his acknowledgment here of his king's responsiblity for the turn in his historical interests need not be taken literally. The "patriotic history" which he resumed writing some two years before the unification was not the Prussian-German variety to which he must have been encouraged by King William but the imperial German variety of which he was reminded by the unsatisfying stage of German unity in his contemporary situation. The German history he now wrote took up not from the political history of eighteenth-century Prussia he had started in the 40s but from the constitutional and religious history of the sixteenth-century German Empire he had started in the 30s, with his perspective relocated now to reflect the convergent influence of his contemporary political experience and his recent historiographical experience of writing discrete histories of individual European nations in the early-modern period. The provenance of the history in question is no mere point of biographical precision—it is crucial to the understanding of Ranke's approach to it. Thus the two main scholarly products of these pre-unification years, *On German History from the Religious Peace to the Thirty Years' War* and the *History of Wallenstein* (published in 1868 and 1869 respectively), were continuous rather with his approach to universal history from a national perspective than with his approach to native history as official historiographer of the Prussian state. The interweaving of national and universal elements in the theme of a frustrated German unity was taken up again as an extension of his concern with the German Empire after the revolution of 1830, while the deliberate preoccupation with integrating individual agents into the general movements of history and the blend of judiciously external with sympathetically internal criticism in the form of these preunification books showed the carry-over of the universal criteria which had characterized his French and English histories into his studies on German history.

In the short volume *On German History* the connection with Ranke's interest in German imperial history after the revolution of 1830 was literal. For the book consisted of two extended essays on the post-Reformation empire, the first of which—covering the empire for the twenty years after Augsburg—was a reprint of an article which he had originally published in the *Historisch-Politische Zeitschrift* of 1832, while the other began in 1575, where the first stopped, and continued the story until 1619 with a focus on the same theme of German unity and the same question of how it failed of realization.[33] But though the issue and the answer were the same the emphasis was not, and the difference between the two parts was an index of the path that Ranke had traveled through the thirty-six years and the more convulsive revolution that separated their composition. Within the cumulative divisiveness of the German culture that was his historical answer in both parts to his initial query about the reason for the growth of German political disunity after the relative harmony at the religious Peace of Augsburg, Ranke's later essay manifested a more articulate concern with rooting the German developments in the general historical process of western humanity and a more actual, because more substantive, interpenetration of individual roles and "the elemental forces of the moral and the politicoreligious world." Starting from his familiar universal theme of the medieval union between spiritual and worldly powers, Ranke now introduced the German imperial problem of the sixteenth and early seventeenth centuries as a prominent case of the general question posed by the challenge of reconstituting this union under the conditions of a divided Christian church. "The variegated character of the European states rests largely on the way this problem was handled." The character of Germany was fundamentally determined, then, by the "clash between two opposed systems and world orders which was to be decided here in Germany." The conflict was not merely transitory but "an opposition of the general tendencies, of the large-scale interests of both parties, . . . the one holding fast to the old center of western Christianity, the other to the cause of dissent."[34]

With this literal identification of the general factors in history as actual parties espousing universal principles, German disunity became a function of the unequal confrontation between the general forces making for conflict and the individual agents of unity. In this context Ranke tended to view the whole historical process, no longer as one in which individuals strive to transcend the necessary conditions of their actions as so many formal universals antithetical to their creative freedom, but now as one in which individuals are inextricably engaged with general forces which are more powerful than they and which they can at best manipulate. What was decisive in the German as in all "such great conflicts" was not so much the action of personalities as "the authority inherent in a fixed party posture and in the will which the principle behind this posture represents." Ranke now defined "politics" as "the attempt, in the midst of the conflict of world powers—both the ideal and the real world powers—which one cannot master, to preserve and promote one's own interest." The political failure of individual German emperors like Rudolf II and Matthias—their failure to control the elemental powers, the antagonists of rival world orders, that they should have controlled—was thus seen in terms of a failure to reconcile the "general" and "particular" point of view, a failure of the individual to make of the nation a true concrete universal.[35]

The extension of Ranke's universal themes to the substance of early-modern German history and the association of Germany especially with the dualistic phase of universalism obviously ran parallel to Ranke's anxiety about German disunity and the world revolution of his own time. This universal connection between the German present and the German past had a methodological as well as a substantive impact upon Ranke's approach to history. With patriotic history sanitized by its larger context, Ranke could now make a historiographical principle of the historian's involvement which he had only admitted apologetically before. "I hear it said in artistic circles," he wrote in the later part of *On German History,* "that it is not good to choose materials in which men have been partisan, because one easily hurts one or the other party. But the historian is assigned to this; it is his most characteristic business."[36] He was ready to write sympathetically of German history with a good historical conscience.

The *History of Wallenstein,* Ranke's only full-length historical biography, in form obviously continued the preoccupation with the interaction of historical universals and personality to which he had addressed himself so intensively in his recent French and English histories, but it also developed the substantive theme of imperial German history which he had just resumed in his essay on the empire around the turn of the seventeenth century. Indeed, the meaning of the book for the historian's own development lay in the combination of this form and this theme, for Ranke's Wallenstein was a man whose association of his personal ambitions with a general force of the empire while retaining the discrete identities of both turned the problematic relationship of individuals and universals into a manageable historical reality. The ultimate failure of this political general to fulfill either his own aims or the goal of German unity to which he attached them gave Ranke historical confirmation that it was indeed through the association of a general movement with particular legitimacy, but not through its specific association in the imperial tradition, that a viable order could be established in modern Germany.

Ranke's whole approach to the Wallenstein problem mirrored his rising appreciation of the power of actual universal movements and his effort to discover in history a harmonious relationship of individuals to them, in the service of both integral historical knowledge and the implications of this knowledge for his own living. "How much more powerful, more profound, and more comprehensive is the general life which fills the centuries in a continuous stream than the personal life to which only a short span of time is granted and which appears to exist only to begin, not to complete," he wrote at the beginning of the book. Setting "on the other side," as had been his custom, "the personalities [who] inhabit a moral world order in which they belong entirely to themselves and have an independent life of original force," he now announced that in Wallenstein he had an individual and a period which permitted the integration of the two sides—which permitted Ranke, that is, to realize his "attempt to write a biography that is at the same time history." In contrast to his earlier ruminations, taking off from Luther, that periods of convulsive change are periods that favor the exercise of individual freedom rather than the submission to general necessity, Ranke now saw in such periods occasions for the fruitful interaction of

free individuals and general necessities. "In times of violen
commotion, when the personality can develop its inherent nature
most strongly and its energy can set purposes for itself . . . every
change of conditions dominates the world or seems to dominate it
every stage of world development offers new tasks and new point
of view to the enterprising spirit; the general and the particula
must be kept equally in mind if both the action which is affected
and the reaction which is experienced are to be understood. Event
develop in the concurrence of individual force with the objective
world-constellation."[37]

Even in the prefatory methodological comments which ir
earlier scholarly productions had usually celebrated the particu
larizing historical method, Ranke now paid tribute to the validity
of the explicit universal factors which he now deemed determinan
in modern German history. As was usual with him he justified hi
treatment of Wallenstein in part by the inadequate and partisan
character of earlier histories. But now he included archival mate
rials themselves in his critique, for, as was the case with hi
universal approach to the French and English histories, not the
errors but the "merely one-sided answers" in the former account
and source materials alike were the grounds of dissatisfaction
Ranke's claim to have "attained an objective view of the facts o
the case," based on the more neutral archives in Saxony and
Belgium, turns out consistently with the nature of these stricture
to consist not so much in factual revisions as in his acknowl
edgment of the reality which objective universal connections in
the German situation held for Wallenstein.[38]

The moral which Ranke spread throughout the contents of hi
history was consistent with this methodological attitude. Hi
Wallenstein was a sovereign individual who succeeded when he
associated his own interests with universal movements and failed
when he was opposed by counteruniversal movements. In essentia
ways, moreover, his Wallenstein was a representative not only o
the political generals who, like Cromwell and Napoleon, have
loomed so large on the landscape of modern history but of moderr
individuality in general, which has sought to reconcile persona
independence with integration into a postreligious order of things
Wallenstein, in Ranke's depiction of him, was a parvenu, a
military entrepreneur of striking originality and prescience whose

recognition of "the military principle in and for itself, without consideration for the purpose of war" was "in line with the thinking of the century and a half that followed." He rose to be generalissimo of the Hapsburg armies, landed magnate, and German imperial prince with pretensions to an electorate—that elite office within the princely estate—by combining "the most extravagant egotistic plans" with "purposes oriented toward a definite, attainable goal," by "always following his own inspirations," and by maintaining "the impossibility of forcing his spirit so far that it obeys another's command." But he also was a man addicted to the "well-considered plan" and the "comprehensive combination," who cherished "the deliberate aim of making the decision of large issues go his way" and who combined "an ambition striving for the ideal" with his "exaggerated pride." Hence he "self-consciously and constantly" kept both "his personal" and "general interests" in mind "at the same time," and if in this "mixture of public interest and private purpose the latter predominated," the mixture still was not reducible to such private concerns: his plans could involve "the assertion of the national character and integrity of the German Empire."[39]

The coherent theme of the *History of Wallenstein* consisted, consequently, in the succession of general movements with which Wallenstein associated his own interests and in the conjunctures of disengaged ambition and countermovements that dissolved each association and prepared his final "catastrophe." Ranke made it clear early in the book that despite Wallenstein's nominal Catholicism, "the idea of religion" receded far behind politics for him, and if this mentality set him at odds with "the destiny of the German Empire and the destiny of the world which saw the religious idea ... if not destroy yet loosen and cast doubt upon the political community," it also made his career relevant to the history of the power-state in early-modern times, when religion could be an ingredient but no longer an independent ally of political power. The three main stages of Wallenstein's career, then, were all defined by political universals. In the first stage he represented the German emperor against both the Catholic and the Protestant versions of the Christian world religion, and against the German princes as well; in the second stage he strove for restoration of imperial unity, entailing toleration and equality of the religious confessions and pacification of the princes, in conjunction with the emperor and against all international powers; in the third stage he planned for the restoration of the imperial constitution, including religious equivalence and the recognition of princely rights, against the emperor and in conjunction with international powers.[40]

Wallenstein's constant enemies in all these stages were the Catholic hierarchy and the Spanish monarchy, both of whom embodied, albeit in different ways, "the political-theological concept of the Middle Ages in which worldly interests appear identified with those of the church as a divine cause." Although Wallenstein stood for modernity in this opposition, what was continuous in his advocacy was the universal nature of the causes he espoused. The imperial authority which in the first stage he "represented" and "on which he based his own activity" was "a universal authority," and Wallenstein supported the whole gamut of its "imperialistic" claims, from Italy to Constantinople. In the next two stages his association of his ambitions for the electoral dignities of the Palatinate and Bohemia with the revival of the religious toleration and the traditional constitution of the German Empire, whether with or without the Hapsburg emperor, was to Ranke based on "both an ideal endeavor directed at the satisfaction of the most fundamental desire of the German nation and Wallenstein's own nature, at once ambitious and rebellious, expansive and impulsive."[41]

Wallenstein's failures to achieve a lasting realization of either the personal or the general side of these associations Ranke attributed seriatim to the hostility of the German princes, the enmity of the papal and Spanish parties at the Austrian court, the suspicions of the Protestants, and finally to the "remarkable" confluence of "the various European nationalities" that led to his assassination. But Ranke's final word on this score had an evident bearing on the great confrontation, which he considered to be universal, of his own time. Wallenstein's ultimate fate, according to Ranke, which entailed the subsequent devastation of Germany and "dissolution of the empire," was attributable to his break with his legitimate ruler, not only because in his own particular case "everything he had ever done and established depended on the authority of the emperor" but because in general "all had failed who undertook to impugn the hereditary powers on which the European realms and social conditions were based.'' Wallenstein failed, in short, because he fought against "hereditary princes whose authority had been firmly rooted for centuries and was bound up with all other national institutions.'' Napoleon, on the other hand, could succeed in founding a durable regime—durable since "in our own day from the ruins of the fallen empire a new one could arise as the continuation of the first"—because he worked on the basis not only of a republic but of "a social revolution of the most fundamental kind.''[42]

So Ranke brought his history to the level of what he considered to be the great global encounter of his own period. He was obviously generalizing from his own experience when at this time, in what he called his "historical testament," he characterized the distinctive quality and comparative advantage of German historiography to consist "in the universal-historical consideration of the whole.'' He saw in the German nation's relationship to history the integral union of the national and the universal which he had been seeking. "The national element in historiography lies not in the material only but also in the perspective on it; our national perspective is the more universal one.'' And yet he was aware that there was something missing, something whose "combination with that general tendency has always hovered before me.'' This missing factor he defined as "the force to grasp the fullness of the moment," and although he couched his longing in historiographical terms, the definition betrayed his readiness for some momentous event to supply a final link to his view of human history.[43] Clearly he was prepared for one last convulsion to resolve the remaining tensions barring his complete integration as an historian, and thereby as a man.

IV The German unification which followed hard upon the successful war of 1870 against France had the historiographical effect of pushing Ranke's frustrated imperial nationalism of the preceding period into two overlapping resolutions: he deflected his German history into a Prussian channel for the purpose of investigating the origins of the victorious Prussian-German historical theme; and he embarked on the actual composition of world history to celebrate the achievement in actuality of the final union between national individuality and human universality in history. Although his focus on these themes tended to be successive, for he dwelt primarily on Prussia and Germany in the decade after the unification and began to publish his *World History* in 1880, there was some temporal intersection (notably in the universal theme which went into the study of the *Origin and Beginning of the Revolutionary Wars, 1791 and 1792,* published in 1875, and in the preparatory reading for the *World History* which he initiated as early as 1878), but, more important, the Prussian and universal historical themes were joined conceptually by his persepctive on the global meaning of the Prussian triumph in 1870 and 1871.

There can be little doubt of the fact that his contemporary political experience had a profound impact upon his historical production, for now Ranke not only admitted but paraded the connection, both in his correspondence and in the published works themselves. The direction of this impact is equally clear, for he showed in this period an overall commitment to the general side of history that postdated the unification in its emphasis and that made his rekindled interest in Prussian history and his new confidence in the scientific respectability of world history a continuous expression of a single, seamless approach.

The keynote of the period which he struck in a personal context—"past and present unite in a single great impression"—[44] he also sounded in a professional historical capacity. For in the same well-known letter to Bismarck which denied that a historian could be both a historian and a politician, Ranke also asserted the fruitfulness of present politics for the historian as a historian. "I have always thought that the historian must become old, that he must experience much and witness the whole development of a great epoch in order to become capable of judging earlier conditions," he wrote, adding fulsomely: "The historian can learn from you, Highness."[45] Despite the note of subservience, Ranke was sincere in his conviction that the historian must be an observer of large-scale contemporary life. In an unpublished diary note of the same year he stipulated that while the historian need participate in the daily life of politics only in the special case of his research on detailed administrative history, for "a universal development of the historian"—and especially of "a modern historian"—what is necessary is that "great events happen before his eyes, revolutions occur, innovations are essayed."[46]

Nor did Ranke shrink from the frank acknowledgment of present influences in his published scholarship of the period. He prefaced the treatise on the origins of the seven-year war which he published in 1871 with the frank declaration that "the completion and publication of this work is connected with the events of the day." Explaining that he had worked on it long before without being able to finish it because of its "deficiencies," he attributed his productive resumption of it to its status not only as a historical antecedent but as a historical analogue of the war of 1870. Thus he acknowledged the role of "the events of the day" in supplying both incentive and interpretive categories to a scholarly historical torso which had furnished neither adequate motive nor adequate theme on its own account. During the war of 1870, he elaborated, it was impossible to be occupied with anything unconnected with it, and he specified the connection of the Seven Years' War with his contemporary scene both in genetic and structural terms. "The gaze of the historian turned to the events of an earlier period which had prepared this clash," he revealed in the familiar accents of a historian using the past to explain the present, and he proceeded to indicate an even more daring substantive connection when he added that "the affinity of the historical object made the difference of periods less perceptible." What he had especially in mind here was the heroic and successful resistance of Frederick the Great to international pressures, for this precedent sponsored the generalization, which he found common to both ages, that "the great wars are destined to develop further the destinies of the world." Well might he conclude that "with this piece I present my tribute to the events and actions of the past year."[47]

He followed this extended essay with a longer work on *The German Powers and the League of Princes,* a sequel in his investigation of the eighteenth-century origins of the Prussian-German theme and a sequel too in his conscious connection of these origins with the present. "I submit to the German nation a piece of its history which reaches close to our own times," he began, and early in his account he noted that the Austro-Prussian confrontation of 1778 "reminds one of another campaign that followed eighty-eight years later almost more than it does of the preceding confrontations" between these German powers. The body of the work comprehended three main strands, all of which adumbrated this future, which was now. First, each of the Prussian kings—Frederick the Great and then, in his own way, Frederick William II—followed the policy of "uniting the large interests of the German Empire with the preservation and growth of his own state." Second, the League of Princes itself, organized around the Prussian initiative, stood for the renovation of the traditional imperial constitution but now on the postreligious, political basis consonant with the times—that is, "the reestablishment of the old system with the inclusion of the organization of the Catholic Church." Third, this great attempt at the rehabilitation of the imperial constitution in the service of a modern political unity failed under the pressure of "the great oppositions [Gegensätzen] which condition general development," triggered first by the Austrian despotism of Joseph II and then by the French Revolution in a conflict "which destroyed the constitutional forms of the empire down to the ground." Only "the idea of the empire" and "the spirit of national unification" survived, to "rise again in full force" under a different aegis "when the right age and hour struck."[48]

Even in such a technically scholarly enterprise as the selection and edition of King Frederick William IV's correspondence and in such a neutral format as his composition of the article for the standard German biographical dictionary (the *Allgemeine Deutsche Biographie*) on the same Prussian king—two historical projects which engaged Ranke's attention during the 70s—the historian's newly avowed present-mindedness was in evidence. Certainly the recency of the subject (Frederick William reigned actively from 1840 to 1858) did not suspend Ranke's scruples about the objective standards binding upon the historian. The publication of the edited correspondence in 1873, indeed, was the occasion for what would become a famous "Sunday afternoon sermon" (in his parlance) on the historian's duty to be objective and to preserve his view of the past from the influences of its present connections: "Historical scholarship and literature is a calling which is comparable only to the priestly, however worldly its object may be. For the continuous current seeks to dominate the past and interprets it only according to the current's own lights. The historian exists to understand and to teach others to understand the meaning of each epoch in and for itself. He must have in mind, with complete impartiality, only the object itself and nothing else."[49] But what he had specifically in mind here was the presumably liberal current of public opinion, which he felt would not be pleased by the book and which he did not deign to please. Not only did he not deny other kinds of connection between the recent past represented by Frederick William IV and his own present, but he even evinced unalloyed pleasure at perceiving them. Thus he noted with satisfaction that Frederick William IV "grasped the basic idea" that would be realized in the new German Empire of 1871, and he declared, in reference to his own biographical sketch of the king, that "I am really not dissatisfied that historical research, insofar as it can really get a handle on things, should penetrate thus into the history of our times."[50]

Careful though he was to guard his responsibility as an independent historian against the friendly pressure of the state that paid and employed him as well as against the unfriendly pressure of public opinion, he again associated his scholarly work with the great political movement extending to his own time in the edition and commentary which he based on the papers of the Prussian prime minister, Prince Karl August von Hardenberg, and published at the end of the decade. Admitting the occasion of the work to have been the "rich archival material available to me," especially after the government had charged him as its official historiographer to peruse the recently released Hardenberg papers, he yet insisted that the form of his work—i.e., a history of Hardenberg's epoch followed by an edition of his memoirs—was dictated by the material's coverage of "the most important period of modern world history, [with] illumination . . . decisive for the whole course of Prussian history to be found therein." He presented the first volumes of the work to Emperor William I together with congratulations on the latter's recent success as Prussian king and German emperor and spelled out the present relevance of the historical work by pointing out that in it "this great turn-about of things . . . is explained in its origin." The "misery" of the Hardenberg period was connected with the present period of glory by "great designs" (*Geschicken*), in which "one can do no other but recognize the finger of Providence."[51]

The concomitant of these concessions to the juncture between past and present in his works on national history was Ranke's insistence upon the universal orientation of the patriotic historian, and it was this insistence, indeed, that made the juncture tenable to one who still clothed the responsibility of the historian in the ethic of impartiality. Thus he could assert, in the context of his Prussian-German studies, that "it would be impossible, amid . . . all the great decisions, to have no opinion concerning them" and still hold in the same breath that "yet the essence of impartiality can be maintained" precisely because he now completed the reorientation of objectivity from his original naive designation of it as the immersion of the historian-subject in the historical object to a more subtle signification of participation of both subject and object in a worldly general process of history that transcended them both. He had always had the notion of and still retained the language about an otherworldly "divine order of things, not precisely demonstrable, yet intuitable," which "floated above" particular objects and their historians alike, associating them in an ineffable way. As he had developed the historical identities of the universal themes connecting various past ages, he had inchoately shifted the meaning of historical objectivity to a hybrid of immersion in particular objects and participation in general process and thus accommodated this secularization of the con- nection. Now, with the recognition of the last, contemporary link in the human historical process he dissolved the hybrid and went over decisively to the transcendent meaning of objectivity. He added that "the historian must comprehend [*auffassen*] the divine order" as "identical with the succession of the ages," and he defined the historical role of "important individuals" by "their place in it." He triumphantly concluded that "the historical method, which seeks only what is authentic and true, thereby comes into immediate connection with the most fundamental issues of the human race."[52]

Hence Ranke could save a role for both the impartiality and the sympathy of the historian through the method of comprehension: the historian is responsible for "recognizing" all parties, "the relationships particular to each, . . . their mutual opposition and struggle," whatever the opinion he may espouse and express, "for in this opposition events and world-dominant destinies are de- cided." In this inclusive sense which joins individuals to one another and the historian to them all, "objectivity is at the same time impartiality."[53] Analogously he who, forty years earlier, had

approached the relationship between history and present politics
from the point of view of showing the valid influence of the history
on the politics now developed the relationship between the two
fields for the independent historian who yet applies lessons of
politics to history in terms of history's distinctive universality: "The
historian can never at the same time be a practicing politician,
because the historical idea has value only in its generality, in the
light which it diffuses over the course of world affairs, while the
practical statesman must, on the basis of a general view, above all
seize the moment at hand."[54]

The shift from the objectivity of the historian's self-abnegation to
the objectivity of his participation in a secular transcendence helped
to determine the main line of Ranke's interpretation in his
Prusso-German works of the 70s. The notion of a human object as
an integrated process which expressed the reality of mankind far
more truly than the individual events it connected enabled Ranke to
give his sympathy for his Prussian protagonists the objective form of
their superior coherence. He grounded his claim to have laid the
basis for a favorable judgment of Frederick William IV in his edition
of that king's correspondence on "the demonstration, in particular
edicts which seemed capricious and inconsistent, of a coherence and
a consistency that escaped the politicians in the everyday course of
business." The demonstration of such qualities in the king by
history was for Ranke not so much the exhibition of virtue as the
revelation of a profound truth, for "in this inner coherence consists
the essence of man, and especially of the prince."[55]

Again, both in "The Origin of the Seven Years' War" and in *The
German Powers,* he was dutifully explicit about the Austrians, but
he showed obvious preference for Frederick the Great, absolving
him even in his dubious preventive strikes and self-seeking League
of Princes; and one of the historian's chief grounds for such loving
care was the explanation that the variety of European circumstances
and policies was actually held together "in most vital coherence" by
the ruler who was also the cynosure of Europe.[56] Ranke elevated his
semiofficial publication on Hardenberg to the dignity of history,
similarly, by emphasizing both the generalizing nature of his
approach and the universal resonance of his subject's actual role in
the historical process. "General movement is the real life of
history," Ranke declared, and from this point of view he now

denied that the historian could penetrate the internality of individual persons, defining ascertainable historical truth itself in terms of what was general and thereby verifiable. There is a categorical difference between memoirs and history, he wrote. "It is not the calling of the historian" to render judgments on the personal relationships reported in memoirs because "the personal can often not be verified, even when one hears both parties. For the muse of history, if I understand it aright, there are things that can be allowed to rest undisturbed." But what the historian can validly do is "to abstract from the contingencies of personal life that memoirs communicate, for his attention is fixed above all on general affairs."[57]

Hence Ranke considered Hardenberg and his administration in the light of "the world-historical question [which] inhered in the relationship of the revolutionary power, located in France, to the European powers with which it was embroiled in internal opposition and external struggle." In this struggle Hardenberg both led a resistant European power and "represented at the same time the tendencies of European life which were to some extent responsive to the revolution." "The general course of affairs," indeed, in a very real sense became primary, for "who could only touch on it without being swept away by it?" Ranke insisted, indeed, that the span of the work was determined by "the inner unity of my presentation. . . . For the epochs, in the comprehension of the historian, are not determined by the year and the day but by the tendencies that prevail in the events." Corresponding to the general scope he predicated, Ranke devoted the bulk of the work to the relations of Prussia and Europe. He indicated, moreover, that the connections of the historical process were not only collateral but temporal, extending to the historian's own age. For he admitted to deviations from Hardenberg's memoirs which were accountable not only to the historian's larger knowledge of the facts but also to "the necessarily changed point of view of a much later age." He concluded, in good world-historical fashion, that the formation of the German Confederation in 1815 "could not then be brought further. It was not the end but a stage of German development."[58]

The new comprehensive perspective which the Prussian victory and German unification of 1870-71 brought to Ranke's native history received a final confirmation in the revision of his *Nine*

Books of Prussian History which appeared in 1878 under the title *Twelve Books of Prussian History*. In the preface he wrote for the new edition he added a general dimension missing in the original preface. While still maintaining that ''historical research is directed by its very nature to the particular,'' he now explicitly warned against ''remaining caught in it,'' and he went on to define the formerly vague ''universal connection'' as ''the vital moments of a general development'' which ''formed an equally appropriate object of research'' and stood in a relationship of ''mutual inspiration, mutual influence, and mutual complementarity'' with research into particulars. His revision, moreover, consisted essentially of expanding the original first section on the seventeenth-century origins of modern Prussia into four ''books'' (he published the expanded sections separately as the *Genesis of the Prussian State*), and the noteworthy feature of the addition was the combination, so characteristic of his thinking after 1871, of a focus on Prussia with a coverage of its international involvements that went far beyond the original conception of the Prussian history.[59]

The publication of the reworked Prussian history in 1878 did not end Ranke's patriotic concerns, either as historian or as citizen, for he would still see the new edition of his book on Hardenberg through the press in 1879, and to the end of his life his attention would be attracted again and again to national affairs through his continuing correspondence with German political leaders, steadily and friendlily with his old crony Edwin von Manteuffel (now stadholder of Alsace-Lorraine), sporadically and formally with the imperial couple and their Chancellor Bismarck. But, whatever the overlap, clearly by the late 1870s his primary concern as a historian—and, since by this time his preoccupation with history was very nearly total, as a man too—shifted to the larger field of world history, which at long last he felt himself qualified to confront directly and responsibly, armed with all the honed tools of his more modestly acquired scholarship.

13
The Final Resolution:
World History in Universal Perspective
(1875–86)

Ranke's new-found confidence in the scientific viability of general history found its most remarkable expression in his determined plunge, after the events of 1870 and 1871, directly into those enterprises of universal history in which he had previously been either frustrated entirely or limited to sketchy and unscholarly lectures. Now he found a format for carrying through the early history of the French Revolution, whose political impact he had recognized almost a half-century before and whose history he had started and dropped some thirty years before. And finally, when he was well into his eighties, he undertook the writing of a *World History* on the level he had always dreamed and despaired of attaining—a world history which "includes the events of all nations and ages, but with the more precise definition which alone makes its scientific treatment possible" and with "the appropriation of the verified [*evidenten*] results of research."[1]

I   Like the general orientation of his Prusso-German history, Ranke's enterprises in universal history too were triggered by the war and unification of 1870 and 1871. However dubious Ranke's ad hominem protestations of the specific connection between the

world-revolutionary study he published in 1875 and his simultaneous involvement with Prusso-German history may have
been—he told the emperor that *The Origin and Beginning of the
Revolutionary War, 1791 and 1792* was devoted to "the undertaking which the late King Frederick William II began in 1792 . . .
and Your Imperial and Royal Majesty . . . accomplished under
entirely different circumstances," and he told Bismarck that the
same book was, "although independent, at the same time a
preparatory school for the comprehensive work on Hardenberg's
Memoirs"—the association of the work with the events of 1870
and 1871, as Ranke perceived them, is undeniable. "The destinies of the world have depended for a long time on the
relationship between France and Germany," he wrote in reference
to the German occupation of France, and this generalized perception of the contemporary experience made it possible for him to
feel that "the year 1870 is directly·related to the year 1792," the
year which "started the tangle of recent history."[2]

The book itself confirmed the connection, for Ranke started by
asserting it categorically: "That the struggle with the revolution,
as it broke out in 1792, has dominated the whole epoch that has
passed since then, in action and reaction, and still goes on today
can be recognized in everything that happens."[3] In the body of
the book, moreover, when he came to the outbreak of the actual
wars of the revolution in 1792, he drew a categorical distinction
between the preceding and following periods which aligned the
decisive events under consideration with the issues of his own age.
"Hitherto," he generalized from the outbreak of the war between
revolutionary France and the eastern powers, "Europe still moved
in the long-established political relations of the great powers; in
1792 it emerged from these and a struggle began in which the
opposed world forces, torn loose from every other consideration,
took each other's measure according to their inherent impulses. . . . The great conflict of powers began which has filled
Europe ever since. One may perhaps say that at least in respect to
foreign relations it was only decided in 1870."[4]

The conceptual link between the last of Ranke's convulsive
political experiences and his ultimate commitment to universal
history was even more striking in the case of the *World History*, for
he planned to end it with the fifteenth century—that is, with the

beginning of modern times—and thus there could be no question in this instance of the temporal continuity with 1870 that could be adduced for *The Origin and Beginning of the Revolutionary Wars.* Yet we have Ranke's own testimony, simple, direct, and timely— for he dictated it while he was composing the *World History*—that the resoluble effect of the Prussian victories motivated him to undertake this final work on the largest of human scales. The Prussian wars with Austria and France, he concluded, appropriately ending his memoirs with an accounting for this belated professional fulfillment of his youthful personal yearning, had as "its chief result that political relations have since developed on a uniformly even basis. The universal prospect for Germany and the world then caused me to devote my last energies to a work on world history, in which I am still engaged."[5] There is evidence, too, that this universal political prospect remained very much on his mind during his composition of the *World History.* In a notebook item entered shortly before the publication of the first volume, Ranke concluded a political resume of the perilous events leading up to and following upon the unification with a defiant declaration of faith in the "society's instinct of self-preservation which must inevitably be effective," and he sealed the declaration with a reference to the Persian divinities which would appear in that first volume. "Ormuzd and Ahriman fight always," he analogized about the gods of creation and of evil. "Ahriman works always at the convulsion of the world, but he does not succeed."[6]

Behind this connection lay Ranke's conviction that the Prussian donouement was itself a piece of world history, representing the stage of that process which was converting the unmanageable variety of the extensive world into a perceptible connectedness of all its parts. "It is an important section of world history that we have experienced since our nurture in the previous century," he wrote to his brother at a point midway between the German unification and his beginning of the *World History.* "Most unexpected is the turn which things have taken precisely in recent years. . . . All empires and states are placed in the closest and quickest communication with one another through locomotive and telegraph, just as the nations of the earth stand like a single nation. . . . On the whole wide globe there is no longer any absolute division. Who still talks about the life of humanity? The demand for it now goes without saying."[7] We can only guess at the part played in this awareness of human cohesion by Ranke's long quest for the world-historical unity of mankind and by his perception of its crystallization in the recent victory of the Germanic principle under the Prussian aegis, but the converse is incontestable: the man who had become aware of the unified human community as a verified reality was prepared to undertake its history. Certainly we find just this conjunctive vision of humanity, including its present reference, in the preface of the *World History* itself, where Ranke defined "the task of world-historical science" as "the perception of the connection of things, the ascertainment of the course of the great events which unites and dominates all nations" and based it squarely on the world historian's contemporary experience. "Personal observation [*Augenschein*] teaches that such a community occurs."[8]

Precisely because of the overbalance of universal coherence in the two main world-historical enterprises which Ranke pursued after 1870—the *Origin and Beginning of the Revolutionary Wars, 1791 and 1792,* and the unfinished *World History*—they remain important less for the history that is in them than for their exhibition of the devices through which he made universal history scientifically authentic in terms of the critical historical method. The two works were addressed to different areas and dealt with different realms of world history. The *Origin and Beginning of the Revolutionary Wars* filled the gap in the general process of modern history which had been filled out heretofore only in the particular histories he had written or already had under way—the gap between the plural system of great power-states, monarchical and constitutional, which dominated the early-modern period, and dual conflict between monarchy and popular sovereignty in the subsequent revolutionary age which had just been resolved in favor of constitutionalized monarchy. The *World History* was designed to present the whole premodern past from the perspective of the "historical life which moves progressively from one nation to another, from one group of peoples to another" and, "in the struggle of the various systems of peoples," produces "general history"—a perspective which Ranke had spent a career in developing for modern history.[9] The different levels on which these two exercises in universal history were pitched led to different emphases in both. The limited work on modern history assumed the universal themes and concentrated on the specifically empirical sequence of events in which they were realized. The large-scale work on premodern history started from the empirical variety of its far-flung individual subjects and singled out the factors of continuity that became the universal factors in human destiny. But the differences in scale should not obscure the congruity of approach: the insistence upon scientific rigor in method and upon the articulation of general processes into the substantive actions of individual persons, nations, and states was designed in both to make universal coherence in the human past historically knowable and verifiable.

In the *Origin and Beginning of the Revolutionary Wars,* Ranke applied three devices to make the methodically ascertained doings of individual agents and succession of particular events representative of the universal themes which gave them their historical meaning. First, people and events in France were viewed as representing the general principle of revolution, and the Prussian monarchy was viewed as representing the general principle of legitimate resistance to it. The former part of this historical incarnation was easier to manage than the latter. "Not France alone but the whole continent was reorganized by the French Revolution of 1789 and as a consequence of the war aroused by it," Ranke set forth at the start of his account, and he proceeded to show how the revolution grew out of a "pan-European age of reform movements" that had been dominated by "the French spirit"; how French internal debates during the revolution "pitted against each other two tendencies that spanned the world"; and how "the coupling of the republican idea with the national" in France associated the revolution with the principle of "the national rights of every people and every state," whose repression would have meant "the repression of all the spontaneous movements of nations, . . . contrary to the meaning and nature of the European community [and] contradicting the whole course of European history in recent centuries."[10] Thus he acknowledged the French Revolution to have been the expression of a fundamental and universal movement in the history of humanity, and correspondingly he accounted for each step of the revolution by blending demonstrable particular factors which had reference to local French conditions with imputed general factors which had reference to the ineluctable general character of the revolution as such. The four-cornered division of France between king, corporations, bourgeoisie, and common people; the French hatred for the Austrian alliance; the character and policies of Louis XVI and Marie Antoinette; the specific French parties, their leaders, and the drama of their conflicts: all these were brought to the fore with good, solid, balanced evidence at once to describe and explain the events of the revolution.

But at the same time the consistent radicalizing tendency of these same events was given an explanation on quite another level: it was assigned to an inherent necessity of the revolution that transcended any particular event of it and indeed the French locale itself. The power of the National Assembly grew "step by step, as with the force of nature," so that by June 1789 the revolution was "already impossible" to reverse. With the storming of the Bastille and the removal of Court and Assembly from Versailles to Paris, "the horizon under which French destinies would develop was irrevocably determined." By October 5 "any deviation from the revolutionary principle became completely impossible." The reason for this inevitable radicalization lay not so much in the French personalities and conditions that produced the particular events but in the "fatalism of the event.... The revolutionary event was driven ever forward by its own inner logic, ... [by] the inner impulse of things, ... [by] revolutionary passion [which] could not be held in check with constitutional forms."[11] Efficient and final cause—to use Aristotelian terms which Ranke did not use—cooperated to present a history of the revolution in France that was at once scientifically precise and intellectually comprehensive.

Ranke's attempt to make Prussia an analogous embodiment of "the historical formation of Europe" against the revolution showed even more clearly the mechanism of representation, for if such embodiment was called for by the subsequent assumption by Prussia of the universal antirevolutionary principle, it was also gainsaid for the historical period of the early revolution by the actual prominence of Austria rather than Prussia in the leadership of the cause. As in the French case, Ranke joined a circumstantial account of the antirevolutionary camp, with the Austrians the chief protagonists, to a general accounting for its ultimate stand, where Prussia became central. From this general perspective, whereas the Austrian government sought merely to "muddle through between . . . these two different phases of world history," Prussian ideas "had a content oriented toward general principle [*das Allgemeine*] and the great phases of politics." "The interests of the old Europe were united in the Prussian camp," wrote Ranke once he came to the war itself. "The opposition of the two great tendencies appears therewith in its universal significance."[12] The overriding concern of Prussia for its own independence and the gradual rise of its concern about the revolution was thus preeminently representative of the legitimate powers as a whole.

The second device for an empirical channel to general history was an adaptation to the revolutionary situation of a wonted Rankean procedure—the interweaving of internal and international affairs. The adaptation, in Ranke's view, was to make the relationship of the internal and the international a seamless continuity, since it was in the very nature of the revolution to be domestic and universal at once. "The characteristic of the revolutionary event is the constant interpenetration of the internal movement and external relations." Revolutionary excesses provoked foreign attacks "as it were necessarily. It became destiny. The French event thereby gained a European imprint." The connection whereby the domestic acts of the French revolutionaries aroused the resistance of foreign powers thus translated these acts into issues in the world arena and made them appropriate to universal history. "The issue of war and peace became identical with the issue of whether the constitution with royal prerogative would be maintained or not. It was a double conflict, which involved the future of the world: monarchy or republic, war or peace with Europe."[13]

The third and final way of turning universal history into a sequence of critically researched events stemmed from Ranke's interpretation of the early revolutionary years as a multifarious, unsystematic period of transition between two systematic "phases" of world history. His scholarly interest in correcting previous accounts by a more judicious and more expanded use of the sources for individual policies and motivations joined his interest in finding a particular sequential format for his general scheme to produce a staggered view of his period in which the historic concerns of the great powers moved slowly, haltingly, convergently, through a graduated series of actions and reactions toward their ultimate principled position on one side of the universal conflict in the age of revolution. He was careful to show that for the first two years of the revolution the concerns of the great powers in eastern Europe remained separate from the problem of revolutionary France—in Ranke's terms, the east and west of Europe were "two different worlds"—and that even this problem was viewed by the powers more with a view to French power than to the French Revolution. Only with the radicalization surrounding Louis XVI's flight to Verennes in mid-1791 was there a felt need to "extend a general, all-embracing politics" over the two worlds. Then the fear of international revolution initiated "a development which went far beyond the previous relationships of states and conferred a different character on the life of the European community." But this development too, in Ranke's presentation, was a devious one, with traditional considerations constantly deflecting and inhibiting the new factor of monarchical solidarity against the revolution until finally the triumph of the explicit idea of popular sovereignty in France and the French declaration of war in 1792 brought on the moment in which "the opposition of legitimacy and revolution" appeared "in its full strength."[14]

Even more to the purpose of historicizing the universal pattern than this serial quality of his presentation was Ranke's reinterpretation of what "legitimacy" meant to the powers that came to defend it against revolution. Time and again he took special pains to insist that the purpose of the monarchical powers was never counterrevolutionary, that it was simply to save the independence of royal authority as it was originally established in the French constitution of 1791. Undoubtedly this view was central to the revisionist scholarship which he focused particularly on Austrian policy, and it fit well with the thesis of the powers' belated focus on the revolution, his other main revision; but the peculiar stress and extension which he gave to the rebuttal of counterrevolution hints at a more basic function for it in the pattern of universal history which now had its *terminus ad quem* in the national unification of 1871. Whereas the pre-1870 Ranke had conceived the global issue of his age to have been hereditary monarchy versus popular or national sovereignty, each with a derivative constitution which he endorsed and rejected respectively (usually differentiated, in his language, by the favorably connotative *Verfassung* vis-à-vis the reprobated *Constitution*), after the unification he acknowledged a larger validity in the ideas of political nationalism and constitutionalism as such.

Thus in the *Origin and Beginning of the Revolutionary Wars* Ranke's alignment of the "old-European powers" with the dualistic French constitution of 1791 against the radical democratic glosses on it should be taken together with his general argument in favor of national constitutional monarchy as contrasted with both republicanism and restored absolutism. Whereas he had formerly admired the historic institutions of the old Europe for their capacity to withstand the revolution and to retain their vitality in the nineteenth century, he now supported the general inference, from a critique of the old regime, that "it certainly cannot be considered the chief requirement of historical life only to affirm what is merely established" (*das eben Bestehende*). Even after the enactment of the French revolutionary constitution of 1791 he defended the share of national self-determination in the revolution against the claim to intervention on the part of the European "concert." Although granting the validity of the concert in principle, as "the basis of the European community," he declared "the rights of every nation, of every state" to be "even clearer and more undeniable," and he maintained that "in this respect the admissibility of revolutionary ideas is only secondary"; primacy must be accorded the question of "whether a nation's right of self-determination may be asserted without reservation or may be limited by the rest of Europe." The answer to this question, he concluded in a present tense that indicated the persistent relevance of the historical lesson, "cannot be decided by reflection, but only by the power of the parties in the conflict." His own explicit démenti of revolutionary principles, consequently, took the form of an attack neither against constitutionalism nor against national sovereignty but rather against the version of them that violated the independent prerogative of the executive. "I dare to assert that all subsequent revolutionary confusions are rooted in the impossibility of institutionalizing a dependent executive power."[15]

Clearly, Ranke's presentation of the actual historical transition to the age of revolutions was calculated to bear out his conviction of their ineradicability from the permanent register of universal history and to support the concessions made by legitimate monarchy to constitutionalism and to political nationalism in his own Prussian-dominated, postrevolutionary era.

II From this final connecting link of modern universal history Ranke moved backward in time to fill up the whole vast canvas of human development that had led up to it. He decided to use the notes and lecture drafts which he had compiled over the years as the bases of a scholarly *World History*. He started to collect additional materials explicitly for it from the late 70s; he began publishing it in 1880; and he devoted his main attention to it until his death in 1886. In it he sought at long last to fulfill his ambition of "researching and understanding the general life of humanity and the particular life of at least the leading nations," of "keeping one's gaze ever fixed on general truth" (*das Allgemeine*) while "yet not violating the laws of historical criticism which are laid down for every detailed investigation. For only critically researched history can count as history at all," and thus "critical research on the one hand and comprehensive understanding on the other are mutually sustaining." He still admitted that "it is not possible to satisfy the requirements for perfection" in such an enterprise, but now insisted that "it is necessary to try."[16]

What made it possible for him to meet the dual stipulations sufficiently to carry on the enterprise for the first time on a scholarly basis to his own satisfaction was the definite shape he gave to the general side of the equation. Of the two kinds of desiderata Ranke's approach to the *World History* undoubtedly favored the general over the particular, both in the historical process and in historical method, but his conception of universal history here was such as to delimit it and thereby to make it compatible with national history and manageable by the standards of particularistic research. He insisted that the common "cultural aspirations" of the various nations constitute "one of the effective motives of their internal development," but he insisted too on the resistance to them of "the native pecularities of the different nations and tribes," pecularities which "also have their own original warrant and invincible essence." He insisted similarly that historians "cannot cling only to the ground of national histories," for the great nationalities "are creations not so much of the country and the race as of the fundamental changes of conditions," but he also warned against "tearing loose from the firm ground of national histories." What enabled him, in his own mind, to do both was to define universal history in terms of its coherence, that is, in terms of the common strand formed by the actual intersections of the sundry nations and by the continuity of this strand through time. As he defined the field, "nations can be considered in no other connection than insofar as, influencing one another, they appear after one another and constitute a vital totality [*Gesamtheit*] with one another." Thus he would focus on the cultural crossroads of the Near East in his history of ancient times because "it has always been one of the most important arenas of world-historical development," and he could refer the succession of empires to "events on which the progress of general history depends."[17]

There was, in addition, something more substantive and more integrated than mere mutual contact, shared setting, and chronological succession that went into the coherence of Ranke's universal history at this point. The idea of progress, so limited, so ambiguous, and so ancillary in his previous formulations, was now exalted to a univocal and central position in world history, with the function of providing a temporal articulation, at once intelligible and researchable, of the universal themes which made up the essence of human history. Hence Ranke characterized as his "directive point of view" in the book the effort to recall "the memories of the events, the institutions, and the great men of past ages transmitted by one generation to the next," alongside "the immortal works of genius in poetry and literature, science and art which . . . represent what is universally human." Both are parts of the "treasure" (*Besitz*) which "the human race has acquired in the course of the centuries" and "which consists in the material and social progress it enjoys, but especially too in its religious development."[18]

Ranke's elaborations of this formulation showed clearly that the attribution of progress to the cultural heritage that formed the material of universal history was for the sake not of the progress but of the compatibility between generality and selectivity, between continuity and individuality, that he associated with it. In these elaborations Ranke identified the "distinctive principle of universal history" with what was permanent in human knowledge and value, and progress in this "concept of humanity" or "cultural world," as he called this principle variously, established its distinctive historicity and its continuing interaction with the evenescent passage of the individual events that were the materials of standard history. The principle of universal history, then, has an objective existence in the historical process and calls for an approach by the historian that is appropriate to it. The concept of humanity—humanity's "consciousness of its own interrelatedness, its own unity"—has a genesis like all historical events and simply has its own over-arching continuity, articulated in its progress. "It is almost the most important object of historical research to determine . . . how the concept of humanity first originated and then was expanded and developed." The concept is, indeed, itself "a universal historical event on which all others depend and this must actually be searched for and, in a manner of speaking, discovered." The world historian can do this by identifying a "cultural world" in the broad sense of culture as the object of universal history. It is based on "no separate endeavor" of men but rather "embraces the free development of all forces oriented toward the ideal"—religion and state as well as the arts and sciences—and it "is indissolubly bound up with politics and war, with all events which make up the facts of history." This cultural world is thus not a segregated arena but a permeable dimension of continuity that cuts through all the fields of history: it "includes all the knowledge which, once acquired, is never lost; the achievements [Fertigkeiten] which one century inherits from another; the general concepts of morality and justice which are indeed innate in men but strive to be developed and raised into clear consciousness; in general, everything that makes for and befits the honor of men." Or, to put it more substantively, the concept of humanity whose "development" it is the task of world history to describe is neither culture in the narrow sense of a field, nor science, nor the state, nor religion but "an idea which encompasses all of this and which is not any and yet is all of them at once."[19]

The concept of humanity and the cultural world in which the historian discovers it consequently are independent of individual nations in principle but are conjoined with their history in both historical and historiographical practice. If "the existence of individual modern nations cannot be imagined without some contact with the general idea [of humanity]," it is also true that "no people can exist in whom nothing else but this idea is represented," so that universal history can be traced not only in the striving for humanity as such but also in "the internal relationship of events to each other" and in "the mutual contact of peoples." The cultural world, as the principle of a universal history which "I assert alongside and above the history of individual nations," is autonomous in its address to "the collective life of the human race which unites and dominates the nations without dissolving in them," but still it makes its appearance "in the most various forms" according to "the particular life of the nations"— especially their "constant conflicts and struggles" with which this "world-historical factor" is always engaged—and progress stands for the enduring line of development through the ebb and flow of the contests. "The universal-historical movement is a dynamic Something which moves forward powerfully amid all storms by its own force." This progressive drive historicizes the strand of permanence in human history not only distributively, through the events produced by the internal opposition involving the various partisans of its development, but also negatively, through the resistance it meets from "degenerate culture bearers" whose conduct "violates the inner command of human honor and the moral world order" and from "the unceasing attacks of those who do not participate in the cultural world."[20]

Now the positive tendency of this idea of progress, with its predication of a developmental continuity across the ages, is patently averse to the skeptical strictures on progress which Ranke had previously expounded at length and with which his name has been primarily associated. The puzzle has been compounded by the decision of Ranke's former student and official editor, Alfred Dove, to publish as the conclusion of the *World History* the manuscript lectures *On the Epochs of Modern History*, which Ranke had delivered privately to King Maximilian of Bavaria some thirty years before and which contain the most memorable formulations of Ranke's stance against progress and for the equivalence of historical ages. The inclusion had the merit of underlining Ranke's conception of the *World History* as the prolegomenous

complement of the work he had already done in the name of
universal history for modern times, and it serves too as a reminder
of the limiting assumptions which should be brought to bear on
the idea of historical progress which lies behind the *World History*.
For this idea undoubtedly corresponded to what the earlier Ranke
had endorsed as "extensive" progress—in terms of the *World
History*, "the formation, maintenance, and diffusion of the
cultural world"[21]—and at least two of the most prominent
characteristics attributed to historical progress by Ranke in the
World History are explicable by this delimitation. The association
of even the favorable approach to progress with constant traits of
human nature and standards of morality, including the random
spontaneity of creative genius, like the attribution of progress
rather to the efflorescent push of genetic force than to the
convergent pull of a telic end, assumed the existence of an inner
life that was not subject to progress at all.

But however compatible in ultimate logic, the difference in
emphasis between the two stages of Ranke's progressive thinking is
crucial to the understanding both of the *World History* and of
Ranke's own development. The fact is that the Ranke of the 1850s
stressed the antiprogressive character of the individual creations
and the epochal dominant tendencies which for him then belonged to the essence of human history, and the Ranke of the
World History effectively excluded this variegated kind of essence
from the purview of universal history, stressing instead the quantitative realization and extension of historical culture in the
continuous world that linked the destiny of nations. The two
approaches reflect their different vintages: the earlier followed
from a contemporary situation dominated by a chronic duality
whose resolution was uncertain; the later followed from a contemporary situation dominated by what appeared to Ranke as an
unprecedented resolution of the main universal conflicts—religion
versus politics, and revolution versus legitimate monarchy—of
human history.

Ranke's later emphasis on the progressive continuity of man's
history enabled him to operate a methodological principle of
exclusion that was hardly available to him when he was pro-
pounding the equivalence of all ages under God, and it was this
principle of exclusion that made it possible for him to apply

scientific standards of exact research to the vast panorama of world history. For despite the handicap of his failing eyesight he based his *World History* primarily on original sources and on a critical evaluation of the commentaries, in a way that was characteristic of his scholarly history and quite at odds with the "rhapsodic" attitude and casual methods of *On the Epochs*. His effective definition of world history as the historical process running consecutively from the cultures of the ancient Near East and Mediterranean through the Roman Empire to the medieval Europe of Christianity and Islam was based on the coincidence of scholarly criteria and historical continuity. In principle he excluded primitive cultures because he claimed that only written records delivered reliable evidence, and he excluded the Chinese and Indian cultures because he claimed their own lack of a historical sense makes their sources equally unreliable.[22]

Both judgments undoubtedly have something in them of his original dependence on philological canons and of his earlier reservations about the applicability of western historical standards to nonwestern, nonhistorical peoples, but his complaint about the "fragmentary" character of both the primitive and eastern sources and the canons he applied to universal history in the body of the *World History* made it clear that the scientific grounding of these exclusions was connected with their heterogeneity when measured by the requirements of historical coherence. This coherence was both lateral—that is, the central intersection of nations in any age—and vertical—that is, continuous—through time. Thus he defined the "universal-historical side" of events or movements both as "the engagement in the general [i.e., international] relationships of states and in the ideas which occasion them" and as the participation in "forces of development" which "produce the uninterrupted life of humanity that is bound by the past but struggles ever for new goals" and "in which each present is influenced by the past and visibly contains the seeds of the future—a relationship on which the inner connection of world-historical events in general depends." Events which fell within the orbit of world history included, for example, the conquests of the Macedonian Empire both because they had a "universal-historical side" which pertained to the crucial Near Eastern and Mediterranean cockpit of nations and because they had the "universal-historical value" of diffusing that Greek culture "toward which all humanity must strive" and which conferred on the Macedonian monarchy "an immeasurable importance for all future centuries." Hannibal's crossing of the Alps, similarly, "has a world-historical character" both because he achieved it "in a general interest" (that is, in a duel for domination of the Mediterranean) and with a multinational involvement and because it removed the chief barrier to the communication "on which the progress of western European culture depends."[23] Whatever did not measure up to both criteria—because of either its spatial or its temporal insulation—did not have the character of universal history and was irrelevant to world history.

These two dimensions of universal history furnished Ranke with his principles not only of selection but also of organization, for they governed the two related levels on which he wrote the book. The detailed political narrative of international relations—particularly conflicts—and of the national histories which conditioned them made up the empirical bulk of the voluminous work, while the analyses of long-range political tendencies—under the aegis of "the abstract, which is always effective in the depths but is not directly engaged in action"—and the description of spiritual movements—notably of religion and literature, which are directed to "the Ideal" and "on a deeper level than politics, at once connected with and divergent from it, modifying contemporary events and preparing future ones"—tied the series of synchronic accounts to the progressive temporal movement of universal history.[24]

In early—i.e., pre-Roman—world history, the emphasis was on the first of these two types of universalism, since mankind was organized primarily into "local societies, forming particular communities of distinctive energy and vitality," and interacting only through membership in more inclusive tribal connections and through domination of or subjection to one of the series of ancient empires that conquered without assimilating. Only through Hebrew monotheism and Greek culture (in the narrow sense of literature, philosophy, and history) did men in this phase participate in the second, or temporal, connections of universal history. Monotheism dissociated religion from time as well as space, grounded an idea of religion that "is everlasting and for the whole world," and "first made possible a history of humanity." Greek culture itself "resolved problems in unbroken continuity" and "has become the common property of other nations and of the following centuries"—indeed, "has become the antecedent [*Vorort*] of the spiritual culture of mankind."[25]

Muted and sporadic but already recognizable were the two dialectical themes which Ranke had long identified at the core of modern history and which yielded some coherence to their respective levels even in this early going of world history. On the empirical, synchronic level of narrative events the recurrent conflicts between the independent "nations" (*Völkerschaften*) and the successive "empires" (*Reichen*) manifested, however brokenly and restrictedly, the political engagement of the national and universal principles in human history. On the analytical, diachronic level, the detachment of God, in the form of monotheism, from local earthly phenomena was even more occasional, perceptible as it was directly only in Israel and indirectly only in Greek philosophy, but where it did appear it adumbrated what would become the continuing opposition between the spiritual and the temporal powers. "The natural conflict between the spiritual impulses and the tendencies inherent in worldly power, as it emerged here, is symbolic for all times." At this early stage the actual preeminence of national over universal organization of life entailed the preeminence of the empirical political over the developmental cultural level of universal history. Even the prevailing religion, to which monotheism was an exception, was particular national "idolatry," and for the most part considerations of a universal-historical sort on any level took the apologetic form of reading "needs of the world" into speculations about "world-historical necessities in their connectedness."[26]

The decisive change—indeed, progress—out of this situation in the thematic history of mankind was registered in the history of ancient Rome, which "takes the most important place among all national histories in world history" and is the "central point in the historical development of the human race" because it made universalism an historical fact on both of the levels of world history. In the republican period, it was especially Rome's elevation of political universalism to primacy in its contemporary world that "raised the human [*das Menschliche*] out of the national and above it,'' for ''the disappearance of the particular national cultures'' with ''their subjection to the Roman republic, in which the whole of the entire world movement was now concentrated,'' was ''one of the greatest world-historical events that has ever happened.'' The contemporary meaning of this achievement was secured by the crucial role of Roman domestic and military history in it. The equal conflict of patricians and plebeians in Roman internal affairs was ''a universal-historical event'' which had ''great importance for the universal position of the Romans in the world,'' since it constituted a popular basis for its appeal abroad, while ''the rise of the military principle to independence'' was a distinctive Roman contribution to world conquest. Through these indubitable historical facts, the universal connections stemming from supremacy over the ancient national powers became themselves literal historical facts. They could thus ''be considered as the first part of the world history that is accessible to historical science.''[27]

Albeit subordinate in significance to the contemporary attainment, contributions to the progressive development of humanity were also perceptible in the republican period. The fundamental motive for the reform movement—especially the Gracchian—against ''existing conditions'' was ''political idealism,'' and ''the modern movement of the world''—equivalent to ''what men call progress,'' which is incompatible with a strict maintenance of existing customs and conditions—''has largely stemmed from this idealism.''[28] More important was the Roman appropriation of Greek culture, for the Romans thereby gave to the forms of ''universal culture'' a ''new ingredient'' of their own that made this culture viable for the later world. Hence what the Romans called ''the world'' (*orbis terrarum*) coincides with ''what we call the cultural world'' (*Culturwelt*), and ''later generations . . . have really never been able to break through the limits'' which were then set up in Asia to their definition of the world.[29]

The imperial period of Rome perpetuated the ascendency of the universal in history but reversed the proportionate weights of its two dimensions: its contributions to the development of humanity overbore its role in the contemporary organization of the world. Not, of course, that there was no such role. The empire was ''a kind of hegemony . . . which represented the idea of totality''

(*Gesamtheit*) and "had a universal-historical task of the broadest scope—to unite the originally very different nationalities which had developed around the Mediterranean into a homogeneous whole" and to extend it westward, maintaining by military power what had been founded on military power. But in itself this universal unity was both too little and too much, finding its limits particularly in the Germanic tribes that remained outside it and tending to form "a central cultural world in perpetuity," with its corollary of "a spiritual and religious slavery" that "could not possibly be the aim of the universal-historical movement."[30]

Hence the salient function of the empire was rather to be "the condition for the further development of the world" through "the formation of a consistent cultural world whose existence has been of infinite importance to the human race." The crucial factor in this progressive function was "the development of Christianity to a world religion" and its union with the empire, for Christianity "conceived the human race as a coherent whole," produced "the greatest ideas which the later world has recognized as essentially Christian," and did most to substantiate "the ideal core of human history," where "there rise ever higher potencies which transform the general course of things accordingly and always confer a new character upon it." This Christianity, in short, was itself essentially developmental in its historical role and endowed the empire with this same quality. In Christianity, the past—i.e., "the principle of the oldest religion"—was introduced into the Roman Empire and made "the common property of the world," in a universal form bereft of its Jewish nationalist roots, oriented toward "the all-inclusive community of mankind," and "therewith opening a new path for humanity." The tension between the spiritual and political powers that arose now from the combination of Christianity's connection with and separation from an empire, together with the persistent doctrinal divisions within the Christian church itself, gave to Christianity a forward-looking posture based on "the unity of its further development in the future" and on its open-ended participation in "the progress of the centuries."[31]

Notably through its Christian religion, then, "the goal of the universal-historical movement" referred the Roman Empire both spatially and temporally beyond itself. For "the religion of humanity" would not permit a universal subjection to Rome: "it was necessary to be able to transmit the products of historical life to other nations, for only in their union with these nations could they become the common property of humanity.'' Hence not so much the geographical limitations on Roman domination as the necessity of opposition and multiplicity for human progress made it impossible for Rome to be the end of universal history. ''It would not have conformed to the spirit of the history of humanity for oppositional nations simply to have been absorbed in the Roman-Greek Empire, for the particular life of the various nations in their involvement with one another and in their connection with the ideal community is the condition of progress in the history of mankind.'' Of these nations the preeminent one for world history was the German, in part because the German tribes dominated the western world that was outside the Roman Empire at a time when the eastern empire was losing its power of acculturation, but more fundamentally because it ''produced an inner force which pre-determined it to an entirely different destiny than to be a Roman province'' and because the German tribes were both individually variegated among themselves and susceptible to general unifi-cation under Roman cultural influence. The third and final—both in the chronological and the progressive senses of that attribute—period of premodern world history, therefore, was the period of the Germanically-dominated western Middle Ages.[32]

The dominant tendency of the period was an interaction of general and particular factors which approximated the ideal and set the stage for the mutual penetration of individuality and universality in modern history. Through the meeting of Roman Empire and German tribes the western world became organized into ''Germano-Romanic realms'' which, through the juncture of Roman administration, law, and above all church ''with the native German way of thinking,'' established ''the system'' of indepen-dent states united by the ''common spiritual horizon which was filled by the concept of *Imperium.*'' With the enervation of Byzantium and the rise of an Islam which, whatever ''ferment'' it brought to world history, was so narrowly national that it ''con-tained no faith for the world,'' both ''the connection of the modern world with the ancient'' and ''the future of the world depended on the existence and the development'' of the Ger-mano-Romanic empire in the west. ''The new realms'' which composed that empire considered "the ancient world," transmitted through "the universal-historical force" of the Roman church, to be their own past, and themselves "became the workshops of the general and particular life of mankind."[33]

Since the new states shared a common religion and common imperial tradition even when they were at their most independent, and since the medieval empire—once it became wholly Germanized with the Saxon dynasty—respected national autonomy even when it was most unified, it is hardly surprising to find that Ranke collapsed the two levels of universal history along with his meshing of the general and the particular at this age of world history.[34] First he now minimized the distinction between the temporally "later judgment of events according to their results" and the interest of research "in the events themselves," stipulating for the former "the need for the cultural world . . . to attract the alien without destroying its independence" as a criterion of human progress and for the latter the closely related proposition that "everything moves in the inevitable oppositions of general life grasped in its development" as the principle of empirical scholarship in its contemporary orientation to the historical facts. Then, as if to underline the interchangeability of temporal development and spatial comprehension in the universal history of man at this stage, he deprecated the method of abstraction which he had used to demonstrate the relationship of events to human progress in the earlier phases of the *World History* and purported to find all the generality he needed in the actors and the events themselves. Admitting that "for general world history it would suffice to present the decisive moments in a certain abstraction," he now insisted that to apply such a method to the founding of the German empire by Otto the Great "would not conform to the sense of this work, which is rather concerned with merging detailed events with the situation as a whole, allowing the latter to be recognized in the former." But he also insisted now that "it is not the case that the facts contradict the general hypothesis," for he held for this whole period both that "the interlacing of situations depends on the movement of particular forces . . . from whose mutual connections the historical life of the world goes forth" and that "their common action was required for the duration and progress of things."[35]

Substantively, this integral union of particular and general factors in history was guaranteed for this stage of human development by the overlap of the now persistent long-range religious-political theme on the everchanging contemporaneity of the universal-national relationship. Thus "the opposition between clergy and worldly power," which "forms the outstanding character trait of the western world," ran unresolved through the whole period, but it did not preclude either the integrating function of the same Latin Christian church or the recurrent collaboration of the spiritual and worldly powers in universal tasks. Thus the church organization was "indispensable for ... the inclusion of nationalities of various kinds in the collective community of Christianity," while the congruence of "religion and nationality" led to the "fusion" of dependent tribes into the "Germano-Romanic realms" of Europe. Hence the conjunction of Catholic church and Germanic nations conferred a general function on religion even when it meant the opposition of pope and emperor. The papal foundation of a German national church had the effect of "connecting the German nation with the greatest product of the human race," and the break between state and church on the imperial level collaborated with the rise of nationality against the multinational empire to form "a condition for the progress of the destinies of the world." Well might Ranke repeat for the church what he had declared for the Germano-Romanic cultural world as such: "Everything was connected with both general and particular interests."[36]

Ranke made a significant adaptation in his method as well, which enabled him to satisfy the joint requirements of precise research into particular facts and the intelligible interpretation of general continuity. He frankly professed his reliance on "tradition," both legendary and historical, and his confidence in his ability to elicit historical truth from such a medium entailed a notion of factuality which had generality and continuity built into it. In part, to be sure, Ranke depended on such a source because, unlike the rich documentation he found for modern history, it was all he had. "Where the complete historical truth is not to be found," he wrote about the origins of Rome, "an old tradition, legendary as it may be, also has its value." But usually he went far beyond this grudging position to make a virtue of his necessity, and the virtue was the delivery by tradition of a historical reality that was both scientifically verifiable and of universal import at the same time. This reality was one of two kinds. There was a distinctively "traditional truth," on different occasions also characterized as "inner" and "symbolic," which Ranke derived from scripture, legend, and poetry in "periods when tradition and history are inextricably entwined with each other" and which was valid as a characteristic expression of the culture which emitted it. There was also discoverable within tradition a factual truth, a truth that was applicable only to "the principal facts, ... linked in a whole." Like the symbolic truth that is embodied in the whole of a tradition, the selective "historical fact" which "comes to us only in this form" is a cross between particular and general reality. When "actuality appears" in "circumstantial traditions, ... it will be possible to combine research, which strives for the exact knowledge of the particular, with the general view of things."[37]

III So at the very end of his life Ranke found the ultimate satisfaction which he had sought so long. Both in the historical process of humanity and in the historiographical methods by which he demonstrated it he perceived the smooth and unqualified dovetailing of the divergent values to which he was equally committed. With the conservative hegemony of his native Germany serving him both as the historical exponent of individuality and as the representative descendent of the universal principles to which, in one form or another, the historically relevant section of mankind had adhered for some two thousand years, his view of history took on the aspect of a differentiated continuum. In "The Confession," which he wrote for himself during 1880, the year when his *World History* began to appear, he explicitly formulated at last his principled acceptance of the continuum. "I accept above all things an individual life of the spirit ... ," he wrote. "I go further and accept a spiritual life in humanity generally, which manifests itself in national origins but becomes a whole through the unification of them so that the whole culture rests upon it. We live in the midst of the expansive tendency of this great movement, which takes possession not only of the various parts of the world but also of all classes internally. . . . All the positive products of this movement ... will have the force to persist, and at the same time the range of participation in the spiritual life itself ever broadens."[38]

It took Ranke an entire historical career to attain the ease of this progressive optimism. Having absorbed the world's dissonances, he now projected back on it his own hard-won integrity. Truly he could now rest in peace.

Conclusion: The Meaning of History

The meaning of history has two senses. It refers both to what has meaning in history and to what about history confers meaning on the present life outside it. The initial condition of any debt we may owe to Ranke is that for him, and for us as his heirs, the two senses overlap. He found meaningful within history precisely those dimensions of human reality which illuminated the fundamental relations of life outside of history. Coincidentally, our loss of faith in the automatic value of history as the study of pastness leads us too to identify meaning in history with meaning from history, and we deny the one if we fail to discover the other. The question is, then: what did Ranke bequeath us of this joint meaning, and what can we take from the bequest?

I   Ranke's discovery of the actual relatedness of universal themes and individual actions in the process of western history made it possible for him to resolve on historiographical solutions for the fundamental political and philosophical problems which remained antinomies for him on their own level. Samples of these problems and his solutions should illustrate specifically what history meant to him.

The political problem which he was unable to resolve satis-
factorily either in his own practical attitude or in his theoretical
utterances was the problem of the relationship between the
nation and the state. In practical politics he espoused political
nationalism in the form of the German policy to be undertaken by
the particular states—above all, by Prussia—but he disapproved of
the political movements for German unification, whether under
liberal or Bismarckian auspices. In his political theorizing he
vacillated between the separate attribution of a moral base to both
the nation and the state as autonomous incorporations of the
human spirit and the single attribution of a spiritual moral core to
the "national principles" as the vital principle of the state, which
"could hardly sustain itself without this principle."[1] But, as
Ranke's historiographical biography indicates, what he could not
thus resolve, either in practice or in theory, at any present moment
of contemporary politics, resolved itself once it could be inserted in
the line of historical process. The policy of unification which he
opposed in the making because it violated both the integrity of the
Prussian state and the spirituality of the German nationality he
accepted as a historical fact because the meaning of the event then
superseded its intention and took on the moral character of the
whole national development which it capped.

Again, his theoretical vacillation between the equivalent and
the subsidiary worth of the state vis-à-vis the nation in political
crises gave way to his unhesitating merger of both under the same
spiritual aegis on the plane of world history. For once Ranke
conceived the process of world history as the movement from the
opposition of spirit and nature, manifest first in the degeneration
of the world religions and then in the violence of universal
revolution, to the harmony of spirit and nature, as manifest in the
organic unity of historic nation and modern state, then the
political history of modern times became at once the record of
states which were by definition incorporations of national spirit,
and the record of nations which were realities only through the
activity of the states they inspired. On a more concrete level, his
uncertainty about the political desirability of a representative
constitution which was at once necessary to a state for the
transcendence of the destructive conflict between monarchy and
revolution and dangerous to the state for the limitation of the

salubrious monarchical power gave way to the acceptance of constitutionalism in the form of a national representation bound to the preestablished institutions of the historical state.

Of the three philosophical dilemmas which were eased for Ranke by their translation into the actual historical arenas, the easiest of solution was the problem of progress, which in a sense solved itself with Ranke's climactic execution of a continuous world history limited in fact to the single process of western development. The problem was severe enough in itself to have led at least one authority to conclude that there simply was a conflict between Ranke's antiprogressive theory and his progressive practice of history.[2] The conclusion is true enough in its notice of the disparate dominant tendencies in the theory and the practice and in its implication of the different modes of thinking that went into each level. But since the opposition between equivalence and progressivism appears on both levels, albeit in varying proportions, the essential conflict between the levels consists not so much of this opposition as of the antithetical results that were produced by Ranke's capacity to reconcile in historical practice the opposition he merely stated in historical theory. This practical resolution, in turn, was made possible by the thematic universal realities which he identified in actual history. For it was in connection with these general real connections—"the conflict of opposites" which have developed "European Christianity," "the community of European nations," and the permanent human treasury of "inherited culture"—that Ranke endorsed "the universal-historical progress which links the several centuries and nations to one another" and constitutes "the progress of the human race." (See chap. 10, III.)

But from the historian's perspective on the particular constituents rather than the universalizable results of these vital conflicts, the individual acts and agents of history took their historical meaning not from any contribution to a progressive chain in time but from their immediate bilateral relation to an eternal and unchanging standard of good. Since there were historical realities corresponding to both the universal and the individual perspectives—realities connected by the unity of opposites—progress and equivalence became a matter of deliberately shifting perspectives on the same historical process.

More difficult, albeit equally soluble in historiographical terms, was the problem of freedom and necessity. For these principles were essentially contradictory to Ranke. "Freedom determines itself individually, morally," while necessity "joins . . . effect and cause with unbroken continuity in all things," and in philosophical contexts Ranke could provide only an arbitrary and exceptional coexistence: "Freedom . . . produces itself very rarely and only in the most important moments."[3]

But in his later years Ranke, like Marx, absorbed his philosophical foundation into the structure of his science, and, like economics for Marx, history for Ranke became coextensive with his conceptual world. In this later historical dimension freedom and necessity became existentially compatible and historiographically complementary. They "exist side by side." If necessity is still "a deep, pervasive connection . . . which penetrates everywhere" and "inheres in all that has been formed and cannot be undone," now freedom too "makes its appearance everywhere." Not only are "the scenes of this freedom" and the necessary connections which are its "basis" equally the proper objects of historical knowledge, but the proportions resulting precisely from "the clash of the antagonistic principles of freedom and necessity" constitute the respective characters of various ages whose "sequence" is universal history. In his histories, moreover—starting with the *History of the Popes*—Ranke found no difficulty in alternating freedom and necessity, in their interactive hisorical guises, within epochs as well. Thus, depending on the occasion, men cannot "resist the . . . tendency of the times"; "original minds" which are "affected by the course" of such a general tendency "themselves impress on it a powerful reaction"; or "the human intellect" is even, dialectically, "left at liberty to seek a new development in a totally altered direction" by the very "mechanism" of events—their "connected reality"—which constricted men's freedom too far.[4]

By the 1860s, indeed, he had come far enough in resolving human duality in its historical version to advance it as a direct replacement of the ontological opposition between freedom and determinism which, on this level, he could not resolve. The historian is not so much concerned with the philosophical issue of freedom and necessity, he noted then. "What matters to him most of all is the other issue, concerning the connection of the general and the particular—concerning their earthly, real meshing."[5]

The last of Ranke's fundamental antinomies which was converted into compatible functions through the synthetic medium of
his mature history was the crucial subject-object relationship. In the
abstract contexts of his theology, philosophy, and theory of history
he committed himself both to the knowable existence of the
object, in which the subject should immerse himself, and to the
distinctive angle of the subject, from which the object must
necessarily be viewed.[6] The same dualism extended to his general
statements about historical methodology. Despite his repeated
tributes to the possibility and desirability of "objective historical
truth," attainable through research, as against the "political and
religious bias of the present," Ranke also acknowledged throughout his career both the undeniable actuality of each generation's
imposition of its own values upon history and the welcome
actuality of present influences upon the historian. "History is
always being rewritten. . . . The prevailing tendency of every age
makes history its own and transfers the ideas of the age to history,
assigning praise and blame according to it." And more approv-
ingly: "Everything that concerns, threatens, and inspires us seeks
to be expressed in the study of history, for the past has it all in
embryo."[7]

Nor was Ranke any more able to reconcile these positions in his
general methodology than in his general theory of history. Usually
he did not even try, confining himself to the simple assertion of
preference for objectivity as a somehow realizable norm or to the
vague romantic invocation of "pure intuition" for the linkage of
historical object and historian-subject. On the rare occasion when
he did confront the two poles of historical knowledge—when he
asked himself, after postulating "the return to the most original
source" as the remedy for historical relativism, "But would one
study it at all without the impulse of the present?"—he had no
answer. "However that may be," he concluded evasively, "pure
intuition remains the norm."[8]

But in his mature historical practice Ranke found the answer: he
assigned the explicit priority of the historical object to foreign
history, the explicit role of the historian's subjectivity to native
history, and the synthesis of both to world history. Thus he
emphasized his "impartiality" and his refusal "to import the
interests of the present into historical work," particularly in
reference to his *History of the Popes* and his *English History,* and

it was in the latter, indeed, that he made the explicit connection between foreign history and objectivity. He justified his undertaking, as a German, to write a history of England precisely on this score. "It is good," he wrote, "that alongside the native accounts which give expression to the sympathies and antipathies passed down in tradition and developed in the polemics of opinionated literature, there should be foreign accounts, which are independent of such sympathies and antipathies." It was in connection with the *English History* too, let us remember, that Ranke described his effort "to extinguish my own self . . . , to let . . . things speak."[9] It was, conversely, in connection with his Prussian and German history that he asserted the historiographical validity of his own subjective point of view. In this genre as well, to be sure, he strove to present "as objective a perception as possible," but privately he admitted, as we may recall, not only that as a matter of fact "I show a lively sympathy [*Anteil*] with the event I describe, the rise of the Prussian state," but that as a matter of principle "a book of this kind would be impossible without such sympathy."[10]

The obvious question is why Ranke found a division of function between objectivity and subjectivity satisfactory in history when he could find this satisfaction nowhere else. In part the reason was psychological: he was aware from his own emotional experience that historians tend to identify themselves with the history of their native land and to remain outside the history of foreign lands. From an early point of his career as a historian, he frankly asserted his preference for German over other histories precisely on this ground. "I was born for German history," he wrote,[11] and this feeling during the 1830s diverted his treatment of the Reformation into the framework of the "native" (*vaterländischen*) history which he was planning at the same time. Ranke's heart-felt sympathy for the history of his own Germany permeated the whole book and led him at times dangerously close to violation of his own cherished rules of objective history. Because "the unity of the nation" found expression in the sessions of the sixteenth-century German Reichstag, he felt justified in characterizing his intention to write the first coherent history of that national institution with a term otherwise anathema to the motivation of his history: he wanted to write it, he said, because like every man he wanted to do something "useful" in his life.[12] Again, it was in the context of this history of the Reformation in Germany that Ranke first acknowledged a pattern of spiritual progress that ran counter to his general commitment to the equivalence of all ages in the sight of God. The Reformation, he judged in the midst of his account of it, was "an enterprise of the greatest importance and prospect for the progress of the human race, but it had first to establish itself in Germany."[13] Thus Ranke could draw from his own experience the clear lesson that the subjective component in native history and the objectivity of foreign history signified a satisfying allocation of values because it was simply fitting to the psyche of historians who felt themselves to be directly involved in the one but not in the other.

But there was a second, more intellectual and more fundamental, reason for Ranke's satisfaction with his solution of the subject-object problem in terms of native and foreign history, for this solution cinched the ultimate coherence of his history. The classification of history into native and foreign became, for him, the middle term between the subject-object relationship, which was his original antimony, and the relationship between national and universal history, which was his final resolution of it. He associated native with national and foreign with universal history, and since he had come to see national and universal history as different aspects of a single and continuous historical process, native and foreign history, with their subjective and objective implications, became simple matters of perspective. "Great peoples and states have a double calling, one national and the other world-historical," he wrote in his *French History*, "and so their history also offers a double side. Insofar as it forms an essential element in the general development of humanity . . . it attracts the attention of foreigners beyond the nationality to it. It can perhaps be asserted that the chief distinction between Greek and Roman historians on the history of ancient Rome in its prime was that they grasped the world-historical side and the national interpretation respectively. *The object is the same; the authors are distinguished by their point of view.*"[14]

The result of this association was to make a perspectival reconciliation not only of nativist and foreign history but of subjectivity and objectivity in history. In his early theorizing Ranke had categorically validated subjectivity in the realm of universals and objectivity in the realm of particular facts, on the grounds that only in a "Greater" (that is, a universal) could a subject truly experience and yet himself be preserved. But as his historical career wore on he tended increasingly to stress the universal connectedness of things: he vested individuality no longer so much in persons as in nations, with their larger and more compatible proportion of coherence in their particular actions, and he identified objective truth not so much with such actions as with the general processes in which they participated. Thus particularity and generality were now conceived to be continuous with each other, with events themselves more general than the facts which composed them and general processes endowed with the historical reality formerly vouchsafed to their individual agents. As an historian he claimed that "the fact is not the outer limit of our knowledge," but rather "only from a spiritually combined series of facts does the event result"; that, in a significant restatement of his famous old formula, "our task is thus to discern what has really happened [*eigentlich geschehen ist*] in the series of facts . . .—to discern their total [*Summe*]"; and that "the objective spirit implanted in the human race manifests itself in different stages which are linked to one another with an inner necessity if not with logical compulsion," for "a certain security of perception"— indeed, "the historical approach" as such—results from "our viewing relationships in the large . . . the course of events in general."[15]

This shift in the modes of subjectivity and objectivity, mediated through the valid subjective sympathy Ranke accorded to the history of his own single nation and through the authentic objectivity he increasingly found in universal history, was important not so much for their reversal as for their convergence. The philosophical categories of subject and object each received an infusion of the other from their historical employment, permitting a harmonious interaction in the practice of history not apparent in its theory. The intimacy of the interaction varied with the relations between national and universal history, and we have found a progression in these relations, within the later Ranke, from complementarity to integration. As long as he made the distinction between national and universal in the operational terms of native history and foreign history, as he did until the German unification, subjective sympathy and objective coherence were juxtaposed for different historians or for the same historian in different postures. He denied, it will be recalled, the characterization "national history" to his studies of both France and England since in each case, as "the historian of a nation not his own," if he were to make a claim of national history for them, it "would be a contradiction in terms."[16] But after 1870, his native national history of Prussianized Germany acquired the universal mission which had been assumed and frustrated sporadically during the Reformation and the reign of Frederick the Great, and he developed enterprises of scholarly world history wherein the merger of national and universal elements in the historical process itself empowered the same historian not only to treat both alike but even to apply the objective standards of humanity's general and continuous progress as the canons of his own sympathetic internal judgments. For the universal coherence in the process of world history joined both the particular facts to the general connections within the past and the individual events of the past to the individual life of the historian in the present.

It has been cogently demonstrated by others that Ranke validated the distinctive claims of both the knowing subject and the knowable object as necessary products of the diffraction of God's essence in earthly reality, and by dint of this differential relationship to the divine the historian's subjective preconceptions in his approach to the historical object were rooted not so much in the fortuitous limits of actual existence as in the essential constitution of humanity.[17] What we can add now is an appreciation of the temporal connection of subject and object through the common participation of this historian-subject and the historical agent who is his object in the same process of human history, a connection perhaps less fundamental but at once more perceptible, more verifiable, and more satisfying than the posited juncture of origins in the will of an inscrutable God.

II What history meant to Ranke is clear enough. But what we can learn from him about its meaning for us is not so clear. Certainly we should register the explicit legacy which has done so much to make the study of history a scientific profession, and certainly we should correct this legacy for the subliminal effects of the universal preoccupations which have gotten lost in the transmission; but the legacy assumes a meaningfulness for history which we must again prove, and the very fact of its distortion indicates that what sufficed as proof for Ranke no longer suffices for us.

Unquestionably the growing vogue of scientism through the nineteenth century and of social scientism through our share of the twentieth, a vogue which has dominated the partial reception of the Rankean bequest and remains the common basis of our routinized historical vocation, had an early imprimatur in the endorsement of Ranke himself. His express insistence upon the scientific nature of the historical discipline, with its communicable method and its neutral stance, appeared early, and it was confirmed and even accentuated in his later development. It was evident both in the scholarly instruments which he founded—the *Jahrbuecher der Deutschen Kaiser,* the Munich Commission of Historical Science, and the encyclopedia of German biography (*Allgemeine Deutsche Biographie*)—and in the mode of integration which made his theological and philosophical concerns amenable to historical discipline. Indeed, the "great facts" which gave him access to world history have some analogy with the general facts which contemporary positivists were identifying with the invariable laws of phenomena to insure the scientific rather than the metaphysical grounding of such laws.

But Ranke's own constant devotion to the scientific method in history does not in itself explain why later historians so underplayed the general level of history which he combined with it. Later historians, formed by different experiences, no longer saw, as he did, a universal and developing pattern in the actual history of man. For them the actual process of history was composed of discrete and discontinuous actions, and when they used Ranke's method it was only to this kind of history that they applied it.

But Ranke's method had always been predicated upon the existence of a continuous general process in actual history—at first discoverable, then discovered—for only if this were so could the historian have common ground with the temporally obscured event he was to grasp. No wonder, then, that in addition to the empirical scientific history which he immediately spawned, toward the end of the century philosophical historians like Dilthey and

Meinecke, who sought to explain how the formal universals implicit in the historian's method could fit a discontinuous historical reality, also looked back to Ranke for their point of departure. He had found what he sought in history rather than in the historian, but his heirs were indebted to him because, like them, he had sought the general connections without which the empirical history of individual events can never be raised to the status of an authentic science.

Yet, despite the persistent subscription to scientific history and despite the revisionist recall of a larger generalizing and therefore sophisticated scientific attitude in Ranke than the main line of descent would have it, a palpable distance subsists between Ranke's approach to history and our own. The host of informed commentators who have resurrected Ranke's "doctrine of ideas" (*Ideenlehre,* or the theory of ideas as divine manifestations of connectedness in this world of fragmented appearances) and have underlined thereby the intellectual character of his universalism through space and time alike, have rehabilitated him only for the small group of practitioners who are already committed to history and, indeed, to the specialized history of ideas within the generic discipline. To the bulk of professional historians and, more important, to the great body of the literate public, he must seem simply archaic, and the more he is himself historically restored the more archaic must he seem.

Neither Ranke's beliefs nor his concerns are ours. We do not hold with a moral world order; our gods, when we have any, are even more inscrutable than his and are surely less responsible for and intuitable through human behavior; nor do we believe that the historical process evinces a continuity endowing history with a comparative advantage over other kinds of experience or that general ideas and organizations extending over many countries and many ages are the most important factors in human history; and assuredly many of us have lost our confidence in the factual association of the past and the present, particularly in the form of viable, established, historically rooted institutions. We are correspondingly less intent on knowing God through His works, on resolving ontological antinomies like the dualism between subject and object or freedom and determinism, and on discovering a literal connection between our contemporary experience and our study of history. Clearly, we share with Ranke neither the assumptions nor the problems which led him to history as the medium which worked both to integrate his attitudes toward life and to organize his experience of life.

One thing, however, we may well learn, figurative as the lesson may be. History remains for us, as it was for Ranke, an inimitable way of rendering comprehensible modes of humanity which must otherwise be incomprehensible. The concatenation of diverse motives, ideas, and actions; the discrepant linkages between policies and their unintended results; the frictional dimensions of the settled past and the open present: when such heterogeneous relationships cannot be understood by the logics of either propositional thinking or the analytical sciences, they may still be manageable by a kind of thinking that makes sense of arranging things, however incongruous in themselves, along the time line. There is, then, a distinctive kind of historical logic which is geared to the actual rather than to the possibles or probables of other logics and which finds its satisfaction in things taking place before, after, or simultaneously with other things. If we think of history thus as a logic of the actual, then we have a modern version of Ranke's focus on history as the meeting ground of philosophy, science, and cataclysmic experience.

But our version suffers from a comparative disadvantage. Because Ranke believed in an eternal moral law and in a conservative continuity between past and present, he could be more fundamentally content with historical solutions and with historical analogies than can we with our pervasive doubts about the applicability of any historical truth outside its own orbit, however satisfied we may be with it. Even if, in short, our historical logic enlarges our understanding of men by providing us with a rationale for what has been irreducibly indifferent or contrary to reason in what he has irrevocably done, how can we use such understanding for our personal salvation or our political information, as Ranke did, when we no longer have the connecting lines for its transfer? We cannot follow Ranke substantively, but yet, both in what he did and in what he failed to do, he guides us to the beginning of an answer.

Ranke sensed that history occupied a dimension of life different from that of either formal thought or aesthetic creation, and the frequent inaptness of his own theorizing about history like the stylistic and imaginative limitations of his own writing served to confirm the general point. As a discipline devoted to the actual but equipped with a language of commonsense organized around the categorical, history seems to offer lessons that inevitably suffer distortion on every occasion that general inferences are linguistically drawn from the actual relations of history. Between the nominalist position that no lessons can be drawn and the realist position that didactic or analogical precepts may be drawn there is a realm of general truth which is at once transferable and untranslatable. When the present is viewed as contemporary history, with an indefinite beginning and a tentative end, and when past history is read with an eye to the knowledge it affords about the logic of the actual—that is, about the possible combinations of motives, actions, and results which men have actually undergone—then these insights from the verifiable past part of the historical process may be applied to the more uncertain mediated present part of the historical process by anyone who has developed his distinctive historical sense from his reading of the past. For the historical sense refers precisely to the understanding that the human combinations that have been struck through time, however ill-assorted or incongruous they may be, derive a meaning simply from their having actually happened in conjunction; that this meaning is inimitable; and that each instance adds its increment of this meaning to the general feeling for the way men circumstantially behave.

The historical sense is a cumulative wisdom. It grows with the reading of history that aims beyond history. There are no substitutes. There are no shortcuts.

Notes

1. The Dubious Legacy

1. For a superb comparison of Thucydides and Ranke as critical historians, see Hajo Holborn, "The Science of History," in Hajo Holborn, *History and the Humanities* (Garden City, N.Y., 1972), pp. 84-96.

2. Ranke to Barthold George Niebuhr, Dec. 14, 1824, in Ranke, *Das Briefwerk,* ed. Walther Peter Fuchs (Hamburg, 1949), p. 69; Ranke, *Sämmtliche Werke,* 3d ed. (Leipzig, 1888), 51-52: 588-89. For Niebuhr, philology was at the heart of historical method—"I dissect words as the anatomist dissects bodies"—and it was this kind of assumption that led Ranke to deem "writing [*die Schrift*] . . . the exclusive basis of history," and the appearance of "authentic written records . . . the beginning of history." Ranke, *Weltgeschichte,* 9 vols., 1st-3rd ed. (Leipzig, 1881-88), 1¹:v-vi.

3. Ernst Schulin, "Rankes erstes Buch," *Historische Zeitschrift* 203 (1966): 584-85. Two recent analyses, indeed, see in Ranke's presentational forms— i.e., in his dramatic style and in the metaphorical organicism of his narrative form respectively—the essential mode of his coherence as an historian. See Peter Gay, *Style in History* (New York, 1974), pp. 59-67, 94; and Hayden White, *Metahistory: The Historical Imagination in Nineteenth-Century Europe* (Baltimore, 1973), pp. 167-78, 187-90.

4. John Emerich Edward Dalberg-Acton, First Baron Acton, *Historical Essays and Studies* (London, 1907), p. 352.

5. Ranke, *Geschichten der romanischen und germanischen Völker von 1494-1514,* in *Fürsten und Völker,* ed. Willy Andreas (Wiesbaden, 1957), p. 4.

6. Ranke to King Maximilian II of Bavaria, Nov. 26, 1859, in *Briefwerk,* p. 432.

7. "Vom Einfluss der Theorie," in Ranke, *Geschichte und Politik: Aus-*

gewählte Aufsätze und Meisterschriften, ed. Hans Hofmann (Stuttgart, 1942), p. 73.

8. In Hans Herzfeld, "Vorwort," in Ranke, *Über die Epochen der neueren Geschichte,* ed. Hans Herzfeld (Schloss Laupheim, n.d.), p. 19.

9. Ranke to Heinrich Ranke, Nov. 21, 1831, and to Friedrich Perthes, May 21, 1832, in *Briefwerk,* pp. 246, 250.

10. Ranke, *A Dialogue on Politics,* in Theodore H. Von Laue, *Leopold Ranke: The Formative Years* (Princeton, 1950), p. 165.

11. Ranke, *Geschichten der romanischen und germanischen Völker,* p. 4; Ranke, *Preussische Geschichte,* ed. Willy Andreas (Wiesbaden, 1957), 1:51.

12. Ranke to Heinrich Ranke, Dec. 28, 1823, and Mar. 27, 1826, in *Briefwerk,* pp. 51, 98.

13. Ranke, *Französische Geschichte, vornehmlich im sechzehnten und siebzehnten Jahrhundert* (Leipzig, 1868-70) (vols. 8-11 of *Sämmtliche Werke*) 1:vi; 5:6, 31; Ranke, "Idee der Universalhistorie," in Eberhard Kessel, "Rankes Idee der Universalhistorie," *Historische Zeitschrift* 178 (1954): 298; Ranke, *Zur Kritik neuerer Geschichtschreiber,* 3d ed. (Leipzig, 1884) (vols. 33-34 of *Sämmtliche Werke*), p. iii.

14. Ranke, *Über die Epochen,* p. 30. References here will be made to this traditional edition, since it is the traditional Ranke that is being presented. The recent critical edition of *Über die Epochen der neueren Geschichte,* published as vol. 2 of Ranke's *Aus Werk und Nachlass,* 4 vols. (Munich, 1964-75), will be used below for chapter 10 for the historical reconstruction of Ranke's development.

15. Ranke to Heinrich Ranke, May 22, 1823, in *Briefwerk,* p. 44.

16. "Geschichte und Philosophie," in Ranke, *Geschichte und Politik,* p. 135.

17. Ibid., p. 136.

18. Ranke, *Dialogue on Politics,* pp. 159, 162, 166, 168-69, 180.

19. "Über die Verwandtschaft und den Unterschied der Historie und der Politik," in Ranke, *Geschichte und Politik,* pp. 127-28.

20. Ranke to Heinrich Ranke, May 5, 1827, and Nov. 30, 1832, in *Briefwerk,* pp. 107, 252.

21. Ranke to Heinrich Ranke, April 9, 1824; Nov. 1827; May 26, 1831; to Ernst Ranke, Dec. 4, 1836, in ibid., pp. 59, 124, 241, 283.

2. The Unscientific Counterpoint

1. Ranke to Anton Richter, Apr. 13, 1823, in *Briefwerk,* p. 38.

2. Ranke to King Frederick William IV, Dec. 24, 1847, in Ranke, *Neue Briefe,* ed. Bernhard Hoeft and Hans Herzfeld (Hamburg, 1949), p. 326.

3. Ranke, *Aus Werk und Nachlass,* ed. Walther Peter Fuchs and Theodor Schieder, 3 vols. (Munich, 1964-73), 2:75. Ranke to Heinrich Ranke, Nov. 20, 1820, in *Briefwerk,* p. 24.

4. Ranke to Heinrich Ritter, Oct. 28, 1827, and to Karl Varnhagen von Ense, Dec. 9, 1827, in *Briefwerk,* pp. 123, 126.

5. Ranke, *Nachlass,* 1:120.

6. Ranke to Heinrich Ranke, Nov. 30, 1832, in *Briefwerk,* p. 252.

7. Ibid.; Ranke to Heinrich Ranke, May 26, 1831, in *Briefwerk,* p. 241.

8. Ranke to Heinrich Ranke, Feb. 1827, in ibid., pp. 104-5.

9. Ranke to Heinrich Ranke, Nov. 20/21, 1828, in ibid., p. 174.

10. Ranke to Heinrich Ranke, May 5, 1827, in ibid., p. 107.
11. Ranke, "Über die Verwandtschaft," p. 121.
12. Ranke to Heinrich Ritter, Feb. 18, 1835, in *Briefwerk*, p. 265.
13. Ranke to Heinrich Ranke, Mar. 1820, in ibid., p. 18. The relationship between historical coherence and the presence of God in history is clearer in the full quotation than the usual focus on the excerpted phrase "holy hieroglyph" indicates. The complete quotation reads: "God dwells, lives, and can be known in all of history. Every deed attests to Him, every moment preaches His name, but most of all, it seems to me, the connectedness of history in the large. It [the connectedness] stands there like a holy hieroglyph.... May we, for our part, decipher this holy hieroglyph! Even so do we serve God. Even so are we priests. Even so are we teachers."
14. Ranke, *Nachlass*, 2:66; Theodor Schieder, *Begegnungen mit der Geschichte* (Göttingen, 1962), pp. 107, 121.
15. Ranke, *Französische Geschichte*, 5:5.
16. Ibid., 5:28, 269-72.
17. For the complementary thesis, see Rudolf Vierhaus, *Ranke und die soziale Welt*) Münster, 1957), pp. 17-18, and Von Laue, *Ranke*, pp. 122-23. For the tensile thesis, Schieder, *Begegnungen*, pp. 123-24.
18. Ranke, *Nachlass*, 1:238; Ranke to Karl August Varnhagen von Ense, Dec. 9, 1827, in *Briefwerk*, p. 128; Schieder, *Begegnungen*, p. 122.
19. Ranke, *Nachlass*, 1:238. For the variety of Rankean quotations on this problem, see K. G. Lamprecht, *Alte und neue Richtungen in der Geschichtswissenschaft* (Berlin, 1896).
20. Ranke, *Nachlass*, 1:120.
21. Ranke to Heinrich Ranke, Nov. 30, 1832, in *Briefwerk*, p. 256.
22. For a fuller discussion of this distinction, see below, chapter 7.
23. Ranke to Heinrich Ranke, Nov. 30, 1832, and May 26, 1831, in *Briefwerk*, pp. 256, 241.
24. For a thorough analysis of Ranke's commitment to world history, see Gerhard Masur, *Rankes Begriff der Weltgeschichte* (Berlin, 1926), pp. 52-129.
25. Ranke to Heinrich Ranke, Nov. 3, 1825, and Feb. 1827, in *Briefwerk*, pp. 92, 104.
26. Ranke to Heinrich Ranke, Nov. 24, 1826, and Nov. 1827, in ibid., pp. 102, 125.
27. Ranke to Heinrich Ranke, Nov. 30, 1834, in *Neue Briefe*, p. 195; to Heinrich Ranke, April 1830, in *Briefwerk*, p. 209; to Heinrich Ritter, Feb. 18, 1835, in ibid., p. 265; to King Maximilian of Bavaria, Feb. 17, 1852, in ibid., p. 356.
28. Ranke, *Über die Epochen*, p. 31.
29. Ibid., pp. 29-31, 33.
30. Theodor Schieder, "Die Entstehung von Rankes *Über die Epochen der neueren Geschichte*," *Historische Zeitschrift* 199 (1964): 21.
31. Ranke, "Geschichte und Philosophie," p. 136; *Über die Epochen*, p. 30; *History of the Popes in the Last Four Centuries*, trans. E. Fowler (London, 1912), 1:464.
32. Ranke, *Über die Epochen*, pp. 32, 34, 194; *Weltgeschichte*, 1:viii-x.
33. Thus two of his most explicit arguments against ideas and progress in history are to be found in an article on the philosophy of history ("Geschichte und

Philosophie'') and his lectures on the epochs of modern world history. The mutual reference of ideas and progress in his opposition to ''philosophy of history'' is self-evident. For his mixing of the two categories in his direction of the lectures against Schelling's philosophy of history, see Schieder, ''Rankes *Über die Epochen,*'' pp. 18-21.

34. Masur, *Rankes Begriff der Weltgeschichte,* p. 105.
35. Ranke, *Dialogue on Politics,* in Von Laue, *Ranke,* pp. 166, 175; Hans Hofmann, ''Zur Einführung,'' in *Geschichte und Politik,* p. xix; Ranke, *Die grossen Mächte,* in ibid., pp. 49, 52.
36. Ranke to Heinrich Ranke, April 1830, in *Briefwerk,* p. 208. See chapter 4 below.
37. Ranke, ''Idee der Universalhistorie,'' p. 297.
38. Quoted in Holborn, ''The Science of History,'' p. 95.

3. The Limits of Theory

1. Philosophie und Geschichte,'' in Ranke, *Geschichte und Politik,* p. 134.
2. Ranke, *Nachlass,* 2:19, 70-75.
3. Über die Verwandtschaft,'' pp. 119-20, 126-71.
4. *Die grossen Mächte,* and ''Vom Einfluss der Theorie,'' in *Geschichte und Politik,* p. 75.
5. Ranke, ''Geschichte und Philosophie,'' p. 36.
6. Ranke to Heinrich Ranke, Apr. 1830, in *Briefwerk,* p. 208.
7. See chapter 5 below.
8. Ranke to Heinrich Ranke, Mar. 1820, Oct. 18, 1822, Feb. 18, 1824, Aug. 25, 1827, Nov. 15, 1829, in *Briefwerk,* pp. 16-18, 32, 54, 111, 203; Hans Herzfeld, ''Vorwort,'' in Ranke, *Über die Epochen,* p. 18; Ranke, *Weltgeschichte,* vol. 1, pt. 1, p. ix.
9. See especially Carl Hinrichs, *Ranke und die Geschichtstheologie der Goethezeit* (Göttingen, 1954), and Ernst Simon, *Ranke und Hegel* (Berlin, 1928), pp. 194-204.
10. Ranke to Heinrich Ranke, Apr. 25, 1823, in *Briefwerk,* p. 39.
11. Ranke to Heinrich Ranke, July 11, 1825, in ibid., p. 86.
12. Ranke to Heinrich Ranke, Dec. 23, 1820, in *Neue Briefe,* p. 19.
13. ''Über die Verwandtschaft,'' p. 124.
14. Ranke to Heinrich Ranke, Feb. 17, 1825, in *Briefwerk,* p. 74.
15. Ranke to Heinrich Ranke, Nov. 28, 1822, and Aug. 25, 1827, in ibid., pp. 34, 110.
16. Ranke, *Sämmtliche Werke,* 51/52: 588-89, 592-95.
17. See below, first part of chapter 4.
18. Ranke's excerpts from Fichte (circa 1817) in Ranke, *Deutsche Geschichte im Zeitalter der Reformation,* ed. Paul Joachimsen, (Gesamtausgabe der Deutschen Akademie (Munich, 1926), 6:363-66; *Nachlass,* 1:493-501; Ranke to Heinrich Ranke, Mar. 1820, in *Briefwerk,* p. 18.
19. Ranke, *Nachlass,* 1:142, 145-46.
20. Ibid., p. 154; Simon, *Ranke und Hegel,* p. 108; Ranke to Heinrich Ritter, Oct. 28, 1827, in *Briefwerk,* p. 120; Ranke, *Sämmtliche Werke,* 53-54:573; ''Schiller als Historiker,'' in Schieder, *Begegnungen,* p. 57.
21. Ranke to Gotthilf Heinrich Schubert, Dec. 13, 1826, and Jan. 6 (?), 1832, in *Neue Briefe,* pp. 92, 165; to Heinrich Ritter, Feb. 21, 1834, in ibid,

p. 259. But philosophically it was only to the young Schelling—the philosopher of identity—that Ranke was close. Of the later Schelling—the philosopher of history—he was as critical as he was of all philosophers of history. See Schieder, "Die Rankes "Über die Epochen," p. 20.
22. Simon, *Ranke und Hegel,* pp. 36-45.

4. The Preconditions of History

1. Ranke to Ferdinand Ranke, Aug. 9, 1838, in *Neue Briefe,* p. 259.
2. Ranke, *Zur eigenen Lebensgeschichte,* ed. Alfred Dove, in *Sämmtliche Werke* (Leipzig, 1890), 53-54:7-12.
3. For Ranke's social background, see especially Vierhaus, *Ranke und die soziale Welt,* pp. 6-22.
4. For this revision see the doctoral dissertation by Günter Johannes Henz, *Leopold von Ranke: Leben, Denken, Wort, 1795-1814* (Cologne, 1968).
5. Ibid., pp. 117-19, 139-41.
6. Ibid., pp. 62-64, 118-21.
7. Ranke, *Lebensgeschichte,* pp. 4-6.
8. Henz, *Ranke,* pp. 146-49.
9. For Ranke's concerns along this line at Pforta, see ibid., pp. 218-28. For Ranke's later judgments on German classicists and romantics, see pp. 27-30 above.
10. Ranke, *Nachlass,* 1:258-64.
11. Ranke to Friedrich Thierach, Apr. 28, 1822, in *Briefwerk,* pp. 28-29; to Ferdinand Ranke, Apr. 12, 1822, in *Neue Briefe,* p. 27.
12. Ranke to Gotthill Heinrich Schubert, Dec. 13, 1826, in ibid., p. 92.
13. Von Laue, *Ranke,* p. 18.
14. Ranke to King Frederick William IV, Dec. 24, 1847, in *Neue Briefe,* p. 326.
15. Ranke to Heinrich Ranke, Mar. 22, 1853, in *Briefwerk,* pp. 368-69.
16. Ranke to King William I of Prussia, Jan. 1, 1867, in ibid, p. 487.
17. "Über die Wechselwirkung zwischen Staat, Publikum, Lehrern, and Schülern in Beziehung auf ein Gymnasium," in Ranke, *Zwei Jugendreden,* ed. Kurt Borries (Berlin, 1927), pp. 28-35.
18. Entry of Dec. 5, 1843, in *Tagebücher von K. A. Varnhagen von Ense* (reprint, Bern, 1972), 2:234.
19. "Tagebuchdiktate Leopold v. Rankes aus dem Jahre 1881," *Historische Zeitschrift* 151 (1935): 332-34.
20. See especially Carl Hinrichs, "Rankes Lutherfragment von 1817 und der Ursprung seiner universalhistorischen Anschauung," in *Festschrift für Gerhard Ritter* (Tübingen, 1950); and idem, *Ranke und die Geschichtstheologie der Goethezeit.*
21. Hinrichs, "Rankes Lutherfragment" pp. 310-11; Ranke to Heinrich Ranke, Mar. 1820, and to Otto von Ranke, May 25, 1873, in *Briefwerk,* pp. 18, 518.
22. Ranke to Otto von Ranke, May 25, 1873, in *Briefwerk,* p. 518; "Das Lutherfragment von 1817," in Ranke, *Deutsche Geschichte im Zeitalter der Reformation,* ed. Elisabeth Schweitzer, Gesamtausgabe (Munich , 1925-26), 6:331.
23. Most commentators have applied neither the term nor the idea of conversion to Ranke's concern with Luther in Leipzig from late 1816 to early 1818. I follow the first editor of Ranke's "Luther Fragment," Elisabeth Schweitzer,

in using both the term and the interpretation for this religious concern. I have not followed her, however, in her subsequent elaboration of the conversion's positive historiographical effect upon Ranke. See her discussion in ibid., pp. 382, 385-86.

24. Ranke, *Lebensgeschichte,* p. 29.
25. Ranke, *Nachlass,* 1:116.
26. Ranke, *Lebensgeschichte,* pp. 31, 59. In this account I have combined formulations from his autobiographical dictations of 1863 and 1885. There are differences of emphasis and detail between the two versions, but they need not concern us here.
27. For this revision, see editorial note in Ranke, *Nachlass,* 3:331-33. The notes on Ranke's abortive Luther work that are published in this volume are more extensive and the editorial comment more critical than in Elisabeth Schweitzer's earlier edition of the material. But the decision, in the later edition, to separate out and publish in another volume (vol. 1) the entries in Ranke's notebooks which are mixed in with the Luther material but are deemed to be independent of it makes it difficult to collate these materials with the collateral and relevant Rankean items which are included in the Schweitzer edition. Since the order of items in the notebooks does not correspond to any order of insertion by Ranke, they cannot be arranged on any scale of priority or succession. The most revealing classification of the items is substantive, between those that indicate Ranke's state of mind prior to or outside his intra-Lutheran conversion, whether these items deal with Luther or not, and those that reveal his state of mind as it was affected by the conversion.
28. Ranke, *Lebensgeschichte,* pp. 29-30.
29. Ranke, "Luther-Fragment," ed. Schweitzer, p. 316.
30. Johann Gottlieb Fichte, *Über das Wesen des Gelehrten, und seine Erscheinungen in dem Gebiete der Freiheit* (Berlin, 1806) pp. 5, 15. For Ranke's excerpts from Fichte, see Ranke, *Nachlass,* 1:493-501.
31. Hinrichs, "Rankes Lutherfragment," pp. 314-16, 326.
32. Ranke, "Luther-Fragment," ed. Schweitzer, pp. 317-18.
33. Ibid., p. 326. Hinrichs, "Rankes Lutherfragment," pp. 315-17.
34. Fitche, *Über das Wesen des Gelehrten,* pp. 135-36, 154, 172, 196.
35. Ranke, "Luther-Fragment," ed. Schweitzer, p. 318.
36. Fichte, *Über das Wesen der Gelehrten,* p. 60.
37. Ranke, "Luther-Fragment, ed. Schweitzer, p. 364.
38. Ranke, *Lebensgeschichte,* pp. 31, 60.
39. Entry of 1816/17, in Ranke, *Nachlass,* 1:28.
40. Ranke, "Luther-Fragment," ed. Schweitzer, p. 327.
41. Entry of 1816/17, in Ranke, *Nachlass,* 1:28.
42. Ranke, "Luther-Fragment," ed. Schweitzer, pp. 315-16.
43. Ibid., 6:316-17.
44. Ibid., 6:326.
45. Ranke, *Nachlass,* 3:389-90.
46. Ranke, "Luther-Fragment," ed. Schweitzer, p. 319.
47. Ibid., pp. 325, 327.
48. Ibid., pp. 323, 331.
49. Ibid., pp. 316-17.
50. Ibid., p. 318.
51. Ranke, *Nachlass,* 3:398.

52. Ranke, "Luther-Fragment," ed. Schweitzer, p. 321.
53. Ibid., pp. 318-19, 337, 360.
54. Ibid., p. 319.
55. Ibid., pp. 326-27, 338.
56. Ibid., p. 328.
57. Ibid., pp. 320, 361.
58. Ibid., p. 361.
59. Ibid., pp. 338-39.
60. Ibid., p. 362.
61. Ibid., pp. 361-62.
62. Ibid., p. 342; Ranke, *Nachlass,* 3:457-58, 465-66.
63. Ibid., 3:456, 462-65.
64. Ranke, "Luther-Fragment," ed. Schweitzer, p. 340.
65. Ibid., p. 338.
66. For his alternative reference to his project of Luther's biography" and Luther's "history," see Ranke, *Lebensgeschichte,* pp. 31, 59; "Luther-Fragment," ed. Schweitzer, p. 387.
67. Ibid., p. 320.
68. Ranke, *Nachlass,* 3:389; "Luther-Fragment," ed. Schweitzer, p. 337.
69. Ranke, *Lebensgeschichte,* p. 31; *Nachlass,* 3:466.
70. Fuchs, introduction to Ranke's Luther notes in *Nachlass,* 3:334.
71. Ranke, *Lebensgeschichte,* p. 59. Along the same line is the mooted report that in Leipzig Ranke had answered in the negative the direct question, Do you want to devote yourself to history? The presumed questioner was Gustav Stenzel, Ranke's college friend and a future historian. See "Luther-Fragment," ed. Schweitzer, p. 385n.
72. Ibid., p. 333.
73. Ibid., p. 320. The association of art and history also led Ranke to compare the reconstructions of the present and of the past in terms of what they meant to poets. Ibid., p. 315.
74. Ibid., pp. 330, 388.
75. Ibid., p. 350.
76. Ibid., pp. 330-31.
77. Ibid., p. 315.

5. The Conditions of History

1. See below, chap. 6, esp. sec. 2.
2. Sarah Austin's diary, entries of Nov. 22 and 30, 1842, in Janet Ross, *Three Generations of English Women,* new ed. (London, 1893), pp. 185-86.
3. Ranke to Karl August Varnhagen von Ense, June 9, 1829, in *Briefwerk,* p. 188. Ranke's social poise was further undermined by his inability to hold his liquor. According to an admirer who was far from malicious, "Ranke cannot tolerate wine," and he gave embarrassing point to the judgment by relating how the historian vomited at the dinner table during a princely party and had to be put to bed in his host's chamber. Otto von Bismarck, *Die gesammelten Werke* (Berlin, 1926), 8:498.
4. Ranke to Karl von Raumer, July 12, 1825, and to Heinrich Ranke, May 5, 1827, in *Briefwerk,* pp. 89, 107-8.
5. Ranke, "Luther-Fragment," ed. Schweitzer, 6:315-16.

6. Leopold to Heinrich Ranke, Apr. 25, 1823, and Dec. 28, 1823, in *Briefwerk,* pp. 39, 51.
7. Ranke, *Lebensgeschichte,* pp. 31, 35. Ranke's correspondence from his Frankfurt years, often detailing his conversations and social life, conveyed the same impression. See, for instance, his report on the celebration of his birthday in his letter to Heinrich Ranke, Jan. 1821, in *Briefwerk,* p. 27. But there was another side to his social existence in Frankfurt, as will appear later in this section.
8. Ranke to "A President," i.e., Prussian *Regierungspräsident,* Aug. 4, 1819, in *Briefwerk,* p. 8.
9. Ranke, *Nachlass,* 3:485.
10. Kurt Borries' introduction, in Ranke, *Zwei Jugendreden,* ed. Borries, (Berlin, 1927), p. 3.
11. Ranke, *Nachlass,* 3:496.
12. Ibid.
13. Ibid., 3:586.
14. Ranke to Heinrich Ranke, May 22, 1823, in *Briefwerke,* p. 44.
15. Ranke to Heinrich Ranke, Feb. 18, 1824, in ibid., p. 53.
16. Alfred Dove, "Leopold von Ranke," in *Deutsche allgemeine Biographie* (Leipzig, 1888), 27:248.
17. Ranke, *Nachlass,* 3:496.
18. Gunter Berg, *Leopold von Ranke als akademischer Lehrer: Studien zu seinen Vorlesungen und seinem Geschichtsdenken* (Göttingen, 1968), p. 19.
19. For the scholarly interest in Munich, vis-à-vis Frankfurt, see Ranke to Friedrich Thiersch, Apr. 28, 1822, in *Briefwerk,* p. 29.
20. Ranke to Heinrich Ranke, Dec. 23, 1820, in *Neue Briefe,* p. 19.
21. Ranke to Heinrich Ranke, May 22–June, 1820, and Apr. 25, 1823, in *Briefwerk,* pp. 20, 39.
22. Ranke to Heinrich Ranke, Mar. 1820, Apr. 25, 1823, and May 22, 1823, in ibid., pp. 18, 40, 44.
23. Ranke to Heinrich Ranke, May 22–June 1820, in ibid., pp. 20–21.
24. Ranke to Heinrich Ranke, Nov. 1820, in ibid., pp. 24–25.
25. Ibid.
26. Ranke to Heinrich Ranke, Jan. 1821, in *Neue Briefe,* p. 20.
27. Ranke to Heinrich Ranke, Apr. 23, 1823, in *Briefwerk,* p. 39.
28. Ranke to Heinrich Ranke, Feb. 18, 1824, in ibid., pp. 54–55.
29. Thus he claimed to find less truth "among the historians ... who know and emulate antiquity and have the education which we ourselves disseminate" than among those "who neither know nor imitate it." Ranke to Heinrich Ranke, Apr. 25, 1823, in ibid., p. 40.
30. Ranke to Heinrich Ranke, Mar. 1820, in ibid., pp. 17–18.
31. Ibid., p. 17.
32. Ranke to Heinrich Ranke, May 23, 1823, in ibid., p. 44.
33. Ranke to Heinrich Ranke, Feb. 17, 1825, in ibid., pp. 75–76; Heinrich Ritter von Srbik, *Geist und Geschichte des deutschen Humanismus bis zur Gegenwart* (Salzburg, 1950), 1: 161–64. Ranke's recollection of Müller's formulation was vague and only approximate. The context of Müller's actual statement made it clear that the Swiss historian's original point was to envisage an academic afterlife that would compensate for this life's deficiency

in his study of universal history. It was as an immediate sequel to his characterization of earthly sources as "the incomplete A B C" of his research into "everything that has happened and recorded about the history of man since the beginning of the species" that he added: "For as soon as I get to heaven I shall ask for the central archive of the ways of God [*Hauptarchiv der Wege Gottes*], then compile everything from star to star, and after a few million years write a manual of universal history [*Universalhistorie*] for newcomers." Johannes von Müller, *Sämmtliche Werke*, ed. Johann Georg Müller. (Stuttgart, 1834), 30:245. It is tempting to think that, despite Ranke's distortion of this notion into a blessing on historical scholarship in general, he subliminally retained the original reference to universal history. What is certain is that as Ranke progressed toward his own solution for harmonizing particular and general history, his early admiration for Müller turned into indifference. See Preface, above.

34. Quoted in Otto Berdrow, *Rahel Varnhagen: Ein Lebens- und Zeitbild* (Stuttgart, 1902), p. 317-18.
35. *Rahel Varnhagen und ihre Zeit: Briefe 1800-1833* (Munich, 1868), pp. 290-91.
36. Berdrow, *Rahel Varnhagen*, p. 317.
37. Herbert Scurla, *Begegnungen mit Rahel: Der Salon der Rahel Levin* (Verlag der Nation, n.p., n.d.), p. 454. The later work was Ranke's *Ursprung und Beginn der Revolutionskriege 1791 und 1792* (1875).
38. Ranke, *Briefwerk*, p. 76 note; Berdrow, *Rahel Varnhagen*, p. 317; Ranke to Heinrich Ranke, July 11, 1825, and Feb. 1827, in *Briefwerk*, pp. 87, 104; Karl Varnhagen von Ense to Ranke, Mar. 28, 1828, and Aug. 17, 1829, in Herman Oncken, *Aus Rankes Frühzeit* (Gotha, 1922), pp. 32-33, 35.
39. Ranke to Karl August Varnhagen von Ense, June 9, 1829 and Oct. 10, 1829, in *Briefwerk*, pp. 188, 197-98.
40. Rahel to Karl August Varnhagen von Ense, Sep. 1827, in Augusta Weldler-Steinberg, ed., *Rahel Varnhagen: ein Frauenleben in Briefen* ed. Augusta Weldler-Steinberg 3d ed. (Potsdam, 1925), pp. 479-80; Ranke to Heinrich Ritter, Mar. 27, 1829, in *Briefwerk*, p. 184.
41. Ingeborg Drewitz, *Bettine von Arnim: Romantik, Revolution, Utopie* (Cologne, 1969), p. 130.
42. Berdrow, *Rahel Varnhagen*, p. 318.
43. Ranke to Heinrich Ranke, Feb. 1827, in *Briefwerk*, p. 106.
44. Ranke to Karl August Varnhagen von Ense, Apr. 8, 1828, in ibid., pp. 152-53.
45. Ranke to Bettina von Arnim, Oct. 21, 1827, Feb. 6, 1828, Oct. 10, 1829, in ibid., pp. 117, 139, 197; Ranke to Karl August von Varnhagen, May 25, 1830, in ibid., p. 213; Rahel to Karl Varnhagen von Ense, Sep. 1827, in *Rahel Varnhagen*, ed. Weldler-Steinberg, pp. 480-81.
46. Scurla, *Begegnungen*, pp. 451-54.
47. Ranke to Karl August Varnhagen von Ense, June 9, 1829, in *Briefwerk*, p. 188.
48. Drewitz, *Bettine von Arnim*, p. 130.
49. Ranke to Karl August Varnhagen von Ense, Apr. 8, 1828, in *Briefwerk*, p. 153.
50. Ranke to Heinrich Ranke, Feb. 1827, in ibid., p. 106.

51. Ranke to Heinrich Ritter, Feb. 18, 1835, in ibid., p. 266.
52. Rahel to Karl Varnhagen von Ense, Sept. 1827, in *Rahel Varnhagen,* ed. Weldler-Steinberg, p. 481.
53. Ranke to Heinrich Ranke, Nov. 3, 1825, and Nov. 1827, in *Briefwerk,* pp. 92, 125.
54. Ranke to Karl August Varnhagen von Ense, Dec. 9, 1827, in ibid., pp. 127-28; to Rahel Varnhagen von Ense, Apr. 25, 1828, in ibid., pp. 157-58.
55. Ranke to Heinrich Ranke, Nov. 24, 1826, and Nov. 1827, in ibid., pp. 103, 125; to Heinrich Ritter, Dec. 9, 1827, in ibid., p. 130.
56. Ranke to Bettina von Arnim, Oct. 10, 1829, in ibid., p. 197.
57. The belletristic interest was still not entirely avocational. Ranke taught a course in modern literature during his early years at the University of Berlin.
58. Leopold Ranke, *Zur Geschichte der italienischen Poesie* (Berlin, 1837), p. 1. The literal translation of this title is *Contribution to the History of Italian Poetry,* as the title of the work on art is *Contribution to the History of Italian Art.* These titles are acknowledgments of Ranke's focus on one period of Italian poetry and art. I have used abbreviations of these titles in the text for convenience.
59. Ranke, *Poesie,* p. 85.
60. Ranke to Heinrich Ranke, Apr. 1830, in *Briefwerk,* p. 208.
61. Ranke, *Zur Geschichte der italienischen Kunst,* in *Sämmtliche Werke,* 51-52: 248-49, 314.
62. See above, chap. 2.
63. *Kunst,* p. 1 (emphasis added).
64. Lecture "Über die Entwicklung der Literatur seit den Anfängen des 18. Jahrhunderts" ("On the development of literature since the beginning of the eighteenth century") (1827), in Ranke, *Nachless,* 4:63-71.
65. Lecture on "Einleitung zur neueren Geschichte" ("Introduction to modern history") (1832/33) and "Vorlesungen über die neuere Geschichte" ("Lectures on modern history") (1833/34), in ibid., 4:95, 102-3.
66. Ranke, "Vom Einfluss der Theorie," pp. 72-75.
67. *Tagebücher von K. A. Varnhagen von Ense* (reprint, Bern, 1972), 2:42; 4:129-30, 234; Berdrow, *Rahel Varnhagen,* p. 353.
68. Bettina is not explicitly named in this diary note of Ranke's, but the probability is high that the reference is to her. See Ranke, *Nachlass,* 1:179 and editorial note.
69. Ranke to Heinrich Ranke, June 1832, in *Neue Briefe,* p. 172.

6. The Incomplete Historian

1. Ranke, *Nachlass* 1:233-35.
2. Ranke, *Sämmtliche Werke,* 53-54:60.
3. Ibid., p. 61.
4. Ranke to Heinrich Ranke, Feb. 18, 1824, in *Briefwerk,* p. 54.
5. *Sämmtliche Werke,* 53-54:60; Ranke to the Ministry (of Education), Dec. 28, 1824, in *Briefwerk,* p. 59; Ranke to Christian von Bernstorff, Jan. 20, 1825, in *Neue Briefe,* p. 60. On Ranke's disinclination to compete with similarly oriented historians in the field of medieval history and on the vocational ambition which helped to stimulate his first excursion into the

field of modern history, see E. Schulin, "Rankes erstes Buch," pp. 582, 586.
6. Ranke to Friedrich Perthes, June 12, 1825, in *Briefwerk*, pp. 84-85.
7. Fuchs, in *Nachlass*, 3:428-502; Ranke, *Lebensgeschichte*, pp. 39-40.
8. Ranke to Heinrich Ranke, Sept. 25, 1819, and Mar. 1820, in *Briefwerk*, pp. 10, 18.
9. Ranke to Heinrich Ranke, Feb. 24, 1824, in ibid., p. 53; to Heinrich Ritter, Mar. 29, 1830, in ibid., p. 206.
10. Ranke to Heinrich Ranke, Nov. 3, 1825, and Feb. 1827, in ibid., pp. 92, 104-5.
11. For Ranke's later uses of "universal history," see *Nachlass*, 1:240; Helen Liebel, "Ranke's Fragments on Universal History," *Clio* 2 (1973): 145-59; Kessel, "Rankes Idee der Universalhistorie," *Historische Zeitschrift* 178: 269-308. An early example of the plurality of meanings in *Universalhistorie* that was analogous to the mixture of meanings in *Weltgeschichte* can be found in Ranke's fragmentary note, "The Scope of Universal History ("Idee der Universalhistorie")," probably written in the mid-1820s. Here he distinguished between universality of scope and the general tendency to be found in every particular phenomenon, but he included both in "universal history." In Kessel, "Rankes Idee," p. 287. Ranke's imprecision in terminology appeared also in his occasional usage of *Welthistorie* synonymously with *Universalhistorie*, both during the 20s and later.
12. Ranke, "Idee der Universalhistorie," p. 303.
13. Ranke, of course, knew the term "universal history" during the Restoration period, but at this time he used it sparingly, in contrast to his frequent use of "world history," and habitually without any distinctive connotation. The undated manuscript fragment "The Scope of Universal History," to which reference has already been made and which has been attributed to the 20s, is an isolated specimen of exposition for the period. Ranke's other references to universal history before 1830 are much more casual. Among his first courses at the Frankfurt gymnasium was the "Universal History (*Universalgeschichte*) of the ancient World to the End of the Western Empire," a course which he soon narrowed to the histories of Greece and Rome. At the very end of the decade Ranke did make a literal reference to "a universal history of the modern centuries" (*eine universale Geschichte der neueren Jahrhunderte*), but the context made it clear that the term in this case too was being used in no specific sense: it was merely alternative language for an extensive world history within a specific period. But he entitled the course on world history as such which he gave at the University of Berlin from 1825 to 1827 "General World History" (*Allgemeine Weltgeschichte*). In 1832, after he had become emphatically concerned with coherence and connections, he called the course "World History in its Universal Coherence (*Weltgeschichte in universalem Zusammenhang*), and a year later he stressed the unitary cast even further by renaming the course "Universal History" (*Die Universalgeschichte*) and appending the parenthetical description "(in its general and internal coherence)." Ranke, *Nachlass*, 3:498; Ranke to Friedrich Perthes, Dec. 14, 1829, in *Neue Briefe*, p. 131; "Chronological Catalogue of Ranke's Lectures," in Berg, *Ranke als Lehrer*, p. 243; Ranke, *Nachlass*, 4:35-36.
14. Ranke to Heinrich Ranke, Oct. 18, 1822, and Nov. 24, 1826, in *Briefwerk*, pp. 32, 102-3; to Varnhagen von Ense, Oct. 10, 1829, in ibid., p. 199.

15. Ranke to Heinrich Ranke, Feb. 1827, in ibid., pp. 104-5.
16. Ranke to Heinrich Ranke, Nov. 1827, in ibid., pp. 126-27; to Heinrich Ritter, Dec. 9, 1827, in ibid., p. 130.
17. Ranke to Heinrich Ranke, Nov. 3, 1825, in ibid., p. 92. Even the manuscript notes on universal history which Ranke wrote down in his most theoretical period, the 1830s and 1840s, were for introductory lectures in his general courses. See Kessel, "Rankes Idee," pp. 273 ff. The function of the fragments on universal history which bear the date of 1877 is not so clear, but it is probable that Ranke was preparing himself for the *Weltgeschichte* which he would soon dictate.
18. Ranke "Idee der Universalhistorie," p. 292; *Nachlass* 4:43-44, 120, 134-45.
19. Published posthumously under the editor's title, *On the Epochs of Modern History* (*Über die Epochen der neueren Geschichte*), the transcript in one of its manuscript versions carried the more revealing title: "Essay on the Definition of Characterization of the World-Historical Epochs of the Modern Age" (*Versuch die welthistorischen Epochen der neueren Zeit zu bestimmen und charakterisieren*). Schieder, "Rankes *Über die Epochen*," p. 9.
20. Dove, "Ranke," p. 252; Berg, *Ranke als Lehrer*, p. 56.
21. E.g., Simon, *Ranke und Hegel*, pp. 196-97, and Von Laue, *Ranke*, p. 45. The motto *labor ipse voluptas*, which Ranke chose for his coat of arms, is one of the items usually cited as evidence of the mystical-erotic tone.
22. Ranke to Heinrich Ranke, Apr. 25, 1823, in *Briefwerk*, p. 39; to Bettina von Arnim, Feb. 6, 1828, in ibid., p. 139; to Rahel Varnhagen von Ense, Apr. 25, 1828, in ibid., pp. 157-58; to Heinrich Ritter, Oct. 28, 1827, in ibid., pp. 121-22; to Ferdinand Ranke, Nov. 11, 1836, in *Neue Briefe*, p. 230.
23. Ranke to Clara Ranke, June 1862, in *Briefwerk*, p. 441.
24. Ranke to Clara Ranke, May 13, 1865, in ibid., p. 460.
25. Ranke to Prussian Ministry, Dec. 28, 1824, in *Neue Briefe*, p. 56; to Freiherr von Stein zum Altenstein, Oct. 1, 1829, in ibid., p. 129.
26. Ranke to Heinrich Ranke, Mar. 27, 1826, in *Briefwerk*, pp. 102-3; Antoine Guillaud, *Modern Germany and Her Historians* (New York, 1915), pp. 87-88, note.
27. Ranke, *Nachlass*, 1:234-35.
28. Leopold von Ranke, *Fürsten und Völker: Geschichten*, p. 4; Ranke, *Zur Kritik neuerer Geschichtschreiber*, pp. iii, v, 24.
29. Schulin, "Rankes erstes Buch," pp. 590-603.
30. Ranke, *Fürsten und Völker: Geschichten*, pp. 3-4.
31. Ibid., pp. 4-5.
32. Ibid., pp. 7-8, 17.
33. Ibid., pp. 4, 28, 47, 168-69, 220.
34. Ibid., p. 7.
35. Ibid., pp. 43, 61.
36. Ibid., pp. 24, 29-30, 59, 99.
37. Ibid., pp. 103, 181-82.
38. Ranke, *Kritik*, pp. iii-iv, 147-48.
39. Ibid., pp. v, 24, 39, 144, 149.
40. The subsequent volumes of *Princes and Nations of Southern Europe*— volumes 2, 3, and 4—would comprise the first edition of the *History of the Popes*, but this was published from 1834 to 1836 when Ranke was writing

under quite different assumptions. Like *The Ottoman Turks and the Spanish Monarchy*, later editions of *The History of the Popes* would drop the original series title. The collection of brief biographies of fifteenth- and sixteenth-century Italians was published as *Historisch-biographische Studien* (Leipzig, 1877).

41. Ranke to Friedrich Perthes, July 10, 1828, in *Briefwerk*, p. 166. The friend was the Slavicist Stephanowitsch Karadschitsch Wuk, who, according to Ranke's later definition of their respective roles in the work, collected the materials, checked the evidence, and wrote the draft, while Ranke merely "took over the composition" *(Fassung)*. Leopold von Ranke, *Serbien und die Turkei im 19. Jahrhundert* (Leipzig, 1879), p. v. This latter work, an expanded edition of *The Serbian Revolution*, not only contained an extension of Serbian history in the nineteenth century but also collected the three other pieces on the contemporary history of Turkey and Serbia which Ranke wrote (but had not published) seriatum during the half-century between the two editions. These additions were not based on ready-made sources, as the original *Serbian Revolution* had been, and they stemmed from broader historiographical motives than the virtuoso processing of materials, but they also were written under essentially international auspices—one in the thirties under the aegis of international revolution and the others to demonstrate the interaction of general European with national Turkish and Serbian affairs. See *Serbian und die Türkei*, pp. vi-xi, and Ranke to Alfred von Reumont, Apr. 15, 1879, in *Briefwerk*, p. 563.
42. Ranke to Friedrich Perthes, Aug. 24, 1825, in ibid., p. 89; to Alfred von Arneth, Aug. 26, 1868, in ibid., p. 494.
43. Ranke to Friedrich Perthes, June 12, 1825, and Dec. 7, 1825, in ibid., pp. 85, 93.
44. Ranke, *Französische Geschichte*, 5:31-32.
45. Ranke, *Fürsten und Völker: Geschichten*, pp. 234, 239.
46. Ibid., pp. 251-52.
47. Ibid., pp. 421-22.
48. Ibid., pp. 240-93.
49. Ibid., pp. 243-53.
50. Ibid., p. 294.
51. Ibid., p. 239; Ranke to Heinrich Ranke, Nov. 24, 1826, in *Briefwerk*, p. 103.
52. Ranke to Friedrich Perthes, Dec. 14, 1829, in *Neue Briefe*, p. 130.
53. Ranke to Friedrich Perthes, Mar. 20, 1826, in *Briefwerk*, p. 95. He excepted only English history from the generalization.
54. Ranke, *Fürsten und Völker: Geschichten*, pp. 288-89.
55. Ibid., pp. 294, 348, 422.
56. Ibid., 294; Ranke to Friedrich Perthes, Mar. 20, 1826, in *Briefwerk*, p. 96.
57. Ranke, *Fürsten und Völker: Geschichten*, p. 269.
58. Andreas, in ibid., p. 228.
59. Ranke, quoted in Kessel, "Rankes Idee," pp. 287, 302-4.
60. Ranke tried to learn the Serb language, but admittedly "not with great success." Ranke, *Lebensgeschichte*, p. 48.
61. Ranke, *A History of Serbia and the Serbian Revolution*, trans. Mrs. Alexander Kerr (London, 1847), p. 40.
62. Ibid., pp. 4-5 (emphasis added).

7. The First Synthesis

1. Clemens Theodor Perthes, *Friedrich Perthes Leben,* 4th ed. (Gotha, 1857), 3:346–52.
2. Ranke to Heinrich Ritter, Oct. 4, 1830, in *Briefwerk,* p. 223.
3. Ranke, "Einleitung zur historisch-politischen Zeitschrift" (1832), in *Sämmtliche Werke,* 49–50:5–7.
4. Ranke to Heinrich Ritter, Oct. 4, 1830, in *Briefwerk,* p. 224; to Christian Gunther Graf v. Bernstorff, Nov. 1, 1831, in ibid., p. 243; to Johann Kaspar Bluntschli, Aug. 21, 1832, in ibid., p. 251.
5. Ranke, "Idee der Universalhistorie," pp. 298–300.
6. Quoted in Friedrich Meinecke, *Die Entstehung des Historismus* (Munich and Berlin, 1936), 2:636.
7. Ibid., pp. 640–42. To be sure, in a reconsideration of Ranke more than an eventful decade later, Meinecke drastically revised his interpretation by assigning to Ranke the concept of "development"—that is, the concern with "the general course of world history" on the lines of Hegel's objective spirit —in explicit contrast to the concept of "individuality." "Ranke . . . finally merges all individualities, no matter how brightly illuminated they may stand out in his work, into the powerful stream of a total development." But this revision has not had the resonance of Meinecke's original interpretation, in part because the reclassification of Ranke is obviously dominated by Meinecke's need to set him up as a dialectical opposite to Burckhardt, newly appreciated as the avatar of individuality, and in part because it is so casually argued. The slight evidence that Meinecke did adduce indicates that the developmental Ranke he had in mind was the aging Ranke at the much later stage of his *World History.* In any event it hardly applies to the Ranke of the early 1830s, as Meinecke's earlier notion of Ranke's essential commitment to historistic individuality and as Ranke's more empirical and compatible idea of universal development indicated in the following pages of my text do. Friedrich Meinecke, "Ranke and Burckhardt," Hans Kohn, ed., *German History: Some New German Views* (trans. Herbert H Rowen, Boston, 1954), pp. 145, 154.
8. Ranke, *Dialogue on Politics,* pp. 156, 157.
9. Ranke to Karl August Varnhagen von Ense, May 25, 1830, in *Briefwerk,* p. 211; to Ludwig I of Bavaria, June 11, 1846, in ibid., p. 335.
10. Ranke to Heinrich Ritter, Aug. 6, 1830, in *Briefwerk,* p. 216; Kessel, "Rankes Idee," p. 285.
11. This is not to say that Ranke had no interest in historical theory during his later years. It is to say that his theoretical considerations were never as focused or developed as they were in the 1830s and that they tended much more to be commentaries on the historical work he was actually doing than disquisitions on history's role in the whole corpus of knowledge.
12. Ranke, *Sämmtliche Werke,* 51–52:588.
13. Ranke, "Geschichte und Philosophie," p. 134; Kessel, "Rankes Idee," pp. 301, 303–4.
14. Ibid., pp. 291–95. The notes for this lecture have been reedited by Volker Dotterweich and Walther Peter Fuchs and have been republished, with additions, in Ranke, *Nachlass,* 4:72–86.
15. Ranke, "Idee der Universalhistorie," pp. 296–98.

16. Ibid., pp. 178, 301, 302.
17. Ranke, "Geschichte und Philosophie," pp. 134, 136.
18. Ranke, "Schluss einer Einleitung zur Vorlesung über neueste Geschichte," in Kessel, "Rankes Idee," pp. 303-4.
19. Ranke, *Nachlass,* 4:85-86.
20. See chap. 10.
21. Ranke, 4:124, 134-35.
22. Ibid., pp. 119, 124, 133, 140-41.
23. Ibid., pp. 144, 183.
24. Ibid., pp. 127, 161.
25. Ibid., p. 120 (emphasis added).
26. Ibid., pp. 85, 126.
27. Ibid., pp. 133-35, 177.
28. Ibid., pp. 121, 126, 132, 133, 138.
29. Ranke, *Die grossen Mächte,* pp. 1, 47-53.
30. Ranke, *Politisches Gespräch,* in *Geschichte und Politik,* pp. 90-91.
31. *Die grossen Mächte,* pp. 1, 52.
32. Ranke to Friedrich Perthes, Mar. 20, 1826, in *Briefwerk,* p. 95.
33. Leopold Ranke to Heinrich Ranke, Aug. 25, 1827, in ibid., p. 110; to Karl August Varnhagen von Ense, Mar. 10, 1828, in ibid., p. 146; to Edwin Freiherr von Manteuffel, July 12, 1852, in *Neue Briefe,* p. 34; Schieder, "Rankes *Über die Epochen,*" p. 22; Ranke, *Nachlass,* 2:442.
34. Leopold von Ranke, *Die Verschwörung gegen Venedig im Jahre 1618,* in *Studien und Portraits zur italienischen Geschichte,* ed. Willy Andreas (Wiesbaden, 1957), Vorwort, pp. 63, 118; Ranke to Friedrich Perthes, Feb. 5, 1831, in *Briefwerk,* p. 231; to Crown Prince Friedrich Wilhelm of Prussia, Aug. 29, 1831, in *Neue Briefe,* p. 158.
35. Ranke, *Verschwörung,* pp. 63, 124-25; Ranke to Friedrich Perthes, Feb. 5, 1831, in *Briefwerk,* pp. 230-32; to Crown Prince Friedrich Wilhelm, Aug. 29, 1831, in *Neue Briefe,* p. 158.
36. The essay was published in *Serbien und die Türkei.* See Ranke's preface, p. vi.
37. Ranke to Friedrich Perthes, Feb. 5, 1831, in *Briefwerk,* p. 231; to Crown Prince Friederick William of Prussia, Aug. 29, 1831, in *Neue Briefe,* p. 158; Dove, "Ranke," p. 258; Berg, *Ranke als Lehrer,* pp. 51-56.

8. The Complete Historian

1. Ranke, *Fürsten und Völker von Süd-Europa im 16. und 17. Jahrhundert,* 4 vols. (Berlin, 1837-45). See chap. 6 above, sec. 4.
2. Ranke to Heinrich Ranke, Nov. 24, 1826, and Feb. 1827, in *Briefwerk,* pp. 103, 105.
3. Ranke to Heinrich Ritter, Feb. 18, 1835, in ibid., p. 265; to Heinrich Ranke, Nov. 26, 1835, in ibid., p. 271.
4. See Von Laue, *Ranke,* pp. 126-32, for a substantial summary of the *History of the Popes,* and Iggers and Moltke's edition of Ranke, *The Theory and Practice of History* (Indianapolis, 1973), pp. 165-496, for an intelligent abridgment.
5. Ranke, *History of the Popes,* 1:431; Ranke, *Die römischen Päpste in den letzten vier Jahrhunderten,* 11th ed. (Leipzig, 1970), 2:377.
6. Ranke, *History of the Popes,* 1:27, 277; 2:54.

7. Ibid., 1:4-8, 26, 407, 408, 542; 2:142; Ranke, *Die römischen Päpste*, 1:128; 2:111.
8. Ranke to Friedrich Gentz, Apr. 26, 1830, in *Briefwerk*, p. 210; to Heinrich Ranke, in *Neue Briefe*, p. 215; to J. J. Stolz, Mar. 2, 1838, in *Briefwerk*, p. 292.
9. E.g., Ranke, *History of the Popes*, 1:103-4, 248-49, 428, 453; Ranke, *Die römischen Päpste*, 1:83, 41, 83.
10. Ranke, *History of the Popes*, 1:296, 410.
11. Ibid., pp. 410-11.
12. Ranke to King Maximilian of Bavaria, Feb. 17, 1852, in *Briefwerk*, p. 356.
13. Ranke, *History of the Popes*, 1:309-17.
14. Ibid., pp. 48-59, 376-99.
15. Ibid., 1:105, 256, 333; 2:3-4.
16. For this dispute, see Berg, *Ranke als Lehrer*, pp. 110-13.
17. See chapter 5 above.
18. Ranke to Heinrich Ritter, Feb. 18, 1835, in *Briefwerk*, p. 265.
19. Quoted in Berg, *Ranke als Lehrer*, p. 115.
20. Ranke to Heinrich Ranke, Nov. 24, 1826, in *Briefwerk*, p. 103; to Karl Varnhagen von Ense, Dec. 9, 1827, in ibid., p. 127.
21. Ranke reprinted the long article as the first section of the book *On German History from the Religious Peace to the Thirty Years' War*. See Ranke, *Zur deutschen Geschichte vom Religionsfrieden bis zum dreissigjährigen Krieg*, 2d ed. (Leipzig, 1874), esp. pp. 3-4, 94-95. (Vol. 7 of *Sämmtliche Werke*.)
22. Ranke to an unknown addressee, Oct./Nov. 1835, in *Briefwerk*, p. 270; to Heinrich Ranke, Nov. 26, 1835, in ibid., p. 272; to Georg Friedrich von Guaita, Sept. 21, 1836, in *Neue Briefe*, p. 220. Ranke made his discovery and his resolve to write a German history in September 1835, but he did not actually begin his research on it until a year later, after he had finished his *Popes*.
23. Leopold von Ranke, *Deutsche Geschichte*, 1:1-2.
24. Ranke, 4:129, 139, 177.
25. Ranke, *Deutsche Geschichte*, 1:1; also see chap. 6 above, sec. 3.
26. Ranke, *Nachlass*, 4:130-31, 139.
27. Ranke, *Deutsche Geschichte*, 1:2-3.
28. Ranke to Sarah Austin, Apr. 1841, in Ross, *Three Generations*, p. 164.
29. Ranke, *Deutsche Geschichte*, 1:5-6.
30. Berg, *Ranke als Lehrer*, pp. 130-40.
31. Ranke, *Deutsche Geschichte*, 1:86, 132, 241, 566; 2:7-8, 254.
32. Ibid., 1:488; 2:307-8.
33. Ibid., 1:110, 288, 439; 2:148.
34. Ibid., 1:447; 2:609, 638.
35. Ibid., 1:109-10, 288, 439.
36. Ibid., pp. 142, 212.
37. Ibid., p. 295.
38. Ibid., pp. 201, 227.
39. Ibid., pp. 137; 2:174, 609.
40. Ibid., 1:239; 2:524, 609.
41. Ibid., 1:447-48; 2:148-49, 174.
42. Ibid., 2:498.
43. Ibid., 1:386; 2:470.

44. Ibid., 2:567, 588, 609-10, 621-23.
45. Ibid., 1:140, 142.
46. Ibid., 1:110, 386; 2:150.
47. Ibid., 2:90, 524.
48. Ibid., pp. 89, 505.
49. Ibid., 1:241.
50. Ibid., 1:483, 2:36.
51. Ibid., 2:583.
52. Ibid., 2:175.
53. Ibid., 1:318, 446; 2:470.
54. Ibid., 1:86, 227, 318, 563, 566; 2:606-7.
55. Ibid., 2:175.
56. Ibid., pp. 147, 607.
57. Ranke, *Deutsche Geschichte*, 6: 381, note. A half-century later, in his *World History* (*Weltgeschichte*), he would resume his more characteristic stance by explicitly reversing the formula, assigning "research" to particular and "perception" (*Wahrnehmung*) to general historical truth. Kessel, "Rankes Idee," p. 286.
58. Ranke, *Nachlass*, 1:240.
59. Ibid., 2:606-7, 624, 639-40.

9. Conservative Retrenchment and Patriotic History

1. Ranke, *Lebensgeschichte*, pp. 52, 71.
2. Varnhagen von Ense, *Tagebücher*, 1:342; 2:42; Ranke to Ferdinand Ranke, June 22, 1840, in *Neue Briefe*, p. 273. As an example of the private familial tone that his friends brought to his relations with the Prussian government, reference may be made to his intercession with Eichhorn on behalf of brother Ferdinand Ranke's candidacy for the director's post in the Friedrich-Wilhelm Gymnasium of Berlin. Leopold reported to Ferdinand that Eichhorn and he had talked, in this connection of "fatherland, family, friends, and our brotherly relationship!" Ranke to Ferdinand Ranke, Oct. 26, 1841, in ibid., p. 281.
3. Ranke, *Nachlass*, 1:464.
4. Bettina von Arnim, *Andacht zum Menschenbild* ed. Wilhelm Schellberg and Friedrich Fuchs (Jena, 1942), pp. 322-23, 345.
5. Varnhagen von Ense, *Tagebücher*, 1:243.
6. Ranke's attitude to these "fashionable parties" in the Berlin of the 1840s was revealed in his remark to an acquaintance that "one is hunted" to secure his attendance. Sarah Austin's diary, Jan. 1843, in Ross, *Three Generations* p. 187. See also Varnhagen von Ense, *Tagebücher*, 2:234.
7. Ranke, *Nachlass*, 1:7; Ranke to Empress Augusta, Apr. 1, 1876, in *Neue Briefe*, p. 630.
8. Ranke to Heinrich Ranke, May 5, 1841, in *Briefwerk*, p. 308.
9. Ranke to Ernst Ranke, Sept. 1, 1842, in ibid., p. 315.
10. Ranke to Clara Graves, Oct. 17, 1843, in ibid., p. 320.
11. Ranke to Ernst Ranke, Sept. 1, 1842, in ibid., p. 315.
12. Alexander von Humboldt to Sarah Austin, June 7, 1844, in Ross, *Three Generations*, p. 206.
13. Ranke, *Lebensgeschichte*, p. 72.

376 · NOTES TO PAGES 186-192

14. Ranke to Heinrich Ranke, Oct. 1844, in *Briefwerk*, p. 328.
15. Ranke to Clara Ranke, Apr. 16, 1857, and July 1860, in *Neue Briefe*, pp. 378, 400.
16. Ranke to Klara Ranke, Oct. 27, 1852, July 13, 1854, Apr. 16, 1857, June 18, 1857, June 11, 1862, July 18, 1862, May 21, 1865, in ibid., pp. 351, 364, 378, 385, 414, 418, 441.
17. Ranke to Heinrich Ranke, Aug. 20, 1844 and Nov. 26, 1844, in *Briefwerk*, pp. 327, 329; to Klara Ranke, Apr. 26, 1857, Aug. 27, 1861, Aug. 27, 1862, Oct. 5, 1864, in *Neue Briefe*, pp. 382, 407, 422, 435; to Selma Carius, nee Ranke, Apr. 30, 1871, in ibid., p. 549.
18. Ranke to Heinrich Ranke, Nov. 26, 1844, in *Briefwerk*, p. 329.
19. Ranke, *Nachlass*, 1:69. What makes the note of desolation in this jotting all the more remarkable is the probability that he had his bride-to-be with him. See the arch reference to the "very pleasant company" in his description later of presumably the same trip, in Ranke to Ferdinand Ranke, July 30, 1843, in *Neue Briefe*, p. 299.
20. Ranke, *Nachlass*, 1:181, 184.
21. Ibid., p. 186.
22. Ibid., pp. 127-28.
23. Ibid., pp. 118, 129.
24. Ibid., pp. 119, 128.
25. Ibid., pp. 129, 132. For his earlier counterrevolutionary idea of freedom, see Von Laue, *Ranke*, pp. 96-97.
26. Ranke to Ferdinand Ranke, July 30, 1843, in *Neue Briefe*, p. 299.
27. Berg, *Ranke als Lehrer*, pp. 28-33.
28. Ranke to Heinrich Ranke, Nov. 27, 1845, in *Neue Briefe*, p. 316.
29. Varnhagen von Ense, *Tagebücher*, 3:55.
30. Ranke to Wilhelm Dieterici, Dec. 27, 1843, in *Neue Briefe*, pp. 305-6.
31. Ibid., p. 306.
32. Entry of July 1846, in Varnhagen von Ense, *Tagebücher*, 3:379.
33. For the impact of Ranke's "inner alienation from contemporary ideas and men" during the 40s on his writing of history, see Hans Herzfeld, "Politik und Geschichte bei Leopold von Ranke im Zeitraum von 1848-1871," in *Festschrift für Gerhard Ritter* (Tübingen, 1950), pp. 328-30.
34. An article on the French Revolution did come out of Ranke's Paris visit: "Über die Versammlung der französischen Notabeln im Jahre 1787," published in the *Allgemeine Zeitschrift für Geschichte* during 1846. The article evinced little of the universal-historical interest and of the revolutionary theme with which Ranke presumably went to Paris. In it he deliberately eschewed the general context represented by "the ideas of the century" and, "holding to our standpoint," simply wrote an internal account of the French financial crisis, the tortuous attempts at reform by the government under Calonne and Brienne, and their frustration by corporate resistance. The article emphasized the distinctive corruption and debility of the French state at that time, as it was exemplified in the episode of the notables, and concluded with finality that the episode had no lasting importance but only "revealed the difficulty and the meaning of the French situation." See the reprint of the essay in Ranke's *French History*. Leopold von Ranke *Französische Geschichte*, 5:338-73. Clearly such an article could hardly inhibit Ranke's main preoccupation now with Prussian history. When

he left Paris for England in 1843, it was to get married and to gather more materials on Frederick the Great.

35. Ranke, *Origin and Beginning of the Revolutionary Wars: 1791 and 1792* (*Ursprung und Beginn der Revolutionskriege 1791 und 1792*), published in 1875.

36. That is, until after his final synthesis in 1870.

37. Ranke's own retrospective rationale is of limited use in establishing the proportions of continuity and break in his choice of a Prussian history as his scholarly enterprise of the 40s, because his own later accounting came in two stages and varied only between vagueness and ambiguity. In 1848, just after he had completed the second volume of the *Prussian History*, he betrayed his own uncertainty about his motivation by employing a hollow terminology to combine the motifs of continuity and new circumstance and, apparently unsatisfied, laying the decision in hands of Providence. "A personal Providence rules over us," he explained to his brother. "Who would have believed that I should ever be destined to write the history of Frederick II! The course of my previous works determined my inclination, but it took the coincidence of manifold circumstances to make it possible in my way" Ranke to Heinrich Ranke, Jan. 1948, in *Neue Briefe*, p. 322. When he returned to the subject much later in the reminiscences of his old age he was at once more definite and more plural: his account varied substantially with the context in which he raised it. Hence he wavered between the view of his new work as an extension of the universal or national themes of his *German History in the Age of the Reformation* which became fundamentally "limited by wholly different vital forces"—i.e., by "the particularistic life of the Prussian state"—in the course of his thinking and working on it, and the view that his aim of tracing "the rise of the Brandenburg Electorate to a European power" was "an entirely different approach" from the thesis of continuity, whether in its universal or national guise. Ranke, *Lebensgeschichte*, pp. 72-74. The contemporary evidence from the 1840s suggests that neither of these later formulations precisely corresponded to Ranke's mentality at the time but that the second version was closer to it than the first.

38. Ranke, *Preussische Geschichte*, 2:14.

39. Ranke, *Nachlass*, 1:241.

40. Ibid.; Ranke, "The Pitfalls of a Philosophy of History (Introduction to a Lecture on Universal History: A Manuscript of the 1840's)," trans. Wilma A. Iggers. In Ranke, *The Theory and Practice of History*, pp. 47-50.

41. Ranke, *Nachlass*, 4:181-82.

42. Ibid., pp. 192-94.

43. Ranke to King Frederick William IV, Apr. 23, 1943, in *Neue Briefe*, p. 291; to Prince zu Sayn-Wittgenstein, Count zu Stolberg-Wernigerode and Baron Heinrich von Bülow, Feb. 21, 1844, in ibid., p. 308; to Gustav Adolf Stenzel, Oct. 6, 1845, in *Briefwerk*, p. 331.

44. Ranke, *Preussische Geschichte*, 1:47-48.

45. Ibid., p. 49.

46. Ranke to Frederick William IV, Dec. 24, 1848, in *Neue Briefe*, p. 326.

47. Ranke, *Preussische Geschichte*, 1:50-51.

48. Ibid., 1:54-56; 2:50-51.

49. Ibid., 2:356, 412-13.

50. Ibid., 1:521.
51. Ibid., 2:9, 404, 406, 408-9.
52. Ibid., pp. 12-13, 35, 394, 411.
53. Ibid., p. 394.
54. Andreas, in ibid., 1:41-42.
55. Entries of Aug. 9, 1847, Aug. 11, 1847, Oct. 20, 1847, Jan. 14, 1848, and Aug. 7, 1848, in Varnhagen von Ense, *Tagebücher*, 4:129-30, 150, 234; 5:152. His most frequently repeated indictment was that the book "lacks character." Varnhagen's indictment of covert present bias has been indirectly confirmed by publication of Ranke's letter to Frederick William IV in June 1847 when he sent the king the first volume of the *Prussian History* along with an oblique comment on its relevance as a counter to the obstreperous United Diet which recently met in Berlin: "After so many . . . confused and confusing speeches, . . . may the nation get acquainted in this book with the picture of the old-Prussian kingdom, in the simplicity, seriousness, and necessity of its exalted calling." Ranke to Frederick William IV, June 24, 1847, in *Neue Briefe*, p. 325.
56. Ranke to Crown Prince Maximilian of Bavaria, Dec. 26, 1847, in *Briefwerk*, p. 338.

10. The Second Synthesis

1. Ranke to Heinrich Ranke, Nov. 27, 1845, in *Neue Briefe*, p. 317.
2. Ranke, *Nachlass*, 1:320-26, 332-34.
3. Ibid., pp. 338-40, 350; Ranke to Heinrich Ranke, Apr. 22, 1847, in *Neue Briefe*, p. 323.
4. Ibid.
5. Ranke, *Nachlass*, 1:334, 339-42, 344, 350-51.
6. Berg, *Ranke als Lehrer*, pp. 170-71; Herzfeld, "Politik und Geschichte," pp. 330-31. Ranke, *Nachlass*, 4:216.
7. Entry of Mar. 28, 1848, Varnhagen von Ense, *Tagebücher*, 4:355.
8. Ranke, *Nachlass*, 1:464-65.
9. Ranke's diary entry of March 1848, in *Briefwerk*, p. 339 note; Ranke to Heinrich Ranke, Aug. 11, 1848, in ibid., p. 339; "Politische Denkschriften aus den Jahren 1848-1851," *Sämmtliche Werke*, 49-50:588-89, 591.
10. Ranke, *Nachlass*, 1:341; Ranke to Heinrich Ranke, Aug. 12, 1848, in *Neue Briefe*, p. 331.
11. Ranke, "Politische Denkschriften," pp. 590-91.
12. Ranke, *Nachlass*, 4:198.
13. Ibid., pp. 214-16, 219-220, 238; Berg, *Ranke als Lehrer*, pp. 271-72.
14. Ranke, *Nachlass*, 4:239-41.
15. Ranke, "Politische Denkschriften," pp. 611, 614.
16. Ibid., pp. 592-94, 609-10, 621.
17. Ibid., pp. 594, 604, 610, 619.
18. Ibid., pp. 601-5, 610.
19. Ibid., pp. 593, 596, 601, 603, 607, 612.
20. Ranke, *Nachlass*, 1:255. The precise dating of the diary note in question is not certain.
21. Ranke, "Politische Denkschriften," pp. 595, 597, 610.
22. Ranke, *Nachlass*, 1:253-56.
23. Ibid., 4:215.

24. Ibid., pp. 198, 201.
25. Ibid., pp. 199, 203, 211.
26. Ranke, "Politische Denkschriften," pp. 595, 597, 610.
27. Theodor Schieder, coeditor of the recent critical edition of the work. See his introduction to this edition in Ranke, *Nachlass*, 2:7.
28. Ibid., p. 10.
29. Ranke to Friedrich Perthes, Aug. 24, 1825, Mar. 20, 1826, Feb. 25, 1828, in *Briefwerk*, pp. 89, 95–96, 144–45; to Heinrich Ranke, Nov. 20 and 21, 1828, in ibid., p. 177. In contrast to his disappointment of the 40s, indeed, during 1850 Ranke was boasting of his discoveries in the Parisian archives, and two years later in the preface of the *French History* he did write he made a strong point of the plethora of materials at his disposal. Ranke to Clara Ranke, Sept. 21, 1850, in *Neue Briefe*, pp. 343–44; Ranke, *Französische Geschichte*, 1:vii–viii. Also see p. 000 above.
30. Ranke, *Lebensgeschichte*, p. 75.
31. Schieder, in Ranke, *Nachlass*, 2: 26–28, 38; Fuchs, in Ranke, *Briefwerk*, pp. xlix–l. The trias idea covered the various proposals which envisaged the organization of a "third Germany," under the leadership of middle-sized states like Württemberg, Saxony, and/or Bavaria, to exercise a condominium over the German Confederation alongside Austria and Prussia.
32. Schieder, in Ranke, *Nachlass*, 2:10.
33. Ranke to King Maximilian, Feb. 17, 1852, in *Briefwerk*, p. 356.
34. Ranke to Clara Ranke, Oct. 1, 1854, in ibid., p. 390; to King Maximilian II, Dec. 30, 1854, in ibid., p. 395.
35. Ranke, in Karl Alexander von Müller, "Ein unbekannter Vortrag Rankes aus dem Jahr 1862," *Historische Zeitschrift* 151 (1935): 313.
36. Ranke, *Lebensgeschichte*, pp. 52, 54, 75. Since the discrepancy appears within the same segment of his reminiscences—the dictation of December 1875—it can hardly be attributed to changing memory or shifting perspective.
37. Ranke to Edwin von Manteuffel, May 31, 1865, in *Neue Briefe*, p. 443.
38. Ranke, *Französische Geschichte*, 1:v–vi.
39. Ranke to Clara Ranke, Mar. 26, 1857, in *Briefwerke*, p. 415; to King Maximilian II, May 25, 1857, in ibid., p. 423.
40. Ranke, *Englische Geschichte, vornehmlich im siebzehnten Jahrhundert*, (4th ed., Leipzig, 1877), 1:v–vi, ix, 3–4.
41. Ranke to Edwin von Manteuffel, July 12, 1852, in *Briefwerk*, p. 345.
42. Ranke, *Nachlass*, 1:132–33, 242.
43. Ibid., p. 357.
44. Ranke to King Maximilian II, Jan. 26, 1855, and Mar. 19, 1855, in *Briefwerk*, pp. 397, 405–6.
45. Ranke to Franz Xaver Pfistermeister, Aug. 14, 1857, in ibid., p. 425; Ranke, *Nachlass*, 1:355.
46. Ranke, *Nachlass*, 1:369–80; Ranke, in Müller, "Ein unbekannter Vortrag," pp. 313–14, 324–26.
47. Ranke, *Nachlass*, 1:369–80, 390–91.
48. Ibid., pp. 385–86, 394; Ranke to Edwin von Manteuffel, May 31, 1865, in *Neue Briefe*, p. 445; to Ernst Ranke, Sept. 1, 1865, in *Briefwerk*, p. 483.
49. Ranke, in Müller, "Ein unbekannter Vortrag," p. 314.
50. Ibid., pp. 313, 327.

51. Ranke to Franz Xaver Pfistermeister, Aug. 14, 1857, and Sept. 6, 1857, in *Briefwerk,* pp. 425-26.
52. Ranke to Georg Waitz, Sept. 1863, in ibid., pp. 443-44.
53. For this context, see Ranke's wavering between the synthetic notion that "the great antagonism in which the world is caught up cuts right through the middle of Germany" and the particularistic notion that overlapping divisions among the princes inhibit action against revolutionary radicalism, in Müller, "Ein unbekannter Vortrag, p. 327.
54. Ranke, *Nachlass,* 2:59-61, 63. This critical edition of *On the Epochs of Modern History* contains both the original stenograph of Ranke's lectures and the revised transcript on which the publication was based. I have used the latter save where differences in meaning require recourse to the former.
55. Ibid., pp. 54-56, 68-69, 77.
56. Ibid., pp. 58-59, 66-67.
57. Ibid., pp. 74-75.
58. Ranke to King Maximilian II, Nov. 26, 1859, in *Briefwerk,* p. 432.
59. See above, chap. 7, sec. II.
60. On Ranke's perception of the connection between Maximilian and Schelling, see Ranke to King Maximilian II, Dec. 30, 1854, in *Briefwerk,* p. 395; Ranke's own notes in *Nachlass,* 1:164-65 (from the 1850s, but including a later reflection from 1875); and Schieder, in Ranke, *Nachlass,* 2:26-28, 38.
61. For Kierkegaard and Nietzsche in this respect, see Maurice Mandelbaum, *History, Man, and Reason: A Study in Nineteenth-Century Thought* (Baltimore, 1971), p. 328, and Walter Kaufmann, *Nietzsche: Philosopher, Psychologist, Anti-Christ* (New York, 1956), pp. 204-6.
62. Ranke to Heinrich Ritter, Nov. 20, 1853, in *Briefwerk,* p. 377.
63. Ranke, *Nachlass,* 2:77.
64. Ibid., pp. 60-62. The important qualification does appear in the transcript, but separated from the idea it qualifies and set several sentences away, whence it is seldom associated with the main historicist idea of individuality which has tended to come undiluted down to posterity. On this point, see Schieder, in ibid., p. 17.
65. Ranke to King Maximilian II, Nov. 26, 1859, in *Briefwerk,* p. 433. Although Ranke did not make the point so categorically in the introductory lecture of October 1954 to *On the Epochs of Modern History,* it was definitely implied in his choice of Asian and North American aboriginal examples in his argument against historical progress and in his distinction between the development of western culture and the stagnation of all other cultures in his argument against the uniformity of progress. *Nachlass,* 2:72-75.
66. Ibid., pp. 53, 139, 156-58.
67. Ranke to Clara Ranke, Oct. 1, 1854, in *Briefwerk,* p. 390.
68. Ranke, *Nachlass,* 2: 96, 107, 122-23, 155-58.
69. Ibid., pp. 174, 206, 235, 258-59.
70. Ibid., pp. 264, 266, 269-70, 279-81, 288-93, 311-15.
71. Ibid., pp. 329, 345, 366-67, 401-2.
72. Ibid., p. 402.
73. Ibid., pp. 402, 409-17, 439-40.
74. Ibid., p. 440. It may be recalled that Ranke had adumbrated the same point, identifying the postecclesiastical European unity vaguely as "culture and power" before the revolution of 1848, in the final volume of his *German History in the Age of Reformation.* See chapter 6 above.

75. Ranke, *Nachlass,* 2:160, 441–45. Emphasis added.
76. See above, pp. 000–00.
77. Ranke, *Nachlass,* 2:261–63, 442–43, 446–47.
78. Ibid., 4:256–58.
79. Ibid., pp. 258–59.
80. Ibid., pp. 259–61.
81. Ibid., pp. 268–69.

11. The Mature Historian

1. Ranke published his *French History* between 1852 and 1861, the *English History* between 1859 and 1866.
2. Ranke, *Nachlass,* 4:281–83, 316.
3. Ibid., p. 280. In the preface to his *English History* Ranke even denied that the history of a country not the historian's own could be called "national history." But in his lectures he used the label freely for his historical studies of non-German nations, and the denial may be accounted simply a rhetorical device to highlight his distinction between a self-regarding native history and a world-regarding national history.
4. Ibid., pp. 275, 288–89, 318–19.
5. Ranke, *Französische Geschichte,* 5:31.
6. Ibid., 1:viii.
7. Ibid., 5:28–30, 272; 6:vii–viii, xxv.
8. Ibid., 1:57, 396; 2:3; 3:1, 113; 4:5.
9. Ibid., 1:13–14; 2:322, 399; 3:52.
10. Ibid., 1:383, 410; 2:379; 3:157, 276, 397, 418; 4:6.
11. Ibid., 1:85, 186; 3:415.
12. Ibid., 4:5.
13. Ibid., 2:61; 3:81, 209.
14. Ibid., 8:242.
15. Ibid., 1:232–36.
16. Ibid., 2:213; 3:169, 199.
17. Ibid., 3:217, 279, 281, 320, 329.
18. Ibid., 4:14, 299–300, 311, 315, 319.
19. Ibid., 1:276–78; 2:107; 3:262, 276.
20. Ibid., 1:84–85, 109, 151, 295; 2:3–4, 87–88, 185; 3:86–87, 113.
21. Ibid., 2:280, 320; 3:153–54, 280, 372, 397; 4:306.
22. Ibid., 3:335, 372, 420; 4:77, 82.
23. Ibid., 1:324; 3:157, 208; 4:309–11.
24. Ibid., 2:18, 308; 3:37, 66, 98–99, 113, 119, 140–41, 281; 4:3–4.
25. Ibid., 1:64; 4:3, 7, 306.
26. Ibid., 1:85, 419; 2:113; 3:287–88, 421.
27. Ibid., 1:164–65, 245–46, 381–83; 2:166–67; 3:287.
28. Ibid., 2:144.
29. See above, pp. 222–22.
30. Ranke, *Französische Geschichte,* 4:407.
31. Ibid., pp. 393–94, 422.
32. Ibid., pp. 422–23.
33. Ranke to Friedrich Perthes, Mar. 20, 1826, in *Briefwerk,* pp. 95–96; to Heinrich Ranke, Nov. 20 and 21, 1828, in ibid., pp. 176–77; Ranke, *Nachlass,* 1:280.

34. Ranke, *Englische Geschichte*, 2:103; 6:142.
35. Ibid., 8:113-14.
36. Ibid., 1:x; 8:261.
37. Ibid., 8:114.
38. Ranke, *Nachlass*, 4:295, 301-7, 412-13, 458-59.
39. Ranke, *Englische Geschichte*, 1:ix-x.
40. Ibid., 1:166; 2:181, 188; 3:43; 4:250, 360; 7:259, 291-93.
41. Ibid., 4:301, 367; 6:199.
42. Ibid., 1:275; 8:27.
43. Ibid., 1:4, 37; 2:270; 5:295; 6:220; 7:9.
44. Ibid., 7:59, 107.
45. Ibid., 8:52.
46. Ibid., 1:89; 6:147, 212-13.
47. Ibid., 1:11; 7:3.
48. Ibid., 4:54-55, 203-4; 6:234-35, 286-87.
49. Ibid., 6:148, 234.
50. Ibid., 2:271; 4:338, 365; 5:242, 243; 6:235, 282, 339.
51. Ibid., 6:239.
52. Ibid., 5:161-62, 175. Ranke confirmed the centrality of the parliamentary constitution in his view of English history by devoting lecture courses to the Parliamentary History of England, in 1864 and again in 1865. In an earlier course he had singled out "power and constitution" as "comprising the whole history of the English nation." Ranke, *Nachlass*, 4:290.
53. Ranke, *Englische Geschichte*, 4:271.
54. Ibid., 1:328; 6:280; 7:62; 8:3, 11, 107.
55. Ibid., 1:323; 4:36, 111, 304; 6:252; 8:6.
56. Ibid., 6:235.
57. Ibid., 8:107.
58. Ibid., 3:327-28; 4:210; 5:108, 111.
59. Ibid., 4:305; 5:46; 7:105, 294.
60. Ibid., 1:40, 324; 4:374; 5:51, 158; 6:162, 287; 7:290.
61. Ibid., 1:347.
62. Ibid., 3:117, 4:259-64, 280; 5:229; 6:180, 264.
63. Ranke, "Fragment of the 60's," in Fritz Stern, ed. and trans., *Varieties of History* (New York, 1973), p. 60. The original German version of this fragment can be found in Ranke, *Nachlass*, 4:296-98. The label of the piece, significantly, is "Die Notwendigkeit Universalgeschichtlicher Betrachtung" ("The necessity of a universal-historical approach").
64. Ibid., pp. 61-62.
65. Ibid., p. 62.
66. Ranke, *Englische Geschichte*, 8:36, 70, 109-10.

12. The Third Synthesis

1. Ranke to Ferdinand Ranke, May 21, 1862, in *Briefwerk*, p. 440.
2. Ranke to Clara Ranke, June 1862, in ibid., p. 441; to Georg Waitz, Sept. 1863, in ibid., p. 444; to Heinrich Ranke, Oct. 18, 1866, in *Neue Briefe*, pp. 465-67.
3. Ranke to Maximiliane von Kotze, nee von Ranke, May 26, 1871, in *Neue Briefe*, p. 555; to Ernst Ranke, July 9, 1875, and Mar. 31, 1876, in *Briefwerk*, pp. 529, 533; to Heinrich Ranke, Aug. 1, 1876, in ibid., pp. 534-36; to

Amalie Helferich, nee Ranke, Dec. 11, 1876, in ibid., p. 541. Ranke's wife died in 1871, and both of the younger brothers (Heinrich and Ferdinand) with whom he had always been intimate in 1876.

4. Ranke to Maximiliane von Kotze, nee Ranke, Apr. 30, 1884, in *Neue Briefe*, p. 718.
5. Ranke to Clara von Ranke and the children, Sept. 28, 1869, in ibid., p. 448; Ranke to Heinrich and Selma Ranke, Mar. 29, 1876, in ibid., p. 532; to Alfred von Reumont, Apr. 15, 1879, in ibid., p. 564.
6. Ranke to Edwin von Manteuffel, Jan. 1, 1866, in ibid., pp. 459-60; to Heinrich Ranke, Jan. 20, 1867, in ibid., p. 472; to Otto Ranke, May 25, 1873, in *Briefwerk*, p. 520; to Kaiser Wilhelm I, Jan. 1, 1877, in ibid., p. 543.
7. Ranke to Clara von Ranke and the children, June 11, 1865, in *Briefwerk*, p. 466; to Heinrich Ranke, Nov. 28, 1869, in *Neue Briefe*, p. 535.
8. Ranke to Edwin von Manteuffel, Feb. 23, 1869, in *Neue Briefe*, pp. 520-21.
9. Ranke to Georg Waitz, Mar. 2, 1867, in *Briefwerk*, p. 490; to Edwin von Manteuffel, May 26, 1867, and Oct. 4, 1869 (date of reception), in *Neue Briefe*, pp. 497, 528.
10. Ranke to Edwin von Manteuffel, May 26, 1867, in *Neue Briefe*, p. 497.
11. Ranke to Edwin von Manteuffel, Feb. 23, 1867, and May 26, 1867, in ibid., pp. 473, 497.
12. Ranke to Edwin von Manteuffel, Oct. 2, 1865, Jan. 1, 1866, May 22, 1866, May 26, 1867, Feb. 23, 1869, Oct. 4, 1869, Jan. 14, 1879, in ibid., pp. 456, 459, 463, 497, 520-21, 528, 539. Also see Herzfeld, "Politik und Geschichte," pp. 337-38.
13. Ranke to Clara von Ranke and children, Sept. 26 and 28, 1869, in *Briefwerk*, pp. 497-98.
14. Ranke, *Nachlass*, 4:453-57, 461.
15. Ibid., pp. 395-96, 450, 462-67.
16. Ibid., pp. 405, 411-13, 433-35, 463.
17. Ibid., pp. 455, 461, 467.
18. Ibid., pp. 400-403, 464.
19. Ibid., p. 340; Ranke to Wilhelm von Giesebrecht, Aug. 23, 1870, in *Briefwerk*, p. 502; to Edwin von Manteuffel, Nov. 1870, in ibid., p. 508; to Edwin von Manteuffel, Sept. 10, 1871, in *Neue Briefe*, p. 561.
20. Ranke, *Nachlass*, 4:468, 473.
21. Ibid., 1:402, 405, 413; Ranke to Emperor William I, Mar. 22, 1871, in *Neue Briefe*, p. 548; to Hans Lothar von Schweinitz, Oct. 12, 1870, in *Briefwerk*, pp. 503-4; to Edwin von Manteuffel, Nov. 1870, in ibid., p. 508.
22. Ranke to Edwin von Manteuffel, Jan. 1, 1866, and Feb. 23, 1869, in *Neue Briefe*, pp. 459, 521.
23. Ranke, *Nachlass*, 1:445; Ranke to Edwin von Manteuffel, Jan. 1, 1866, Feb. 23, 1869, Nov. 20, 1870, in *Neue Briefe*, pp. 459, 521, 544; Ranke, *Nachlass*, 1:409; Ranke to the Munich Historical Commission, Sept. 26, 1883, in *Briefwerk*, pp. 581-82.
24. Ranke to Hermann Heiberg, Apr. 1, 1885, in ibid., pp. 589-91.
25. Ranke to Bismarck, Feb. 13, 1882, in ibid., p. 574.
26. Ranke to Edwin von Manteuffel, Sept. 10, 1871, in *Neue Briefe*, pp. 560, 562.
27. Entry of January 1877, in Ranke, *Nachlass*, 1:79-80.

28. Ranke to Edwin von Manteuffel, Nov. 29, 1882, in *Neue Briefe*, p. 706. The role of Ranke's historical filter in preparing his acceptance of Bismarckian Germany can be glimpsed in the comparison between this acceptance and the rigid monarchical, anti-Bismarckian stance of his intimate friend, von Manteuffel, whose political views were congenial to Ranke's own. On Manteuffel's politics, see Gordon A. Craig, "Portrait of a Political General: Edwin von Manteuffel and the Constitutional Conflict in Prussia," *Political Science Quarterly* 66 (1951): 4-5.

29. It should be recalled that Ranke denied that either his *French History* or his *English History* were classifiable as "national history" since he dealt with them from a universal rather than from an internal perspective. See above, chap. 10, sec. I.

30. The addressee of Ranke's justification was Georg Waitz, formerly a student and strictly a German medievalist. Ranke to Georg Waitz, Oct. 28, 1865, in *Briefwerk*, pp. 484-85.

31. Ranke to the Academy of Germany Natural Scientists, Feb. 26, 1867, in *Neue Briefe*, pp. 479-80; to King William I of Prussia, Mar. 22, 1868, and Dec. 4, 1871, in ibid., pp. 507, 568.

32. See, for example, Ranke to King William I of Prussia, Jan. 1, 1867, in *Briefwerk*, pp. 486-87; and Ranke, *Lebensgeschichte*, p. 75.

33. See chap. 8, sec. II above, esp. n. 21.

34. Ranke, *Zur deutschen Geschichte*, 7:101, 167, 175, 206.

35. Ibid., pp. 184, 223, 227-28.

36. Ibid., p. 105.

37. Ranke, *Geschichte Wallensteins*, 2d ed. (Leipzig, 1879), pp. vi, viii-ix.

38. Ibid., pp. vi-viii.

39. Ibid., pp. 230, 268, 283, 314-15, 345, 349, 428, 434.

40. Ibid., pp. 119, 145, 166-67, 230.

41. Ibid., pp. 97, 99, 144, 159, 177-78, 370, 372.

42. Ibid., pp. 435, 450, 455-456.

43. Ranke, "Ansprachen, gehalten an persönlichen Feiertagen" (1867), in *Sämmtliche Werke*, 51-52:590.

44. Ranke to Wilhelm von Geisebrecht, Mar. 5, 1877, in *Briefwerk*, p. 550.

45. Ranke to Otto von Bismarck, Feb. 22, 1877, in ibid., pp. 546-47.

46. Entry of January 1877 in Ranke, *Nachlass,* 4:79-80.

47. Ranke, "Der Ursprung des siebenjährigen Krieges," in *Zur Geschichte von Oesterreich und Preussen zwischen den Friedensschlussen zu Aachen und Hubertusberg* (Leipzig, 1875), in *Sämmtliche Werke*, 30:63-64, 235.

48. Ranke, *Die deutschen Mächte und der Fürstenbund: Deutsche Geschichte von 1780 bis 1790*, 2d ed. (Leipzig, 1875), in *Sämmtliche Werke*, 31-32: v-vi, 20, 147, 156-59, 269, 288-89, 453.

49. Ranke to Otto Ranke, May 25, 1873, in *Briefwerk*, p. 518. The work in question was a selective edition of correspondence between the king and Baron Christian Karl Josias von Bunsen, royal friend and diplomat. It was published as *Aus dem Briefwechsel Friedrich Wilhelms IV. mit Bunsen*, ed. Leopold von Ranke (Berlin, 1873).

50. Ranke to Edwin von Manteuffel, Jan. 25, 1873, in *Neue Briefe*, p. 594; to Carl Geibel, July 1, 1877, in *Briefwerk*, p. 551.

51. Ranke, *Hardenberg und die Geschichte des preussischen Staates, 1793-1813*, 2d ed. (Leipzig, 1879), in *Sämmtliche Werke*, 46:viii-ix; Ranke to Emperor

William I, Jan. 1, 1877, in *Briefwerk,* pp. 542-43. The first edition was published under the title *Denkwürdigkeiten des Staatskanzlers Fürsten von Hardenbergs,* 5 vols., ed. Leopold von Ranke (Berlin, 1877-78), after Ranke had successfully petitioned Bismarck to drop "commissioned by the government" and the editor's title of official historiographer from the title page. Ranke to Carl Geibel, Nov. 3, 1876, in *Briefwerk,* p. 537.

52. Ranke to Otto Ranke, May 25, 1873, in *Briefwerk,* pp. 518-19.
53. Ranke, *Deutsche Mächte,* pp. vii-viii. Ranke's definitive alignment of history and objective idealism against the speculative objective idealism of Schelling is a product of this period as well. In a dictated note of 1875, he rejected Schelling's later philosophy, which sought to link the speculative idea of God to natural and human history, as "theosophical"—i.e., the application of reason to the realm of "the positive, which lay beyond reason." "The limit of all human existence," said Ranke in this context, is that "one can never get from the quid to the quod." This paean to quiddity left only theology and history to share the truths of heaven and earth between them. Ranke, *Nachlass,* 1:165.
54. Ranke to Bismarck, Feb. 22, 1877, in *Briefwerk,* p. 546. Cf. his earlier "Über die Verwandtschaft" (1836).
55. Ranke to Alfred von Reumont, June 8, 1874, in *Briefwerk,* p. 542.
56. Ranke, *Hardenberg,* pp. iv, x-xiii, 353.
57. Ibid., pp. vi, x-xiii.
58. Ibid., pp. vi, x-xiii, 353.
59. Ranke, *Preussische Geschichte,* 1:44, 50-51. The first four sections of the Twelve Books were published, without the new preface, in 1874.

13. The Final Resolution

1. Ranke, *Weltgeschichte,* 1¹:iv (i.e., vol. 1, pt. I, p. iv).
2. Ranke to Edwin von Manteuffel, July 10, 1872, in *Neue Briefe,* p. 579; to Emperor William I, Mar. 9, 1875, in ibid., p. 620; to Bismarck, Apr. 1875, in ibid., p. 622.
3. Ranke, *Ursprung und Beginn der Revolutionskriege,* p. v.
4. Ibid., pp. 196, 247.
5. Ranke, *Lebensgeschichte,* p. 76.
6. Ranke, *Nachlass,* 1:448.
7. Ranke to Heinrich Ranke, Nov. 28, 1874, in *Briefwerk,* p. 528.
8. Ranke, *Weltgeschichte,* 1¹:v.
9. Ibid., 1¹:vii.
10. Ranke, *Ursprung und Beginn der Revolutionskriege,* pp. v, 1, 4, 149-50, 181, 239-40.
11. Ibid., pp. 39-40, 50-51, 95, 99, 113.
12. Ibid., pp. 109, 225.
13. Ibid., pp. 131, 232.
14. Ibid., pp. 60-61, 69, 109, 179.
15. Ibid., pp. 8, 143, 149-50.
16. Ranke, *Weltgeschichte,* 1¹:vii. Ranke completed six "parts," each consisting of two volume-length "sections" and reached the eleventh-century Salian dynasty of Holy Roman Emperors in the middle of the seventh part, when his dictation was broken off by the unbearable pain immediately before his

death. The volume, in one section, was completed on the basis of sundry pieces which Ranke had dictated on the occasions of his readings and designed for inclusion in the book. The subsequent posthumous publication of parts 8 and 9 was arranged by a team of editors, led by Dove, who used a few remaining dictated pieces and, for the bulk, Ranke's earlier lecture notes.

17. Ibid., 1^1:vi-vii, 93, 111-13.
18. Ibid., 1^1:viii.
19. For the elaboration in terms of the concept of humanity, see "Some Fragments on Universal History" (1877), in Liebel, "Ranke's Fragments on Universal History," pp. 154-57; for the elaboration in terms of "the cultural world" see the posthumous reconstruction of Ranke's dictation in Ranke, *Weltgeschichte*, 8^1:4-5.
20. *Weltgeschichte*, 8^1:4-5.
21. Ibid. For Ranke's earlier views on progress and the puzzle resulting from the juxtaposition of the earlier and later, see above, chap. 2, and chap. 11, sec. III.
22. Ranke, *Weltgeschichte*, 1^1:iv-vi; Ranke, in Liebel, "Ranke's Fragments," p. 155.
23. Ranke, *Weltgeschichte*, 1^1:332-33; 1^2:153-54, 169-70; 4^1:8-9.
24. Ranke, *Weltgeschichte*, 1^2:1; 2^1:174, 299; 3^1:127, 183.
25. Ibid., 1^1:38, 88, 104, 155, 375; 1^2:1.
26. Ibid., 1^1:28-29, 79, 155; 2^1:299.
27. Ibid., 2^1:78, 386, 411; 2^2:1, 27, 44, 71-72, 153; 3^1:1.
28. Ibid., 2^2:19.
29. Ibid., 2^1:392; 2^2:256, 411-16.
30. Ibid., 3^1:3-5.
31. Ibid., 3^1:3-6, 166, 170, 175, 315-16, 542-46.
32. Ibid., 3^1:5-6, 546. This division of the *World History* into three periods is mine, not Ranke's, but it does roughly follow his volume divisions. According to this scheme, the first volume covers the first period; the next two—on Rome—deal with the second; the fourth volume considers the transition between the second and third—i.e., the Roman and German—periods; and the final two plus volumes of Ranke's own composition focus on the Germanic empires and the Germano-Romanic national states.
33. Ibid., 4^2:242-43; 5^1:104-5.
34. Even the Carolingian Empire, which Ranke found deficient in its respect for the national tribal principle, he characterized as simultaneously a unified empire and a society of nations." Ibid., 5^2:234.
35. Ibid., 6^1:96-97.
36. Ibid., 4^2:442; 5^1:323-24; 5^2:242-43; 6^1:4.
37. Ibid., 1^1:55, 79, 161-62; 2^1:8, 79; 6^2:97-98.
38. Ranke, *Nachlass*, 1:166-67.

Conclusion: The Meaning of History

1. See above, pp. 7, 19-20.
2. Simon, *Hegel und Ranke*, p. 188.
3. Ranke to Heinrich Ritter, Apr. 1837, in *Briefwerk*, p. 285.
4. Ranke, "Fragment of the 60's," p. 61; Ranke, *History of the Popes*, 1:48-49, 105-333.
5. Ranke, quoted in Berg, *Ranke als Lehrer*, p. 206.

6. For the analysis of Ranke's views on the subject-object relationship which demonstrates his commitment to both sides of it, see Berg, *Ranke als Lehrer,* pp. 180–218.
7. Ranke, *Sämmtliche Werke,* 51–52; 520; *Nachlass,* 1:241.
8. Ranke, *Nachlass,* 1:241.
9. Ranke, *Englische Geschichte,* 1:vi; 2:103.
10. Ranke, *Preussische Geschichte,* 1:49; Ranke to Crown Prince Maximilian of Bavaria, Dec. 26, 1847, in *Briefwerk,* p. 338.
11. Ranke to Heinrich Ranke, Nov. 24, 1826, in *Briefwerk,* p. 103; to Karl August Varnhagen von Ense, Dec. 9, 1827, in ibid., p. 127.
12. Ranke, *Deutsche Geschichte,* 1:1.
13. Ibid., p. 447.
14. Ranke, *Französische Geschichte,* 1:v. Italics mine.
15. Ranke, quoted in Berg, *Ranke als Lehrer,* pp. 191, 204–5, 212.
16. Ranke, *Englische Geschichte,* 1:vi.
17. E.g., Berg, *Ranke als Lehrer,* p. 216.

Bibliography

1. Ranke's Works: Collections

Aus Werk und Nachlass. Vol. 1: Tagebücher, ed. Walther Peter Fuchs. Vol. 2: Über die Epochen der neueren Geschichte, ed. Theodor Schieder and Helmut Berding. Vol. 3: Frühe Schriften, ed. Walther Peter Fuchs with the collaboration of Gunter Berg and Volker Dotterweich. Vol. 4: Vorlesungseinleitung, ed. Volker Dotterweich and Walther Peter Fuchs. Munich, 1964-75.

Das Briefwerk. Ed. Walther Peter Fuchs. Hamburg, 1949.

Geschichte und Politik: Ausgewählte Aufsätze und Meisterschriften. Ed. Hans Hofmann. Stuttgart, 1942.

Neue Briefe. Ed. Bernhard Hoeft and Hans Herzfeld. Hamburg, 1949.

Sämmtliche Werke. 54 vols. Leipzig, 1867-90.

The Theory and Practice of History. Ed. Georg C. Iggers and Konrad von Moltke. Indianapolis, 1973.

2. Ranke's Works: Books

Deutsche Geschichte im Zeitalter der Reformation. Ed. Willy Andreas. Wiesbaden, 1957. Eng. tr., History of the Reformation in Germany, trans. S. Austin. London, 1845-47.

Deutsche Geschichte im Zeitalter der Reformation. Ed. Paul Joachimsen. Gesamtausgabe der Deutschen Akademie, 6 vols. Munich, 1925-26.

Die deutschen Mächte und der Fürstenbund: Deutsche Geschichte von 1780 bis 1790. 2d ed. Leipzig, 1875. In Sämmtliche Werke, vols. 31-32.

A Dialogue on Politics. Trans. Theodore Von Laue. In Von Laue, Leopold Ranke: The Formative Years (see below). (See Politisches Gespräch, below).

Englische Geschichte, vornehmlich im siebzehnten Jahrhundert. 4th ed. Leipzig, 1877. In *Sämmtliche Werke,* vols. 14-22. Eng. tr., *A History of England, Principally in the Seventeenth Century.* Oxford, 1875.

Französische Geschichte, vornehmlich im sechzehnten und siebzehnten Jahrhundert. Leipzig, 1868-70. In *Sämmtliche Werke,* vols. 8-11. Eng. tr. of first part, *Civil Wars and Monarchy in France,* trans. M. A. Garvey. London, 1852.

Fürsten und Völker: Geschichten der romanischen und germanischen Völker von 1494-1514; Die Osmanen und die spanische Monarchie im 16. und 17. Jahrhundert. Ed. Willy Andreas. Wiesbaden, 1957.

Fürsten und Völker von Süd-Europa im 16. und 17. Jahrhundert. 4 vols. Berlin, 1837-45.

Geschichte Wallensteins. 2d ed. Leipzig, 1879.

Geschichten der romanischen und germanischen Völker von 1494-1514. See *Fürsten und Völker.* Eng. tr., *History of the Latin and Teutonic Nations, 1494-1514,* trans. S. R. Dennis. London, 1909.

Die grossen Mächte. In *Geschichte und Politik.* Eng. tr., *The Great Powers,* trans. Theodore Von Laue, in Von Laue, *Leopold Ranke: The Formative Years.*

Hardenberg und die Geschichte des preussischen Staates, 1793-1813. 2d ed. Leipzig, 1879. In *Sämmtliche Werke,* vol. 46. See Ranke, ed., *Denkwürdigkeiten des Staatskanzlers Fürsten von Hardenbergs.*

Historisch-biographische Studien. Leipzig, 1877.

History of the Popes in the Last Four Centuries. 3 vols. Trans. E. Fowler. London, 1912. See *Die römischen Päpste.*

A History of Serbia and the Serbian Revolution. Trans. Mrs. Alexander Kerr. London, 1847. See *Die serbische Revolution.*

Die Osmanen und die spanische Monarchie im 16. und 17. Jahrhundert. See *Fürsten und Völker.* Eng. tr., *The Ottoman and Spanish Empires, in the Sixteenth and Seventeenth Centuries,* trans. Walter K. Kelly. London, 1843.

Politisches Gespräch. In *Geschichte und Politik.* Eng. tr., *A Dialogue on Politics* (see above).

Preussische Geschichte. 2 vols. Ed. Willy Andreas. Wiesbaden, 1957. New edition of *Zwölf Bücher preussischer Geschichte,* 2d ed. (Berlin, 1874). First edition published as *Neun Bücher preussischer Geschichte* (Berlin, 1847). Eng. tr. of 1st ed., *Memoirs of the House of Brandenberg and History of Prussia During the 17th and 18th Centuries,* trans. Sir Alexander and Lady Duff Gordon. London, 1849.

Die römischen Päpste in den letzen vier Jahrhunderten. 11th ed. Leipzig, 1907. Eng. tr., *History of the Popes in the Last Four Centuries* (see above).

Serbien und die Türkei im 19. Jahrhundert. Leipzig, 1879. Second edition of *Die serbische Revolution.*

Die serbische Revolution. Hamburg, 1829. Eng. tr., *A History of Serbia and the Serbian Revolution* (see above).

Über die Epochen der neueren Geschichte. Ed. Hans Herzfeld. Schloss Laupheim, n.d. Recent critical edition in *Aus Werk und Nachlass,* vol. 2.

Ursprung und Beginn der Revolutionskriege 1791 und 1792. Leipzig, 1875; 2d ed., 1879.

Die Verschwörung gegen Venedig im Jahre 1618. In *Studien und Portraits zur italienischen Geschichte,* ed. Willy Andreas. Wiesbaden, 1957.

Weltgeschichte. 9 vols. 1st-3d ed. Leipzig, 1881-1888. Eng. tr. of 1st vol., *Universal History: The Oldest Historical Group of Nations and the Greeks,* ed. G. W. Prothero. New York, 1885.

Zur deutschen Geschichte vom Religionsfrieden bis zum dreissigjährigen Krieg.
2d ed. Leipzig, 1874. In *Sämmtliche Werke,* vol. 7. Eng. tr. of 1st part,
Ferdinand I and Maximilian II: State of Germany after the Reformation,
trans. Lady Duff Gordon. London, 1853.
Zur eigenen Lebensgeschichte. Ed. Alfred Dove. In *Sämmtliche Werke,* vols.
53-54.
Zur Geschichte der italienischen Kunst. In *Sämmtliche Werke,* vols. 51-52.
Zur Geschichte der italienischen Poesie. Berlin, 1837.
*Zur Geschichte von Oesterreich und Preussen zwischen den Friedensschlüssen zu
Aachen und Hubertusberg.* In *Sämmtliche Werke,* vol. 30.
Zur Kritik neuerer Geschichtschreiber. In *Sämmtliche Werke,* vols. 33-34.

3. Ranke's Works: Articles. (*Unless otherwise noted, these pieces were not
published in Ranke's lifetime.*)

"Ansprachen, gehalten an persönlichen Feiertagen." In *Sämmtliche Werke,*
vols. 51-52.
"Einleitung zur historisch politischen Zeitschrift." In *Sämmtliche Werke,*
vols. 49-50.
"Fragment of the 60's." In Fritz Stern, ed. and trans., *Varieties of History.* New
York, 1973.
"Some Fragments on Universal History." In Helen Liebel, "Ranke's Fragments
on Universal History" (see below).
"Geschichte und Philosophie." In *Geschichte und Politik.*
"Idee der Universalhistorie." In Eberhard Kessel, "Rankes idee der Universal-
historie" (see below).
"Das Luther-Fragment von 1817," ed. Elisabeth Schweitzer. In *Deutsche
Geschichte im Zeitalter der Reformation,* ed. Paul Joachimsen. Gesamtausgabe
der Deutschen Akademie, 6 vols. Munich, 1925-26. Also in *Aus Werk und
Nachlass,* vol. 3.
"The Pitfalls of a Philosophy of History (Introduction to a lecture on Universal
History: A Manuscript of the 1840's)." Trans. Wilma A. Iggers. In *The Theory
and Practice of History.*
"Politische Denkschriften aus den Jahren 1848-1851." In *Sämmtliche Werke,*
vols. 49-50..
"Schluss einer Einleitung zur Vorlesung über die neueste Geschichte." In
Kessel, "Rankes Idee der Universalhistorie" (see below).
"Tagebuchdiktate Leopold v. Rankes aus dem Jahre 1881." *Historische Zeit-
schrift* 151 (1935).
"Über die Verwandtschaft und den Unterschied der Historie und der Politik."
In *Geschichte und Politik.* Published.
"Ein unbekannter Vortrag Rankes aus dem Jahr 1862." Ed. Karl Alexander von
Müller. *Historische Zeitschrift* 151 (1935).
"Über die Versammlung der französischen Notabeln im Jahre 1787." In
Französische Geschichte, vol. 5. Published.
"Der Ursprung des siebenjährigen Krieges." In *Zur Geschichte von Oesterreich
und Preussen zwischen den Friedenschlussen zu Aachen und Hubertusberg.*
Published.
"Vom Einfluss der Theorie." In *Geschichte und Politik.* Published.
Zwei Jugendreden, ed. Kurt Borries. Berlin, 1927.

4. Ranke's Works: Editions

Aus dem Briefwechsel Friedrich Wilhelms IV mit Bunsen. Ed. Leopold von Ranke. Berlin, 1873.

Denkwürdigkeiten des Staatskanzlers Fürsten von Hardenbergs. Ed. Leopold von Ranke. Berlin, 1877-78. For 2d edition, see Ranke, *Hardenberg und die Geschichte des preussischen Staates.*

Historisch-Politische Zeitschrift. 1832-36. Ed. Leopold Ranke.

5. Contemporary Sources

Arnim, Bettina von. *Andacht zum Menschenbild.* Ed. Wilhelm Schellberg and Friedrich Fuchs. Jena, 1942. For another edition, see *Die Andacht zum Menschenbild: Unbekannte Briefe von Bettine Brentano.* Bern, 1970.

———. *Werke und Briefe.* Frechen, 1961.

Bismarck, Otto von. *Die Gesammelten Werke.* Berlin, 1926. Vol. 8.

Fichte, Johann Gottlieb. *Die Anweisung zum seligen Leben.* Berlin, 1906.

———. *Ueber das Wesen des Gelehrten, und seine Erscheinungen in dem Gebiete der Freiheit.* Berlin, 1806.

Müller, Johannes von. *Sämmtliche Werke.* 40 vols. Ed. Johann Georg Müller, Stuttgart, 1831-35.

Perthes, Clemens Theodor. *Friedrich Perthes Leben.* 4th ed. Gotha, 1857. Eng. tr., *Memoirs of Frederick Perthes, or Literary, Religious, and Political Life in Germany from 1789 to 1843.* 2d ed. London, 1857.

Ross, Janet. *Three Generations of English Women.* New ed. London, 1893.

Sybel, Heinrich von. *Gedächtnisrede auf Leopold von Ranke.* Berlin, 1886.

Varnhagen von Ense, K. A. *Tagebücher von K. A. Varnhagen von Ense.* 15 vols. Reprint, Bern, 1972.

Varnhagen, Rahel. *Rahel Varnhagen: ein Frauenleben in Briefen.* Ed. Augusta Weldler-Steinberg. 3d ed. Potsdam, 1925.

———. *Rahel Varnhagen und ihre Zeit (Briefe 1800-1833).* Munich, 1868.

6. Commentaries

Dalberg-Acton, John Emerich Edward, First Baron Acton. *Historical Essays and Studies.* London, 1907.

Berdrow, Otto. *Rahel Varnhagen: Ein Lebens- und Zeitbild.* Stuttgart, 1902.

Berg, Gunter, *Leopold von Ranke als akademischer Lehrer: Studien zu seinen Vorlesungen und seinem Geschichtsdenken.* Göttingen, 1968.

Craig, Gordon A. "Portrait of a Political General: Edwin von Manteuffel and the Constitutional Conflict in Prussia." *Political Science Quarterly* 66 (1951).

Dove, Alfred. "Leopold von Ranke." In *Deutsche allgemeine Biographie*, vol. 27. Leipzig, 1888.

Drewitz, Ingeborg. *Bettine von Arnim: Romantik, Revolution, Utopie.* Cologne, 1969.

Gay, Peter. *Style in History.* New York, 1974.

Guillaud, Antoine. *Modern Germany and Her Historians.* New York, 1915.

Hahn, Karl-Heinz. *Bettina von Arnim in ihrem Verhältnis zu Staat und Politik.* Weimar, 1959.

Henz, Günter Johannes. *Leopold von Ranke: Leben, Denken, Wort, 1795-1814.* Cologne, 1968.

Herzfeld, Hans. "Politik und Geschichte bei Leopold von Ranke im Zeitraum von 1848-1871." In *Festschrift für Gerhard Ritter,* ed. Richard Nürnberger. Tübingen, 1950.

Hinrichs, Carl. *Ranke und die Geschichtstheologie der Goethezeit.* Göttingen, 1954.

―――. "Rankes Lutherfragment von 1817 und der Ursprung seiner universalhistorischen Anschauung." In *Festschrift für Gerhard Ritter,* ed. Richard Nürnberger. Tübingen, 1950.

Holborn, Hajo. "The Science of History." In *History and the Humanities.* Garden City, N.Y., 1972.

Iggers, Georg C. *The German Conception of History: The National Tradition of History.* Middletown, Conn., 1968.

Kaufmann, Walter. *Nietzsche: Philosopher, Psychologist, Anti-Christ.* New York, 1956.

Kessel, Eberhard. "Rankes Idee der Universalhistorie." *Historische Zeitschrift* 178 (1954).

Lamprecht, K. G. *Alte und neue Richtungen in den Geschichtswissenschaft.* Berlin, 1896.

Liebel, Helen. "Ranke's Fragments on Universal History." *Clio* 2 (1973).

Mandelbaum, Maurice. *History, Man, and Reason: A Study in Nineteenth-Century Thought.* Baltimore, 1971.

Masur, Gerhard. *Imperial Berlin.* New York, 1970.

―――. *Rankes Begriff der Weltgeschichte.* Berlin, 1926.

Meinecke, Friedrich. *Die Entstehung des Historismus.* Munich and Berlin, 1936.

―――. "Ranke and Burckhardt." In *German History: Some New German Views,* ed. Hans Kohn. Trans. Herbert H. Rowen. Boston, 1954.

Oncken, Herman. *Aus Rankes Frühzeit.* Gotha, 1922.

Schieder, Theodor. *Begegnungen mit der Geschichte.* Göttingen, 1962.

―――. "Die Entstehung von Rankes *Über die Epochen der neueren Geschichte.*" *Historische Zeitschrift* 199 (1964).

Schulin, Ernst. "Rankes erstes Buch." *Historische Zeitschrift* 203 (1966).

Scurla, Herbert. *Begegnungen mit Rahel: Der Salon der Rahel Levin.* Verlag der Nation, n.p., n.d.

Simon, Ernst. *Ranke und Hegel.* Berlin, 1928.

Srbik, Heinrich Ritter von. *Geist und Geschichte vom deutschen Humanismus bis zur Gegenwart.* 2 vols. Salzburg, 1950-51.

Vierhaus, Rudolf. *Ranke und die soziale Welt.* Munster, 1957.

Von Laue, Theodore. *Leopold Ranke: The Formative Years.* Princeton, 1950.

White, Hayden. *Metahistory: The Historical Imagination in Nineteenth-Century Europe.* Baltimore, 1973.

Index

355, 361; divine, 28, 44, 50-51, 162
impartiality, 46, 150, 156, 270-72, 316, 349-50
India, 101, 334
individuality (and individuals, personality), 6, 7, 14-18, 21, 23-25, 35, 46, 50, 53-58, 60, 61, 63, 64, 80, 100, 110, 130-32, 141, 143-47, 158-59, 163-64, 178, 179, 188-90, 195, 198, 201, 211, 214, 215, 222, 226-30, 232, 233, 235, 236, 239, 242-45, 248, 253, 254, 258, 260, 267, 269, 272, 273, 276, 279, 284, 285, 295, 296, 298, 299, 303, 304, 306-8, 312, 316, 318, 324, 330, 333, 339, 342, 345, 352, 355, 372
intellectual history, 157-58, 199
Ireland, 276, 277
Islam, 126, 339
Israel, 335, 336
Italy, 80, 81, 84, 90, 94, 95, 110, 111, 113, 114, 116, 128, 160, 224, 310

Jacobi, Friedrich Heinrich, 28, 29
Jahn, Friedrich Ludwig ("Father"), 69, 70, 97-98, 206
Jahrbuecher der Deutschen Kaiser, 354
James II, king of England, 273
Jansenists, 154-55
Jesuits, 154-55, 263
Jews, 44-45
Joseph II, Holy Roman Emperor, 314

Kant, Immanuel, xi, 3, 29, 36
Kierkegaard, Sören, 233

lectures, 22, 73-74, 102-3, 125-26, 130, 134-42, 149, 194-95, 207, 213-14, 217-19, 224-26, 228, 231, 232, 235-47, 271-72, 290, 295-300, 329, 362
legitimacy, 307, 327, 333. *See also* conservatism; monarchy
Leipzig, 40, 45, 69, 365; University of, 41, 47, 48, 53, 54, 63, 96, 97
Lessing, Gotthold Ephraim, 40
liberalism, 69, 70, 82, 95, 191, 200, 203, 204, 220, 224, 264, 268, 293, 295, 315, 345
literature, 20, 40, 48-50, 70, 71, 74,

79, 80, 84, 89-94, 99, 157, 179, 188-89, 243, 257, 266, 279, 295, 330, 335, 368; poetry, 97, 303, 330
London, 187
Lords, House of (England), 280
Louis XIV, king of France, 239, 249, 251, 253-57, 259-62, 265, 300
Louis XV, king of France, 265, 266
Louis XVI, king of France, 325, 327
Loyola, Ignatius, 154
Luther, Martin, xi, 28, 48, 49, 51, 53, 54, 56-63, 79, 154, 159, 166-67, 169, 171, 307, 363-65; Lutheran, 8, 26, 36-38, 44, 69-70, 173-75

Mabillon, Jean, 3
Macaulay, George Babington, 220-21
Macedonian Empire, 334-35
Machiavelli, Niccolo, 1
Manteuffel, Edwin von, 95, 183, 205, 208, 220, 294, 319, 384
Maria Theresa, archduchess of Austria, queen of Hungary and Bohemia, 200
Marie-Antoinette, queen of France, 325
Marx, Karl, 1, 348
Masur, Gerhard, 19
Matthias, Holy Roman Emperor, 306
Maximilian I, Holy Roman Emperor, 112-13, 172
Maximilian II, king of Bavaria, 22, 95, 103, 216-19, 224-25, 230-32, 240, 241, 243, 247, 332, 380
Mazarin, Cardinal Jules, 254, 255, 259, 261, 262
Mediterranean, 101, 221, 334
Meinecke, Friedrich, 130-31, 355, 372
Memoirs of Chancellor Prince Hardenberg, 317-19, 321
Middle Ages, 90, 138-40, 237-39, 241, 248, 253, 258, 261, 262, 264-66, 277, 298, 301, 305, 310, 334, 339; medieval history, 2, 3, 71, 100, 243, 298, 368
military principle, 211, 224, 294, 309
moderation, 7-8, 131, 296
modern history (and early-modern history), 3, 74, 79, 93-94, 97, 98, 100, 108, 115, 117, 120, 139, 185-86, 195, 216, 246, 248, 260, 298, 299,

Parliament (English), 221, 239, 274-76, 278-85, 289, 382
particular history (and empirical history, specific history), 21, 23, 63, 67, 102, 104, 105, 107, 108, 115, 117, 119, 121, 124, 125, 137, 139, 143, 146, 152, 158, 161, 169-70, 179, 181, 222, 226, 247, 251, 264, 272, 323
particular truth (and particularizing method), 5, 6, 14, 15, 17, 30, 66, 80, 81, 88, 93, 97, 104, 106, 123, 127, 132, 134, 136, 138, 143-46, 159, 172, 193, 194, 199, 201, 214-16, 225, 228, 237, 241, 242, 244-45, 248, 269, 272, 273, 286-88, 296-99, 301-3, 308, 324, 329, 339, 341, 342, 348, 352, 353, 375
parties, 111, 228, 251, 258, 259, 266, 280, 296, 305, 306, 316. See also duality .
patriotic history. See national history
pattern. See theme
Paul, Jean, 28
personality. See individuality
Perthes, Friedrich, 128
Pfistermeister, Franz, 227
Pforta, 40
Philip II, king of Spain, 254
philology, 13, 14, 48-50, 74, 78, 98, 334
philosophy, 22, 24, 29, 35, 49, 54, 62, 63, 97, 104, 132-38, 232-33, 287, 295, 298, 335, 336, 349, 356
philosophy of history, 19, 21, 24, 361-63
pietism. See religion
Pindar, 49
Pius V, pope, 155
Plato, xi
plurality (and diversity, fragments, multiplicity, variety), 102, 104, 107, 109, 121, 141, 156, 159, 177, 222, 224, 226, 233, 235, 238-40, 244, 247-50, 253, 255, 268, 269, 275, 280-81, 299, 301-2, 323, 334, 339
poetry. See literature
Poland, 202
political history, 92-94, 158, 165, 182, 260, 269

politics, 4, 7, 8, 19, 36, 39, 41, 42, 67, 86, 92, 94, 95, 98, 129, 138, 148, 158, 159, 161, 166, 173, 175, 179, 184, 188, 190, 203, 204, 212, 227, 242, 257, 290, 293, 295, 296, 302, 306, 309, 312, 317, 333, 345-46
Poppo, E. F., 71, 72, 75
popular sovereignty, 206, 209, 212, 215, 235, 240, 264, 266, 274, 282-83, 323, 327, 328. See also national sovereignty
Portugal, 112
power, 179, 211-12, 238-39, 242, 251, 257, 259, 298, 380, 382
pragmatism, 135-36
Prague, Peace of (1866), 293
Presbyterianism, English (and Nonconformity, Puritanism), 274, 277, 279
present, 218-28, 231, 234-36, 239-43, 265, 270, 271, 286, 287, 296, 301, 306, 312-15, 334, 349, 353, 355
princes, 113, 172, 174-75, 198, 299, 309-11, 380
Princes and nations of Europe, 116
Princes and Nations of Southern Europe, 81, 90, 116, 151, 370
process, historical, 126, 134, 137, 141, 146, 166, 181, 233, 271, 299, 301, 305, 306, 316, 317, 324, 347, 352-54, 357
profession, academic, 36, 38, 41, 43-46, 51, 52, 66, 68-70, 74, 78, 96-100, 184-88, 190-91, 290, 291, 304, 353
progress, 17-19, 21, 109, 127, 138, 139, 141, 142, 168, 176, 177, 228-31, 233-34, 239-44, 272, 330-43, 347, 351, 353, 361, 380
Protectorate (England), 282, 283
Protestantism, 45, 60, 62, 154-55, 158, 160, 165-67, 169-75, 198, 238, 257-59, 264, 268, 272, 274-78, 289, 292, 309, 310; Huguenots, 263
Providence. See God, in history
Prussia, 11, 40-43, 75, 83, 128, 182-84, 186, 193, 196, 206, 208-9, 212, 218, 220, 222-24, 239, 246-47,

293-94, 299, 301, 302, 304, 312,
318, 323-26, 345, 375, 379; Prus-
sian-German idea, 301, 304, 311,
313, 316, 317, 320, 321, 353;
United Diet (1847), 202-4, 378
Prussian history, 192, 312, 315, 350.
See also *Nine Books of Prussian
History*

radicalism, political, 203, 380
radicalism, religious, 171, 173, 176,
190, 282
Ranke, Clara (née Graves), 184-88,
219, 383
Ranke, Ernst, 184-85
Ranke, Ferdinand, 184, 375, 383
Ranke, Heinrich, 26, 69, 70, 76, 77,
97-98, 184, 383
Ranke, Otto, 292-93
rationalism, 38, 47, 240
Reformation, 60-64, 72, 80, 108, 198,
238, 239, 247, 257, 260, 268, 276,
298, 350, 351, 353. See also *German
History in the Age of the Reformation*
Reichstag: Holy Roman, 161-62, 223,
350; North German Confederation,
294
religion, 15, 20, 25, 26, 35, 41, 45-65,
70, 75-77, 79, 80, 90-92, 96, 104,
140, 155, 159, 163-64, 166, 168,
173, 175, 189, 203, 213, 231, 243,
257, 258, 261, 263, 276, 271-78,
284, 291, 295, 298, 309, 331, 333,
335, 336, 346, 363-64; pietism,
37, 38, 47, 69. *See also* Christianity
Renaissance, 79, 108
republic, 211, 236, 263, 264, 301,
302, 311, 324, 326, 328. *See also*
democracy
Restoration: European (1815-30),
27, 28, 369; English (1660), 277,
278, 283, 284
revolution, 28, 30, 126, 127, 129, 130,
145, 158, 207-9, 211, 228, 239,
240, 248, 253, 263-68, 283, 288-
90, 295, 298, 299, 301, 303, 311,
312, 318, 323-29, 333, 346, 371;
Puritan (English), 281, 282, 284;
Glorious (English), of 1688, 239,

277, 280, 283; French, of 1789,
79, 83, 103, 192-93, 208, 217, 240,
246, 265, 282, 283, 301, 314, 320,
324; European, of 1830, 41, 94,
95, 128-30, 132-33, 137-39, 145,
147, 148, 158, 159, 180, 201, 203,
211, 232, 301, 304, 305; European,
of 1848, 180, 181, 192, 201-28,
232, 246, 380
Richelieu, Cardinal Armand Jean Du-
plessis de, 251, 254, 259
Romano-Germanic nations (and Germano-Romanic nations, Latin-
Germanic nations), 105, 108-12,
116, 120, 174, 236, 239-42, 250,
253, 254, 256, 260-61, 265, 274-
76, 278, 279, 339-41
romanticism, 8, 16, 28, 30, 40, 47, 82,
100
Rome, ancient, 71, 235-38, 267, 334,
336-41; Roman history, 3, 63, 71,
213, 351
Rome, modern, 152, 153, 157
Rousseau, Jean-Jacques, 36
Rudolf II, Holy Roman Emperor, 306
Russia, 239

Saint Bartholomew Massacre, 18
Saint-Simon, Louis de Rouvroy, Duke,
14
Savigny, Friedrich Karl von, 84, 183,
205
Saxon dynasty (Holy Roman Empire),
340
Saxony, electoral, 36, 37, 40, 42
Saxony, royal, 40, 42, 198, 308, 379
Scandinavia, 110
Schelling, Friedrich Wilhelm Joseph
von, 19, 28, 29, 82, 218, 232-33,
362, 363, 380
Schiller, Johann Christoph Friedrich
von, 1, 29, 40
Schlegel brothers, 82; Karl Wilhelm
Friedrich von, 28, 29, 46, 98
Schleiermacher, Friedrich Daniel
Ernst, 29, 30
Schlosser, Friedrich Christoph, xi
Schlözer, August Ludwig von, xi
science, 13, 20, 62, 68, 133, 140, 158,
179, 214, 215, 218, 249, 250, 296,